GUYANA

THE LOST EL DORADO

This book is dedicated to my darling granddaughter Karen,
for all her love, dedication and support.

GUYANA: THE LOST EL DORADO

A Report on My Work and Life Experiences in Guyana
1925-1980

MATTHEW FRENCH YOUNG M.S.

PEEPAL TREE

First published in Great Britain in 1998
by Peepal Tree Press Ltd
17 King's Avenue
Leeds LS6 1QS
England

ISBN 0 900715 25 2

FOREWORD

Brigadier Joseph G Singh, MSS, DPA, M Inst D, FIMgt, FRGS, psc, rcds.
Chief of Staff, Guyana Defence Force

There are those in the history of mankind who, through their pioneering efforts, have given to their own time and to future generations an enabling environment within which improvements in the quality of life, the development of science and technology, and the creation of spiritual and material wealth can flourish and provide impetus for further achievements.

It is in this context that the life, activities and experiences of Matthew Young, documented in this autobiography, must be assessed.

In the fifty-five years of his working life (1925-1980), Matthew Young, whom I had the privilege of meeting in 1970 at Camp 1 (Camp Young) Madhia, and in 1978 at Matthews Ridge, made a remarkable contribution to the difficult process of enabling Guyana to gain access to the resources of its interior. His contribution was in developing an infrastructure both of geographic knowledge and of practical road construction. He pioneered and developed lines of communication in most of the geographical areas of Guyana which are shown on the maps in this book. What is more, whether in his work in the mining, forestry, rice, sugar, road survey and construction and aviation sectors – both private and public, Matthew Young provided a remarkable example for all Guyanese to follow, of industry, ingenious resourcefulness and practical invention.

In writing his autobiography he has further contributed to our awareness of our national history and culture. In his account of life in Guyana from the 1920s to the late 1970s he gives a lively picture of our changing social life, glimpses of the lifestyles of the Amerindians peoples of the interior (and their unsung contribution to our country's knowledge of the hinterland), and of our rich flora and fauna which too few Guyanese have the chance to see. Perhaps his descriptions of creeks, forests and savannahs will whet the appetite of our people to know their country better.

The paintings, a few of which are included in the book, give credence to this multi-talented gentleman's commitment to sharing his knowledge of and love of Guyana and to providing motivation and focus to the efforts of current and future Guyanese.

My publishing of this book as a non profit-making undertaking was realised with the approval of Mr. Young's granddaughter, Ms. Karen Caballero, the encouragement of former President Mr. Desmond Hoyte, SC, and the advice and assistance of Dr. David Dabydeen, Director of Caribbean Studies, University of Warwick.

My deep appreciation is extended to all those who subscribed to the cost of publication, and in particular, to the Guyana Sugar Corporation.

The typing of the contents onto IBM compatible diskette was done by Ms Agnes Duke and Mrs. Claudia Ogle, ably assisted by Mrs. Gloria Abrahams, all of the Guyana Defence Force.

Finally, my grateful thanks for the cooperation of Peepal Tree Press in realising this project.

May you, dear reader, be enlightened and entertained by the life and works of the remarkable Mr. Matthew Young, MS, 1905-1996.

AUTHOR'S INTRODUCTION

It must be remembered that for quite a long time after the European discovery of the New World, the territory known as Guiana was very much more
extensive than it is today, embracing the whole north-eastern section of the
continent between the Amazon and the Orinoco Rivers. This region was the
source of a famous myth, firmly believed by cold-blooded businessmen and
hot-blooded adventurers who alike poured out their bullion and their blood
in search of it, that somewhere in the hinterland of Guiana there was a large
lake, situated between the Takatu and the Rupununi rivers. On that lake
there was an island and on that island was a city called Manoa. The streets
of Manoa were paved with gold and the King of Manoa had his oil-anointed
body daily covered with gold dust. He was the Golden One, the El Dorado.

It is possible that it was the wretched Incas, enslaved and tortured by the
Spanish Conquistadores in their tireless hunt for gold, who started the story
of the golden city across the mountains to the east – as far away as possible
from their own country – in the vain hope of ridding themselves of their
tormentors. It is possible that the idea of the golden man arose from old Inca
customs when, on ceremonial occasions, the Inca or High Priest did actually have powdered gold fixed to his body by means of odoriferous resins.

But why the lake? This in time, apart from the stories of its vastness and
the existence of the city, proved to be the one element which had a basis in
truth. As early as 1739, practical doubts as to the physical existence of El
Dorado began to take shape when, in that year, the Dutch Commander of
Essequibo, Gelskerke, dispatched one Nicholas Hortzman, a native of
Hildesheim, up the Essequibo River to find a connection with the Amazon
River. Accompanied by two Dutch soldiers and four able Creoles to serve as
guides and interpreters, Hortzman left Kartabo, at the Mazaruni and Cuyuni
River junction, on the 3rd November 1739, on one of the epic journeys of
Guiana. On May 11th, 1740, the party entered the lake which the Indians
called *Amucu*. This lake had two islands and was filled with reeds. From
this lake they entered the Pirara river which took them out of the Ireng or
Takatu river, then downriver to Para in the Amazon.

In my own journeys into the interior, I encountered the contemporary
pursuers of the myth of El Dorado, the pork-knockers or prospectors for diamonds and gold in Guyana's rivers. I myself had some success in finding
valuable deposits of these minerals, though also the equally harsh experience of the fatal hazards which accompanied the search for such wealth.
However, in time, what I came to see was that it was not the gold which
should be the true subject of the search for El Dorado but what was inciden-

tal to the original myth: the lakes and the water they contained. Here, for the Guyana of the future, lies a source of power and of vast acres of irrigated and fertile farming lands in the interior. During my working life the goal of developing such riches from the interior remained more dream than reality. Hence my title.

This narrative is the result of constant promptings from my Guyanese friends and foreigners alike. On my return from trips into the interior I found there were many who were curious to hear about my experiences, my descriptions of the country I traversed, my life among the Amerindians and the practicalities of the work I was engaged in.

It must be understood, from the nature of things, that the great majority of pioneers in the hinterland of Guyana were men to whom the axe and the gun, the paddle and the pick, were more familiar than the pen and pencil; consequently the bibliography on the bush is relatively limited. Some, too, of what has been written has been both notoriously self-advertising and exaggerated, fantastic and often quite simply false. Not that they do not make good reading – as fiction – but unfortunately they purported to be factual and give an exceedingly distorted, if not unkind, picture of things as they really are. Fortunately, however, there were exceptions, men who were able to and did record their impressions of our little known interior. In a modest way I hope my account will add to our store of knowledge of the interior.

I fell in love with the bush and savannahs of our vast interior from my very first journey in 1925 when I first saw the mighty Kaieteur falls. That love and curiosity has taken me on foot to the Brazilian and Venezuelan frontiers, has carried me by boat up most of our rivers. I have cut lines through the bush from river to river, and traversed possible communication routes which later surveyors and road builders have followed. I have seen the possibilities of agriculture on a large scale, the vast stretches of valuable timber which require our careful husbandry, the indications of further gold and diamond deposits. I have repeatedly argued that our capital city was built in the wrong place, on the narrow strip of coastland where all our commercial activity is based, and not in the interior where all the possibilities of future development lie.

Over the years I have tried to persuade my fellow Guyanese of the beauties and the opportunities of the interior. In later years I tried to show the beauties through my paintings: the towering ranges, the rolling north and south savannahs, the spectacular waterfalls, the cool shadowed creeks and the vast forest dressed in their mantles of variegated colours.

Guyanese, see and know our country and enjoy what God has blessed us with.

CHAPTER 1

Diamond Prospecting in the Upper Potaro – 1925

GUYANA is an Amerindian name meaning Land of Many Waters. There are approximately four thousand, four hundred miles of rivers and creeks encompassed within a landmass of eighty-three thousand square miles, stretching from the Atlantic Coast to the Dutch frontier in the East, to the Brazilian in the South and the Venezuelan in the West.

In the early years, the only means of travel into the hinterland was by boat, using our natural waterways.

In February, 1925, I left Georgetown accompanied by the now late Edwin Haynes, a retired government surveyor, who had asked me to accompany him as his assistant into fifty square miles of a diamond concession situated at the Potaro River head, in the Pakaraima mountains.

I travelled up the Demerara River by the *S.S. Essequibo*, one of Sprostons riverboats, to Wismar some 60 miles from the coast, arriving at 3:30 p.m. I stacked our cargo on the railway platform in preparation for loading on the train to Rockstone the following morning. Our baggage was carried by our cookman to Sprostons Hotel, high on a hill bordering the river.

I was up early next morning. The air had a nip to it, but what caught my eye from the hotel veranda was the nest of activity across the river, with ocean-going ships loading bauxite ore from the Mackenzie plant; the beautiful view of distant forests up and down the river, the mines and the railroad showing in the distance.

Up to the close of the last century, Plantation Christianburg and the adjoining estate of Wismar had been owned by the Scottish family of Patterson. They operated a sawmill worked by a water wheel near which was the family mansion, which is now the Government Rest House and Magistrate's Court. Then, in 1896, because the Pattersons became involved in a court action against Sprostons, whose plans to build a railroad involved trespass on the Patterson property, the Government bought both estates. It was here in Wismar in 1910, that Professor Harrison, the director of Science and Agriculture, stuck his walking stick into the earth and barked 'BAUXITE, the future of British Guiana!' A couple of years later, a tall, weather-beaten and grizzled

Scottish-American appeared on the river and began to buy up all the privately owned lands, at an average price of two dollars per acre, to grow oranges on. His name was George Bain MacKenzie, after whom was named the first great bauxite centre of the country. But in 1925, Wismar still consisted mainly of one road running along the river front down to Christianburg. There were shady forests on the hill slopes bordering the river and a few scattered houses and shops.

The train for Rockstone left at 7:30 a.m., after the steamer had departed on its return to Georgetown. One thing I recollect clearly was that the tiny carriages were equipped with wire gauge windows to prevent sparks from the wood-burning engine damaging our garments or baggage. This train was like a toy, having to be nursed up the gradients of the white sand hills. I eventually arrived at Rockstone on the right bank of the Essequibo River at noon having travelled a distance of only 17 miles with many stops on the way. I stayed at yet another Sprostons Hotel, a rambling old house with accommodation for about a dozen guests. Its situation by the river was peaceful and serene; in view was Gluck Island one of the larger group of islands in the Upper Essequibo River, which lies just off and upstream of Rockstone.

Next morning, it was the intense cold that awoke me from my slumber. I was later to learn that Rockstone is one of the coldest spots in the interior.

Our baggage and cargo was carried from the hotel and stowed in an old steel-hulled launch. This was powered by an old 'hot ball' Kelvin engine which had to be heated with a blow torch before it would start.

Travelling at the same time with his party was the Anglican Bishop. Their effects were stowed in a small tent boat which our launch would have to tow upstream and on to Tumatumari, our destination in the Potaro River. This arrangement proved to be feasible until we were steaming up Crab Falls rough water. Just above the falls, the engine in the launch failed. We watched the Bishop's boat drifting into danger. Only quick thinking and fast action on the part of our engineer prevented an accident as he managed to get the engine working again. The entire party arrived at Tumatumari near dusk; we discharged our cargo at the road end below the falls where, at a later date, a Hydro-power plant was to be installed to power the machinery put down to recover the gold discovered there.

I slept in Tumatumari Hotel, built on top of a laterite rock hill and overlooking the falls, but I had to kill an eighteen inch black centipede which I discovered climbing up my mosquito net before I could rest in peace, lulled to sleep by the thunder of the falls. Sprostons really had an eye for the tourist trade, for both the Wismar and the Tumatumari Hotels were built at vantage points overlooking the river with scenic views of the surrounding country.

I was up bright and early. I walked down the road to the river to check our cargo, and arrange for a lorry to transport it to the upper boat landing above the falls. After lunch, Mr. Haynes asked me to accompany him over the river below the falls to a Patamona Amerindian Village where he thought he might be able to recruit some labour. This was my first chance to meet with the real indigenous people of Guyana. The village consisted of four or five large-leafed huts into which were packed men, women and children, their dogs and fowls. These Amerindians do not wear any clothes, just the women's tribal bead aprons and the men's red sallow cotton laps. I could not speak the language, so I just followed everything I saw Mr. Haynes do. We were invited to partake of their evening meal.

I was handed a large piece of Cassava bread about three-quarter inch in thickness, which would act as a plate on which to put the pieces of fish or meat I took out of the clay pot in which the Amerindians boil their meat or fish mixed with casareep (this is a product of the cassava root) a black substance similar to molasses, to which is added the red pepper. The Amerindians keep this pot continually over the fire and when the contents diminish, fresh meat, fish or frog legs are added, as the Amerindians always want a continuous supply of meat to eat with their cassava bread.

I really received a shock when I took my first mouthful of food, for it was really a pot of pepper. This mouthful was the end of my meal. I felt as if my breath was cut. Tears ran from my eyes, my nose started to run and I imagined smoke coming out of my ears.

When Mr. Haynes explained to the Amerindians what had occurred, there were peals of laughter at my expense, but one young woman took pity on me and brought a calabash (gourd) of casiri, a cooling drink made from fermented cassava mash. To make the casiri drink, which is a sort of beer, the old women used to chew the cassava root until it turned into a paste. This they spat into a large stone jar. Water was added and the mixture left to ferment for three days before it was ready to use. Some Amerindians strain the drink and colour it with the juice of the purple potato. In these modern days, the cassava is grated and not chewed.

The following morning, the lorry collected us from the hotel and transported us to the top of the falls. The road was over laterite rock bordered on both sides with flourishing cashew trees that seem to thrive on this rocky terrain. Our party proceeded up river by another boat from this point above the falls to Garraway Stream, the road-landing below the Kangaruma Range of falls. A lorry took us still higher, some three miles along the shady forest road to Mr. Austin's shop at Kangaruma landing. There our cargo was discharged because this would be our jumping off point into the bush.

Mr. Haynes enquired from Mr. Austin if any of his Amerindians had arrived from Chinapow landing above Kaieteur Falls. On learning they had not, Mr. Haynes arranged for Mr. Austin to transport us and our cargo through the river to Tukeit. After dinner, I retired to bed, the last bed I was to sleep in for the next eighteen months.

As day dawned, I was up and into the river for a swim. The men were engaged in loading the boat with our cargo, waiting for the river mists to lift, before the captain or rather the steersman felt it safe enough to push off the boat, which was powered with an outboard Archimedes motor. Coming out of the river bushes, I could see the distant mountains bordering Amatuk Falls. They were shrouded with the vapour rising from the surrounding forests. After a few hours of travel on this wide open river, I had a beautiful view of the entrance to the Kaieteur gorge and had my first view of Amatuk Falls of which I took some snap shots. At this point, we had to discharge our cargo and portage it across the falls to another boat.

We proceeded up river, which was much narrower than the lower reaches. This was the real gorge with the mountains pressing in on both sides and towering above us. We arrived at Waratuk Falls. During the rainy season, a boat can steam over, but as the water was low, the boat had to be hauled over by ropes. The party took lunch here. Some years after I had passed here, a pork-knocker discovered, in a pot hole in these rocks, a cache of diamonds valued at $25,000.00. At this point, I could clearly hear the echo of the thunder of the Kaieteur Falls and saw the blobs of white foam floating down river.

Our boat arrived at Tukeit landing, a clearing on the left bank of the river in which nestled our Rest House. At 3:30 p.m. our cargo was discharged and stored in the house. Tukeit is at the foot of the range of rapids that lead up the gorge to the foot of the main falls. From this point one has to follow a path through the forest leading to the escarpment.

The Rest House consisted of two fair-sized rooms, furnished with about ten cots. There is a fall back which acts as a kitchen and a gallery facing the river.

I peeled off my clothes and donned a pair of swimming trunks. I dived into the dark brown waters of the river and swam out to a pile of rocks in the middle of the river. I was recalled by a shrill blast from a police whistle and frantic signs from both Mr. Haynes and Mr. Austin. I was then warned never to swim in these dark brown waters again as there were things under the water dangerous to anything moving, such as the 'water tiger', known lo-

cally as the "massacuruman", something in the shape of a human form covered with hair, having small ears set in a head armed with the fangs of a
tiger with webbed hands and feet armed with terrible claws and having a
tail. It was said to be approximately five feet tall. There is also the dreaded
pirai or carib fish which can take off a finger or a toe or a piece of flesh from
one's body with one bite from its powerful jaws. The taint of blood in the
water drives the pirai crazy and they become at once raging, savage de-
mons, blindly attacking anything, no matter what, from which blood is flowing. They grow up to sixteen inches in length and are of a bluish black tint
with silvery sides and fiery red eyes. The jaws are furnished with large triangular and extremely sharp cutting teeth.

When I woke next morning, I was surprised to see the foot of my white
cotton hammock covered with blood. I drew Mr. Haynes' attention to this.
He informed me that Dr. Blair (the bushman's name for the vampire bat)
had paid me a visit. This Bat has a body length of about four inches and a
wing span of between twelve to sixteen inches and is readily distinguish-
able from all other bats by the structure of the teeth. Their most obvious
characteristic is that the two upper cutting teeth (incisors) are as large as
the canines, gouge shaped and very sharp, fitted for acting on the skin much
as a razor would. These are the only bats which have ever been caught drinking the blood of animals.

Mr. Haynes welcomed some newly arrived Patamona Amerindians in their
own language (of which I later learnt a few words), introducing me as his
son.

There were women and children in this group. The women wore no clothing, their breasts and buttocks naked. Their only covering was a small bead
apron worn in front and tied at the waist. (These quayos are only eighteen
inches wide by twelve inches deep). The men and boys are also naked with
only a red sallow cotton cloth tied around their waists and passed between
their legs. The women wear strings of coloured beads around their necks
and bind their upper arms, wrists, and legs below the knee and the ankle
with strings of coloured beads. This is said to give their limbs a good shape.
They are heavily tattooed on their faces, which is their beauty mark. Their
babies are carried in a woven shoulder hammock.

During the afternoon, I was surprised to see the women and girls engaged
in gashing the thighs and upper arms of the men with pieces of broken bottle, the blood flowing freely. I was told they did this prior to the day they
were to drough heavy loads to safeguard against cramp while climbing the
mountain escarpment. Not only the men but some of the more mature women

were treated to this letting of blood. These Amerindians are equipped with warashis, a carrying basket plaited from the split nibbi vine which is approximately two and a half feet long, twelve inches wide with six inch sides. This is hung from the shoulders and the head with strips from the inner bark of the mahoe tree. The weight of the load must be equally balanced between the head and the shoulders. These Amerindians carry from 100 to 200 pounds. The women usually carry more load than the men, to allow the men the freedom to hunt on the trail.

When we moved from Tukeit rest house the following morning, I saw men, women and even some of the children picking up loads. I too, although not having a warashi, but being fairly strong, picked up a half bag of flour, 100 pounds, and tossing it over my shoulder, started on my walk through the forest some three miles to climb the escarpment to the top of the falls some 700 feet up. I walked along a narrow rock-strewn path crossing occasional streams and ever mounting the approach to the wall. I passed some of the early starters resting at various points along the path of the climb. A covey of powis crossed my path; about five of them going about their business. These birds are black all over with soft white feathers on their breasts and inner legs and carry a curled plume close to their heads. They are about eight to ten pounds in weight and resemble our house turkey. They are sought after as they are good eating.

One or two akuri (accourie) were disturbed in my passing, giving off their "frank-frank" sound. These small animals are the size of a rabbit and belong to the rodent family having two pairs of long front teeth, those on the upper jaw generally being much larger than those on the lower one. They gnaw their food which consists mostly of seeds from the numerous palms that grow in the forests. Their bodies are a dark greenish brown but their backs are covered with long orange coloured hair. They utter a short shrill whistle which the Amerindians imitate, calling the animal to within gunshot range.

I had now met the escarpment and started my climb. There were spots where I had to hold onto tree roots to pull myself up and over some huge rocks and step over the many fallen trees. At some parts of the wall, I met water penetrating through the rock formation running over the lower rocks to join the numerous streams. By this time, I was feeling the weight of the bag of flour and was glad when I reached the escarpment top to emerge from the forest onto a flat rock plateau covered by clumps of scrub bush. I glimpsed the mountains looking faintly blue in the far distance. I rested by a huge rock on which I eased the bag of flour, then I proceeded for another three quarters of a mile to the rest house where I threw down the bag of flour. When I tried to straighten up, I found I could not without suffering severe pain.

Of course, when the Amerindians learned of my dilemma, there were many jokes and laughter at my expense, but I was learning. I was up early next morning feeling a little sore. The Amerindians, who had slept in their hammocks outside were dispatched, back to Tukeit rest house to bring up the balance of our supplies.

I accompanied Mr. Haynes who had promised to show me this mighty fall. We followed a rock-strewn path through the scrub bush. I could distinctly hear the echo of the falls, but I was unprepared for the sight that met my eyes.

I was struck by the stupendous beauty that opened up before me, unable to express in mere words the surge of deep emotion I felt to see nature in its element as I watched this volume of rare black water as it rushed past to fall over the edge of the rock precipice, disappearing into a vast chasm to send back a thunderous echo.

The spray from the falling waters swirled around the surrounding cliffs, through which hundreds of swallows were darting, the spray at all times hiding the gorge. I walked through the shallow water to stand on a large rock which jutted out and over the falling waters. From this vantage point named Look-Out-Rock, I had glimpses of the mighty basin 740 feet below and witnessed nature in its element, where the falling waters formed a boiling cauldron of white water which was rushing out into the rocky gorge. The rock ledges and projecting rocks divided the falling waters into spray. I felt as if I was floating in a white cloud of mist. The morning sun created a beautiful rainbow in the swirling spray above the falls. I have witnessed other falling waters and the beauty of it in many parts of Guyana is more picturesque, but never having the grandeur of this father of waters. This first impression has been locked in my memory never to be forgotten.

It was here exposed on this projecting rock that I received the biggest fright of my life. A gust of wind sweeping up the gorge hit the face of the falling water and swept upwards snatching my white pith helmet from my head. I automatically stretched out my hand to retrieve it, only to find myself frozen in fright, realising I was leaning over the direct drop of the falls in this deep gorge. I was not man enough to walk back, but got down on my hands and knees and crawled back to the river bank.

I spent another pleasant night here on this high plateau, though when I woke with the intense cold, I was glad that I had brought my blanket with me. I found the Amerindians encamped outside having brought up the balance of our cargo from Tukeit.

The Amerindians made two trips from the rest house to the boat landing and stowed everything in the boat. We had no engine to power our boat and had to depend on the manpower of the Amerindians paddlers to propel it. After an early lunch we set off at 10:00 a.m..

The river in these upper reaches was about 500 feet wide. The high walls of the gorge had given way to more open country, though now we were enclosed by the ever-changing jungle, with now and again a glimpse of a deer drinking at the river edge. At one point we disturbed a tapir (bush cow) which dashed off through the bush.

The tapir's body is stout and clumsy with thick short legs. The head is peculiarly shaped with a long and very flexible snout or short trunk and a high crest or poll. The local tapir feeds on various wild fruits, especially the seed of the ité palm as well as the leaves of small trees. It needs to put away twenty pounds of fallen fruit, low growing leaves, grass and aquatic plants each day. Essentially a loner, tapirs pair up for mating. After thirteen months, the baby is born; by age four the young tapir is ready to mate. Its torpedo shaped body weighs about 600 pounds and, combined with the strength of a military tank, sends the tapir crashing through tangles and thickets impenetrable to almost any other creature, often scraping off would-be predators such as jaguars as it heads for the nearest water.

A tarpaulin was erected for our overnight camp on a high river bank. The Amerindians slung their hammocks between the trees surrounding our clearing. They usually build a small fire under their hammocks, as they do not have blankets. One never sees an Amerindian with a white hammock. They are always smoke grimed.

It was the barking and howling of the red baboons that awoke me before dawn, followed by the screeching of the parrots and parakeets. Some of the Amerindians caught a few fish with the raw meat or guts from an animal or bird they had shot as bait. They were either pirai or haimara, a sweet eating fish, steamed with garlic and onions or fried. Our cook prepared a cooked meal to carry with as we had far to go and could not afford to stop to cook. The Amerindians exist on their cassava bread with some dried meat or take a cup of farine and sugar which is very filling.

Our journey up river was uneventful. Although we had glimpses of monkeys jumping from tree to tree, the bush did not vary very much and it was rather tedious sitting in the boat hour after hour watching the same scene. I was fascinated by the muscles in the backs and shoulders of the boys pulling the paddles. To see the muscles rippling in their effort to propel the boat, it was evident these Amerindians were in good condition. I do not recollect ever having seen a fat Amerindian. It was late in the afternoon when we arrived at the Chinapow Creek on whose bank was the landing and a store. I was introduced to Joseph, the storekeeper, who was an aged Amerindian with greying hair. I learned that this man had grown up with a Jesuit Priest. He had received a good education and had travelled abroad, but on his return to British Guiana, he could get no one to employ him so he reverted to the aboriginal way of life.

Joseph assisted our cook in preparing the evening meal and showed us where we could sling our hammocks. Everyone was a little tired so we retired to sleep early. Next morning, the cargo was discharged from the bateau and checked before being stored away. Mr. Haynes had requested that certain supplies be put aside for the Amerindian droughers to start carrying to Anandabaru the following day, things much needed for the main store at our destination, some thirty miles inland.

I secured a warashi from Joseph the storekeeper in which I packed my hammock and a change of clothes and picking up my gun, I joined the first batch of men and women who had already picked up their loads. At one point, when one of the women was crossing over a deep ravine on a fallen log, she cried out to her partner for help as she was carrying a large trunk in her warashi and felt as if she was overbalancing. He stretched out his hand and steadied her and they both inched over slowly to the other side.

I walked through these cool shady forests in company with my Amerindians, resting periodically and quenching my thirst at the small creeks we crossed. It was my first walk through this mountainous area. There were stretches of level land, much like park lands, with the immense trees towering above us. Other areas, such as the creek lands, were covered with a more dense and vine-tangled bush. It was here on these high ridges that I first heard the distant tolling of that snow white bird, sounding like a bell, from high tree or mountain spur. Here too, I heard the call of the calf bird, so realistic that it had me peering into the bush expecting to see a cow calf.

The Amerindians do not measure distances by miles, so when I queried them how far I had to travel, they pointed to the sun and made a sign with their hands to the side of their heads, meaning sleep one night. The Amerindians never hurry when carrying loads, but if a herd of wild hogs is scented or any other game is seen, the loads are thrown down and they run after the game to shoot it. All Amerindian trails follow the easiest course, similar to the tapir who is dubbed the surveyor of the bush, as it follows the contours of the hills and not the more tedious ups and downs. The miles are longer but one gets to one's destination with less fatigue.

As the forest starts to get dark at approximately 4:00 p.m., I had to select a camp site near a clear water stream. I slung my hammock between two good sized trees and built a small fire with dry wood over which I put my saucepan to heat water for coffee.

On trips such as this where one cannot travel with kitchen utensils for cooking, I learned to travel light, carrying a small sack of farine, about half a pound of sugar, a tin of condensed milk, a piece of dried meat or fish and a small bottle of ground coffee beans. The Amerindians always have their cassava bread to eat with whatever they have, such as a piece of meat roasted on the end of a stick. The Amerindians were encamped around me, two or three of them sharing a hammock, with their little fires underneath to keep them warm. When the fire dies down, one of them would jump out to stir it up and then jump back inside. There was much giggling and laughter among the younger boys and girls for these children of the forest have much laughter in them.

In the silence of the night, a distant thud of a fallen tree could be heard. The sound of the red baboons was ever present. Occasionally one hears the passing of an opossum or other night animals in their quest for food, but what I really noticed were the darting fireflies, looking as if they were searching for something. I noted the hum of the insects in their search for food. When the forest is still, the silence seems to press on one's ears. It was in this silence I was to be treated to the sweet tune of the small brown quadril bird, its whistle taking all the notes like a flute, the scales mounting up and down. Old bushmen say this small bird likes to occupy areas around camps.

CHAPTER II
Among the Amerindians of Anandabaru Creek – 1926

On my arrival at Anandabaru Creek, Mr. Haynes told me I had met our base camp, which was to be my home for the next eighteen months. The administrative compound was built on a high hill on the other bank of the creek, on which were erected three fairly large leaf-roofed huts. The walls were of balamanie bark, beaten and peeled off the tree. The bark is about three-quarter inch in thickness and the floors can also use this bark with spaced beams two feet apart to bear them. There was also a large trading store. All were built with wattle sides with open windows, but having doors of wood boards. Because of the intense cold at this 2,000 feet altitude, clay firesides were installed in each house; old kerosene tins (four gallon cans) were cut open and nailed to the wattle wall to prevent fire catching the dry wattles.

I was introduced to Innis, a coloured man, who was in charge of the trading store and did the bookkeeping. There was one other young black man about my own age who hailed from the Berbice district.

On the hill top, Mr. Haynes had a cultivation of approximately ten acres; mostly ground provisions were grown here to supply our needs. There were fruit trees and sugar cane. From this hill top, I had a clear view of Mt. Kowatipu, rising some 3,000 feet from the forest floor like some sentinel, sheer sided and having a flat top.

On our arrival at base camp, the Amerindians from the outlying areas started to come in, some having travelled for days either walking or by corial. There were mostly the Patamona but Acawaio and Warrau tribes were intermingled. They were coming to meet Mr. Haynes's son. This was I.

I was presented with a beautiful nine foot blow pipe made from the awara palm. The inside shone like a rifle barrel. Its entire length was intricately carved and coloured with signs of snakes and birds and animals. It carried two accouri teeth mounted on the pipe to act as sights, just like a rifle. With the blow pipe, I was given a small plaited quake of Amerindian cotton - light and fluffy picked from the cotton tree and about two dozen sharp pointed darts made from hardwood, about the size of an ordinary match, and a small clay container of "curare" poison, dark green in colour. This clay container has to be heated over a fire to melt the poison in preparation for dipping the tips of the darts.

I was instructed in the use of the blow pipe. A little of the cotton is inserted into the mouth of the pipe, through which a dart is pushed at the mouth's edge. The blow pipe is then aimed at the victim (I chose an ordinary chicken). The dart is then blown from the pipe in a spitting gesture. The instant the dart penetrates the victim, it causes instant paralysis and eventually death.

I received numerous bows of hardwood made from the letter wood and purple heart with cane arrows tipped with hardwood, bone and metal. There were arrows for shooting fish, game, and some dum-dum for knocking birds out of trees. I was also presented with a beautifully decorated headdress of parrot feathers and a beautiful shoulder cloak, wonderfully woven from the three coloured macaw feathers (red, yellow, blue) and a necklace of some brown beans which the Amerindians claim, if worn all the time, will prevent sickness. For each present I received, I in turn had to present the giver some small token such as a kitchen knife or a cutlass, a looking-glass or a little lead shot or a flask of gun powder or a plate and spoon. Amerindians rarely steal, they believe in barter. If an Amerindian covets something you own, he will bring a gift for you, then in turn, ask for what he wishes.

Mr. Haynes took me in hand to instruct me in the use of a prismatic compass. As we had to open up our concession lines, encompassing some fifty square miles, some boundaries marked by creeks, our lines were not less than fifty feet wide, allowing freedom of travel. He also instructed me in the art of prospecting for gold and diamonds, what outcrops to be on the outlook for, and how to make cross cuts in the creek flats when tracing for gold.

The Amerindians lived at the foot of our hill, but on the other side of the creek, slinging their hammocks under rude leaf shelters or in between the trees. Our permanent work force consisted of fifty men and women with a scattering of children. They worked for a period of three months, then were permitted to return to their villages to reap the cassava from their fields and to cut away new clearings. This they burn, then they plant a next crop of cassava. When the field work is completed, they send out the huntsmen and the fishermen. The women work on the grating of the cassava root to make and bake the cassava bread and farine which is their staple food. They also make a sour kind of beer by grating the root and placing it in a large stone jar to which water is added and then left to ferment for three days. They go through about a week of feasting and drinking which gives them a good purging. When the Amerindians leave our place of work they look very pale, but on their return after three weeks, they have a robust look, their skins having a pink complexion. The cassava plant is said to contain a certain amount of strychnine whose properties give the Amerindians this pink colouring.

Our Amerindians were not paid in cash but in trade goods. Some of the men received a muzzle-loading gun, caps and gun powder and a bag of shot. Others received an axe or a cutlass. The boys got kitchen knives which they used in hunting and carving pieces of wood. The women and girls selected pieces of printed material to make dresses, beads with which to adorn themselves and looking glasses and combs. Spoons were in great demand.

No alcoholic beverages were allowed on the concession. It was strictly against Government regulations. When under the influence of liquor, the men became gregarious, losing all sense of responsibility and self-respect, or in a fighting mood. They would demand items from the store which were only for sale and not presents. Not getting what they want, their mood sometimes turned ugly. The women and young girls, when under the influence of alcohol, turned very amorous and practically demanded sex. A woman would think nothing of taking a man other than her husband, boasting of the act to the whole village, much to the amusement of all.

Once, a pork-knocker (prospector) managed somehow to penetrate our area and gave the Amerindians three or four bottles of rum. I knew nothing of this until the night when I was invaded by three young women demanding to be let into my quarters. They were very merry and making obscene gestures which left little doubt what they wanted. When I would not open the door, they departed with much laughter. I was later to learn that these young women had given me their Amerindian name of "AMOKO", meaning old man or one who was incapable of having sex with three young women.

Our work force was divided into three groups, two of twenty and one of ten. The latter did the prospecting in advance of the work parties. It was Jonas, the young black man, who directed my party of twenty in the art of stripping the top soil, felling and junking of trees in the area I had selected to make a pit of thirty by thirty feet. The clearing and excavation of the top earth was done by the men, the women assisting in the removal of branches and logs. When all the top soil had been thrown out, exposing the diamond gravel, a small area near the pit was levelled and boxed in by heavy logs to retain, in an area of 144 square feet, the diamond gravel.

The head or end of a tom-box, seven feet long, two and a half feet wide, with one foot sides, is built from sawn boards and strengthened with a wooden lathe nailed across the bottom at the intake end and the discharge end. This box rests on the edge of the pit; the rear end rests on a wooden crossbar resting in two forked sticks. A perforated iron plate with three-quarter inch holes rests against the rear crossbar about two feet from the end of the tom on an angle of 45°, held in place by bush wood wattles in the bottom of the tom-box. The tom-box discharges the concentrates into a square receiving box approximately three feet by three feet and two feet deep.

Water from a nearby waterway or small creek is led into the entrance of the tom-box, the flow of which is controlled by one man. Two spade men will constantly spade gravel from the heap going into the tom. This concentrate is washed by two hoe-men pulling the concentrates against the perforated iron in a rubbing motion. The finer ones pass through to the settling box. The "cooley" or larger stones are gathered by hand against the tom iron and thrown aside in a heap.

A stand of round bush wood two inches thick and sixteen feet long is set up in the pool, parallel to each other and resting on hardwood forked sticks, near the settling box. This stand is used for a rest for the sieves which the men use in "jigging" for the recovery of the diamonds. These sieves are a wooden band four inches wide tacked at the two ends to form a hoop. The bottom is a piece of copper wire, a sixteenth of an inch gauge, and is fixed by an outer hoop to the bottom of the sieve. I was instructed in the art of jigging by Jonas, the young black man. I had three young girls dipping the concentrates from the settling box with galvanized bailers and filling the sieves which were then operated in the water of the pit with a gentle pumping motion, spinning slowly at the same time, to centre the heavier stones and the diamonds. The sieve is then spun at a faster rate and brought out of the water to rest on the stand; the lighter and larger concentrates are scooped out from the outer edges of the sieve, then a careful search is made of the centre. A diamond, when once seen, can never be mistaken for anything but a diamond. There is a hard brilliance that shines out, be it blue white, bottle green, black, silver cape or any other colour. I was in charge of the collection of all stones found, which I kept in a brass cartridge shell.

Our work day started with a blast from a bottle horn. Then a dip in the icy waters of Anandabaru creek. After coffee, there was a walk through the forest for a distance of about half a mile. Both boys and girls work naked in the pit and the pool. There is never a dull moment, for these Amerindians liked to laugh and play, the boys teasing the girls working with Jonas and I. Two young girls between the ages of fourteen and sixteen were assigned to me, to bring my lunch from the main encampment to the work site, every working day, wash my hammock and my clothes, and light the fire in my bedroom on cold nights, not reluctant to spend the night keeping my hammock warm.

One night one of these girls came after dark to throw herself into my hammock.

Mr. Haynes, who occupied the next room, suffered severely from asthma and rarely had a good night's sleep, asked me the next morning what had been wrong with me the previous night because he had heard me turning continually in my hammock. I told him I had had a little fever. He sternly told me that that kind of fever could cost me six months in jail. The Amerindians were the wards of the Government. No one was allowed to have sex with them unless they were lawfully married.

On one occasion, I travelled from Aranadabaru camp in company with Mr. Haynes and two Amerindians, walking through the cool forests up and down hills, crossing numerous creeks and then across the Ireng River into Brazilian territory. Mr. Haynes had a contract with one of the Brazilian Ranchers to supply us with beef. The cattle were driven from this ranch, swimming the Ireng River to Anandabaru. There they were slaughtered. The men cut the meat into strips, salting it and hanging the strips on wooden racks to dry in the sun. This is called "tasso" and forms one of the basic foods of the Savannah Amerindians. The other is the cassava bread.

The Brazilians grow and smoke their own leaf tobacco "Lingo de-Yac", narrow like the tongue of the cow. I fell in love with the aroma of this tobacco. The first pipeful I smoked made me as sick as a dog, but for years after, up to 1980, I smoked nothing else but this tobacco.

During the rainy season, May to July, the Ireng River is swollen by the waters coming down from the mountains, cutting off some transportation overland, but river boats of a fair size travelled up river from Boa Vista to visit farmers and ranchers who were isolated by the dry river from their supplies. During exceptionally dry weather there are areas where the river bed is practically dry, enabling some rustling of cattle from Brazil to Guyana or vice versa. The Government, at a later date, built a wire fence from the Mt. Egerton - Good Hope area - down to the Dadanawa Ranch, the other side of the Kanaku Mountains, to prevent cattle from Brazil crossing into Guyanese territory on the occasional outbreaks of Foot and Mouth disease. I was privileged to travel some miles down stream to the town of Boa Vista, which in 1925 was a township of mostly adobe and leaf structures. In later years it improved greatly and today is a modern city.

I found the language barrier a little frustrating but Mr. Haynes was on hand to translate. I found the people most hospitable and kind. Miniature cups of sweetened black coffee was served as refreshment to all visitors when entering a home, much as we would offer a refreshing drink of alcohol. Brazil in those days produced the most coffee in the world.

I was engaged for some months prospecting the various creeks of the concession for indications of diamonds as well as cutting lines of communication from point to point. I was always very fond of hunting, carrying my gun on all my walks. On one occasion, while hunting alone, some distance from the compound in the silence of the forest, I heard a light pattering sound as if a light rain was falling, accompanied by the chirping of numerous small birds, but it was a clear brilliant day without a cloud in the sky. I looked about me, only to be electrified with shock when I saw the floor of the forest, the tree branches and the shrubs simply swarming with thousands of army ants which devour every living thing that cannot get out of their way. Having heard various stories of the danger, I literally took to my heels and headed for the nearest creek. I followed the downward course of the creek, which carried me some miles from camp. I did not return to the camp ground until late in the afternoon only to find Mr. Haynes organizing a search party, fearing I was lost in the bush. I explained to him what had happened. He then gave me some incidents of the yakman or soldier ants which travel through the forest in hundreds of thousands, cleaning out entire villages. I was, at a later date, to see the skeleton of a monkey that had been tied to a house post, when the inhabitants had moved out on the approach of these ants. They travel in columns three inches wide, sending out encircling arms, like a pincer movement to trap their prey, which once encircled stand no chance of escape.

I was good at pencil sketching whilst a boy at school in England and continued to carry a sketch pad for all the years I was in the bush, sketching everything of interest on my travels. From our hill top, I made a sketch of Mt. Kowatipu standing out from the surrounding country, sheer sided with a flat top. The sides are unscalable but the Amerindians say there is a large cave at the foot, through which animals and beasts pass to climb to the top. On one occasion, while I was hunting in the vicinity of that mountain with two of my Amerindians, I heard the sound of some beast approaching accompanied by a jabbering in a guttural tone, so we hid in the bush not knowing what to expect. I could hardly believe my eyes when I saw two huge beasts resembling apes or gorillas or bush men, covered with a sort of brown hair walking upright like a man. They were about six feet tall. When they had passed, I noted the size of their foot prints with splayed toes. Following this occurrence, the Amerindians would not hunt in that area any more as they said it was a bushman we had seen. This brought to my mind an article I had read in *Readers Digest* where a photograph was actually taken of a beast such as this in the Rocky Mountains. Later an associate surveyor told me babracot

his cook had been missing some smoked meat from his babracot. He heard someone bang a saucepan in the leaf fall back which acted as a kitchen at about 2:30 a.m. On shining his torch light in the direction of the sound he was surprised to see this huge hairy form with a leg of meat in its hand. He shot at the vague form but it crashed away into the bush. The next morning blood spots were found in the vicinity but no sign of a beast. Were these beasts any relation to the gorilla family or were they remnants of prehistoric man? It would be interesting to investigate these remote regions of the bush to see if there are any traces of their habitation.

When one is lost in the bush, one usually bangs on the spur of a large mora tree. This gives off a loud booming sound, drawing the attention of anyone in the neighbourhood who could lend assistance. I was on my way out to Chinapow landing with ten Amerindians to bring in some more stores. I had to spend one night on the trail. After slinging our hammocks on the nearby trees, I prepared my evening meal of a piece of tasso and farine and prepared to rest. Some of the Amerindians were gathered around the camp fire talking and eating when we heard this distant booming sound which seemed to be coming in our direction. Everyone stopped eating and talking and looked in the direction from which the sound was coming, expecting to see someone emerge from the bush into the fire light. Then, after a silence of maybe one full minute, the sound started again, going away to die out in the distance.

The Amerindians were all afraid. They said this was not a good place as there were spirits. I examined the ground around our camp the following morning but could discern no sign of any intruders. On another occasion, I heard a sound as if someone was beating clothes on the rocks at the river side, so I took my five cell torchlight which gave me a brilliant beam of light and shone it on the rocks by the river side, but I did not see anything although the sound continued. When nothing could be seen nor any explanation given for it, the Amerindians put it down to spirits. There are times in the silence of the night when a long low whistle is heard. The old bushmen say it is made by a snake, but the Amerindians, on hearing this whistle, cower in fear as they say it is made by the kanaima or Amerindian avenger.

To understand exactly what a kanaima is and what he does, one must know something about the conditions under which the Amerindians lived in the days of long ago. In urban societies, when someone steals our property or any one injures us, we telephone the police who come and enquire into the matter and we trust that the courts will see that the person is punished. But the Amerindians lived in small family groups separated from each other by many miles of forest with no telephones, no policemen, or courts. So when an Amerindian was robbed of a canoe, his bow and arrows or even his wife, he would pack his hammock and cassava bread in his shoulder basket, and set off on a walking or canoe journey of many miles to the house of an Amerindian he knew to be a kanaima. He would lodge his complaint to the kanaima and ask that the thief be punished. The kanaima would then tell him the fee – ten quakes of cassava if you wanted the thief made really ill, but if you wanted him killed, it would cost one of your daughters.

If the latter course was decided, the kanaima would smear his body with anaconda fat, tie his bark loincloth around his waist; across his shoulder he slung his little tigerskin pouch and grasping his heavy four-sided club of purpleheart wood, he would set out for the culprit's house. If night had fallen by the time he approached it, he would sleep between the great spurs of a mora tree. He would wake just as dawn was getting light between the trees and see the culprit making his way to hunt. As the culprit passed the mora tree the kanaima would spring out and knock the culprit on the head to make him unconscious. A kanaima never kills his victims outright. From his pouch the kanaima would take a splinter of greenheart wood no bigger than a match and pointed at each end. Kneeling he would pull out the culprit's tongue and force the greenheart splinter through it, pushing back the bleeding tongue into the mouth. He would go down to the creek and wash off the snake's fat from his body knowing he had earned his fee.

Presently the culprit's wives would come along the trail on their way to the cassava fields and would be horrified to find their husband lying unconscious at the foot of the mora tree. Seeing the blood oozing from his mouth, they knew at once he had been attacked by a Kanaima. The poison from the greenheart splinter would have so swollen his tongue, it would completely fill his mouth so the splinter could not be removed. He could not speak to tell his wives who had attacked him neither could he eat or drink and in three days he would have died of blood poisoning. This is what I mean when I describe the kanaima as being the Amerindians' policeman, judge, prison warden or executioner. In short, the whole machinery for keeping the peace through FEAR. An Amerindian will rarely talk of the kanaima, but when he does, it is with hushed voice as though he were speaking of something very dreadful indeed.

At Chinapow Landing, I was shown an Amerindian woman whose face was hideously disfigured. As a child, she had been bathing at the riverside whilst her mother was washing clothes. On hearing the child scream, the mother turned to see a creature, the "massacuraman" come out of the river and make a grab at the child. It was only the mother's intervention that saved the child, but the claws from the creature's hand left the child's face scarred for life.

On my walk back over the thirty odd miles to Anandabaru, my overnight camp was overrun by a drove of wild hogs. A hardwood club wielded properly can kill a hog when hit over the snout. My boys simply ran wild, killing as many as five. Of course, this delayed our departure, as the hogs had to be cleaned and cut up for transportation in our warashis. There are two species known locally as the kairuni and the abouya. The peccary (abouya) carries the white markings of a collar around its neck and differs from other pigs in possessing four instead of six incisor teeth, in lacking a tail and the fourth hind toe. They all have a peculiar dorsal gland opening on the hinder part of the back containing a liquid of a strong and disagreeable odour. They are found in small droves not exceeding ten in number and are difficult to approach. When hunted by dogs, they run into holes under tree roots or into a hollow log. Peccary are very fond of frequenting the swampy flats where they root about for grubs and the seeds that fall from the numerous palms growing there. The white lipped peccary or kairuni as it is locally called, is a larger animal and moves in droves of sometimes two hundred or more. These are more easily approached to within twenty yards and can be killed with a charge of B.B. shot from my gun. There is generally a puma or deer tiger following the drove, killing and eating the stragglers from time to time when he wants food, but should the puma allow the hogs to surround him, he would be torn to pieces and eaten.

On one occasion I was walking through some low lands covered by wild lily bush, I had my dog with me. The hogs must have scented the dog for the whole area seemed to erupt with the dreaded sound of hundreds of clicking tusks. I beat a hasty retreat for there was no low branched tree in the vicinity which I could have climbed had I been attacked. A friend of mine who was attacked by a drove of these kairuni. They ate his dog and put him up a thorn palm for about an hour before they left. My friend had to be treated with soft grease to remove the thorns from his chest, arms and legs.

On another occasion when I was returning to my camp from a hunting trip and carrying a baby wild hog which was crying, I was startled to see three pumas jump into the trail ahead. Two disappeared but the largest squatted in the middle of the trail awaiting me and the piglet which had attracted its attention. Not having a gun, but remembering as a young boy that the act of stooping to pick up a stone to throw at a dog usually scared it off, I stooped and gathered up a handful of dry leaves and shouting at the top of my voice, ran towards the puma and threw the handful of leaves in its direction. The puma streaked off into the bush and I streaked up the trail to my camp.

The bush has its dry and rainy seasons. During the dry season, the Amerindians use the haiari vine to poison the creeks. The vine is collected and cut into two feet lengths and carried in bundles to a creek selected for this operation. The men and women sit on a rock in the flowing stream and pound the vine with a hardwood stick. The juice from the vine runs into the water turning it a milky white colour. This drugs the fish which float to the surface and are caught by the younger boys and girls. If a fish floats beyond the poison, it is liable to survive. It is here the boys use their bows and arrows to shoot the fish.

They spend some days in this operation, during which time they smoke their catch over a fire before carrying it back to their village. It was during this operation that I was first shown the ancient art of making fire by one of these Amerindians. He chose a piece of dry wood into which he placed a pointed piece of hardwood. Then sitting down and placing his feet on each end of the piece of dry wood, he spun the pointed piece of hardwood between the palms of his hands at the same time keeping a pressure downward. After a short time, the constant spinning pressure of the hardwood on the softwood caused a wisp of smoke to appear. Fine scrapings of dry wood were placed around the point of friction. When the smoke increased the Amerindian gently blew into the tiny spark until a flame appeared between the dry scrapings. This he nursed into a brighter flame, adding fine chips until he had a strong fire burning.

The rainy season is indicated by the changing colour of the leaves on the trees, especially the mora tree whose leaves change from green to yellows, reds and browns. The other softwoods and some hardwoods bloom into brilliant yellow that can be picked out from a distance between the deeper greens, brilliant heliotrope, reds, orange and many other hues. Vines blossom and wild plants are found with their beautiful blooms, but with all this beauty lies danger.

I saw the skies darkening and there was a stillness in the bush as if nature was listening. I heard distant rumblings heralded by vivid flashes of lighting and claps of thunder. I heard the approach of rushing winds which had the forest giants swaying, the foliage overhead hissing and roaring and small branches and leaves falling in showers. I heard the sound of the approaching tropical rain storm coming from a distance. When the storm arrived there was a roaring all around making conversation impossible. This was the time to look up and listen for falling trees. Unfortunately I could not hear every danger signal. I was just standing there when my companion yelled RUN. As I leaped forward, there was a terrific thud. On the ground, right behind me, lay a piece of dead tree limb measuring some three feet in length and a foot in thickness half buried in the mud. Had I not leaped ahead, I would have been struck dead. The bushman will tell you there is far more danger in the forest from falling trees than from snakes and jaguars. The other hazard of the rainy season is the swiftness of flood. The rivers can rise in level as much as fifteen to twenty feet overnight.

However, it was during the great drought of 1926, whilst still in the mountains that Mr. Bracewell, a geologist, and Mr. Lord, a land surveyor, paid us a visit. These gentlemen had been doing some surveys in the surrounding area and were on their way back to the city. Mr. Bracewell, who was later to be appointed Director of Geological Surveys, gave me at a later date some insight into geology which served me greatly in my prospecting for gold and diamonds and other precious minerals. Mr. Lord was later appointed Commissioner of Lands and Mines.

Mr. Haynes asked me to assist these gentlemen through the forests and down the rivers from Anandabaru back to Georgetown. I sent out a runner to Chinapow landing with a message to Joseph to have the bateau ready for our arrival in two days time. I selected six men and four young women to act as porters as far as Tukeit. They would also act as part of the boat crew. I had been receiving news of bush fires for some time, so I knew that the party would have to be on the lookout for falling trees whose roots had been weakened by the fires.

I made a forced march to the river landing, the smoke from the forest burning my eyes. Mr. Bracewell had a narrow escape as a poisonous butterfly snake fell on his shoulder whilst ducking under a tree. One of the Amerindians was quick to strike it off his shoulder before it could strike at Mr. Bracewell's neck. I arrived at Chinapow landing at 6:30 p.m. very tired and after a light supper, retired to my hammock. I had told Joseph to inform Johnson, the boat Captain, to be ready to travel to Kaieteur falls the following day.

Joseph informed me that the level of the river had dropped alarmingly and doubted our progress through the lower reaches of the rivers would be free from trouble. Our troubles began at once, for there were many exposed sand banks and rocks where there had been deep water on our trip up. However, without a heavy cargo our boat floated high and with the current in our favour, the trip to the falls was done in a day. Our baggage was carried from the boat to the rest house. There I sensed something was missing. It was the thunder of the falling waters. I walked from the rest house with four of my Amerindians to the river. I could hardly believe my eyes, for in place of that mighty volume of water, I saw only exposed rocks scattered over the river bed and a bare stream of water which fell over the edge of the precipice, turning to spray where it fell fifty feet down. The vast chasm was opened to my gaze showing the foot of the immense walls of the gorge. Few people, if any, have been privileged to walk across the river at practically the edge of this mighty fall, stepping from rock to rock and wading the more open spots. I and my Amerindians made it over to stand on the sandy opposite bank.

That night, Mr. Bracewell and Mr. Lord showed me some of their maps covering the areas they had traversed and gave me some of their experiences in those remote areas.

Our descent of the escarpment the following morning was a little precarious, as the recent forest fire had burst some of the rocks in our path and we had to make numerous detours to get over and around fallen trees. There were still signs of fire in the vicinity. Our party eventually arrived at Tukeit Rest House at approximately 3:00 p.m. to find a boat awaiting us.

Our Amerindian porters, both boys and girls, were to return to Anandabaru having completed their job at this point. One boy had been very close to me during my stay in the mountains, accompanying me on hunting and fishing trips. It was to him that I had described the world outside: the trains, electrical trams, the big ships made of iron that float on water, our city houses with electric lights and the big water, the Atlantic Ocean, stretching as far as you can see. This was like some fairy tale to him. He wanted to travel with me to see the city and all the wonderful things I had told him about. One of the young women who had attended to my needs at Anandaburu also wanted to travel to town with me. When Mr. Lord told them that no aboriginal was allowed to travel to town without permission from the Government, the young woman fell on her knees and with tears running down her cheeks beseeched us to take her with us, but her request had to be turned down as I had no permit. I was to look back on this incident with deep regret for on my return some three months later to transport some diamond machinery up river over the Kaiteur escarpment, I learned from the Amerindians who were sent out from Anandabaru to assist with the transportation, that most of the young men and women who worked with me during my stay at Anandabaru had died from an epidemic of Asian flu which had swept through that region. So my little Amerindian boy and girl never lived to see the world outside of their mountains.

I have had to lead a fairly solitary existence and when working in the bush, I find it best to live by myself. Maybe it has something to do with being in tune with the land. Most of my successes in the location of gold and diamond deposits were when I was alone, going where my thoughts led me. Sitting by my camp fire at night or just lying in my hammock, I would listen to the stillness of the jungle. The minutest sound carries: the chirping of the crickets, the rustle of a passing bush-rat, the swish of a swooping bat, the crashing passage of a tapir through the bush, the cough of a hunting jaguar, the death squeal of an accouri, the howling of the red baboons which can be heard at a distance of five or six miles, the rustle of the night monkey passing overhead and pausing to investigate my presence. I would think about the predators and scavengers; of the bush-cows, ants, flies and about their being part of the cycle of nature and of life. The jungle gives a bushman a different outlook. You know things will constantly go wrong that you have no control over. You don't give in, but accept the fact that you have to work around things to come to terms with the land. Living this way involves a full commitment to getting right down to basics. You have to rely on yourself, not on other people, so you develop a very honest relationship with yourself.

I thank God, or whatever or whomever it is, for my being alive and for the earth and the beauty it contains and for the things I am able to experience. We need to get back to the idea that we are all responsible for our own actions, not somebody or something else.

CHAPTER III
Proprietor of Agatash Estate – 1927-1929

When I left the bush, my younger brother Howard and I pooled our resources and purchased Agatash Estate, comprising 1,700 acres of land, 365 acres of which were in lime cultivation. The estate was situated on the left bank of the Essequibo River, four miles up river from the mining town of Bartica and sixty-five miles from the coast. Our sister Margaret, just married to Cecil Pereira, joined us to run the house. Cecil assisted us on the estate.

Our house of three bedrooms and a wide veranda was built on the top of a laterite and granite rock hill, one hundred and fifty feet straight up off the river. I had a wonderful view from here, seeing as far down river as Bartica and Makouria on the opposite bank. The steamer plying between the city and Bartica could be clearly discerned when it arrived on Tuesdays, Thursdays and Saturdays.

I found on examination that fifty percent of the lime cultivation had been lost due to bird vine, that the bridges were in bad repair, the riverside stelling and self-acting koker was broken, and two or three of the labourers' houses were in disrepair. The factory, a steel-framed building of concrete with a roof of a galvanized sheets, was in good order. Approximately three miles of constructed roads were badly eroded.

I decided to work inland from the river. I engaged a number of labourers from the nearby village and some East Indian labour from the coast lands. All the existing cultivation of limes and lemons had to be weeded and cleaned up prior to our picking and shipping our produce. I purchased a launch in which I installed a converted Model "T" Ford engine. This was to be our only means of transportation to and from Bartica where we purchased our supplies and collected our mail.

On my investigation of the lands beyond the first range of hills, I discovered an area of flat sandy loamy soil, on which I decided to try out a crop of peanuts. I engaged a number of Bovianders (of mixed Afro-Guyanese and Amerindian descent) to clear the area: clearing the underbush, felling, junking and burning the bush; stumps were cleared out by means of a stump puller. I used a Fordson tractor and Oliver plough to turn over the soil. A number of women were engaged in planting the peanuts, assisted by some of the men. An area of fifteen acres was selected for this trial.

From the time the first shoots showed above the ground, the cultivation was attacked by the cooshi or kooshai ants, otherwise known as the umbrella ant. These ants dwell in the ground where they dig huge nests which cover several square yards. From these nests radiate well beaten roads, sometimes as much as six inches wide, leading to the forest or field where they obtain the green leaves with which they line the inner chambers of their nests. On these leaves a fungus grows which feeds the ants (cows) in the warm darkness, a fat white insect from which the ants derive a substance apparently in the form of body juice. It is a wonderful sight to see these ants on the march. At first glance it appears that thousands of segments of green leaves have come to life and are walking along the miniature roads, but a closer look will show that each piece is being carried by an ant smaller than its burden which almost hides it like a parasol or umbrella. All the burden-bearing insects are hustling along in the one direction toward the nest and now it can be seen that an equal number, empty handed, are running in the opposite direction to pick up their share of leaves. These ants climb up the tree, shrub or plant and using their sharp front clippers, cut pieces of the leaves, dropping them to the ground. To exterminate these ants, (and this must be done if anything is to be cultivated in the vicinity), is a difficult, heartbreaking and expensive task. The burial of dead carcasses in the nest, the spreading of tar, carbolic acid and equally offensive material on the nest will drive them away, but only to build another nest in the vicinity. The inhabitants of the nest must be exterminated entirely and up to the present the most successful methods are the use of carbon bi-sulfide or their drowning out with water. The former method is dangerous (the chemical being highly inflammable as well as having an atrocious smell) and very expensive, plus the high steamer freight. I had a nasty experience with this chemical when Howard and I were killing some ants which had their large nest under a bunduri thorn bush. I crawled under the bushes and plugged all the outlet holes, then taking a crow bar, I punctured the centre of the nest, into which I poured a tablespoon of the chemical, lit a match, dropped it into the hole and plugged the hole. I could clearly hear the dull explosions underground, but in backing out on my stomach, one of the blowholes gave way and I received the blaze of the explosion, a blue flame right in my eyes.

I could not see when I eventually made my way out and Howard had to hold my arm and lead me. When I reached home I told my sister what had happened and she treated my eyes with the white of an egg, washing them out on the second day, and reapplying more egg white. It was four days before I finally regained the use of my eyes. I was thankful that I had not been blinded for life.

After several severe setbacks in labour and in cash, the time came for me to reap my first crop of peanuts. I purchased some rice bags and employed fresh labour from the village, but on pulling up the plants, it was discovered that the pods had no nuts. Such is the farmer's life. Unless one has patience and a belief in God, one is liable to give up. I decided to travel to the city and seek advice from the Agricultural Department.

I met a Mr. Beckett, an Englishman, who told me he had known my father and had spent many a pleasant day at his house on our rubber estate at Mabaruma, North West Region. Mr. Beckett agreed to accompany me back to Agatash, where he spent a month giving me some very useful information and advice. I had to apply limestone to the fifteen acre patch, re-plough the area, covering the vegetation and replant. On reaping my crop later, I was rewarded with a bumper crop, the pods carrying three instead of two nuts.

I also purchased coffee, cocoa plants and pineapple plants on Mr. Beckett's advice, which I planted on the nearby hill slopes, the cocoa having to be planted under shady trees. I repaired the riverside self-acting koker and decided to put in a rice crop in an empoldered area adjacent to the river from which I could draw irrigation water. Greenheart timbers were felled and shipped out from the more forested areas to the saw mills at Bartica.

I allowed the residents from Bartica to graze their cattle in the low lying creek lands where there was lush grazing and between the lemon and lime cultivation. I later had to close these pastures as too many cows were being killed by the puma or deer tiger. One night though, Howard, accompanied by one of the men from the village, set out to await the return of the puma to a cow it had slain. It was not until approximately 11:00 p.m. that a shadowy form was discerned slinking toward its kill. Howard and his companion were sitting on a wabini (stand) built against a tree about ten feet off the ground. With the aid of a torch light (the puma looked up to the light as it began to eat from the kill), Howard was able to shoot it. This animal proved to be seven feet in length and we kept its skin in the house.

The East Indian labourers were occasionally killing snakes when they were weeding the grass in the overgrown cultivation, mostly the venomous labaria and an occasional land boa constrictor. In this country, there are probably as many as forty different species of snakes, of which probably only seven or eight at most are venomous. Therefore when you meet a snake, the chances are five to one against it being a venomous one. The labaria, though, which rarely exceeds four feet in length, has a bite which, if unattended, has been known to cause death within forty-eight hours. It is known as the dreaded fer-de-lance elsewhere in the West Indies. The land camoodi, land boa, or boa constrictor is remarkably coloured, with browns, russet red and cream which blend with its natural environment. One has to look a second time to distinguish the snake. They are usually found to be below eighteen feet in length but some have been found to be twenty feet and over.

Sakarara Bay, which lay behind our house, was a favourite fishing ground for the night fisherman from Bartica. I too have caught many fish for the table from this vicinity. Once, I was paddling my corial along the shoreline when I heard a piercing scream coming from one of the smaller islands in the bay. Thinking someone was in pain, I went to lend assistance, only to discover that the screams were from two water-dogs (otter) fighting over a fish one had caught. The brown variety are found in rivers all over our country, but the black are most rare, and I have only found them in a black water creek discharging its waters into Sakarara Bay. These water-dogs have an overall length of four feet from nose to tail, webbed feet, and a flat tail. They are fast swimmers, adept at catching the fish in the creeks and lakes. They are not welcome in our fishing reserves as they chase the fish away. Their fur is not as thick as those of their cousin otters of the northern lands. I have seen them made into pets when captured young.

I experienced good hunting in the low lands bordering the bay. There were numerous droves of wild hog, and an occasional red deer. It was in this area where Howard and I first saw a large quarta or spider monkey. We heard a loud crashing in the tree branches and looked up to see this large monkey swinging from branches and jumping from tree to tree. These monkeys have very long arms, legs and tail, which make them appear larger than they really are. I have seen them in captivity, very slow moving and gentle as pets.

Howard and I were standing on our riverside stelling inspecting some workmen repairing the timbers, when we noticed what we thought was a moss covered log float by. It was not until some two hours later that two men from Agatash Village came paddling furiously to report there was a large kaiman (overgrown alligator) lying on the sand beach by the village and requesting that I go and kill it. Howard and I decided to drop down stream in our launch. On my arrival, I saw this huge reptile basking in the sun on the beach in front of the village where a number of people were assembled. I had a Sharps .22 high-powered rifle. I approached the reptile and put a bullet in its right eye. The kaiman tore up the sand in all directions with its powerful tail in its death struggle. I measured its length which proved to be twenty-six feet from nose to tail. The head and jaws alone were five feet. The Amerindians and some of the old bushmen wear a kaiman tooth on a string around their necks. This is said to keep away snakes. The scrapings from a kaiman tooth are said to be a cure for snake bite.

CHAPTER IV
Up the Mazaruni: Shooting Marshall Falls – c. 1927

Bartica, the mining town, was the departure point for riverboats travelling up river to the diamond fields in the Mazaruni river and to the gold fields in the Cuyuni river in the early years. Because fortunes were being made, the shops and liquor stores rarely closed. Men returning from the fields with their fortunes spent their money freely, saying that there was plenty more where that had come from. There was a price to be paid. On my visits to Bartica on a weekend, I was always hearing of the fatalities the tributors suffered in their river travel. It was the same too for the crews and steersmen who took the merchants' boats to supply their up-river shops with much needed supplies. These steersmen were paid on a round trip. The faster they made a trip, the more money they earned, and although the Lands and Mines Department laid down strict laws on river transportation, forbidding the running of certain rapids and falls after dark, these laws were flagrantly disobeyed, to the risk and danger of the lives of the passengers in the boats. Moreover, on their departure from Bartica, the merchants would often overload their boats beyond the insurance mark, increasing the hazard because a heavily laden boat cannot negotiate the swiftly flowing and treacherous currents as well as it should. The gold officer or warden had often to turn back these boats to Bartica and have them off-load sufficient cargo to enable the insurance mark to show.

Fortunately, though, these river boats were built by men who knew the rivers, being forty or forty-two feet long, bateau shaped, having a beam of six or seven feet and a depth of four feet, capable of carrying a cargo of sixteen thousand pounds and a crew of twelve boat hands, including the steersman (captain) and engineer. The captain usually steers on the left-hand side of the stern and has an assistant, whom we term as an awkward paddle man, on the right. The steering paddles are nine feet in length, usually made from the yarulla tree or the pakusanna tree. These paddles are strapped to the side of the boat about two and a half feet from the stern, using a new three-quarter inch diameter manilla rope, passed through a small hole below the gunwale, drawn tight by hand and re-enforced by hardwood wedges driven between the gunwale top and the rope, to prevent any slack. This binding rope was the safety margin between life and death on many trips, especially in steaming up the falls with a heavily laden boat. When the captain pulls on his paddle to get just a little more margin to clear a rock or to approach a convenient way to climb a rapid, and his rope cuts it is, as the saying goes, "All gone". For the boat, after losing steerway, can swing broadside to the strong current, slam into a rock, broach itself and sink or be braced on a rock, take in water and sink. Lives as well as cargoes have been lost. These paddles take a terrific strain in negotiating these swift currents, especially if the boats are powered by 90 HP inboard engines.

It was because so many lives were lost in the years 1924-1926 that the Government decided to build a road, cutting out these miles of falls, following the ridge between the Essequibo and the Mazaruni rivers for a distance of seventy-five miles, at which point, a road fifty-one miles in length was opened to come out at Issano on the right bank of the Mazaruni above the falls. When tributors arrived at Bartica, they would join a transport bus which took two days to cover this distance.

My elder brother, Robert, who was the warden or gold officer, at the time, took a party up to Marshall Falls, so that we could have the experience of shooting down these turbulent waters. The warden's boat measured thirty-two feet in length, was bateau shaped, having a beam of five feet and a depth of two and a half feet. It was loaded with food and drinks, coconuts and ground provisions, spare paddles and rope. Robert and Howard, my two brothers, and I and the steersman left Bartica early Sunday morning and following the right bank of the Mazaruni river proceeded upstream passing Kalcoon lime estate on our left and the Penal Settlement on the left bank of the river to our right. The river at this point being over a mile wide, the settlement is where all the long term prisoners are sent. The original stone buildings were erected by the early Dutch settlers. Today the prisoners have a thriving stock farm, cattle, pigs and poultry. They plant their own vegetables and fruit. About one mile up river from the settlement, we passed the point where the Cuyuni river joins the Mazaruni river. In this wide bay, lies the island of Kyk-Over-Al, on which stands the remnants of an old Dutch fort. The history of this fort goes back to the 1600s. At this point, the river is exceedingly wide and can prove very dangerous to small craft, should a strong wind blow up, causing the waves to swamp it. At the right bank of the Cuyuni river, at its junction with the Mazaruni, there is an old river landing which years before was the entrance of a road leading to Peter's Gold Mine. Eventually, our boat arrived at Baracara Settlement at 10:00 a.m. This settlement consisted of some twenty families mostly of Amerindian and Afro-Guyanese descent.

A throng of happy children ran down the sand beach to meet the boat. Their mothers were engaged in washing clothes at the riverside. The boat was moored and Robert led the way along a narrow track to the house of Peter Vanderhyden, a retired river steersman of exceptional ability. Peter introduced me to his wife and his two buxom daughters. Robert explained the purpose of our visit and asked Peter to accompany us and steer the boat through the falls. Peter agreed, adding that his two daughters would accompany us to assist in preparing our lunch. He said he would also bring six boys from the settlement to form the boat crew, because no boat would venture into Marshall Falls without a full crew to assist in handling the boat operations.

We left Baracara at approximately 11:30 a.m. and proceeded up river enjoying the brilliant sunshine. At points there were gaps in the vegetation on the river bank where people had once lived but had departed to let the bush take over. Iced drinks were served on board. Beer, rum and aerated drinks for the girls, though most river women prefer their drinks on the strong side. After an hour or so, I noticed the increased speed of the current as we approached the rapids. Great blobs of foam were floating downstream. Peter told us we were now in the fallout of the rapids. After another twenty minutes of steaming up river, I could hear the roar of the falling waters. When we rounded a bend in the river, I saw the spectacular sight of surging white water against a background of black rocks and green shrubs growing on the rocks.

This was Marshall Falls. Looking at this wall of fierce water, I wondered how our small boat could ever battle its way through. Peter told my brother that the water was too full and powerful to challenge the main channel, so he would take one of the lesser rapids. The boat was now in the hands of Peter and his crew of river men. He instructed his bowman to take over the bow paddle and the crew to stand by their paddles. The bowman stood on the bow of the boat with his paddle poised ready to ease the boat off any submerged rock. I was thrilled to see the speed of the water as the boat eased up into the current. The young men were called upon to bend their backs to their paddles when the boat hit a hump of surging water. Paddles broke under the strain but a spare one was quickly picked up from the bottom of the boat, where there was a bundle of spares. It was fascinating to watch the play of muscles in the backs and shoulders of the paddlers in their endeavour to pull the boat up this rapid. After about ten minutes, we came up under the lee of a large rock. Here Peter paused to give the crew a breather and for us to readjust ourselves. He then once again swung the boat out into

the swirling waters. It was a wonder to see Peter handling the steering paddle, reading the currents and using them to his advantage. One could feel
the boat respond to his paddle. Approximately a quarter of a mile from the
summit of the falls the boat was tied up under the lee of a small island where
we planned to take lunch. The girls in the boat had been peeling cassava,
sweet potatoes and grating coconuts. As they were preparing a creole dish
of "metagee", whilst awaiting the cooking of this pot, two of the boys had
managed to hook two packu fish to sweeten the pot. These fish are about two
feet in length having a circular shape about three inches thick in the centre.
Their colouring is black along the back, the sides and underbelly a tinge of
reddish brown. They feed on the green moss and other aquatic vegetation
which covers the rocks. They can be caught with a rod and line using the
lanna seed as bait. Some Amerindians use this seed encased in a plaited
basket and tied to a length of string. The scent of the lanna seed dancing in
the current of the rapids draws the Packu to the surface, at which point the
Indian shoots it with an arrow from his bow.

Some of the party swam in the rapids before called to lunch. This was
where the fun started, for when one of the young men finished his share of
metagee, he would look to rob another's plate of the various tidbits. There
was much horse play. My brother Robert swam out to a rock in the rapids,
holding his plate over his head, where he completed his lunch in peace.

After lunch, swimming resumed. There was one spot in the rapids where
you allowed the current to carry you along, to be sucked under for a distance of about a hundred yards. Then the suction bursts, allowing the current to push you up again. At this point you had to catch a turn-tide and
swim out back to the river bank. I tried this run and got my chest, elbows
and knees bruised by the submerged rocks. One of the boys who had drunk
too much liquor missed the turn-tide and was swept downstream to a larger
fall, and was only just rescued in time by two of his friends. This put a stop
to our swimming. Peter was very angry, because the drunk man could have
lost his life. We were all foolhardy, he said, to take these unnecessary risks
in the name of sport. He decided it was time to go because it would still take
about two hours to return, even with the help of the swift water and the falling tide which could be felt up to this fall.

The boat was reloaded and pushed off to enter the narrow twisting channel known as "Tramway Hole" of overhanging trees. At one point, spotting
some ripe papaws on a tree, two of the boys dove overboard and swam ashore
to retrieve them. Peter swore at them because he had no space to swing the
boat round in this narrow channel to pick them up. Fortunately we were able

to hold on to some tree branches on the river bank to hold back the boat until the boys returned with their fruit. Lower down, the boat once more emerged into the main river, where we encountered two cargo boats with miners returning to Bartica who challenged us as to who would 'meet out' first. But they were unprepared for Peter's knowledge of back channels and short cuts. He cut through some even narrower holes in the bush, twisting and turning, some barely having room for the boat to pass. If I had admired his steersmanship in the falls, I really had to take my hat off to him here, for in these narrow confines and travelling at twenty miles an hour, he had to make his decisions without any hesitation. At one point the bowman was thrown off the bow into the dark black water by a sudden twist around a sharp turn, but these boys are like fish for as fast as he was in the water, he surfaced and catching the gunwale, hauled himself back on board, none the worse for his ducking. When the boat eventually did emerge into the main river, we were way ahead of the other two boats. A rope end was shown to them to taunt them.

We arrived back at Baracara at approximately 5:00 p.m. I followed the boys and the girls to the back of the settlement where the waterfall had formed a natural pool of clear, cool water. The girls peeled off all except their panties and the boys down to nature's dress. There was much laughter and play. I returned to Peter's house where I was offered drinks and something to eat. Eventually, everyone tracked down to the beach where the boys brought out their guitars and mandolins and we danced on the cool sands in the moonlight. Most of these river girls have the natural gift of dancing. After thanking Peter for his hospitality, our party returned to Bartica.

I decided to sell the estate in early 1929 because I was incurring too much overhead expense and not getting sufficient return. I had foolishly planted long term instead of short term crops. Mr. De Souza, a saw mill owner from Bartica, purchased the estate. I was sorry to learn a few years later that he had cut all the greenheart timber from the backlands, sold the existing cottages, broken up the lime factory to sell it in parcels to Bartica residents, leaving the rest of the estate to return to virgin forest.

However, there are memories which I will always treasure from my time at Agatash. In particular, the villagers there introduced me to the "Mashramani" way of life, for when there is a house to be erected, or a field to be cleared and burned or planted, or any labour requiring assistance, they send out invitations up and down river for their friends and neighbours to attend a "Mashramani" on such and such a day, describing the work to be done. Huntsmen and fishermen are sent out a day in advance of the occasion to bring in fresh meat and fish. On the morning of the occasion, I have seen corials and boats arriving from up and down river with whole families. The men and boys and some of the more mature women come armed with cutlasses with which to underbush the area, and axes to fell and junk the trees. The women, other than those working in the bush, assist in cooking and preparation of the casiri and sleep-inducing tonic drinks. Work in the field closes at about 2:00 p.m. when everyone takes a dip in the river to wash off the grime. Then the drinks are served followed by a call to eat. When the heat of the sun diminishes, the guitars and violins are brought out, the older men providing the music, the younger boys and girls joining in the dancing. Those who have a far distance to travel leave early; some who have had too much to drink prefer to spend the night right there. Few river people have sufficient cash on hand to pay for this kind of work. For years, this has been their way of life, helping one another when the occasion arises.

CHAPTER V
Sugar Estate Overseer: Plantation Tuschen – 1929-1935

When I left Agatash Estate and my first experience of bush life and farming, I decided to join the firm of Booker Bros. McConnel & Co. Ltd. to further my education in agriculture, in tillage, planting, irrigation and drainage. Booker Bros. and Sandbach Parker & Co. Ltd. were the owners of most of the larger sugar estates. Their factories produced Demerara sugar, molasses and rum.

I was interviewed by Robert Strang at the Georgetown Assembly Rooms, headquarters for all planters when they were in town. He said I resembled my father, who had emigrated from Scotland to British Guiana at the same time as he had. Young men from Scotland and England comprised the staff of most of the sugar estates, along with a good percentage of local men. I was assigned to Plantation "Tuschen-de-Vrenden" which translated from the Dutch means "between the friends". It is situated on the left bank of Boeraserie Creek, which discharges its water into the Essequibo River, thus forming the boundary between the West Coast of Demerara and the East Bank of Essequibo, having De Kindren to the East on the right bank of the Boeraserie Creek and Plantation de Vergenoegen, a rice and coconut estate to the west in the county of Essequibo. Mr. Strang informed me I would be paid the sum of $29.33 per month with a $5.00 allowance to pay my house-boy who would also receive a daily wage of three bits per day or six shillings per week. I would take my meals at the manager's table, for which the manager would receive $30.00 per month from the firm.

On a Sunday afternoon in May 1929, I reported to Mr. Birtles, the manager, who informed me that I was to occupy one of the six rooms in a two storied house (previously housing six overseers when the estate was grinding its own canes). The house had been built on solid brick pillars by the Dutch, twelve feet from the ground. It had a fair size kitchen attached on the first floor, furnished with a large Dover wood-burning stove. The bathroom, located at ground level, was of concrete. There was no running water. A bucket of water was put inside the bathroom and I had to use a calabash (gourd) to throw water over my skin. Rain water collected from the roof was stored in a ten thousand gallon wooden vat. An outhouse or latrine was built over the drainage trench, flushed at every falling tide. I had to furnish my room with a small cot, table and chair and a kerosene lantern as there was no electricity. I would receive one gallon of kerosene oil per month to illuminate my room and to make up my weekly pay sheets and reports. I would also receive two cakes of soap and four pounds of sugar per week. I later purchased a kerosene pressure lamp, 350 C.P., as the kerosene lantern was putting too much strain on my eyes, working up to two and three in the mornings to complete my pay sheets.

On Monday, I returned to Georgetown to purchase my outfit, a riding saddle, bridle and reins, spurs, riding breeches, tunics and a pith helmet, blankets and toilet requisites. I returned to the estate travelling from Vreed-en-hoop by one of the slowest trains, covering the distance of fifteen miles in one whole hour. (British Guiana was the first country in the whole of South America to lay rails and have a train running). A donkey cart conveyed me and baggage from the train station to the overseers' quarters. I reported to Mr. Birtles and I was introduced to Mrs. Birtles, her two sons, and a daughter. (Ted Birtles, one of the sons, was later killed in a bombing run over Berlin in World War 2.)

On Tuesday morning I was awakened by a loud knocking on my door and the night watchman calling "Panch Bajou" – 5:00 a.m.. These watchman were supposed to call out every hour of their watch reporting "all is well". If a watchman is not heard on the hour you could guarantee he was sleeping. On one occasion, I was with Mr. Todd, another manager, when we discovered the factory watchman asleep at his post. Todd, taking a leaf out of his cigarette book, stuck it to the man's bare leg and lit a match. The man leaped to his feet with a startled yell to find the manager and me holding his night stick and lantern. He was given a severe warning and lost a night's pay.

On arising, I had to report to the managers' yard along with Mr. Camacho, the deputy and six Indo-Guyanese sirdars, to await orders from the manager as to where the various gangs of labour were to work. In some seasons it was a punishment awaiting the manager's arrival because the mosquitoes in the rainy season would devour you alive, and in the dry season the sand flies took over, biting and stinging your exposed neck and arms. After orders, I accompanied the sirdars into the labourers' compound, known as the "Nigger Yard", comprised of logies built on the ground in which the labourers lived. The sirdars shouted out orders to the shovel gang or forking gang to go to such and such a field in such and such a section, either Zeelugt or Tuschen; the weeding and boy gangs were sent to their various locations and the creole gang was divided into various groups to work on different jobs.

From the yard, I returned to my quarters where my servant, Babu, had brought my coffee, etc. from the manager's yard. He then bought my riding mule to my house. I had learned to ride horses in England. Riding a mule is similar but the disposition of the animals differ greatly. My first mount was an old black mule named accordingly "Blackie" who took a joy in bracing my leg against any tree she was passing. She was slow but she got me to my destination eventually. After "Blackie", I was given another mule named "Lady Love", but she was trouble, and in the end a killer. One incident occurred on a Saturday morning when the Attorney, Mr. Strang, was riding with the managers to inspect the cultivation. "Lady Love" refused to go forward and was constantly moving back, so I jammed her with my spurs, and she promptly put down her head and bucked me off into the trench, much to my discomfort as Mr. Strang and Mr. Birtles were approaching at the same time. I crawled out of the trench, my nice white tunic and riding breeches soaking wet, my boots full of water, only to meet the baleful eyes of my "Lady Love" and the guffaws of laughter from Bobby Strang and the manager. Worse was to follow because on another day, as she was passing one of the fork men who was carrying his fork on his shoulder, she side-kicked the man, breaking his ribs under the arm which was holding the fork on the shoulder. I jumped off and gathered the man in my arms and carried him to the hospital which was only a couple hundred yards away, but the man died within a couple of hours. The doctor said the ribs had punctured his lungs. At the inquest which I had to attend to give evidence, the Magistrate, Mr. Ruggles, told me to put this mule to pull cane punts, and take another mule to ride. But "Lady Love" continued to prove most unladylike, for although burdened with the harness of a pulling mule with a long steel chain, she waited until one of the women from the weeding gang was passing then kicked the woman into the trench, thence to the hospital where she fortunately recovered.

This put an end to my riding mules. I purchased a gelding, dark red in colour, whom, I named "Bruno". I later broke in a jet black stallion on Leguan Island, whom I named "Ras Kassa" and a cream coloured mare which Mrs. Whyte, the owner of Canefield Estate on Leguan Island, presented to me as a gift. I also received a mouse-coloured racing mare from Kuldip Maraj from the Essequibo Coast. He said the mare had killed a jockey and his men were afraid to ride it. He said the mare was called "Rhonie".

Whenever called upon by Mrs. Whyte to visit her to break in some horses, I would leave the estate on Saturday after paying the labourers, and catch the last train, which connected with the ferry from Parika to Leguan. This ferry was captained by Willie Phillips, an old boxer and a friend. I would sleep at Canefield and break in the horses on the sand beaches the following morning, returning to the estate on Sunday afternoon via the ferry from Leguan to Parika. One afternoon, galloping to catch the ferry, I was thrown off my horse into a stinking muddy trench and had to stop at the police station to wash off the mud before I could board the ferry. By the time I got to the stelling, the boat had already pulled away so I sent a piercing whistle across the water and my friend, Capt. Willie, swung the steamer back to pick me up.

The labour force on the Estate was Indo-Guyanese, either indentured from India or their descendants. I can say that in my day 60% were Mohammedan, 30% Hindu and 10% Madrassi. The sirdars or "drivers" were mostly Mohammedan. Dil Mohamed, the head driver, was in overall charge. He supervised the cane cutting and shovel gangs. Sultan supervised the loading of cane into punts. He was also the ranger for the estate, looking after the coconut cultivation. Najeer and Adalut were in charge of the shovel and forking gangs. Eli Bachs was in charge of the jobbing shovelmen, Manan Khan was in charge of the weeding and boy gangs and Surju (a Hindu) was in charge of the Creole gang.

I was put in charge of the Creole gang, the junior gang on the estate, made up mostly of little children, their ages ranging from ten to fourteen years, a mixture of Indo-Guyanese and Afro-Guyanese, with a few mature Afro-Guyanese women. The children received the sum of one and a half bits per day, the older ones receiving two and a half to three bits per day. The so called "bit" or four penny piece was still in circulation and was a successor to the old quarter guilder, in common use in the early days of the British occupation. In those days, all sugar estate labour was reckoned and paid in guilders, half and quarter guilders (bits) and until recently job work was given out in so many bits per rod. A half bit denoted two pence, bit and a half – sixpence and two bits – eight pence. The Creole gang was engaged in applying sulphate of ammonia to young growing canes from a gallon bucket carried on their arm, and collecting and loading cane tops into the cane punts for transportation to new fields that had to be planted. They also fetched dirt in wooden trays on their heads, to build stop-offs and smousing for the irrigation or flooding of fields. I had to inspect the young growing canes for signs of borer worms that eat into the base of the shoot killing the plant.

These children left home at 7:30 a.m. to walk two or three miles to their work, they would be on their feet the whole day, in the sun and rain, and had to walk back home in the late afternoon. Young women from the weeding gang were often included in the Creole gang to push up the manuring or the supplying of cane tops. These women received three and a half to four bits per day. I had three or four strong Afro-Guyanese boys to handle the heavy manure bags in the punts, and to refill the buckets as fast as the children came back to the punts for more manure. These boys received three and a half bits per day.

At midday, I gave the gang their lunch hour. My lunch was brought from the manager's house by my bateau boy on my mule. I selected a cool spot under a tree and took my lunch, washing it down with a water coconut the boy picked off a nearby tree. In excessively heavy rainfall, I usually stopped work when we were applying manure, but when otherwise engaged, I had to grin and bear it, sheltering some of the children under my umbrella or rain-coat. I really pitied these children as they stood there in their wet clothes shivering, waiting for the rain to stop on the many days it rained during the rainy season. They were wet before they arrived at their work spots and had to work in wet clothes the whole day before they returned home. There were times I have had to pick up a little one and give them a ride home on my mule back.

There was much laughter and play during the lunch hour and in teasing some of the older girls of sixteen to eighteen years I soon found myself in trouble, for some of them were really pretty. One girl of Madrassi origin called Soorsatie cried out in her sleep at home: "No sahib, no sahib". Lochan, her father, came to see me the next day and asked me if I had interfered with his daughter. I explained that there was nothing but play in which the girl was kissed, but nothing more. Another girl of sixteen years of age, from a Mo-hammedan family, with a clear complexion and grey eyes, whose name was Hakikan, was always bringing flowers and plants to my house. She was then making advances to me. She was sent away for about a year to spend time with her grandparents at another village. On her return, she waylaid me in the back dam. I would have passed her on my horse for she had grown and put on weight, but she called out: "Sahib, don't you know me". It was only then that I recognised her. She said she was a big girl now and was ready for me. We walked the side-line dam where I took her virginity before going home. I saw her frequently after this as she was attached to the weeding gang, but I had no further physical contact with her. Some months later, when her mother was presenting Hakikan to a prospective suitor, Hakikan was sent to fetch a bucket of water from the well pipe, as is the custom, so the prospective bridegroom could view his prospective bride. But on lifting the heavy bucket of water, Hakikan took in with pains and delivered a stillborn baby boy. Everyone was shocked, for no one suspected that Hakikan was pregnant.

The next day, I was taking tea when my houseboy told me Dil Mohamed and some of the other sirdars had come to see me. Dil Mohamed's first question was: "Sahib, were you friends with a girl by name of Hakikan". I said yes but only once, and that had been months ago. Then Dil Mohamed explained what had happened. It seemed that one of the sirdars, Eli Bachs, was her father and Najeer and Adalut her uncles. They were very hurt and upset as this incident had spoiled the girl's chance of marriage. I tried to explain matters, telling the sirdars what had led up to the incident and offered to pay for all expenses of the infant's burial and compensation to the girl. Dil Mohamed told me that the entire estate liked and respected me, but had it been otherwise, they would have reported me to the attorney and I would have been dismissed. I learned later that Hakikan did marry the boy and they moved to Vreed-en-hoop.

CHAPTER VI
Hunting in the Backdam

From the Creole gang, I was promoted to be in charge of the 'boy' gang (of young men) whose task was to weed all the riding dams, clean the side-line trenches which provided drainage and the middle-walk trenches in preparation for the grinding season so the cane punts could move freely. They were also used to underbush new areas being taken into cultivation for canes. They worked on a piece rate basis, weeding dams at twenty cents per square rod or cleaning side-line or middle-walk trenches at eight cents or one bit per running rod, depending on the width of the trench. These young men and some of the younger girls also formed a gang of about thirty who were engaged in bleeding the rubber trees adjacent to the Boeraserie Creek and conservancy. They left home very early in the mornings so as to catch the latex when it is running freely before the sun came up. They cut the bark of the tree with special knives, each cut leading into another. At the bottom cut a small tin cup is inserted to catch the latex. By dayclean, 8:00 a.m. all the latex milk was collected and handed to the man in charge of the smoke house who smoked the sheets from which rubber was made. On my first visit to the smoke house, the man in charge, a Mr. Chung, immediately recognised me. He asked me if I was not David Young's son from North West District, as I resembled my father on whose rubber plantation he had worked.

It was whilst I was in charge of the boy gang that I got involved in hunting with dogs. I had always been fond of hunting and I always had a double barrelled Midland gun at hand. There were two strapping Indo-Guyanese brothers, Johnnie and Sarone, who were always accompanied by a pack of seven dogs. These boys explained to me that the creek lands and the area of the rubber fields harboured large red deer, water haas, labba and other game. I joined them to go out hunting on Sunday mornings. At approximately 4:30 to 5:00 a.m. the boys awakened me with a blast from a cow horn and the barking of dogs under my house. I would take a hasty cup of coffee, don a pair of yachting boots and, dressed in khaki, join the boys in a large corial or dug-out which we paddled along the middle-walk trench, the dogs trotting along on the riding dam. At our destination, the last cross dam near the rubber-bush, the boys produced some roti and curry which we ate before the dogs were put in the field. Then two of us would take up positions with our guns to shoot whatever the dogs chased out. Some red deer practically ran me off my feet as they fled to the adjacent Vergenoegen estate and back again before they were shot.

One morning we had hunted without any luck and were about to return home at about midday, when I suggested that we put the dogs back through an abandoned patch of cane they had already been through. I volunteered to go to the cross-canal bucket head near the side-line on the edge of the rubber bush, as the others were tired and reluctant to walk the 120 rods. I walked the dam bed smouse of the field and positioned myself, awaiting the barking of the dogs which would herald the approach of game. The midday heat was oppressive as I awaited impatiently for about twenty minutes. I was about to walk back, thinking the boys might have been correct in saying there was nothing there, when I was alerted by a deep-throated bark from Spot, a white bull with a large brown spot on his back. I then noticed the top leaves of the cane waving where some animal had been disturbed. Some of the other dogs now picked up the scent and joined the chorus of barks and yelps. Eventually I saw a large antlered deer coming across the field from the far side, bobbing as it jumped over the drains between the two rows of cane. When it reached the second bed from me, I aimed at his head, only to break one side of his antlers. The second barrel of shot caught him on his left shoulder but that did not stop his run. He was coming straight for me, so I threw aside my gun and jumped onto the back of the deer, the two of us falling into the cross-canal trench. I took its horns and tried to drown it in the water, at the same time shouting for the boys to come. When they did arrive and saw my position, they all burst into peals of laughter. Johnnie said I resembled Father Neptune emerging from the depths, covered by a mantle of the shrimp grass with which the surface of the canal was covered. The boys cut a twelve-foot sapling two inches thick to which they tied the feet of the deer. Sarone said that this was the largest buck they had shot for a long time. We would occasionally capture a young deer the dogs had run down. I saved three which I had roaming tame in my compound.

Labba or water haas were our other quarry. We would chase them out of their holes under the rubber trees. They would take refuge in the water, but we shot them when they surfaced to breathe. The water haas had long been hunted by the estate authorities as they have a habit of grazing down young canes. A dollar a head was the bounty. The water haas is the largest of our rodents. It is three to four feet long, having a massive body and a heavy, flat head, small eyes and ears, short stout legs with hooflike claws and weighs about 100 pounds. In the grassy wastelands of the lowlands, it is met with in fairly large droves. These rodents, when cornered, can attack with their tusklike cutting teeth, causing severe injury. One of our dogs died from such an attack when a water haas took a large chunk of meat out of its side and it bled to death. When caught young, water haas make splendid pets. In the water, these animals can be traced by a succession of air bubbles from their lungs. I have dived behind a young animal, following these bubbles, and was able to grasp its back legs, slide my other hand up its belly, and lift it out of the water, where the men took it and slid it into an empty rice bag.

During the mango season, I had a good time night hunting for labba. A wabini or a stand is erected in the tree branches eight or ten feet from the ground and mango seeds are collected and piled at a spot which I could see by the beam of my torch light. Labbas usually emerge from their holes at 8:00 p.m. on a dark night, or await the downing of the moon. On a moon lit night, when the labba comes to eat, I would await the cracking of a seed. After a half minute, it would start to eat. This was when I would switch on the beam of the torch light, catching the reflected green of the labba's eyes. I usually used B.B. shot for these animals. One night, a young boy from one of the labourer's logies asked to accompany Johnnie and me. We secured ourselves up in the tree, but when a stray cow approached, thinking it might frighten away the labba, I sent Seepersaud, the boy, to chase it away. I heard him shouting at the cow, then I heard him exclaim in a frightened voice "Oh me mama!" and then silence. Johnnie and I called to him a few times, but on getting no reply we decided to investigate. We called and shone our torch light beams under the surrounding trees and called repeatedly. Eventually, I heard a voice in a tree above my head saying "Look me dey hey, Sahib". I asked him why he had not answered and he said that a tiger (jaguar) had made a rush at him. He was so frightened, he had sprung to the nearest branch and hauled himself into the tree. Johnnie and I examined the bole of the tree and saw claw marks. I was later to shoot this jaguar for it started to raid the pig pens of the residents in the Zeelugt area.

I have been caught waiting up in a mango tree at the beginning of a new day and only realised it when I heard the manager's order bell ringing. I had to run and leave my gun at the gate, hurriedly joining the line to receive my orders and not dressed as I should have been in my working clothes. When orders were finished, the manager said, "Mr. Young, would you wait". He then thanked me for the many times I had presented him with wild meat and fowl but reminded me that a man cannot do justice to his day job if he is up all night in a tree.

During the rice planting season, the people have a lot of trouble with invading wisiwisi ducks which swoop down and eat the paddy seeds. This was a sport I really enjoyed, shooting these and the larger Moscovi ducks when they are on the wing. On two or three occasions, I had had the pleasure of travelling up the Boeraserie conservancy to Waramina where there is a large house at which the overseers from the different estates spend a day or two during the "Phagwah" festival. A book is kept to record the weights of the ducks shot. My score was a whopping twelve pounder. I enjoyed swimming in these waters. But there was one occasion, after I had shot a duck which fell into the waters too far from the bank of the creek, when I decided to swim out and recover it and, about to stretch out my hand to retrieve it, the duck was snatched from my grasp by some denizen of the deep. I did a right about turn and managed to do a record sprint to the creek bank. I suspected it must have been an alligator or a water dog that made a meal of my duck.

In the dry season, fishermen catch a lot of hassar which have been trapped in the small ponds of the savannah. I have caught many such fish by blocking the cross-canal mouths with a seine, then having the boys beat the surface of the water, thus driving the fish before them where they are caught in the seine. Another well known table fish is the cuffum or tarpon which can be caught in areas such as the Mahaica and Mahaicony Creeks, weighing up to 40 lbs. on average with scales over two inches in diameter. However, fishermen are not keen on getting the larger ones in their nets for a large tarpon is like a bull in a china shop. I have seen them in the evening in the Boeraserie Conservancy rolling like porpoises. I have never been lucky enough to catch one on a hook; at the sight of a rod and line, they find they have business elsewhere. They are famed too for their leaping powers. Their frequent leaps into the air seem to be mostly in sporting manifestation of their immense vitality and not for food or from fear. The jumps are accomplished generally by the fish swimming rapidly upward through the surface of the water into the air, giving a sharp flick with its tail as it leaves the water. There is at least one known instance of this leap proving fatal. An Afro-Guyanese man was fishing from his corial at the mouth of the Akawini Creek when a cuffum, said to be seven feet in length, suddenly jumped out of the water and hit him over his heart, killing him instantly. The momentum and weight of the fish were so great that, at the postmortem, it was discovered that all the man's ribs had been stoved in.

A near tragedy occurred when I visited some of my boys who were cleaning a cross canal. I found most of them on the dam bed of the canal shouting to those left in the water to come out. When I asked them the cause of the panic they told me there was a boa constrictor in the water and it had wrapped one of the boys in its coils. I immediately grasped a cutlass from one of the men and jumped into the canal with all my clothes. Feeling for the giant snake, I began to saw at the spot I was grasping (chopping the snake would have made no impression on its body). Soon the head of the snake appeared above the water. I shouted to the other boys to try and catch hold of the head, but they were too afraid, so I told them to help the boy who was still held by the snake by trying to pull him out of the canal. My constant sawing must have had some effect on the snake for it released its hold on the boy and disappeared in the waters of the canal. My action in jumping into the water to assist one of the boys earned me a higher respect from all the labourers on the estate.

The rivers of Guyana have always held a fascination for me, their hidden dangers perhaps a challenge I could not resist. For instance, taking a holiday at Wismar on the Demerara River with some friends, I used to bathe every morning at the riverside, then take a swim over the river and back again. On morning an aged Afro-Guyanese woman stopped me, "My son," she said. "I have seen you swimming this river everyday, but take an old woman's advice, don't swim too far out, for many swimmers have disappeared here." On another occasion I was with Jack Luther, a friend, meeting his brother from the Georgetown steamer. He carried his brother across the river in his corial, but it was too small to accommodate me, so I told Jack I would swim and meet him over the river at MacKenzie. I took off my clothes and, leaving them in a bundle on the river bank, plunged into the dark river and swam under water until I surfaced quite far out from the bank, then continued to the other side. I borrowed a shirt and pants from a friend and later went into town to join Jack. He, meanwhile, after spending a very convivial day with various friends, had decided to return home down river. As night had set in, I decided to go back to Wismar. I took off my clothes again and, strapping them on my head, swam back over the dark river, guided by the light from my friend's house. Back there, I found him most distressed. He said the police had come to his house making inquires for me. It seemed that some women who were washing clothes had reported to the police that they had seen a red man plunge into the river and not return, as his clothes were still there. I went to the Police Station the following morning to explain what had actually happened and recover my clothes.

It was during this same Easter weekend that a group of Boy Scouts from Georgetown were swimming on the MacKenzie side of the river when one of the boys just disappeared without a sound. His body was later found on the mudflat, his chest ripped open and his heart and liver missing. The creature who did this must have had enormous strength. On another occasion, in the upper reaches of the river at Clemwood, some school children were crossing on their way to school when a girl gave a piercing scream, pointing to a large hairy hand with long nails clutching the gunwale of the boat. One boy had reacted quickly, bringing down the paddle he was holding in a sharp cruel arc to hit the hand with a sickening crunch. The thing let loose of the gunwale and broke the surface of the water to disclose a feline face with two protruding fangs. Its head and chest were covered with hair. It did not surface again. There were several other instances over the years of the drowning of children, mostly boys, in the Wismar - Christianburg area. In many cases, according to medical testimony, the heart had been dug out of these victims by the time their bodies were recovered. Is it possible that a monster, the masacuraman or water tiger, unknown to zoology actually exists? I am inclined to believe so, for it brings to mind my first visit to the interior in 1925 when I saw a grown Amerindian woman whose face had been hideously disfigured by such a creature when she was a child, bathing by the river.

CHAPTER VII

An Overseer's Life: Industrial Relations and the Ways of Mules

When I took charge of the weeding gang, I was in charge of approximately four hundred estate and transient women between the ages of eighteen and forty years. Before the piece work was shared out, the sirdar and I had to walk through each field (there might have been ten or more fields) and price the type of work to be done. On Tuesday mornings, the sirdar would share out the amount of work each weeder thinks can be completed by Saturday. The prices ranged from one and a half to two and a half cents per three rod bed for hauling cane trash from the cane roots and the drains and rolling the trash between the rows of young canes. Then there is the weeding and mould-ing of young canes, priced at two to three cents per bed, for two rows of cane. Finally, there is the weeding of high canes. The prices ranging from two to three and a half cents per bed, working out to twenty cents or thirty-five cents per opening (two rows of canes) across ten three rod beds and the cleaning of half of the cross canal at the beginning and at the completion of the work.

It was during the high canes weeding that many jealousies were born, as some women received more money than others. Those receiving less said it was because the sahib or the sirdar was receiving favours from the woman concerned. On one occasion, I was brought up before the manager on a charge from a young woman's husband that "Mr. Young was living with his wife." The Manager called the young woman forward and asked her if this was true. The young woman bluntly denied the accusation. He then asked me the same question. I denied the charge and explained how these jealous feelings came about between the weeders, especially if a woman received extra money for extra work done. Some women took delight in carrying false information and stirring up trouble in their neighbours' households. I do not deny, though, that had the high canes been able to talk, there would have been many stories to be told.

When I was promoted to the cane-cutting and punt-loading gangs, my duties included the burning of the fields to be cut the following day. This was carried out by the foreman of the cane cutters. I had to order the number of cane punts required to transport the cane cut that day. Before the cane was cut, I had to have a man cut a track through the burnt canes, so that the sirdar and I could estimate the yield per acre of cut canes and price the work accordingly. There were times when the price was not agreeable, so I had a couple of 'draw foxes' to whom I gave an extra amount if they would start the work of cutting. Canes have to be cut right down to the root. The top of the cane is lopped off and the leaves thrown away leaving the cane top for use in planting renewed fields.

Oxen or mules were used to pull the loaded cane punts from the cross canals into the main middle-walk trench, where the long dam boys would hook their long steel chains (forty feet) to the punts for transportation to Plantation Uitvlugt, the grinding estate some four miles away. Usually one mule will haul eight fully loaded (four tons each) punts in good weather when the trenches are fully irrigated, but in the dry season, I have seen two or even three mules fighting to pull one or two punts of cane in very shallow water, practically scraping the mud on the bottom of the trench. Another difficulty was that the P.O.J. (a Java cane) is very thin and hard and gives a lot of trouble to load a four ton punt, these canes having a tendency to make a pile whose size was out of proportion to their weight. The old type of bamboo canes were thick and heavy as were the diamond ten. These loaded well under the gunwale and still carried the tonnage. The men loading these punts were paid nine bits or three shillings a day for loading three punts (two men to a punt). The pricing of cutting the canes varies: very light growth, two or three cents per three rod bed; heavy cane from eight to twelve cents. A cane cutting gang would only cut half of the field – what we may term the windside, another gang would cut the remaining five beds on the lowside. Cut cane had to be bundled and carried to the cross canal bed. During the cane cutting season I have been known to leave my house at 7:00 a.m. and spend the entire day and night in the back dam, only to return home at dawn the following day to get a bath and a cup of coffee and return to the fields once again.

The duty of the punt-loading overseer was also to see that all loaded punts passed through the locks to the Boeraserie Creek and safely through the locks into Plantation De Kinderen. There was an Afro-Guyanese in charge of the watchhouse at the creek who operated the winches to open the lock doors. During the very dry season, I spent many nights at the Boeraserie Watch House in his company (being bitten by the mosquitoes and sand flies, although Daniels, the watchman, made smoke and gave me a rice bag into which I put my feet), to make certain all the cane punts had crossed the creek and that the locks had been secured again. During these early years on sugar estates, I had to put up with many privations.

From the cane cutting and punt loading gangs, I was promoted to the forking gang. These men planted the cane tops in fields that had been flooded and were being renewed. They also forked the young canes, burying the cane trash around the cane roots (this is called mulching) and the ordinary plain forking when digging to the depth of the fork is essential. There was much trouble when some of the men only skinned the surface of the soil. I tested their work with my walking stick which was marked from the base in twelve inch marks, the top being three feet two inches in length. If I found I did not have the required depth, I called the men back to overhaul their work. Some did, but one man did not, so I held back his money at the pay table and told him he would have to go back on Monday to put his work right, before he could receive his wages.

The following week the sirdar, who was an Afro-Guyanese – Ralph Lawson, went to check the man's work to see if he had overhauled his forking. The depth was not even four inches on my stick. When I called the man's attention to this he got highly annoyed, said he was not going to do any overhauling and furthermore, he was quitting. I turned my back. Sirdar Lawson shouted to me to look out! Turning back I saw that the forkman had picked up his fork to drive it into my back. Lawson had immediately struck the man's hand with his hackia (hardwood) stick, causing the man to drop the fork. He was then escorted from the field and told never to return for work on the estate.

There was another occasion when I had to condemn the work in three fields. These men were from De Kinderen. I reported the matter to my manager who phoned the manager of De Kinderen, who got highly annoyed with me for condemning the work of his forkmen. The Attorney, Mr. Muirison, had to be called in to settle the matter. When he entered the fields in question, he did not walk more that twenty-five yards before he came out again. He was very angry and told the manager that I had been quite right not to pay for that type of work as there was no depth and patches were left untouched. By this stage I had become much more confident in my role as a manager. For instance, Plantation Tuschen used to receive the last issue of cane punts although we had the furthest distance to transport our canes, so one morning I lined up my long-dam boys at De Kinderen middle-walk trench and commandeered the first set of punts which were bound for De Kinderen back dam. On hearing of my action, the manager from De Kinderen rang my manager and complained. I was reprimanded for my action but when I explained my position to my manager and pointed out that our receiving the last issue of cane punts caused the loaders to finish late and the passing of the punts at the creek locks to finish even later, from that day forward Plantation Tuschen received the first issue of punts from the factory. My actions on these two occasions put me in bad graces with De Kinderen's manager.

I was breaking in a new mule for the manager, when I had the misfortune to fracture my right ankle. The mule tripped on a rubber tree root and I was thrown over its head, landing on my feet. Attempting to mount again, I found I could not bear my weight on my right leg, then I noticed the boots lacing and the bottom fastening of my leggings had burst. I managed to haul myself up on to the saddle and started for home some two and a half miles away. I was lucky to meet my weeding gang sirdar, Manan, with some men in a corial. When I told Manan what had happened and the pain I was suffering, the men lifted me from the saddle and placed me in the corial, where I was conveyed home. The doctor was sent for, who confirmed my leg was broken. I was then taken by car to Georgetown Hospital. I was in the hospital some four weeks before I learned that all the West Coast Estates were on strike. On hearing that my manager had been physically molested, I asked Dr. Romitte, the Surgeon in charge, if I could leave the hospital and return to the estate. He was reluctant to do this as my leg needed another two weeks to heal, but I eventually prevailed upon him to agree to my discharge and return in two weeks to have the cast removed.

After crossing the Demerara River by ferry, I hired a taxi from Vreed-en-Hoop stelling. As I travelled along the coast, I found barricades of donkey carts and drays had been placed across the road at Cornelia Ida and Plantation Leonora. The taxi was stopped but the men on the road recognised me as an overseer and a visitor, because some Sundays I had ridden over on my horse to visit my friend Tommy Kenyon, and I was allowed to pass. The entrance to Plantation Uitvlugt is up a side road so I passed there freely, but at Plantation De Kinderen I was again stopped and told in no uncertain language to get my so and so self out of the car. However, when I was recognised – since many of the men had worked with me – I was allowed to pass over the Boeraserie Creek bridge. From there I travelled to Tuschen High Bridge where I was again stopped and told to get out of the car. I stepped out on my wooden crutches and the boys there who knew me assisted me to the bridge. Here, I spoke to some of the men I knew to be leaders and asked them the cause of the strike. They explained that the punt loading wages had been cut from nine bits per day to eight and a half bits, but it was more or less a sympathy strike originating from Plantation Leonora where the strike had started by the women and children refusing to go out to work. I asked them whether they would agree to return to work if the manager gave then back the half bit, and they said yes. I hobbled across to the main gate of the manager's house where the boys left me. Bowley, the butler, answered my knock and was surprised to see me. When Mr. Baxter, the manager, came out he wanted to know why I had left the hospital before my leg was properly healed. I told him I had heard of the strike and that he had been physically assaulted. He told me that the labourers had only knocked the pith helmet from his head, but he was more worried that all his canes were spoiling in the fields. I told him about my conversation with the labourers and Mr. Baxter said he would give anything to get the men back to work. As I left the office, the manager urged me to take a police escort (there were policemen guarding his house) back to my house. I declined, explaining that it was the labourers who had escorted me from the bridge to his house.

When I reached the workers on the high bridge, I told them that the manager had agreed to my proposal and they could be assured of getting what they wanted. One man in the crowd made some objection. He was promptly subdued as the men lifted him bodily and dropped him over the rail into the trench. I told them I wanted man, woman and child out of their houses and into the cane fields early the following morning to load the cane into the punts for transportation to Uitvlugt. The next morning, at 3:30 a.m., I heard the voices of people on the road for about half an hour. After this silence. I was up and out of bed by 6:30 a.m. I sat in my verandah drinking coffee when I noticed the manager come out of his yard, gaze up and down the estate road, then walk as far as the mule stables, then return to his house. Half an hour later, he came to stand on the high bridge and look up and down the public road, hitting his leggings with his riding crop, then again returned to his house. Fifteen minutes later he again emerged from his compound and crossed the high bridge to enter my compound. He called out to me, "Good morning, Mr. Young. You assured me yesterday the men would be out today prepared to load the cut canes into the punts." I did not answer him for out of the corner of my eye I could see two of my leading punt loaders, Khedan and Eli Bachs, coming along the road from the back dam. When these men saw me on the verandah, they threw their punt-loading ropes into the air, calling out at the same time, "All clear, sahib". I turned to the manager and said "That is your answer, sir". He wanted to know what I meant. I told him that all the canes were loaded and on their way to Uitvlugt, the grinding estate, and that the reason he saw no one on the road was because the people had left for work at 4:00 a.m. Mr. Baxter did not say a word but turned around and re-entered his compound where he telephoned Mr. Muirison, the attorney at Plantation Uitvlugt, to tell him that all the canes from Tuschen were on their way. Mr. Muirison asked him how this could be because Uitvlugt and Leonora were still on strike. Mr. Baxter explained that I had returned from hospital, had spoken to the labourers and got them to turn out.

I was later transferred to La Bonne Intention, a grinding estate on the East Coast of Demerara. I also served at Plantation Schoon Ord on the West Bank of the Demerara River and back to Plantation Enmore on the East Coast of Demerara. I served twelve years with this company before I resigned after a misunderstanding with the management. The company said it was sorry to lose me, as I had a good record for dealing with labour. Mr. Payne, the director, said I was making a mistake because sugar was coming into its own.

CHAPTER VIII
The New York Zoological Expedition: The Rupununi – 1937-1938

Within a few days of returning home from the sugar estate, I received a message from the Commissioner of Lands and Mines to call at his office at the earliest opportunity. He informed me that a Dr. William Holden, an American who was heading an expedition from the New York Zoological Gardens to collect specimens from the bush, was desirous of getting a man to take charge of men and cargo to be shipped up river. I was told to contact Dr. Holden at the Hotel Tower. At my interview with the doctor, he explained that Mr. John Melville, a rancher from the Rupununi district, would be doing all the up river and savannah transportation but he wanted a man who knew the Amerindians and the bush to organise the first stage of the expedition, that is to hire Amerindians to act as boat hands and droughers and to arrange river transportation, boats, engineers and steersmen. Dr. Holden told me that the Commissioner of Lands & Mines had given me a very good recommendation and if I was not presently engaged in anything, he would be glad to have me take on the job and travel through to Brazil with him.

I first went to the aboriginal mission in Georgetown where I met a number of Amerindians, some who had worked with me before. These men hailed from Moruca, North West District and were accustomed to work with geological and other government surveyors. I selected fourteen men and advanced them money to purchase their necessities. I then travelled to Bartica to arrange for a tent boat and two Johnson 25 HP outboard motors and a 40 foot cargo boat powered by a V8 Ford Marine Engine. All food stuffs such as rice, flour, sugar, biscuits, were put into four gallon tins and sealed to keep out the humidity. We would embark from Bartica. The cargo boat would transport most of our food and the tent boat would carry the members of the American expedition and some of their equipment, radio transmitter, specimen boxes, tents and tarpaulins for camps, gasoline for the engines etc. I engaged a river steersman (captain) and his assistant for the cargo boat and an engineer. The tent boat was also assigned a steersman and engineer.

The party consisted of Dr. Holden, Dr. Smith, a botanist, Terry, an entomologist, Dr. Snediger, an expert on snakes, Bill Hassler, the cameraman and Holford, a radiotrician lent to the expedition by the National Broadcasting System of New York. There were fourteen Amerindians, two steersmen and their seconds and two engineers, one cook for the American party and myself. Arrangements were made before I left Bartica that the boats should travel in convoy to ensure the safe arrival of food and personnel at our destination.

We left Bartica in late November 1937 to steam up the Essequibo River. On passing Monkey Jump, the narrowest part of the river at St. Mary's compound, we decided to take lunch before tackling the rapids but could not enter the huts as the sand could be seen actually moving with the hundreds of jigger fleas. The water in the river was so low that when the boats reached the rapids they had to be unloaded, their cargo transported over the rocks and the boats themselves had to be hauled through the rapids by means of a warp rope and reloaded.

The tent boat, which was lighter, was soon hauled over and reloaded. They forged ahead endeavouring to reach Rockstone before dark, not waiting for us, contrary to what we had agreed at Bartica. It was on this first day that things started to go wrong, for at Wabruk Falls, the last before reaching Rockstone, I realised our inboard engine did not have enough power to surmount the falling waters. The captain tried twice with all of us bending to the paddles, but it made no difference. Then one of the boys was sent to swim out with a lifeline to which was attached the warp rope. The warp would then be pulled up to a point where it could be secured, then the boathands would pull themselves through this swift current to the rock on which the warp was tied and then haul up the boat. However, the force of the current swept one of the men from the rope and it was only with luck that I was able to grab his arm as he was passing the boat stern to save him from being swept down the falls. Our manpower, together with the help of the engine, was still inadequate to pull the boat over this fall. As night was approaching, I told the captain we should camp on the rocks before we lost a man in the dark. There was no means of catching a fire, so I opened two tins of corn beef, biscuits and sugar and gave the men something to eat. We would try to get the boat over the falls the following morning by leaving some of the cargo on the rocks. What surprised me was that there was no sign of the other boat whose passengers, not seeing us, should have returned to find out what the problem was.

We spent a miserable night catnapping on the cold rocks. I was glad when day dawned. We unloaded half the cargo from the boat and packed it on the rocks. The boat was then able to surmount the fast water. On the way to

Rockstone, we met the tent boat returning down stream to look for us. I instructed them to load up the balance of our cargo at Wabruk Falls and return.

At Rockstone, I had a showdown with Dr. Holden. I reminded him of the arrangement that had been made at Bartica for the two boats to travel together for safety and told him that I had nearly lost one of my men at Wabruk Falls and that the rest of the Amerindians wanted to return to Georgetown because they felt the doctor showed no regard for their safety. I called a meeting of the two boat captains, the engineers and the men, at which the laws of the Lands & Mines Department were explained to Dr. Holden. He had wanted to travel the whole day and late into the evening (it was all right for his party as the tent boat had a cook and the facilities to prepare meals on a portable stove), but according to the regulations the boats were supposed to stop at midday to allow the men to prepare a meal and then to stop at a proposed camp site at 3:30 p.m. to allow the men to build tarpaulin tents because, in the bush, night sets in at 4:00 p.m. We agreed to travel the whole day, but to allow the men sufficient time to prepare their food for the day and to stop and camp at 4:00 p.m. at the latest.

Higher up river, we began to meet more falls and rapids, especially in the area between Mt. Twasing on the left bank and Mt. Akaiwanna on the right bank where there were about eight rapids. We had no difficulties until we encountered Itanami. This is a shallow stretch of fast water three quarters of a mile in length, through which the men had to transport our entire cargo on their heads or backs over sharp and slippery stones. The entire operation took about three hours, so long that we had to build camp for the night at the head of the rapids, after the boats had been hauled over. At Kurupukari Falls the following day, our cargo again had to be discharged at the foot of the falls near the Police Station, the boats hauled through the falls to the upper river above the Police Station. Only half of the cargo was reloaded, the rest being left at the Police Station so that we would be able to travel faster, as the doctor was anxious to reach Mr. McTurk's ranch at Karanambo in the Rupununi River. It was at this point in the river that cattle from the Rupununi Savannahs were carried across in flat bottomed boats on their way to the coast lands by way of the Berbice River. We spent the night at the Police Station, which was also the Government Rest House and Magistrates Court. There was one constable on duty and a helper to keep him company.

On our arrival at Apoteri, the junction of the Rupununi with the Essequibo River, I was welcomed ashore by the staff of the two balata stations based at this point, the Real Daylight and Balata Co. and Garnett and Co. Balata

Store. Our party was entertained to dinner, after which the Americans were treated to some bush stories by some of the balata bleeders; some very true, others to be taken with a pinch of salt. These balata bleeders lead a lonely and tough life working alone or with a partner. They carry their food and clothing in warashis, cutting lines into the bush in search of the bullet wood trees. Having found these trees, the men build a rough leaf shelter. Unlike rubber trees, only half of the circumference of the bullet wood tree is bled and only as far as the first branch. This will produce on an average four to five gallons of latex. When the scars are thoroughly healed in four to five years time, the other half of the circumference may then be bled, producing a like quantity of latex. The latex collected is then made into sheets of balata. When a man's food is nearly exhausted, he carries his balata to the nearest river point for collection by boat. The collectors regularly encounter jaguars, some get bitten by snakes, others get lost for days but still they come and go. As well as balata, these men also collect some rare orchids, especially in the vicinity of Apoteri.

Our party arrived at Karanambo, Mr. McTurk's ranch, the following day at noon. "Tiny", as Mr. McTurk was known to his friends, and his wife, made us all welcome, preparing food and giving us places to sling our hammocks. At about 2:00 p.m., Dr. Holden asked me to return to Kurupukari with the tent boat to bring up the balance of our cargo. I took Captain Benjamin and a boat crew and left Karanambo at 3:00 p.m. There was brilliant moonlight that night and Captain Benjamin took advantage of this fact to run all the falls, which is really against the law, as the Lands and Mines Department rules no boat shall negotiate the falls after dark. We ran into Kurupakari early next morning, collected our load and started back up river, reaching Karanambo at 4:00 p.m. the same day.

Mr. McTurk (Tiny) and I had met in the Pakaraima Mountains in 1925 on my first trip into the interior. It was Tiny who showed me how to use the Indian blow pipe. On his ranch, he was rearing cattle and horses. He also dealt in balata, his Wapisianna Amerindian employees bringing the balata sheets to the ranch.

The large fresh water lakes in the vicinity of Karanambo harboured our largest fresh water fish. Records show that they attain a length of fifteen feet and weigh as much as 400 pounds. Anyone who wishes to achieve distinction as an angler should visit the Rupununi district, taking with him a complete tarpon outfit. There he will meet with a foe worthy of his steel. No tuna ever caught on the California coast can compete in size and strength with the gigantic arapaima of the Amazon, Rio Branco, Rio Negro and Rupununi.

These fish come across from Brazil, Rio Branco via the Takutu and Rupununi Rivers to the Essequibo River where they have been seen below the mouth of the Potaro River and as far down as Rockstone. Inlets along the banks of the river appear to be their resort, for everywhere can be seen their reddish brown and black tinged tail and dorsal fin (along with the heads of the kaiman) exposed on the surface of the water. The arapaima has a habit of coming to the surface especially at night and bringing its tail flat down on the water with a blow that sounds like a pistol shot, the sound carrying at least half a mile. The Amerindians usually take this fish with a harpoon, but it can be caught with the hook as well as the bow and arrow. This fish has one of the most variegated scaly carcasses imaginable. The salted fish is an industry in Brazil, Para being the market.

Andrew MacDonald, (of Scottish and Macusi Indian parents) who was assisting John Melville in the transportation of our food and equipment, arrived at Karanambo with a long bullock cart and bullocks. In these early days, there were no proper roads or any motor transportation. At certain points on our journey, it was a joke to watch Andrew and his assistant dismantle his cart and carry it and the cargo over a creek or a swamp, then reassemble his cart and reload it with our equipment. This happened not once, but many times. Horses for our party had been provided by Charlie Melville, John's younger brother, who also met us at Karanambo. I bade farewell to Mr. & Mrs. McTurk on the morning of the third day, the party being guided by Charlie to Pirara. This ranch was owned by Mr. Hart, an American who had married into the Melville family, who were also of Scottish and Amerindian stock.

At Pirara there was much to talk about, as American met fellow Americans. Mr. Hart said we must spend the night. When we sat down to dinner, the food was simply swarming with flies, on the beef, rice, farine and vegetables. Old Hart said this was nothing compared to some seasons. As long as one lived on a cattle ranch, there were bound to be flies around. When some of our party were reluctant to eat, Old Hart cracked a joke about eating under these conditions for years. He was in perfect health, standing 6ft 4in and weighing over 200 pounds.

We were supplied with fresh horses the following morning and continued our journey across the savannah to Manari. This ranch was owned by a Basque Frenchman who had also married one of the Melville girls. Mr. Orella told me he had cut and hauled bullet wood trees from the surrounding mountains to form the framework of his house. Termites never eat into this wood, nor do they trouble the wallaba wood. I think that of all the ranches we were to visit, Manari with its surrounding hills and mountains, with the blue tinted water of its lake and river, was the prettiest. Here again the arapaima fish were to be found in the river and lake.

From Manari, the party proceeded to Bon Success, a government outpost on the right bank of the Takutu River, a tributary of the Rio Branco River. This river forms the boundary with Brazil. Here I met an old friend, Mr. Edwin Haynes, with whom I had penetrated the Potaro River head into fifty square miles of a diamond concession in 1925. He now held the post of Commissioner for the entire Rupununi district. He was in charge of all police in the area and had to act as magistrate. The houses in his compound were built of wattles with raised board floors and ité leaf roofing. We were assigned to the house usually used as the magistrates court.

The following day, Mr. Haynes accompanied us across the Takutu River to visit a Brazilian rancher and store owner, Senior Figerido, who, on learning we were visiting Americans, was most gracious and went out of his way to make us welcome to his house at San Salvadore. Sr. Figerido insisted that the party spend the day there to taste Brazilian hospitality, and sent his own boat with invitations to his neighbours to come and meet the Americans. He also arranged to have a "fiesta", so that everyone could join in our entertainment. There was plenty to eat and drink. Guitar music was supplied by his neighbours. I had the pleasure of dancing with Senorita Figerido who told me she had been educated by the nuns at the Ursuline Convent in Church Street, Georgetown.

At dawn the following day, a flotilla of small boats escorted us back to Bon Success. The doctor thanked the Brazilians for the splendid time we had spent in their company. Our party slept most of the day recuperating, then proceeded on to Teddy Melville's Ranch at Lethem. Here I met a Mrs. Myres who had a small ranch adjacent to Teddy's. She was studying the savannah Amerindian's way of life and writing a book. Her husband was a New Zealander who was a geologist. Teddy, who was later to become a very good friend, entertained us. I met his daughter, a very pretty girl who later married an old sugar estate overseer who had migrated to the savannah.

Camp was pitched on the banks of Sand Creek as the water was too high to ford. This was fortunate, for during the late afternoon a Wapisianna Amerindian came to our camp asking for the doctor as one of his boys had been bitten by a rattle snake. Charlie Melville accompanied the doctor and I to act as interpreter. We mounted our horses and followed the man to his village. The boy was about twelve years of age. The doctor gave him an injection and made an incision above the fang bite, then had me assist him by operating suction caps to draw out the poison. We left the village at 2:00 a.m. the following morning after the doctor was satisfied the boy would recover.

Andrew MacDonald, who had been born and raised in the savannah lands and never wore boots or shoes, told me he had been bitten twice by rattlesnakes. On the first occasion he had been driving out his cattle to pasture in the early morning when he was bitten, not regaining consciousness until late afternoon when he managed to crawl home, his foot hugely swollen. The Amerindians attended to him, but it was only his clean living and physical strength that enabled him to recover. When the water subsided at Sand Creek, the party pushed ahead to the Catholic Mission at St. Ignatius at the foot of the Kanaku Mountain. The priest in charge was Fr. Carey Ellis who gave us a lot of useful information and told the Americans he was compiling a book on the languages of the Wapisianna and Macusi peoples.

We left the Mission bordering the right bank of the Takatu River and following the foot of the Kanuku Mountain to enter the Southern Savannah, which is far larger than the north. Eventually we reached Wichibai, John Melville's ranch. This had a well laid out compound and a sprawling, comfortable house. The patio floor was made of red brick tiles made locally from clay dug from the pits near the river. The walls were made of adobe (clay mixed with grass and baked in the sun), two feet thick, keeping the interior cool. The roof was thatched with ité palm leaves which usually last for twenty years before re-thatching. John was married to a Brazilian girl and had a number of children. We spent some time here checking our food and equipment for our journey ahead.

On our trip so far, Dr. Smith had been collecting botanical specimens as well as bush ropes and vines which have a certain medicinal virtue. I had been assisting Dr. Snediger in the collection of frogs, rats and snakes, the rattler and the labaria, both venomous. Dr. Snediger would hold them by the neck and put a glass test tube against their fangs and milk out the poison. I could see the yellow-coloured poison being ejected from the sacks at the base of the fangs every time the test tube was pressed against them. He then injected them with formaldehyde. He then put the snakes. frogs and rats into a formalin solution in lead-lined tanks. These were screwed down in preparation for shipping to the U.S.A.. He wore very thick spectacles. This he said was the result of an experiment in which he had been used as a guinea pig as a young man at the zoo. He had to place his arm into a cage of North American diamondbacks (rattlers) similar to our bushmaster and was bitten. He was given the antidote serum but nearly lost his life. His lungs and heart were damaged and he had almost lost his eyesight, hence the extra thick glasses. Terry, the entomologist, used the brilliant light from our gas lamps to draw into our tarpaulin tent all kinds of bugs and moths. He would reap this harvest and bottled them. Bill Hassler, the cameraman, was busy taking movie and still photographs of the country and people. Dr. Holden visited the Amerindians we contacted, checked their physical condition and extracted bad teeth. There were also set times when Holford, our radioman, contacted the N.B.C., New York. The individual members of our expedition had then to broadcast a short programme of their activities and their findings.

Leaving Wichibai, we passed over endless grass lands dotted here and there with sandpaper trees, whose leaf, when the sun is hot, can act as a piece of sand paper. When we arrived at Isherton, we decided to build our base camp. Holford and Terry were to return to Georgetown at this point, taking back whatever samples were ready for shipment back to the U.S.A..

Whilst camped here, we visited Dadanawa Ranch, operating under the Rupununi Development Co. Theirs was the largest cattle holding in the Rupununi. I met a Mr. Turner who had been a sugar estate overseer but who migrated to the bush. Christmas 1937 was spent at Isherton. Holford managed to make radio contact with the MacGreggor's expedition in the North Pole. Dr. Holden spoke and requested some ice to cool our thirst. MacGreggor's party would have been glad of our tropical heat. As a contribution to our Christmas festivities, John Melville had acquired some Brazilian Rum which is termed "cashash" or bottled dynamite. After drinking some of this liquor, he and Dr. Holden had some altercation about money not yet paid for his transportation services. John pulled out his revolver and fired a shot into the air, at the same time challenging Dr. Holden to a duel. Knowing John very well, I got out my hammock and went across to pacify him. What was the result? John swung around and let me have a blow from his fist which tumbled me flat. (John was extremely strong, being able to lift a horse (savannah pony) off its four feet.) Dr. Snediger and Bill Hassler had to hold me down because I was in a passion and seeing red and threatening to go for my shot gun. After much soft talking by the saner members of the party, things quieted down for the night. John was most ashamed and he did not sleep in camp but slept in the bush, not returning to camp until the following morning. The joke of the whole incident was that because of John's wild shouting and shooting, our Amerindians also took to the bush for the night. I had to go out and shout for them, telling them everything was now all right. It was from Isherton that most of our Amerindians were sent back to the Coast. Cornelius, our camp cook, also decided to leave after the shooting incident. However, John Melville said he had sufficient Wapisianna Amerindians to see us through to the Essequibo River ahead.

Whilst camped at Isherton, a Dr. Davidson, a very tall American who turned out to be a member of the Royal Geographical Society, walked over from his place on the Marudi Mountain. His visit was most interesting. He informed us that he had a small place which he was farming. From the post holes he had dug to erect his house, he had recovered sufficient gold nuggets to finance a trip to Brazil to buy food and supplies to last for some time. There was a gold rush to the Marudi Mountains a couple of years later. During his conversation, he mentioned that he had seen a meteor fall and had taken a compass bearing on its point of contact. Next day he took two Amerindians and cut a line to the spot which was approximately three miles away. Dr. Holden said he too would like to visit the area, so after getting the compass bearing, Charlie Melville, Bill Hassler, Andrew MacDonald, Dr. Holden and I took the walk, having to cut our way through some overgrown areas and fording two or three creeks to reach it. What a sight! The giant trees surrounding the spot had been uprooted, and those not fallen looked as if some giant hand had twisted them. The whole area of about two or three acres had a scorched appearance. The hillside on which the meteor had fallen had been torn away and the meteor buried itself on the flat.

Dr. Smith, the botanist, decided to return to the north savannahs and mountains, there to try and get some more valuable botanical specimens. Dr. Holden, Bill Hassler, Andrew MacDonald, Justine Pierre and Pablo, a Wapisianna Indian and I would form the party to proceed forward into Brazil. Dr. Snediger and John Melville would accompany us as far as the Akarai Mountains which formed the boundary to Brazil. Leaving Isherton with our bullock cart, food and equipment, we passed through this last savannah to Mr. Gorinsky, a white Russian, who was also married to a Melville girl, who had ranched there for some years, as the grazing was good. (Later he had to leave because of the constant loss of cattle killed by the jaguars in the area, and he moved to the northern savannah and settled at Good Hope.) At this point, the bullock cart had to be abandoned and we had to devise a way of carrying all our food and supplies on the Kuyuwini River, seven miles through the bush. This Kuyuwini is a left bank tributary of the Essequibo River.

John Melville instructed the Amerindians to drough in saw pits in which to saw boards from a tree which they had felled. With these boards, a large balahoo (flat bottomed boat) was built, nailed and caulked with oakum and sealed with tar. We spent two nights here under the canopy of trees, (a contrast to the usual open savannah) before pushing off downstream in the balahoo, powered by a 25 HP Johnson motor we had brought with us.

The Kuyuwini River proved to be a shallow river full of sand banks. At one point we encountered a twenty-one foot boa constrictor (water camoodie) which John Melville killed with a charge of dynamite. Dr. Snediger cut off its head to recover its teeth which are curved inwards. He narrowly missed damage to his right hand, for although the snake's head was cut off, its jaws closed with a snap. He cut open the snake and showed us an embryo. He told us the boa constrictor gives birth to its young. When we reached the large Essequibo River, we swung upstream passing a large blackwater tributary, the Kasikaityu, on the left bank and proceeded on to the Onoro Creek, a right bank tributary. It was near this point that the Government surveyors plotting the Brazil - Br. Guiana boundary had been encamped. We built our camp by the river side, but I took a walk into the bush to try to find the surveyors' old camp site. There I located four or five sealed biscuit tins. I found them to contain white broad beans, which the doctor said were a good source of vitamins. Noticing some jiganit fruit, which I knew labba feed on, I decided to sit out the night and I was lucky to shoot a labba before 8:00 p.m.

Next morning, John Melville said he would show us a tributary of the New River. We followed an Amerindian trail for about ten miles and saw land full of diamondiferous rock. The water of the New River comes off the Akarai Mountains to discharge into the Corentyne River which forms the boundary with Dutch Guiana. Whilst traversing this line, I nearly trod on a bushmaster snake. John Melville shot it with his revolver. It measured seven feet with a diameter of five inches. The bushmaster has black diamond markings on its back, the balance of its skin a dirty white, with a pronounced scaly surface. I have learned to handle many snakes, no matter their size, but I have always had a great respect for this large snake, both for its deadly bite and its immense strength. It was here too that John drew my attention to a brilliant green snake with white markings on its skin under a small tree which I was passing. John claimed this snake sleeps for six months and that on awakening, the limb on which it had been sleeping dies or is dead. When cut with a knife, this snake does not bleed red blood but gives off a white substance. Collectors have come from the U.S.A. in search of this snake as they claim the white blood is a cure for cancer.

After leaving Onoro, we pushed ahead to the Chodikar River one of the upper tributaries of the Essequibo River which descends right off the Akarai Mountains. This waterway was very narrow, shallow and full of floating grass. The engine could not operate here so we reverted to the use of pole-sticks cut from the river bank. Unfortunately, one of the poles hit a quakoo marabunta nest and before one could wink, everyone who knew what a sting from one of these large black marabuntas could do was overboard and ducking in the water to avoid being stung. The boat was eventually pushed past the danger spot to the mountain foot where we pitched our camp. John Melville and Dr. Snediger returned to the savannah from here.

CHAPTER IX
The New York Zoological Expedition: Into Brazil

As we crossed the Akarai range of mountains into Brazilian territory, Dr. Holden drew my attention to some greyish and greasy looking rocks at the side of our walking line. He informed me this was oil shale, an indication of oil in this area. (I reported this fact to the Minister for Energy, Minister Jack, when he visited my camp with Minister Hoyte. This was in 1974, some thirty six years later, when Guyana was suffering from oil shortage.) We crossed the mountain and descended to the Mapuera River, an upper tributary of the Trombedas River. At this camp ground, some Wai-Wai Amerindians visited us from their nearby village. Dr. Holden told them, through our interpreter Andrew MacDonald, to come back the following day, but in their ceremonial dress of parrot feather headdress and bone armlets dressed with the soft white feathers of the powis.

The next day a party of six men and four women arrived arrayed in their tribal dress. They danced and sang their songs which Bill Hassler recorded. He also took movies of their dancing. The women wore only a small bead apron tied at the waist and the men a red sallow cloth lap. The men have an average height of 5ft 6in., the women an average of 5ft. They have a fair complexion and are muscular. After their performance, Bill Hassler replayed the tapes for their benefit. The Indians were astounded, gaping and laughing among themselves. They were given some presents from our trade goods. Dr. Holden added to his collection by taking a few bows, arrows and one or two head dresses, paying the Indians in trade goods. Learning from Andrew that our intention was to travel down river to the Brazilian camp, one of the Amerindians agreed to accompany us as our guide.

There was no river transportation from here on, so I decided to make a corial. Justine and Andrew felled a silverballi tree and a length of twenty-one feet was measured and the trunk cut off. An axe was used to junk out the larger pieces from the middle of the opening, then cutlasses and an adze were used to chip out the inner portion. When the tree trunk was dug out to my satisfaction, I was ready to set fire to the dry chips in the bottom of the tree trunk to open it as the heat expands the wood. Hardwood cross members were inserted to keep the required shape of the opening. However, Dr.

Holden requested that he be the one to burn out the interior of the craft. After a little gasoline had been sprinkled into the hull, the doctor, instead of striking a match and tossing it into the hull, foolishly used his cigarette lighter. I only heard the "woosh" of the exploding gasoline and the good doctor was minus his goatee, moustache, eyebrows and the hair on his arm, and his face suffered some blisters which I had to treated with cream. The corial was christened the "HUMBOLDT" after one of our earlier explorers.

After loading our baggage and equipment into the corial, I found there was no room for the passengers. Our Amerindian guide told Andrew I could acquire another corial from an Amerindian village down river, so Andrew and the guide and I left to travel down stream for a distance of about two and a half miles. From there, I had to walk about half a mile from the river before meeting the village which seemed deserted. Our guide seated us in an open round hut at the centre of the village (comprised of some fourteen houses). We were under observation for some time before one of the older inhabitants made his appearance. Our guide stated our need, described who we were and where we were going. Only then did the remainder of Indians — men, women and children put in their appearance. We were given fruit and refreshed with casiri drink. A bargain was struck with the headman to pay him one felling axe and one mattock for a corial, to be delivered at our landing the following morning. Then I returned to our camp up river. I later learnt that the reason for those forest Amerindians living so far from the river without any visible signs of a landing was because Brazil nut collectors and balata bleeders used to raid their villages for food, stealing their provisions and ravishing their women, so they were naturally wary of all visitors coming from the river.

Early next morning, our corial was delivered and paid for. One of the men from the village wanted to join our party to visit some of his relatives lower down river. There were six in our party and two Amerindians guides so I placed one Amerindian in each corial. The cargo was divided and Bill Hassler accompanied by Andrew MacDonald and Pablo, the Wapisianna, were in one corial and Doctor Holden, Justine Pierre and I in another corial with an Amerindian guide from the village. I was very lucky to have obtained these guides for they showed exceptional knowledge and skill in negotiating the numerous rapids, standing in the bow of the corial, which is the correct way to steer, so that any obstruction or submerged rock could be seen before the craft reached it. John Melville had predicted that we would meet the Brazilian Boundary Commission Camp within three days. We did find the camp site but it was deserted because, due to the dry weather, the level of the water had dropped, so the Brazilians had camped further downstream to facilitate the transport of food to other survey parties.

One night whilst the camp was asleep, a tapir, in making its escape from a jaguar, accidentally knocked out a corner post from our tarpaulin tent. The tent collapsed on us. The doctor started to yell and both he and Bill Hassler had the devil's own job to get out of their hammock nets. When the doctor did emerge from the ruins of the camp, he was holding his revolver and asking where it was, not knowing what has smashed our tent. I had another experience some three or four days later. We had slept at one of our riverside camps. Whilst preparing coffee and pancakes for the doctor, Pablo and I heard the sound of powis crowing from across the river, so I dispatched Pablo with a .22 rifle to try and bring in some fresh meat. I distinctly heard him firing numerous shots but he returned empty-handed, and said he had missed.

I covered down the food as the others were still sleeping. Then, Pablo and I recrossed the narrow river to tie up our corial at the other bank. Taking our knives, I started to cut a "sirihi" , an Amerindian hunting line, to act as our guide to follow on our return. Pablo showed me where the powis were located. I shot two, which Pablo collected. I wounded a third bird but it continued to fly from tree to tree. All thoughts of continuing our "sirihi" were forgotten, so much so that when we met a group of quarta monkeys, one which I shot, we were without a "sirihi" or walking line to follow. I turned to Pablo and asked him in which direction we should walk to meet our camp. He pointed in a direction which I felt was wrong. It is said an Amerindian is never lost in the bush, but I failed to understand that Pablo was born and grew up in the savannah grass lands and could find his way by compass bearings or by the sun or the stars, but in this deep jungle of heavy forest trees, he was at a loss. After walking for about two hours following Pablo's cutting, I called a halt as we had left hilly country and were penetrating low lands, vine infested, which slowed our progress. I told Pablo to climb a tree to see if he could see any smoke from our camp After descending from the third tree he had climbed, Pablo burst into tears, said he saw nothing and we were lost. The quickest way to get lost is to panic so I sat down on a fallen tree and, taking my knife, I drew a map showing Pablo at approximately what point we had crossed the river and up to the location we had shot the powis. I estimated we could not have covered more that two miles, but was it from up river or was it down river? I decided to retrace our steps following Pablo's cutting. At the beginning of his line, I took my bearings and decided to cut in the direction I felt our camp was located. I gave Pablo the rifle and the powis. The monkey he discarded as being too heavy. I had been cutting for about half and hour when I came across a portion of our original "sirihi", although the line did not continue. I decided to cut in the same direction. At about 2:00 p.m. I distinctly heard revolver shots and drew Pablo's attention to its direction, which was the same point to which I was cutting. I then came across my original cutting from the river, traversing a rocky hillside. I knew we were near home. Then I heard a loud explosion as if dynamite had exploded in the river.

It seems that the doctor and Andrew, missing Pablo and I from camp for so long, feared we were lost, so the doctor fired six spaced shots from his revolver, then Andrew tied two sticks of dynamite together and threw them into the river after igniting them, which sound I had just heard. We emerged from the forest at exactly the same spot where we had disembarked from the corial, so my sense of direction proved our salvation. If one is really lost in these forests, which stretch for hundreds of square miles, with only isolated Amerindian settlements, the only way to find a way out is by following running water until it meets a main river, then to follow this downstream until some kind of habitation can be found. The doctor warned us all not to stray far from the camp and I vowed that if I heard any more powis crowing, I would leave them strictly alone. I must say that in all my bush experiences, I have strayed a few times but I have never been truly lost. Some men have been lost for more than a week, finally being found with hardly a stitch of clothing on, hungry and practically out of their senses. One man was lost for a day right behind his camp. It was not until he awoke in a tree root at dawn and heard his fowlcock crowing that, on following the sound, he found himself at home.

Because we had received no food supply from our expected source, Andrew, Justine and I used our torch lights and cutlasses to chop fish sleeping between the rocks or in shallow water by the river bank. We boiled these fish with a little salt we had left, and the Amerindians shared with us the cassava bread they had brought.

After travelling downstream for a week, having to get out of our corials on numerous occasions to portage them and our equipment over rapids we could not chance to run, we passed into some beautiful country, rugged and eye-catching with red dirt hills, similar to laterite clay. Numerous Brazilian nut trees were pointed out to us by our guides. During our passage down river, having to be in and out of the river to assist with the corial, I could not wear anything but a "buckta", very brief shorts. Consequently, my skin turned nearly as brown as the Amerindians, my hands were hardened from the paddling and my bare feet were cut in numerous places from the sharp rocks I had to negotiate in the river. The other men suffered the same as I. On the seventh day, we were lucky to meet a party of three boats coming up stream. These proved to be members of the Brazilian Survey party. Andrew explained to them in Portuguese our difficulties. These men promptly decided to camp where they immediately provided us with hot food and coffee. They carried with them 7lb tins of corned beef which, served with their red beans and farine, formed their staple diet, mixed with fresh meat and fish.

There was little sleep in camp that night as these men were curious to learn from where we had come and to where we were bound. I slung my hammock and made much of their hospitality, particularly of their tobacco for a much needed smoke, and their wonderful coffee. They told us we would have to travel down stream for another three days, descending some difficult falls before meeting their No. 7 or Base Camp.

Setting off down river, now fully supplied with food, I saw this immense thing sliding into water from the right bank. The doctor asked me what it was. I told him it was an anaconda, one of the largest of the boa constrictor family. The doctor said this was impossible so I instructed our Indian guide to nose in the corial to the river bank. I jumped out with my cutting knife and kipped a line to the vicinity from which I had seen this monster emerge. I arrived at an area where the bushes had been pressed down as if by some immense weight, measuring an area of about 200 square feet. I then discovered the bones of animals in the vicinity, which the snake had vomited up after digesting the victim it had swallowed. I called to Justine Pierre to escort the doctor through my cut line, then I showed him the impression of the large snake and the bones. I estimated the length of the anaconda to be at least fifty to sixty feet and having a girth of five to six feet. To me, it had resembled a mora tree slipping into the river. Only on seeing did the goodly doctor believe. Records in Brazil prove that anacondas measuring some sixty feet have been known to slide into an Amerindian hut near the river and carry away a victim whose screams and the disturbed water were the only indication of what had happened.

Our Amerindian guides took us to a village approximately a mile from the river where we walked into what seemed to be some kind of celebration, as a good percentage of the villagers were near drunk on casiri or piwarri drink. It seemed as if they were celebrating some tribal war victory, as one fellow who seemed to take a liking to me showed me a missing big toe and the nasty wound left behind, which did not seem to trouble him too much, where a broad arrow had struck. He took me in hand, bringing a calabash of casiri for me to drink and a leg of a roast meat. Dr. Holden again insisted on taking the blood pressure of a number of the Amerindians and extracting the teeth of others and administering aid to the wounded and the sick. It was here that an incident occurred that nearly cost us our lives. As I have mentioned before, Dr. Holden liked to collect anything that caught his eye. Andrew, who was our interpreter, had charge of the suitcase which contained our trade goods. When the doctor took something from the Amerindians, Andrew would open the suitcase and pay for the item, but on this occasion when he opened the suitcase, the villagers, being under the influence of liquor, saw the glitter of looking glasses, brass beads and shiny knives and they grabbed the suitcase from Andrew and started to take out some of the items. Dr. Holden, on seeing this and fearing he was going to lose all his trade goods, grabbed the suitcase back from the Indians. Had the doctor known, these Amerindians rarely stole. They would have taken out each item, examined it, maybe have cracked a joke and passed it on. When everyone was satisfied with their viewing and wanted one of the items, he would, after some time, have gone to his hut and brought out one of his cherished possessions and given it in return for what had caught his eye. But in snatching the goods from them, the doctor did something against their way of life. They felt insulted and cheated of a good bargain. There was an immediate change in their attitude from one of much laughter to angry scowls and mutterings. I sensed what was about to happen and, fearing for the safety of my companions, I called Bill Hassler and Andrew MacDonald and told them to get the doctor out of the village. They were to try to ease out unnoticed and run as fast as possible when they got out of sight of the village back to the river landing and the boats.

Justine Pierre and I ran ahead to prepare the boats. No sooner had our party arrived than I heard the yelling of our pursuers and by the time our corials were out in the stream, a shower of spears followed us but fortunately fell short. Our guides had been left behind in the commotion, but as they were blood relations, I did not fear for their safety. The angry and frustrated shouts from the bank lent us more strength to speed our corials on their way.

It was the following day at about 2:30 p.m. when we eventually sighted the No. 7 Brazilian Outpost. Dr. Holden immediately told us to hoist the Union Jack and the Stars and Stripes flags on the two corials. We were met at the landing by the Commandant, Dr. D'Olivera Correira, a tall bronzed figure with a full black beard and some soldiers. He spoke very little English so Andrew was called upon to translate. On learning we had travelled from British Guiana via the Essequibo River to its head, and over the mountains into Brazil, he was astounded we had reached so far in such small craft. The commandant called his sergeant and asked him to allot us to our quarters. I learned this camp was run under military lines. Dr. D'Olivera Correira invited us to a dinner whose menu comprised soup, fish, meat and vegetables, followed by a sweet, then coffee accompanied by brandy and cigars. What a complete change from the food we had been eating on leaving the frontier, at times nearly starving!

I told the commandant of our encounter with the Amerindians in the village about a day's journey upstream from the outpost. He told me we were very lucky to escape with our lives as the Amerindians in that area were still 'savages', not having frequent contact with civilization. Dr. Holden explained that his purpose in travelling through these jungles was to collect specimens for the New York Zoological Gardens. He wanted permission from the Government at Rio de Janeiro to grant us a free pass through the country. Dr. Correira contacted the Government by radio and relayed Dr. Holden's request. We received a message the next day granting our party a free pass, during which the Brazilian authorities would give us all assistance possible.

Holding a quiet conversation with Dr. Correira on a fallen tree in the compound after dinner, I learned he was born on the Rio Negro, an upper tributary of the Amazon. His father has owned a small sugar estate. In an uprising of the labourers on the estate, his parents had been massacred, but his Nana had managed to save him by smuggling him out in a canoe. Dr. D'Olivera Correira was widely travelled, speaking well on many topics. His greatest wish was to see his country developed.

CHAPTER X
The New York Zoological Expedition: From Brazil to French Guiana

When we left Dr. Correira, he told us he had notified the Base Camp "O" at the Trombedas Falls to expect us. There was a natural bar across the river at Camp "O" location, forming the falls which descended in seven great ranges.

The boats transporting our party were similar to our own bateau or river boats. The outboard motor was a diesel, very heavy and mounted on the reinforced stern of the boat, but instead of having the propeller shaft dropping vertically at the stern, it jutted out horizontally about fifteen feet in length, at the end of which was the propeller, enabling the engineer to operate in shallow water by pressing down on the steering arm of the motor and raising the arm to a normal position when operating in normal water. At each fall, we had to disembark from the boat we were in and walk over, descending to another level, to the next boat awaiting us. From the height of these falls, the open country ahead could be seen stretching towards the distant Amazon River.

We spent two nights in camps between these falls where the army had everything prepared and ready for us. At "O" camp, we were welcomed by the senior officers and entertained handsomely. In the evening after dinner, we boarded a large river launch, powered by two diesel engines and having upper and lower decks. It was a moonlit night. After slinging our hammocks on the open top deck, we enjoyed the smooth water and were lulled to sleep by the purr of the powerful diesel engines.

I was up with the daylight and after breakfast I enjoyed the passing scenery of herds of zebu cattle grazing up to their bellies in the rich blue-green grass. There were scattered country residences, each having white adobe walls and red tile roofs. Senior Campos explained to me that the red tiles were made by hand, the shape of the tiles being shaped on the thighs, then baked in the sun and tied in place on the rafters of the house with strong bush vines or bush rope.

Our party arrived at the mouth of the Trombedas at about 2:30 p.m. to see the mighty Amazon River stretching before us. As far as the eye could see the water was of a muddy (tea) colour, studded with islands and floating

islands of trees and grass that had been torn loose by the force of the mighty
current. The launch travelled a short distance down river to the town of
Obidas, where our disembarkment caused quite a stir – our bearded faces,
our stained and torn clothing with our toes peeping out of our canvas boots.
Senior Campos escorted us uphill to the hotel. He introduced us to the proprietor (who did not seem to like our looks), explaining that we were American scientists just arrived from the jungles. There were no beds but hooks in
the walls from which to sling our hammocks. I had to request a cash advance from Dr. Holden with which to outfit my men and myself with more
presentable clothing. I went to a tailor, accompanied by Bill Hassler, where
all of us were measured for shirts and pants.

The doctor learned of that a steamer was arriving the next day at Obidas,
which he hoped to join on our way down to Para. The tailor was asked to
rush our clothing. When the outfits were delivered, Bill Hassler who is 6 ft
2 in found that he had three-quarter length pants and shirt sleeves to match.
I received pants about a foot too long and a shirt that could double around
me. The other boys were in similar difficulties. We embarked on the steamer
in midstream at 2:00 p.m. the same day. The boat was crowded with students from the University of Manaus, going home for carnival. I had the good
fortune to meet a student who could speak English. He had a brother who
was an engineer and another who was a doctor, who were both engaged in
building a highway up the Amazon Valley to open up their country. He introduced me to a number of other students and gave them a sketch of our
journey. They were especially interested in our narrow escape from the
Amerindians.

There was music and dancing on board at nights. It was the first time I
had danced the Brazilian samba. Meals were our problem. Dr. Holden had
booked first class passages for himself and Bill Hassler, leaving us to travel
deck and to hustle for our food. I had to create quite a stink before he organised proper meals for us. In the bush, where the good doctor had to rely on
us for his daily food and well being, it was smooth sailing, but once he was
back in civilisation and society, he did not want to associate with us. The
steamer stopped at a couple of riverside towns. I purchased some locally
made cheese, which proved to be very nice. At another stop at a wood mill,
they were extracting perfume from the rose wood. I managed to get a piece
of the wood and a small bottle of the perfumed water. The steamer stopped
too at the Henry Ford rubber plantation on the right bank of the Amazon
River for half an hour. The Ford people had done a wonderful job to cut out
such an area in this jungle and transport into it a modern version of civil

living: paved roads, mosquito-proofed bungalows, modern electrical lighting, motors cars and motor boats and every comfort one could wish for.

The steamer arrived off the city of Para the following afternoon. Andrew,
Justine, Pablo and I were not allowed to disembark, having to wait until the
port doctor gave us our yellow fever injections. A taxi was sent to collect us
from the wharf and transport us to the Grand Hotel in the main Plaza. Whilst
Dr. Holden was arranging passages home for us, we spent a pleasant few
days in this old city of Para. Carnival was celebrated during our stay there.
Everyone, young and old, went wild with sport, dancing and drinking. Women
we met on the street threw small paper bags of sweet smelling powder, the
men spraying the women with perfume.

I was introduced to a young Brazilian of German descent at the Grand
Hotel. He had been anxious to meet me when he learnt I was a member of a
recently returned expedition from the bush. He told me his father owned a
twin-diesel schooner which plied up and down the Amazon River from Para
collecting all kinds of skins, both of animals and snakes, butterflies, and
the feathers of rare birds. Alligator skins, he explained, were shipped to the
United States to be made into shoes, handbags, suitcases and other articles.
These items were then shipped back from the States to Rio-de-Janeiro for
the tourist trade. He explained that his father's partner had been handling
the business from the Para end but there had been some questionable dealings, so he, the son, had been sent to take charge. His proposition to me was
that I join forces with him, as I knew the bush so well, and the proceeds
from our collection would be divided equally. I thanked him for his kind
offer but as I had entered the country without a passport I could not accept.
I was also offered a job by a tall American, Mr. Dalton, who was represent-
ing Singer Sewing Machines. I told him I could not speak the language. He
said this was no barrier, for when he had arrived in Brazil, neither could he,
so he had done his business by showing the buyers a picture and then did
the balance of the deal in sign language. I told Dr. Holden of his offer. He
advised that I go to the office of the British Consul which informed me I
would have to return to Guyana to get all my papers and passport fixed up. I
could then return. The Consul kindly assisted me by introducing me to the
Chief of Police who took my photograph, front and side faced, and my finger
prints. I was then given a visa to return at any time.

Over the next few days, I was busy shopping as I found items far cheaper
here than in Guyana. I visited the factory where they made hammocks – all
kinds from the net to the heavy blanket type which are used in the mountains. I selected a plain white hammock with a matching mosquito net. I

changed a five dollar bill and was surprised at the amount of paper money I received in exchange.

A motor schooner was finally located that would transport us to French Guiana. Our party boarded the schooner in the late afternoon and we motored down river to the island of Marajos where we spent the night. This island of Marajos is about half the size of Guyana in square miles and is situated in the mouth of the Amazon River. I learnt that the island does a large trade in alligator skins. In dry weather, when the lakes and ponds are dry, the vaqueros lasso these reptiles from horse back, pull them out of the water and slaughter and skin them. The meat from the tail is prepared and canned, the skins made into leather for use in the manufacture of shoes and baggage. Brazil did a lot of canning even then, for I purchased banana, mangoes, and other fruits which had been crystallised and canned.

After leaving Marajos, we continued down the Amazon, stopping for a time at the Brazilian outpost at the mouth of the river on its left bank. Going ashore, we learned the authorities were holding some Nazi party members behind barbed wire fencing. It seems that they had been causing trouble and had been rounded up. (This was 1938 and the war with Germany was just around the corner.) From there we proceeded along the coast of Brazil until we met the Ouyapok River which forms the boundary to French Guiana, going up river to a Djuka (Bush Negro) Settlement. When the vessel was tied up it was swamped by a flood of black humanity. There was a hum of activity in the air as if we were near a giant bee's nest. Everyone seemed to be talking at the same time. The Djukas were noted for their wonderful wood carvings. I admired the decorative work on their corials and paddles and purchased a wooden chain carved from a single piece of wood. The Djukas just wore a lap or a piece of cloth wrapped around the waist. To these men a penknife was worth its weight in gold.

Leaving this settlement, we continued up river, the water very dark brown or black, to a large village on the left bank of the river where the Captain discharged some cargo and food stuffs for the shops located there. This village was in French territory. The languages spoken were a creole, patois French and their own language. Here we spent the night moored just off the village. Dr. Holden and Bill Hassler went ashore with the Captain to be entertained at one of the trader's shops. I did not go ashore but tied my hammock on deck as it was a clear moonlit night. Next morning, whilst the vessel was being discharged, the sun got very hot on deck so Justine and I decided to take a swim in the cool dark waters of the river. We plunged overboard and were swimming up river when we heard a loud commotion coming from the village. The people were shouting and running toward the river with the Captain in the lead. He was beckoning frantically for Justine and me to get back on board the schooner. He was very relieved to see us safely back, explaining that no one swam in the river as it was infested with the dreaded South American piranha fish. A horse falling overboard had literally disappeared in minutes before their eyes. I immediately thought back to our rivers in Guyana where we have the pirai, a larger version of the cannibal fish, but they do not swarm in their thousands as the piranha of Brazil.

I met a number of islanders from the West Indies who were engaged in mining gold, but because of the approaching war clouds, they were returning to their homes in St. Vincent, St. Lucia, and Martinique. Men, women and children were decked out in gold ornaments. The schooner sailed from this upriver village the same afternoon, travelling throughout the night until we hit the coast lands, thence along the coast to Cayenne in French Guiana. There, we had to report to the police station. To my surprise the Chief of Police proved to be a Guyanese who was very pleased to welcome us on learning we were from Guyana. He kindly accompanied us to a hotel where we could await our next boat connection to Dutch Guiana. He returned later in the evening to have a chat with us, to learn the latest news from Guyana. He said he originated from the village of Stewartville on the West Coast of Demerara.

The proprietor of our hotel was a true Frenchman. He informed me he had fought at the Battle of Verdun during the 1914-1918 war where the French war cry was "They shall not pass". I told him I had been attending school in England during those years and I had experienced many Zeppelin air raids. His two daughters had a perfume store under the hotel. I managed to secure some very expensive Parisienne perfume to present to my sister on my return home. He kindly invited Bill Hassler and me to his house (he did not live in the hotel) where he and his family entertained us. On leaving, he gave us a bottle of liquor he had made specially for his family. Rather than spend all our time in the hotel, Bill Hassler and I hired two cycles to tour the town and countryside, climbing a high hill on the outskirts of the town which held a huge reservoir that supplied the city with water. On one of our excursions, a lorry drew up after overtaking us and a young creole Frenchman approached me to ask if I was a scout as I was wearing my bush hat which looks similar. I told him no, but I had been a scout in England. Bill Hassler introduced us and explained that we were trying to see as much of French Guiana as possible in the few days we had left. We were immediately invited out to Monsieur Jacques estate where he had a little of everything under cultivation. He was also burning wood coals. His labour comprised Frenchmen who had served time on Devil's Island but were not allowed to return to France and had to eke out an existence in French Guiana. These men looked really miserable, barefooted, bareheaded and wearing only tattered clothes in the boiling tropical sun. They were as red as cherries and although the working conditions looked bad in our eyes, Monsieur Jacques said it was nothing to what they had been through on Devil's Island. We were introduced to his mother and two sisters who entertained us to a splendid dinner and the girls played the piano for us. They were very interested to hear of our travels in the bush and asked if we were not afraid of jaguars and snakes.

The following day, Dr. Holden informed me that he had booked passage on the Pan-Am plane for Guyana. He asked that I remain with the men and equipment to see them safely back home. Andrew MacDonald, Justine Pierre, Pablo and I later boarded the Dutch coastal steamer and departed for Paramaribo, Dutch Guiana. We arrived there the same night and engaged rooms in a small hotel. During my six months of travel I was used to my nightly rest. But here I found our beds simply crawling with bugs, so I decided to go out and walk, instead of being devoured alive. In the morning I purchased some souvenirs to carry home, and then we boarded the same steamer, arriving in Guyana the following day. I passed all our expedition stuff through the customs and arranged for the men to meet me the next day. Then I returned home to my sister's house after an absence of six months.

CHAPTER XI
From Motor Mechanic to Ordinary Seaman – 1942-45

Not being presently engaged, I travelled up river to Seeba Quarry where the Elmhurst Contracting Company was blasting granite rock, crushing the stone and shipping it to Atkinson Field, Hyde Park (now Timehri Airport) for the building of an air strip the American Armed Forces were putting down, also for the construction of roads. I managed to secure a job as a motor mechanic to work on the repairs and maintenance of their Mack Trucks. The chief mechanic, Mr. Truelove, asked me if I knew anything about diesel engines. I said no, but I would like to learn. He seemed surprised by my honesty, for he said that many workers claimed that they did, but then bitched up the job. My first job on a diesel shovel was to take out and clean the injectors. I did not put them back correctly and when the starter was pushed down, the engine failed to start. Truelove said we all learned from our mistakes. I lodged with the other mechanics and purchased enough food to last me until I could return to Wismar to collect my belongings and let my friends know where I was before they became too anxious. My immediate boss was a young American, a first class mechanic, but very impetuous. He said he preferred to work on large machines than on small ones. I saw him working on a small 1.5 H.P. water pump. He could not get it started so he just picked it up, heaved it overboard and said the Americans could afford better.

The chief blaster, Andy Kruger, set his charges for 11:00 a.m. every day when a whistle was blown, warning everyone to vacate all buildings in the compound because a large rock had once landed on a house there. When the button at the control house was pushed, I saw a vivid flash of flame, followed by the sound of the explosion, then saw the whole cliff face lift and fall back into the quarry. Diesel shovels were used to load these rocks into the Mack trucks for conveyance to the crusher known as "Old Humphrey". The oversized rocks were blasted again in the quarry by smaller charges. The crusher operated day and night, stopping only to change the jaws. One night a young Afro-Guyanese had the job of keeping one of the conveyor belts from slipping off by the use of a stick. He must have been very sleepy for when his stick got caught in the belt, instead of losing hold of the stick he held on. The belt caught his arm and ripped it from his body. His shout of anguish and pain was heard by a man working nearby. The stopping of the crusher at that hour woke the whole compound to enquire the cause. The site doctor rushed the boy by speed boat to MacKenzie Hospital where his life was saved. I understand he received a life pension from the American Government.

Once, learning of my swimming ability, I and some of the other men were called upon by Andy Kruger to swim out to a sunken barge which was blocking the pontoon channel. We were instructed to place a case of dynamite to each corner of the barge and wire the charges, then swim back with the wire to the shore where it was attached to a plunger. Boats had been warned to keep clear of the area, but some of the river people, learning what we were about to do, paddled their corials downstream to collect the stunned fish after the blast. When all was ready, Andy Kruger asked me to push the plunger. What a sight! The whole river bed seemed to rise up for a 100 feet, hang suspended with flying pieces from the wooden barge, then drop back, sending waves right up the river bank. The shock of the blast must have blown the fishes to fragments as the boat men collected very few.

There was a compound on the other side of the river where rum was sold. On paydays, the launch from Wismar brought up the whores to entertain the workmen from the plant. These women would earn in one night what a man had taken a whole month to earn. Some of the Americans would ask the workmen to buy rum and bring it back over. No American boat was allowed at that landing, nor could the launch tie up at the American wharf. Some of us from the mechanic shop used to swim over at night with money and a small bag tied at the waist to hold three or four bottles of rum and swim back. One night, the watchman on the wharf beckoned me urgently. He told us to come out of the water as he suspected a "massacuraman" was lurking in the area for he had seen a round hairy head appear and disappear into the dark waters. This put a stop to our night swimming.

Mr. Stauning, a tall, grey-haired American who was in charge of operations, took a liking to me and placed me in an administrative post. One night, I was called into the quarry where our truck drivers had picked up an immense toad in the headlights of their truck. The Americans were notified and they took that toad up the hill to their quarters to photograph and measure it. It proved to be two feet high, having a circumference of three and a half feet. It was a most loathsome animal with a slimy skin covered with huge warts.

I left this job at Seeba Quarry to join an American liberty ship in the port of Georgetown, where seamen were jumping ship due to the submarine threat outside of our harbour. The captain of the *William Cullen Bryant* carried me to the American Embassy where I was signed on as an ordinary seaman at a salary of $300.00 U.S. per month. I reported on board with a few personal items, because I could purchase most of what I wanted on board, duty free. The ship ran a first class mess, food was plentiful, the refrigerator was full at all times. When I came off watch at night, there was always hot water, coffee and cocoa, bread, ham and cheese. Our trips up river to Mackenzie City were placid runs. The only unpleasant part of loading the bauxite ore was that the red dust penetrated all parts of the ship, although the doors were shut and heavy curtains placed inside the doorways. On completion of loading operations, I assisted in hosing down the decks on our way downstream.

The ship, after getting clearance from Port Georgetown, usually left at sundown. On passing our lightship, there were strict orders that no one was allowed to smoke cigarettes on deck and all portholes were blacked out. This was a precaution against submarines lurking in the area. On two occasions, an American "blimp" accompanied us part way in the daytime. These airships were always on patrol, on the look out for submarines. I made three trips on this ship. Being the only Guyanese on board, I paid special attention to my duties and got along very well with the crew, so much so that the Chief Mate said I should accompany the ship on its return to New York.

On our fourth trip, as we approached the submarine net off Port of Spain, Trinidad, a German submarine lurking in the area sent a torpedo after us, but through the quick manoeuvring of the steersman, the torpedo barely caught us on the bow. However, the force of the explosion threw me against the hatch, fracturing three ribs. I did not realise this at the time, I just felt a sharp pain. A radio message was dispatched to the air base in Trinidad, and in no time I saw three planes swoop down and around us, dropping bombs in the area of the submarine. The sub tried hard to get clear after doing his damage but one of the bombs must have damaged him in some way. The coming of night saved him, but the "blimp" traced him with flares the whole night and the following day I heard that planes had sunk the submarine. The ship managed to limp into Chaguaramus, where the bauxite was offloaded and the damage from the torpedo checked. This did not prove as serious as was thought because, as a modern ship, the *William Cullen Bryant* had self-sealing holds as a safety factor against torpedoes. On my return home to Georgetown, I was referred to hospital where the x-ray revealed three fractured ribs. This put an end to my chance of visiting the States as the ship had to sail without me – and also an end to my sea career.

During my recuperation at home, I got to know some young pilots from the American Air Force from the 337th squadron who were stationed at Atkinson Field. These pilots use to alarm the residents of Georgetown with their low flying tactics, just skimming the rooftops in the city. A complaint was laid to the Commanding Officer at Atkinson Field and these incidents came to a close. After hearing that I was recovering from a submarine attack whilst serving on an American ship, these young pilots invited me to visit the air base and spend the day there. They arranged with a fishing boat to land me at a spot near the river where I could be picked up by a public works lorry carrying men into the base to work. I was conveyed to their quarters near the runway. Since I did not have permission to be there, they gave me some olive green fatigues, on the sleeves of which were displayed a sergeant's stripes. We then adjourned to the NCOs' mess hall for breakfast. I joined them on a motor-trac-tractor for a ride to where their plane was parked under a camouflage net. I assisted the crew in checking and cleaning the hydraulic system. Whilst employed on this work, I fortunately got some oil on my hands and face, for who should appear but the Flight Lieutenant on inspection. He immediately spotted me and asked the Master Sergeant who I was. The boys replied that I was a Sergeant Young, a Puerto Rican, who had dropped in on an overnight stop and was giving them a hand.

On completion of the overhaul, the Lieutenant said he would take the plane up for a trial, so all of us were bundled aboard. My friends pushed me up into the copilot's seat and said they would tell me what to do. I was on edge the whole time not knowing what questions the Lieutenant might put to me. On our return to barracks, we showered and changed into khaki uniforms. I was issued a suit with complete with my Sergeant's stripes and cap. We adjourned to the NCOs' mess hall for lunch. After lunch, we visited the NCOs' canteen where the boys ordered Golden Wedding whiskey and treated me to rum-soaked cigars. I was introduced to numerous other airmen as Sgt. Young from Puerto Rico. Later, after 'scrounging' around for bread, meat and other canned stuff, a block of ice and drinks, the boys explained to me they had a couple of girls in a house over the river. A truck was commandeered and the provisions stowed in it. Then we left for the river landing, where I had been put ashore that morning, where a boat awaited us.

On our way, we were stopped by the Commanding Officer, Colonel Matthews, who enquired where we were going. The boys said they were going for a boating trip on the river. He told them to be very careful. Praise the

Lord, he did not peep into the lorry where I was sitting with all the stolen stuff. I was glad to get into the boat after this scare and over the river. I spent the night in the house and returned to Georgetown the next day. When I told my friends what had occurred, they told me I did not realise what danger I had been in – no identification papers and posing as a NCO of the USAAF. I could have been arrested as a spy and ended up in a lot of trouble.

After this incident, I was offered a job at Atkinson Air Base to work in the motor pool as a mechanic, by a Major Macaw. I was to work under a Lieutenant Brodie and later under Captain Marsh. Two American mechanics, Sgt. Daymon and another we used to call "Shorty", were our advisors. I soon worked my way up from a mechanic to an administrative post. I was then transferred to the M.P. Station in Georgetown in charge of the vehicles there until the end of the war in 1945.

CHAPTER XII
Gold Prospecting Up the Cuyuni – 1945-1947

Major "Art" Williams (later Colonel) USAAF, who pioneered the development of air transport into our interior, asked me to join his team on his gold concession in Julian Ross Itabu on the right bank of the Cuyuni River and next to the Aurora Gold field. I had five other men with me. Our job was to cut block lines for the purpose of prospecting. We built a tarpaulin camp and later a leaf camp near a clear fresh water stream. Nearing completion of this task, I was unfortunate enough to be taken with severe pains in my abdomen in the area where I had been operated on for gall stones in 1939, whilst at Plantation Schoon Ord. I could not eat, neither could I stand upright or sit down without pain. Grant and Brotherson, two Afro-Guyanese who had been working along with me, had to practically carry me to the river and then down to Aurora Gold Fields Compound to check with the dispenser. Because of the continuing severe pains, I had no rest the whole night. Not having eaten or drunk anything from the time I left camp, the dispenser kindly brought me a glass of milk. Even this proved too much, for the pains intensified. Jimmy McNeil, a Scotsman in charge of bush air strip locations for "Art" Williams found me in this condition and immediately sent for "Art" Williams' pusher plane. Harry Wendt came for me the same day. I was met at the Ramp by an ambulance and rushed to the Public Hospital, Georgetown, where I was lucky enough to meet Dr. Grieson, another Scotsman, who had operated on me for the gall stones in 1939.

I was x-rayed but no further gall stones showed. Dr. Grieson said that sometimes soft gall stones formed which do not show up on x-ray. The best thing to do was to take out the whole gall bladder. This would save any further trouble but it would have to be a major operation, did I agree? I told him I wanted to get well and return to work so to go ahead. I remember the day well, when I was put on the operating table, mother naked and painted with iodine. Dr. Grieson, who was scrubbing at the basin, turned and asked me if I was afraid. I told him that as long as Almighty God was there, and Dr. Grieson was performing the operation, I was not afraid. When I regained consciousness some hours later, I found two nurses in attendance, each holding one of my hands. They were checking my pulse. My feet or rather the bed end was raised higher than my head. The nurses said this was because I had lost a lot of blood. My sister had been twice to see me, but I had still been unconscious.

Ten days after the operation, it was time for the charge nurse to remove the packing of the wound. It so happened she was on leave that day. Another nurse, a strapping coloured woman, attended to me. I do not know where some of these nurses get their certificates, but two of them worked on me, pulling and tugging at the concealed plug in my wound. My backbone felt as if it was coming through my stomach. I had to grit my teeth and grip the side of the bed. I was groaning with pain. Eventually, the plug came out with a rush of blood. I was quickly swabbed off and rebandaged. Fifteen minutes later, I felt a warmness on my stomach. On lifting the sheet, I found all my bandages soaked with blood. I asked the nurse to call the doctor who unfortunately was not in the building so, I asked her to call any doctor in the area. Shortly after, a doctor from the maternity ward appeared. After examining the dressing, he found the nurses had worked loose some of the clips holding the wound when they so roughly pulled out the plug. The doctor told me it would hurt somewhat to renew the clips. I told him to stop the bleeding, as I did not imagine it could be any worse than what I had just been through. When Dr. Grieson visited the ward the following morning and learned what had happened to me the previous evening from one of the other patients in the ward, he really blew up, and told the charge nurse that it was no use him trying to save lives if through her carelessness they were to throw it away.

On my discharge from the hospital, Dr. Grieson told me to do no heavy work for six months, but in four months I was back in the Cuyuni river area where I met Jimmy McNeil and joined him opening an air strip 7 miles inland from Aurora Gold Fields on a high laterite ridge. A compound of three bush houses sheltered the men working on the air strip. One afternoon when I was going to the creek to bathe and fetch up a bucket of water for the camp, I saw a large turtle tiger (so named due to the spots on its back, shaped like a turtle) standing on our washing plank at the creek side. I put down the bucket quietly and ran back to camp for my gun, but I did not get a shot at it for, by the time of my return, it was swimming over the creek and disappearing into the bush on the other bank.

On another occasion in this high-ridge country, early one morning, I was leading the line of men when turning a sharp point in the narrow walking line, I met up with a large jaguar, a beautiful looking animal with the same turtle markings. I had a warashi on my back, my knife was in my right hand and my gun in my left. To drop the knife and swing the gun to my right shoulder would only have taken a second, but the meeting was so sudden that we were both left motionless, no more than twelve feet apart staring at each other. When I did drop the knife, the jaguar sprang into the bush. I fired a shot behind it to give it more speed. Two days later a huntsman shot a large turtle tiger. It could have been the same one I had encountered but we were in jaguar country and it could have been another. I collected its skin, which I still have at home. Early another morning, Grant, one of my men, went to ease his bowels in the nearby bush. He dropped his pants and was about to do his daily duty when he heard a low growl behind him. He turned and saw a large jaguar feeding on an akuri. Grant took off like a jet, arriving in camp with his trousers still around his knees, much to our amusement.

I learned to operate the International bulldozer, which was equipped with a bullcam in front. It was the only piece of equipment we had to clear the air strip and to do all the cutting and grading. I worked from 7:00 a.m. to 5:00 p.m. every day. I had an assistant who did the night shift, David Daniels, an Amerindian. We worked around the clock, only stopping to service the machine and fuel up. On occasions, we had to travel the seven miles out to Aurora pulling a skid trailer to bring in drums of fuel.

The rainy season set in with heavy thunder and lighting. As a boy at school in England, I had loved a good thunder storm. My attitude had changed during my working years in this tropical country. I have seen death in the cane fields when one of my forkmen was struck by lightning and a fellow overseer was killed when lightning struck the steel umbrella he was holding. Many people have been killed sheltering under trees. My men on surveys would wrap their shirts around their cutlasses. I have seen two of my men shocked when holding a steel measuring chain. A thunderstorm experienced in these mountainous areas is nothing like one in England. Here, when a clap of thunder explodes over one's head, one can feel the vibrations in the rock under one's feet. Late one afternoon when I was grading on this high laterite ridge, I saw the rain approaching but continued work because I wanted to complete that portion of the strip as the following day it would be too wet to work. Black clouds were rolling up accompanied by flashes of lightning and peals of thunder. My bulldozer was operating well when, all of a sudden, a brilliant bluish flame exploded over the blade of my machine directly in front of me. At the same time I experienced a severe shock and the machine stopped dead. I was stunned for a moment, then realising what had happened and glad to be still alive, I switched off the engine and put down the canvas blinds and started for my camp through the driving rain. I noticed a huge mora tree ablaze on the edge of the strip that must have been struck by the lightning which had hit my machine. Colonel "Art" Williams warned me never to operate these machines during a storm as they were made of steel and I was lucky to be alive.

As a boy, I always believed lightning struck from the clouds, but today I know different. Storm clouds develop an electrical charge, negative at the bottom and positive on top. This produces a positive charge on the ground that follows the cloud like a shadow. Between the cloud and the ground is a potential of millions of volts. The positive fingers are reaching up from high buildings and trees and the negative fingers from the clouds are reaching down. Finally, the resistance of the air is overcome and a connection is made along a conductive air channel. A monstrous surge of electricity shoots from ground to cloud producing a brilliant flash. Lightning's intense heat violently expands the air along the path of the stroke. So fast does the air rush aside that it makes waves that can be heard as a sharp crack of thunder if the lightning is close, a rumbling if far off.

The construction of the air field, although located and supervised by "Art" Williams of USAAF, was backed financially by Guyanese government money. When the grant was finished before the actual completion of the strip, the Government failed to back "Art" Williams, although we guaranteed to finish the job within the next six weeks. Consequently, the men were retrenched and I was left in charge of all the equipment.

During my period of waiting for a new job, I was initiated into the method of the prospecting and working of alluvial gold. I had with me an Afro-Guyanese, Cambridge by name, alias "Tajam" a drougher. I prospected the same creek tributary on which our camp was built. Tajam bored some holes with a shovel to a depth of three to four feet, bringing up some gravel and he washed it in a battel (gold pan). We discerned "barley grain" gold settled in the thimble. Tajam said this was a good indication so we cleared an area of about twenty by thirty feet, and dug down to gravel. Tajam constructed a tom box and a chest. A piece of rice bag was spread under the tom iron and was held in place by a riffle at the edge of the tom box. This was sprinkled with quicksilver to catch the gold passing through the tom iron. Attached under the tom box edge was the chest with riffles inside. This chest was two and a half feet in length and narrow to about one foot at the discharging end. Our first day's work produced nothing compared to what we expected on our investigation, but then we discovered we were working gravel which rested on a false clay, blue in colour. When we punctured this clay we discovered the real gravel underneath, a reddish brown gravel resting on a red catch-cow mixed with rounded granite boulders. The depth was only three to four feet. Here we reaped a harvest of gold nuggets. The largest nugget I washed out was three and a quarter ounces in weight.

Soon after this I was recalled by "Art" Williams and had to move all my equipment seven miles to the river in preparation for being shipped to Georgetown. At Aurora River landing, I was introduced to two Americans by Colonel Williams who said these men wanted to travel up the Cuyuni River to its tributary, Wenamu, which forms the boundary to Venezuela. He asked me to accompany them in their search for gold. The manager of the Cuyuni Gold Field at Aurora, Mr. Zinkie, supplied a thirty-six foot boat and an inboard engine for this trip up river and supplied food from the ration store. Captain Sugreem Singh was engaged to steer the boat and I was asked to operate the inboard engine. There was the regular boat crew and some men I took with me to prospect for gold. At the Devil's Hole range of falls, (the worst in the Cuyuni River) whilst towing a small boat behind us, there was insufficient power in the engine to steam up the first hump of surging white water. I noticed river water pouring over the gunwale into the boat. I shouted to the Captain who in turn shouted to the assistant steersman to cut the rope towing the small boat. In the excitement of the moment he foolishly cut the paddle steering rope. The boat immediately lost headway and I had to cut the power of the engine as the boat started to swing broadside to the rushing water. Some of the men, fearing what might happen, panicked and started to jump overboard. Others, more level-headed, plunged overboard with the life line, swam to a rock and tied the rope to a tree shrub. From here the warp rope was secured to the tree and the boat made secure, preventing it from running back down the rapids. When the Captain realised what had happened, he was furious with his assistant for cutting his steering paddle rope. He said he could have lost his boat and cargo and maybe some lives.

After the rope was renewed and tied to the steering paddle, the captain ordered the small boat to be left behind, to be brought up later. Then, when everyone was in place, he instructed me to go start up my engine. The cargo boat managed to climb the first five rapids, but on meeting "Big Wamapoo", the tiger of them all, the boat halted behind a large rock, which broke the force of the water. The boat crew was put ashore with the warp rope. Two men were assigned to the bow line and two to the stern line. As the Captain gave the order, the bowman eased out the boat bow into the stream. I gave the engine some power and with the assistance of the men on the ropes, the boat gradually eased ahead against the rushing water. At the apex of the fall,

it was a real strain on the men with the ropes and required the full power of
the engine to climb to the top, where the Captain tied up under an island. To
the right of Big Wamapoo rapids we could see the main falls: a maelstrom of
boiling white water within a jungle of ugly black rocks – so named the devil's cauldron or "Devils Hole".

For the next stage, the cargo from our boat had to be discharged and the
boat hauled on hardwood rollers over a spit of land on this Island, to the
more placid waters of the upper river. On our resumption, we passed Dukwarri
rapids, where we stopped for something to eat. Then the Captain had to take
a back channel at "Itabu", to cut out the more dangerous Kanaima Falls.
This Itabu exits just beyond the beginning of the falls into a long stretch of
still water. Bordering our right, on the left bank of the Cuyuni River, was
Venezuelan territory. At the foot of Kanaima Falls, Akarabisi Creek forms
the boundary between Guyana and Venezuela. There is a Government line
from the Akarabisi Creek mouth, which goes across to the Barama River in
the North West Region of Guyana.

On our left, or the right bank of the river, were the mountainous regions of
the Isenero River head, and the Haimaraka at Makapa Hills was on our right.
We met a man called McNaughton, who was living with an Amerindian
woman. He had large fields of cassava and other provisions. He told us that
he was producing some good diamonds from his workings. On leaving Marwa
Landing, McNaughton's place, we proceeded through the calm waters. I could
see the towering mountains on my left which form a part of the Pakaraima
range. This range crosses the Mazaruni River to form the Peaima Falls. We
stopped at a large blackwater tributary on the right bank, Ekereku, the sands
of which showed grains of gold when washed carefully in a battel. We made
camp here for the night. The following morning we steamed up Bulcan Falls,
at the Ohnopi Creek mouth, passing the Island and onto Eteringbang Falls
where our boat had to be lightened before pulling it over the falls. Then we
proceeded to Mora Falls, the last before we steamed into the Wenamu River
mouth at about midday. After lunch, I paid a visit to the Venezuelan outpost
at this river mouth, which is situated on the left bank. This compound is an
outpost of the National Guard. There was a Sergeant in charge, with approximately twenty men under him. I met a Guyanese, Edwin by name, who
proved to be McNaughton's half brother. He held the post of boatbuilder,
engineer and steersman for the Venezuelans. Edwin informed me the Venezuelans had been raiding and working gold on Guyana's lands.

I built two camps at the Wenamu river mouth, opposite to the Venezuelan
Compound. Here I started my prospecting for gold. Some of the Venezue-

lans came over the river to show me where they had been working the gold. Their method was unlike ours. Whereas I would open a large area, dig out the overburden, then throw out the gravel, the Venezuelans would bore a round hole about three feet in diameter and work their way down to gravel. All excavated material is hauled to the surface through this hole, which they called a "baranca". They would then follow the gravel, working on their stomach, leaving small pillars of gravel for support, so they could wiggle out backwards. The gravel is brought up to the surface and washed in their gold pans at the river's edge. I found that a number of these men and women suffered from rheumatism from lying on this wet and cold ground. I had my men build a V-shaped trough made from sawn boards which extended from the riverbank to the hill foot. Water was pumped from the river with a homelight pump for washing our gravel.

The gold at the hill foot proved to be coated with something resembling black enamel. Only after cracking this coating, could I discern the gold. The men had been throwing away these 'ironstones', as they thought they were, and I had to rework this piece of land to recover them. Some surface gold was picked up at the hill foot, which was nearly white in colour, but proved to be very light. The returns I got here were not up to the expectations of the Americans. They had heard of some gold mines over in Venezuela in the Eteringbang Creek and paid a visit to the workings with the hope of buying or investing, but the government red tape proved too intricate, so they pulled out. Before returning to Aurora, they arranged with me to continue with the prospecting up the Wenamu River for a further six months when "Art" Williams would return on the 15th December 1947 to pick me up in his plane.

CHAPTER XIII
Pork-knockers and Balata Bleeders and A Fortune Lost

My only means of transportation up the Wenamu River was by a woodskin rented from an Amerindian. As this frail craft could not convey my party of five, I decided to send one of my men, Gaskin, with the Amerindian to show him where I intended to camp that night. They would transport all our food and equipment. Westmass, Ouckama, Yan, Veecock 'Johnson and I would walk up the river bank through the bush. When we met some burned out areas where fallen trees had been covered by vine and razor grass, and knowing the speed of our progress would be impeded, I decided to swim across the Wenamu River and walk on the Venezuelan bank. I took off my clothes and instructing the others to do likewise, I tied my clothing on my head, slung my boots around my waist and swam safely over. I had to swim back part way to assist one of my companions who found himself in some difficulties. We eventually arrived opposite the Muruwawe, a large black water creek, where our camp was set up. I hailed the Amerindian with the wood skin and we were carried over to our camp ground. The men did some cleaning up around the camp before they prepared our evening meal. The Amerindians with us, an Akawaio and his wife, told me the source of this creek was high in the mountains dividing the Wenamu from the Ekereku Valley. They said the Venezuelans had reported good deposits of gold at its source.

Early the next morning, I asked Gaskin, one of my companions, to accompany me to prospect the headwaters of this creek. The Amerindians transported us in their woodskin to the mountain foot, where the water was getting too swift. Gaskin and I disembarked and I instructed the Amerindians to await our return. We followed a track leading up into the hills. Presently I detected a wonderful scent coming down with the wind. After scenting like a hound dog, we came across some ground orchids, their stalks about two feet high and bearing a brilliant yellow flower shaped much like English daffodils. I collected some of the bulbs from between the rocks to carry home as I had never seen this species before. At the top of this hill spur, I was surprised to come across a well defined track about eight feet wide and well trodden, as if by plenty of people. I told Gaskin I intended to follow this track to see where it led us. After about half an hour's walk and an estimated two miles, I heard a man calling or shouting. Imagine my surprise when we met up with a string of donkeys being herded by one man, Each donkey (burro) was loaded with two blocks of balata slung from a pack saddle. The man could not speak English but by sign language he indicated his camp was further on.

Late in the afternoon, Gaskin and I entered a small compound of very rough leaf shelters where the balata bleeders lived. We met two other Venezuelans in the camp. They too could not speak English and I knew no Spanish. I was shown the fire pit dug in the earth in which they boiled the latex. These balata bleeders were raiders having no right to be on our territory. In years gone by, the forests of our North West Region were most prolific in bullet wood trees from which balata gum is extracted. Balata was used extensively in the manufacture of machinery belting. Today it is no exaggeration to say that for every standing bullet wood tree in this vast area, ten lie rotting on the ground. As I have said, the legal way to bleed a tree is to take half of the circumference and only up as far as the first branch. This will produce four of five gallons of latex. When these scars are healed in four or five years time, the other half of the tree can be bled, producing the same amount of latex. But over the border in Venezuela, it was the custom to fell the tree and bleed it on the ground, throughout its entire length, even the main branches not escaping the bleeder's cutlass. The latex collected by this method from each tree varied from fifteen to twenty gallons. This was boiled and poured into condensed milk cartons to harden. Each block averaged twenty kilos of dried balata. Our lawful method was to prepare thin sheets of balata but although this block balata did not fetch as high a price in the market as our sheet variety, it nevertheless was to the advantage of the illicit bleeders to prepare blocks, on account of the very much smaller risk of being caught. Two men could fell and bleed a tree and prepare the blocks and be several miles away in thirty-six hours.

The police made numerous raids on suspected areas to catch these illicit bleeders. One particular Afro-Guyanese family was especially noted for its illegal activities, even the sister taking advances from the balata traders and going herself into the forest to secure the easily obtained balata from felled trees. It was this woman though who saved the life of a police officer who had made one of the few successful raids to catch the illicit bleeders actually at work. One of the brothers raised his gun to fire at the officer but his sister knocked it up.

Because I was dressed in khaki shorts and shirt and wearing rubber-top boots and my bush hat turned up at the left side, similar to the uniform of

our bush police, these men took me for a police officer. Gaskin and I had to
make much of our position. We were given bags to sleep on, but our dinner
comprised of very rough fare, a piece of dried fish, cassava bread and a cup
of strong black coffee. They gave us a bottle of Jeyes Fluid and a powis
feather to paint inbetween our toes, as the camp ground was infested with
jiggers which have the habit of boring into one's toes. After spending a miserable night, we set off back at dawn to rejoin the Amerindians who were
camped at the river awaiting our return.

Describing this brush with these illegal balata bleeders reminds me of an
incident which happened some years afterwards when I was in charge of the
Balata Company's depot at the mouth of the Siparuni river. My duties included receiving the balata from the foreman of the various gangs of bleeders. There was one foreman who gave me a lot of trouble. Pompey was from
Surinam, a big burly fellow whom I sometimes believed was a bush Negro
or Djuka. These people who lived in the upper reaches of the rivers were
supposed to have kept alive many of the customs of their African ancestors
including snake worship. This foreman's balata was invariably adulterated
with the gum of the 'cow tree', the addition of which increased the bulk but
diminished the quality of the balata.

Matters came to a head when I refused to accept, even at a reduced rate,
a large consignment of gum he had brought in. Pompey, who was accompanied by two of his men, finally realising that his pleadings were in vain, flew
into a frightful rage and with blazing eyes and frothing mouth, let go a stream
of invective in the 'talki-talki' of his native land, a patois of corrupted Dutch
and English with an admixture of African. I could not follow the whole of his
tirade but gathered that dogs used the graves of my ancestors for purposes
intimately their own. Finally, his frenzy apparently having died down, Pompey
added in plain English that he 'would put a snake on me'.

We had been having several months of dry weather and the river was low
and full of pirai, so I used to perform my evening ablutions in a little annex
behind the house, where my cook would place a bucket of water and a calabash. It was four o'clock when I got the abusing from Pompey and an hour
later when I went to have my evening bath. I had stripped and was about to
pick up the calabash to dash water over my body when, with an instinctive
shudder, I swiftly withdrew my hand from the calabash. In the bottom was a
white tailed labaria six inches in length – one of the smallest and most venomous of snakes. It was marked like its larger namesake except for an inch
of tail, which was a dirty-white in colour. Calling to the cook to bring a kettle

of boiling water, I soon dispatched the deadly little snake and went on with my bath. Then I stretched out my hand for the towel which, on entering the bathroom, I had hung on one of the row of pegs on the wall. Just as I was about to take hold of it, my eye was arrested by the brown and black mottles of a large labaria lying against the wall along the lath which was holding the pegs. The snake's head was not six inches from my towel, the shaking of which would undoubtedly have irritated the reptile into hostile action.

I left the bathroom, delaying not the manner of my going, my naked skin still dripping. I fetched my gun and blew off the snake's head. Retiring to my bedroom, I got into pajamas and, having already put on one mosquito boot, was about to pull on the other when providence drew my attention to the fact it was heavier than usual. Quicker than lightning, a thought flashed through my brain and with a spasmodic jerk, I flung the footgear to the end of the room where it struck the wall and fell to the floor, but it did not come to rest. The doeskin heaved and writhed and a moment later an angry morabanna thrust its broad head out of the boot followed by three feet of blended black and mauve body. Again I waited not on the order of my going but, yelling for my cook, rushed out of the house and down to the store where I got the bookkeeper and his assistant to bring their guns. Walking warily into the bedroom, I found the snake travelling along a corner of the wall and shot it.

Three snakes in the house in half an hour! There must have been something in Pompey's threat.

To cut a long story short, we shot and killed four more in and around the house before morning: one in the woodpile; a second coiled around the dog's food plate, (the animal drawing our attention to it by walking stiff-legged at a safe distance around the plate and whining plaintively); a third was atop of my mosquito net betrayed by the bulge I noticed on my retiring to bed and the fourth, really the seventh and the biggest of the lot, a ten foot camoodie, lurked in the roof space. By this time, I had been reduced almost to a state of idiocy. I could not sleep and was afraid to move. In addition to the two tilley gas lamps that were normally in the house, I had a dozen new Dietz lanterns sent up from the store filled with kerosene oil, lit and placed in every nook and corner of the building so that even a cockroach could not run across the floor without attracting attention.

Fortunately for me, the camoodie must have been the final effort of Pompey's obeah, if such it was, for no more snakes appeared in the house, but morning found me hollow-eyed and nervous. Shortly after dawn, Pompey and two of his cronies came up the hill, apparently to see if I was still alive.

So peeved was I at the sight of him that, getting up from my chair and grasping a prospecting knife that lay on a nearby table, I slashed at the cord holding the rolled-up tarpaulin that served as a verandah blind, it being my intention to shut the sight of him from my eyes. As the tarpaulin fell, there was a deep angry humming sound and imagining I had yet disturbed another snake, I fled to the bedroom. Barely had I reached it and slammed the door than I heard a discordant chorus of agonised yells and calls to God from Pompey and his companions.

Later the cook and the bookkeeper explained to me that when I had cut the cord to open the tarpaulin blind, I had disturbed a nest of quakoo marabuntas that somehow during the dry spell had settled in the rolled-up blind without anyone noticing them. At the sudden disruption of their home, I fortunately having shut myself in my bedroom, they had fallen on the only persons in the vicinity: Pompey and his two friends. The quakoo is the fiercest and most dreaded of all our numerous species of hornets. When several dozen of them landed on and stung Pompey and his friends, their plight was worse by far than mine had ever been. In their agony, they had plunged into the river whence, minus several toes, they were driven ashore again by the pirai. My cook told me that as soon as they regained the use of their eyes, they stole an Amerindian canoe and cleared off down river. Perhaps he wanted nothing more to do with a man who controlled such vastly more powerful 'obeah' than his own.

Obeah or the long arm of coincidence – I never wanted a similar experience with seven snakes in my house in twelve hours, nor did I propose to have any dealings whatsoever with anyone who professed the possession of occult powers.

To return to my account of this earlier journey up the Wenamu river, when we reached our main camp, I was handed a note informing me that two of my men, Westmass and Ouckama, had found the going too tough and were on their way out to get a passage back to the city. However, two other men who happened to be in the area requested permission to join my party.

The next morning, after packing up our equipment, I paid a call to a trading store on the Venezuelan shore. I found to my surprise a woman running the business. She could speak fair English. She admitted that she had been supplying the illicit bleeders with rations and buying the blocks of balata from them. She did, though, tell me that the men I had met the previous day had taken me for a police officer and had run into the bush and were afraid to return to their camp. I told her she was abetting illegal raiders. I did not mind their bleeding according to our laws, but I strongly objected to their utter disregard for the future value of our trees by their method of cutting down the trees to rot on the ground. She kindly offered to put me up for the night. During our conversation over dinner she gave me some very useful information about the surrounding country and the politics in Venezuela. Next day, acting on information from this woman, I continued upstream to Arawai, the foot of a range of falls going up into the Karamuta mountains on the Venezuelan frontier.

The National Guard had another outpost at the foot of these falls staffed by one corporal and one private. They patrolled the bush trails from La Boca at the Wenamu river mouth every two weeks, visiting outlying settlements. I spent the night with these soldiers. They seemed to be very glad of the company. The area opposite their outpost, on the right bank of the Wenamu and stretching to the escarpment wall, was an old burned-out area. The second growth of these trees and stumps reared out of the low bush along with patches of deer calaloo which bushmen use in their food. The leaves are good to eat mixed with rice or meat. The following day, I took two men and started to cut through this dense second growth in my endeavour to locate an old walking line leading up the face of the escarpment. I managed to pick up a trace at the base of the escarpment. Later, coming back to the river we managed to open the line a little wider as this would be our supply line.

After bidding the soldiers farewell, the men and I packed our warashis with our hammocks and food, leaving the heavier tools and tarpaulin to be brought up later. I did not tax the men with too heavy a load as we had to scale the escarpment by what proved to be no more than a goat track, zigzagging up the practically perpendicular face. At some places, stakes had been driven into the wall to provide a handhold, but they were now rotten with age. This climb proved to be about 750 feet up the river. In comparison to my climb up the escarpment of Kaieteur in 1925, this was much more precarious. It took us about an hour and a half from the river to reach the summit of the escarpment. Our reward on reaching the top was to see open savannah lands stretching to trees bordering a creek some distance away. Further away were more islands of bush, with a view of the mountains of the Mazaruni river head showing a lighter blue in the distance. As I sat on the edge of this escarpment, taking in its beauty, I could look down and see the river twisting and turning, glistening threadlike in the sun, and the forest stretching as far as the Cuyuni. There are places where the beauty of orchids and wild flowers can say more than words. Over and over in my travels in our country I have met such places and been unable to express in mere words the wondrous feelings I have had on these occasions.

We picked up our warashis and started across the open savannah towards a line of trees that seemed to demarcate a creek. I picked out a camp site near this beautiful icy-cold clear water coming out of the mountains. I had the men cut hardwood upright posts and beams to frame our camp; larger wood was cut to form a corduroy flooring and turru and manicole palm leaves for roofing and walls. In two days time I had a comfortable leaf hut. I sent back four of the men to bring in the balance of our load from the Venezuelan outpost.

On investigating this creek, I found signs of previous workings. Washing some of the gravel, I saw indications of diamonds but unfortunately I had travelled without any sieves for their recovery. Whilst we were encamped here, some Akawaio Amerindians visited the camp. In their very broken English, I learned they had a very old Afro-Guyanese living in their village. I visited their village the following day and met a wizened old man with silver-white hair. When he saw me he got up with fair agility for his age, then I received another surprise. Before I could speak to him, he asked, "What do you seh, boy?" I asked him if he knew me. He then asked if I was not David Young's son from North West. I said I was. He said he knew it, for I had my father's features. Jacob was the old man's name. He gave me a rundown of some of my father's earlier activities in this area. It seems my father and his partner, Dingalseh, a German, had worked gold here in the late nineteenth and early twentieth centuries. He told me that at that time he used to wash twenty ounces of gold in a battel, so much that the Venezuelans use to raid across the river at nights and guns were fired to repel the raids. Old Jacob then carried me to a small tributary of the Arau River, which proved to be the name of the river on which I was camped. He told me not to expect the old records of twenty ounces to the battel, but I could still collect sufficient gold to cover the cost of my expedition.

The pay dirt in the stream ran in a narrow vein of alluvial workings. I discovered I was working mostly gold nuggets which were very rough, proving they originated from the nearby mountain. If they had travelled from further away, they would have been much more rounded. When our food supplies ran low, I sent two of my men out to the Awarai National Guard outpost with two or three ounces of gold. I had already arranged with them that when they travelled out to Alta Cuyuni, on the upper reaches of the Cuyuni River at Cuidad Bolivar to draw their wages, they would purchase the items I had marked down in my letter and pay for it with the gold I sent out. The food in Venezuela was far cheaper than the food transported from Georgetown to our bush shops. On some weekends, these soldiers would pay us a visit at our workings. They panned gold, for the experience, which I allowed them to keep.

After working in this mountain area for about four and a half months, I decided to move down river to be in time to meet "Art" Williams, as arranged, on the 15th December 1947. I threw down a large purpleheart tree and, using the bark, constructed a good sized woodskin to transport our stuff out to the river mouth. The men had to cut a track through the bush through which we had to haul the woodskin to the river. The woodskin was a little thin and we had to use the craft with care. I packed our gold, some thirteen pounds wrapped in a small blanket, in my small steel canister and strapped it shut. On our arrival at La Boca, the National Guard outpost, I spent some time trying to contact Georgetown by the Venezuelan radio transmitter to learn when the plane would be arriving for us, but I failed to make contact. I had written out a full report on my prospecting and a description of the gold and the amount recovered.

I gave my men some time to relax and we spent some time on Ankoko Island and the gold workings in the Eteringbang Creek. Dances and picnics were organised for our benefit. Edwin said he would transport us to Aurora on his next trip down river on patrol to Akarabisi, but my men were eager to travel at once as they wanted to get home for Christmas. I exchanged our thin-skinned woodskin for a more sturdy craft and Edwin supplied me with a chart of the river, telling me to look for certain landmarks. What was most important was that we should discharge the woodskin at all the rapids and streak them unladen. After we had passed through Devil's Hole range we would be safe. The Venezuelans at the outpost pressed us with food supplies, mostly vegetables and smoked fish. I bade farewell to these very kind people early one morning, estimating that we would be in Georgetown in time for Christmas. But "Man appoints and God disappoints".

When we arrived at Mora Rapids, I followed Edwin's instructions, discharging the woodskin, carried over our load, then slowly let out the woodskin down through the rapids. This operation was repeated at Eteringbang Falls, but at Bulcan rapids at the mouth of the Ohnopi River, the stream looked so smooth the men urged me to run it instead of discharging, the operation taking so long. We learned that it is a bad thing not to follow good instructions and the truth of the Afro-Guyanese saying: "more haste less speed". In no time we reached the fall out. Unfortunately, we had taken no account of the current coming around the island at Ohnopi Creek mouth. This just boiled over the stern of the woodskin leaving us all struggling in the water. It all happened in a flash, for a woodskin does not float. There were five of us.

Veecock from Windsor Forest, West Coast Demerara, Yan, a tall Chinese from Cummings Lodge, East Coast Demerara, Johnson, an Indo-Guyanese from Bartica, a coloured boy who had taken passage with us, and myself. Yan, who had previously confided in me that he could not swim, had asked that should anything happen, I was to assist him. Johnson was seated in the bow, Yan next to him and then Veecock, the coloured boy and me in the stern. When the woodskin sank, Yan held on to Johnson, begging him for assistance. Johnson's cruel reply was: "Move your ass, this is every man for himself".

Veecock turned to Yan, who was a big chap with an outsized foot, and told Yan to follow him and do as he did. Veecock, Yan and the coloured boy, headed for the Venezuelan shore which was closer. Every hand that Yan pulled in the water and every foot that he kicked, he called out, "Oh God – Oh Lord", but he managed to make it to the shore. I swam to the island in the middle of the river, towing our small tarpaulin which contained our hammock bags and clothing. I heard, over the roar of the rushing waters, Johnson crying out for help. "Oh God, help! help! Matthew help me, Oh God! Oh! me mama help me!", but as he had predicted, it was every man for himself. He was going down the main stream away from me and into the turntide at the foot of the fall-out, which I learned later was infested with electric eels. This was no doubt one reason for Johnson's cries for help, because these eels send out an electrical current which numbs the swimmer so that he cannot help himself.

Johnson was a powerful swimmer and although hampered by his clothes, I felt that he would reach the shore. Nevertheless, as soon as my feet touched land on the island, I quickly hauled the tarpaulin ashore and ran to a point on the island where the river was at its narrowest so I could assist Johnson. All I saw in the rushing water were remnants of our cargo, tins and paddles, anything that could float was carried away. But there was no sign of Johnson. Veecock hailed out to me saying Yan had reached shore safely but he had not seen Johnson. We spent half an hour searching the river edge downstream for signs, but to no avail. I had to make up my mind to join the others on the Venezuelan shore as I was still on the island. I walked upstream on the island, estimating the pull of the current before I struck out for the mainland. I was suffering from shock and I found myself tiring, but God had put a rock in my way on which I rested for a minute before continuing. As I neared the other shore, Veecock and Yan came into the water to assist me. Once ashore, I burst into tears, thinking of the loss we had suffered: Johnson drowned and six months work, our gold and belongings lost.

I took stock of our position only to find there was no knife or matches between us. I had swum ashore with my briefs on, no shirt, no boots and bareheaded. Veecock had on a pair of pants and a shirt, the other two men only pants. We searched the area adjacent to where we had come ashore. There were some lines but I did not know how far we would have to walk before we contacted anyone. So I decided to follow the river back to Wenamu or Eteringbang where I knew we could get food and assistance. We had left only that morning, the accident had happened at about 1:30 p.m., but with the swift current we had travelled some miles down river from Wenamu.

I decided to walk back, following the left bank of the river. We took it in turns to bore bush, as we had no cutlass to assist us to cut a line. The bush is always more dense around a river corner. I estimated that night would set in around 4:30 p.m. so we had at least two and a half hours to make some progress. I told the men to keep a look out for some rocks at the river corner where we could camp for the night, because sitting in the vicinity of rocks keeps one warmer than on an exposed sand bank. When we could no longer see to make any progress, we halted for the night, hungry but thankful to be alive. The silence that surrounded us could actually be felt, only the candle flies and other insects there to keep us company. We catnapped throughout the night with our backs pressed against each other for warmth. The following morning at daylight, I went to the river to soak my skin, for my whole skin was paining from the efforts I had made in forcing our way through this dense jungle. The others were in no better shape but bearing up bravely. I took a drink of water and we started on again, taking it in turns to bore the bush, taking an occasional rest at the riverbank on the chance we might spot a boat.

I had the misfortune to step on a thorn vine with barbs about an inch in length which runs along the ground, and at this stage was covered by leaves. The bushmen call this vine "What is man" as the thorn is poisonous and very painful. I spent this night in pain and suffered a fever. On the third day, I was hampered by a painfully swollen right foot, but as we were nearing Mora Falls, which we could discern by the roar echoed down the river, I went, or rather hobbled, to the river for a drink of water. There I saw a flash of red in the river. This proved to be an Amerindian woman fishing from her woodskin. I recognised her as William's wife, the man who had been with me for a short time in Wenamu. I hailed out to her, but she seeing four bearded and practically naked men, was afraid to approach until I made myself known. When she paddled over, I explained what had happened. I told her to paddle back to Wenamu and inform William, her husband, who should go to

Edwin for help. She gave me a piece of cassava bread and a stick of sugar (papilong) which I shared with the others. We did not move from this point in the river, expecting Edwin and the soldiers to come at any moment.

The boat did not arrive until near dusk. They shouted to locate us, then they walked over the falls, as it was too dark to use the boat. I must say they gave us every assistance to get to the boat. Edwin met us at the river with lanterns. He took charge of me and Rosa his wife put me in a hammock with instructions not to move. My men were similarly taken care of. Rosa pampered me like a child for three or four days, hardly allowing me out of my hammock. My skin looked as if I had encountered a tiger. There were scratches and cuts all over, which I had received in penetrating the raw jungle. I gave Edwin an account of what had happened on our journey down river. He promised to travel down river with his boat to locate Johnson's body and bury it. Edwin said he would also try to locate my canister with gold at the first dry weather when the water in the river would drop. I and the other men spent about a week recuperating. The people were most hospitable and kind. We were provided with clothes and food and encouraged to stop and work some diamonds and gold in Venezuela to recoup our losses, but the men were anxious to get back to Georgetown. We had, of course, no boat but Edwin informed me that his half brother, McNaughton, was on his way up river to do some trading with the Venezuelans.

On McNaughton's arrival at Wenamu River mouth, I laid my distress to him, explaining we had no food or clothing and no money, but I was desirous of travelling down to Aurora with my men. Would he loan me his boat for the trip? McNaughton bluntly refused, so I took over the boat at gun point. I told McNaughton I was acting legally, as there was a clause in the Lands and Mines Regulations where it is stated that if one is destitute and has no means of transportation, a boat can be seized and provided it is then handed over to the nearest police station. I stocked up the boat with food from the Venezuelans, had the men make two oars and sufficient paddles, as we had no motor to power the boat, and then departed for Aurora.

I took the steersman's paddle after receiving written instructions from Edwin as to the river channels and what land marks to look out for. We negotiated the rapids down from Wenamu safely, but at the point where we had to cross the river to Hauling over Island, the sight of the rocks and white water dashing this way and that way with the cross currents, aroused in me considerable misgivings. However, following Edwin's instructions, I told the man holding the bow paddle to watch out for the large rock on which the water was dashing itself, which lies in the channel of the fall-out of Big

Wamapoo, the worst of the many drops in this Devil's Hole range of rapids. He had to hold his paddle on the same side as mine, no matter if the boat looked as if it would smash itself on the rock, because the water would assist us by throwing us off.

I cast off the boat and held my breath. The speed of the water was terrific, but we managed to fly past this large rock, but the second and third rapids caught us unprepared. Submerged rocks knocked the steering paddle, throwing me to the bottom of the boat. The current swung the boat around and around, flinging it over submerged rocks and through narrow channels. I could not steer the boat as we ran through Big Wamapoo. It must have been guided by the Almighty who brought us safely to the still waters at the foot of the falls. On our arrival at Aurora landing, (Cuyuni Gold Fields) I reported to Corporal Bacchus, to whom I handed over McNaughton's boat and reported our disaster. I signed a statement to this effect. The men and I were then flown to Georgetown.

When I arrived home, I found everyone mourning my death as they had heard of the drowning in the Cuyuni River and thought it was me.

CHAPTER XIV
Diamond Prospecting Up the Mazaruni – 1948-1950

After recuperating at home for a month or two, I got the bush fever again. I was dead broke but I managed to raise sufficient money to outfit a small expedition. Whilst in the Cuyuni River, I had learned from McNaughton that whilst cutting the concession lines for Carnett and Co. Balata Company, the surveyor, Klautky, had come across two depositions of gold in the region of the Urluowra River on the right bank of the Cuyuni River. The surveyor had reported a deposit some twelve miles from the river, which had been found and worked. However, the larger deposit further inland has never been found. The surveyor had lodged a plan of his survey in the Department of Lands and Mines, but on my enquiring for it, I was informed it was missing.

I decided to travel up the Mazaruni River as far as Awarapari Creek on the left bank of the river. From here I would cut a line across to the Urluowra Creek head, as both the Awarapari and the Urluowra creeks originated from the same source. I formed a crew of young men from Georgetown, my nephew included. I asked Mannie Veecock, who had been with me in the Cuyuni river mishap when I lost everything, to accompany me. I purchased food for the party to cover a three month period and an Evinrude outboard motor. The boat I decided to build when I reached Apaiqua. We travelled up river by Correia's river service, which was an uneventful trip until we met the falls at Apaiqua. The water was high in the river and the outboard motors on Correia's boat really had to strain to get the boat over the hump and across to the shop landing.

Our boat Captain, Moore, introduced me to Mr. Davis, Correia's shop manager at this point. Mr. Correia had told me in town I could get all I required from his shop, should I run short of anything. I purchased boards, oakum and nails and tar here and built a balahoo (flat bottomed boat). When finished, the boat resembled a coffin and that description very nearly proved too apt before we eventually reached our destination. At this point, two Brazilian divers who heard I was travelling up river asked to join our party. I also recruited Manni Studor, a boat-builder from the Pomeroon River. It was Zanie, a clear skinned Brazilian, who pointed out to me the Awarapari Creek the first day on our way up river. I beached our boat and built a tarpaulin camp. The men discharged our cargo, and we spent our first night there.

Next morning, I climbed over the Awarapari Falls, which were near the mouth of the creek, and picked up an old geological line cut by Dr. Bracewell ten years earlier, but still visible. I followed it, crossing a large white-water creek, a left bank tributary of the Awarapari, its origins in the mountains dividing the Haimaraka and Isseneru creeks. Proceeding about one and a half miles from the river, I found myself entering deeper water. It was Zanie who informed me the Awarapari was a vast drainage basin in the rainy season. Since the water had risen to a height of fifteen feet over the land there was no possibility of prospecting that area, so I decided to travel up river the following day to a blackwater creek on the left bank of the Mazaruni River, the Wakawapu Creek, in which Zanie said an old pork-knocker used to work gold. It was here at the foot of Awarapari Falls that I was awakened at 3:00 a.m. by the sound of beating, as if someone was washing clothes. I got out of my hammock and taking my 5-cell torchlight, shone it in the area from which the sound came, but I could see no living object. Up to this day I cannot say what caused this noise. I later learned that there had once been a large Amerindian village in this area.

Early the next morning, I had the men reload the boat and we proceeded up river to the foot of Pot Falls (so called because of the circular holes worn in the rocks by the force of the water). All that could be seen of the falls was a wild turbulence of white water. The men got out of the boat and had to haul it through the trees at the river side, though the water was high in the river which helped. At one point, a strong crosscurrent caught the bow and swung it out towards the fall. The boat started to ship water and it was only quick thinking by the men on the bow rope that saved it from sinking. We arrived at Wakawapu Creek mouth at about 2:00 p.m.. A clearing was quickly made in which I erected the tarpaulin tent and the men discharged the cargo from the boat. They had to lift it up a ten foot embankment to the tent. Rain had started to fall and it continued to fall all night.

Early next morning, Steve, the coloured Brazilian, whose hammock was close to mine, awoke me saying, "Señor, listen". I strained my ears but heard nothing unusual. Steve continued to insist that I listen, and then I heard a faint lapping of water blown by the morning breeze. I realised at once what had happened. I jumped out of my hammock into a foot of water. I aroused the rest of the camp. The river had risen more than ten feet during the night and our boat was floating in front of the camp. I instructed the men to open up the bush about 300 feet higher up the slope from the river. Steve started to fell the overhanging trees. It was right here we received our second and more serious setback. Steve, having built a fourteen foot barbricut to fell a large mora tree, bellied the tree and than descended from the barbricut to get a cigarette. At the same moment, there was a freak wind squall. The large tree fell, crashing right on top of my camp. Our bags of rice, flour and sugar were burst open and our lanterns broken. Because the camp ground was under water, these rations were lost. I had the men build a temporary leaf camp, then dispatched the boat with a crew of four men, with a letter to Mr. Davis at Apaiqua, requesting a new supply of food.

I took my gun and walked up to the left bank of the river to look for some fresh meat. I crossed three small streams which discharged into the river. I reached the foot of a laterite rock ridge about half mile upstream. I shot a small wiribisiri deer and then followed the foot of this ridge which brought me out to the right bank of the Wakawapu black water creek. I shot two powis, then traced a line along the right bank of the creek back out to the river. I told Manni Veecock I had seen some likely creek flats, made up nice and wide. I told him we would take a shovel and battel the next morning and do some prospecting. This proved very encouraging, for in the first hole, about eighteen inches by thirty inches and only eighteen inches deep, we washed out two diamonds, one a grade blue-white stone. You can imagine my feelings. Here I was looking for gold and had fallen upon diamonds. On the return of my men from Apaiqua with fresh supplies, I put them all on to cutting claim lines and nailing up claim boards. Then I sent down river to file these claims.

I had the men build a larger leaf camp measuring thirty feet by twenty-four feet with a fall-back to act as a kitchen. I also put down a plot of provisions – cassava, sweet potatoes and plantains. The first pit we excavated and threw out measured twenty feet by twenty feet with a depth of four feet to gravel, which was four to six inches thick. On completing the washing, I was surprised at the number and quality of the diamonds, a good number being well over a carat in weight and of a blue-white colour.

I pushed ahead with the work of recovering diamonds, putting in two crews with two tom boxes while I went ahead with my prospecting. I was lucky when alone. I found a three feet wide ravine tucked away between the other three creeks. I dug a prospecting shovel hole and washed the gravel in my battel and this proved to be even richer than the other creeks. I immediately cut my claim lines and nailed up my claim boards. On hearing of the strike I had made, I received a visit from a number of pork-knockers (tributors) asking permission to work some of my lands. I gave them some positions on the understanding they paid to me forty percent of their finds. Little did I know at that time the nature of these pork-knockers. At a later date I was to learn some of them had sold their stones at Tumereng, some miles way down river.

I decided to travel to town to bring up some Afro-Guyanese who had worked with me on the sugar estates cutting canes whom I knew to be bushmen. Whilst in Georgetown, I received a radio message from my nephew informing me the last claim I had discovered had been raided. Although my men fired guns over the raiders' heads, the raiders worked at night with bottle torches. My men said short of shooting to kill, they could not stop them. I travelled back accompanied by two policemen to apprehend the raiders, but these men heard of my return by bush telegraph (word of mouth) and made good their escape. I viewed the three foot ravine I had discovered and planned to share with others, only to find a forty foot wide trench which the raiders had opened up.

I was later to learn that Davis, Mr. Correia's shop manager, on seeing me travel to town, had taken the opportunity to outfit as many pork-knockers as possible with boats and rations knowing he would recover big returns from my claims. He had spread the rumour that I would not be returning. I reported this matter to Mr. Correia, as I had lost thousands of dollars by these raiders, and threatened court action. Although I continued to work these claims for some time, I also prospected further up the creek, finding another but poorer deposit. I then went further up river to the foot of Peaima Falls. The ironstone ridge above my camp formed a natural gateway for the approach to the falls. The river above gets very shallow and is full of gravel banks. The Amerindians have a trail from the foot of the ridge up which they walk to the top of the Falls.

I went into a blackwater creek just below the falls. It was what I called a dead bush – large granite boulders towered above me. I penetrated further up the creek accompanied by three of my men. There was no sound of bird or beast, not even the hum of an insect. The inky black waters of the creek left me with a crawly feeling at the nape of my neck. The men started to get jumpy and would penetrate no further. Continuing on my own, I encountered a waracabra tiger, jet black all over, save for a white belly and the underside of the jaw. The Amerindians fear these cats as they say they travel in flocks like their namesake, the waracabra bird (trumpet bird). I heard the "Frank! Frank!" of a startled akuri, which ran in my direction, uttering its frightened cries, then I saw this black form in close pursuit. The akuri passed at speed, then I took a shot at the cat and missed but the akuri was safe. On my return to camp, the men asked me what I had shot. I told them that this was my first contact with one of these cats, which afterwards often visited the vicinity of our camp.

The creek by the camp was simply swarming with haimara fish and the men delighted to go fishing there on Sundays. On one occasion, night caught some of them there. Not seeing them back in camp, I sent out a search party with lanterns, but without result. The following morning the men walked into camp. They told me they had heard the search party and seen the lanterns from a distance, but were afraid to move from where they were sitting on a fallen tree, fearing they might stray. In the river we caught an immense lau-lau fish which measured up to seven or eight feet and weighed about two hundred pounds. These fish used to carry away many hooks and the only way to catch them was when a large spur from a cork wood tree was used as a float and anchored by a large stone. When the lau-lau took the hook, I have known it to drag the float a quarter mile downstream.

From the highest point on the ironstone ridge behind our camp, I could see a waterfall some distance upstream which proved to be a white-water tributary of the Wakawapu, the source of which lies in the "All go round Mountain" or the Marugaru Mountains, the source of the Awarapari and Urluowra Creeks. Diving in the creek to pick up some gravel near the junction of the white water, I brought to the surface some hard whitish pink clay which I later learned from the geological department was bauxite.

We eventually left the upper Mazaruni River to drop back down to the Awarapari Creek to search for the gold I had originally come after. The weather had improved and I thought it a good opportunity to cross the Awarapari Basin before we started in this trip. I dropped down to Apaiqua to purchase some rations. I was at Hamlin's shop when a jaguar entered the shop from the kitchen in search of a dog it had scented. The alarm was raised by the shop assistant who climbed into a hammock over the counter. Hamlin clambered up the partition dividing the shop from his living quarters to get a shot at the jaguar. The animal finding himself cornered and hearing all the shouting, promptly hurled itself against the wire mesh behind which were stacked cartons of beer. This proved no barrier to the jaguar for he moved through these like a bulldozer and bolted through the back door. Night was just setting in. I do not know if the jaguar got confused in all this commotion because it next leaped through the door of Drakes' recreation hall where men were playing billiards and cards and drinking. At the appearance of the jaguar in their midst, there was a general exodus through the nearest windows and doors with the jaguar following.

I had left my own small dog coiled up in the cold fireside of the men's logie which was occupied by tributors (pork-knockers) here to sell their diamonds. There was much drinking and carousing. At approximately 1:30 a.m. these men were disturbed by someone forcing a passage between the sleeping men in their hammocks. There were the usual curses and comments. "Man, you so drunk, you en know your own hammock?" They were further aroused by my dog's "Kai-Kai" when the jaguar grabbed it and disappeared into the bush. The jaguar seems to have a special fondness for domestic animals, cattle, pigs, dogs.

I was told of another incident in Isseneru Creek. A pork-knocker was travelling out to Apaiqua to buy rations when night overtook him. He stopped at a friend's shack. His friend had his lady friend with him and only one room. The traveller had to be content to spend the night on a bench outside covered with a rice bag his friend supplied. About 3:00 a.m. a prowling jaguar sensed a figure on the bench. It took its paw and pulled the bag from the sleeping man's face. On feeling the bag being pulled from his face, the pork-knocker, thinking it was his friend awakening him to travel, opened his eyes. His eyes and the jaguar's made four. Turpentine in the pork-knocker's rear could not have made him move as fast, for he was up and through the balamanie bark wall as if it was tissue paper, yelling that a tiger was about to eat him.

On my return to Awarapari, I built a temporary leaf camp in which I stowed my outboard engine and fuel and other items. My original crew had been cut down to four and myself. I decided to cut a compass line due north on the left bank of the Awarapari, deviating at very low spots, trying to keep to the high ground adjacent to the creek. I discovered the whole area was low lying with little mounds of laterite and quartz gravel and some granite rock outcrops. The first white-water creek I crossed originated in the Haimaraka Mts. to the east. A deposit of gold had been discovered here by an Englishman, but he died before he could do any productive work. I continued upstream for about five miles, before I met the larger stream descending from the mountains to the west. I decided to trace this larger stream. I had to climb to a height of nearly 1,000 feet before I came across a plateau of savannah lands. I took a bearing of approximately north west and walked a distance of approximately three miles. There I came across a tributary of the Ekereku Creek. Veecock washed a battel of gravel and recovered two nine sixteenth carat diamonds. This find proved to me that this mountain range was the source of the Awarapari and that the Urluowra, Ekereku and the Wakawpu must be the source of diamonds. This proved to be true some years later, especially in the Ekereku, so much so a landing strip was opened on the savannah top.

I returned to the main creek and continued cutting north for about another five miles when I noticed water flowing to the north in another tributary which proved to be a hand going into the Urluowra and discharging into the Cuyuni. I had been informed by the local pork-knockers at Apaiqua that cutting from Mazaruni to Cuyuni I would encounter a high mountain. There proved to be a wide valley between the Mauraugaru Mts. to the west and the 1,000 foot mountain at the source of the Isseneru River to the east. The elevation of this watershed could not be more than 500 feet and I saw a lot of laterite and crystallised quartz floats. Here I discovered diamonds at a depth of only three feet in a stiff red clay. The gravel proved to be very thin. I felt that lower downstream I could make a larger discovery. I worked in this area for a few weeks, gathering some diamonds but the stones were nothing in comparison to the area I had left at Wakawapu.

Rain began to fall again. One of my men took sick so I decided to pack up and move out as we were also short of rations. It was lucky I did so, for on reaching the basin, the men had to cut branches and 'tie' from tree to tree because the water was too deep for walking. I feared for my dog, a large brindle bull because it was a far distance to swim. I eventually reached high land and camped for the night. At 2:00 a.m. I heard an animal cracking some bones in our garbage. When I picked up my gun and torchlight, in its beam I saw to my joy, Willie, my dog. He had survived.

There is a ridge between the Awarapari and Isseneru Creek that, if traced, could form a feasible route for a road to Makapa Hills on the right bank of the Cuyuni River. I have a feeling that this area, if properly prospected with the assistance of a road, will open another gold or diamond strike.

I travelled down river and joined forces with a nephew of Correia and Bill Fleming, an Englishman, (he was supposed to be an outside son of King George V – and he certainly had a facial resemblance of the Prince of Wales) and a small crew. We penetrated to the Meanu Creek head which comes out of the mountain. We were finding some diamonds along with gold, often burrowing in between huge conglomerate and granite boulders following the gravel. I said the larger pay must be coming from higher up in the mountain, which proved to be true, for a few years later men with suction pumps reaped a harvest in diamonds.

I later did some skin diving in the icy cold waters of the Karanarg Creek, just above Tiboku Falls. This was an experience I did not forget in a hurry. A pot of hot cocoa was kept continually on the fire, for, after only fifteen minutes in the water collecting gravel, I was glad to get out for a hot cup of cocoa. I then left here to join James Collins, a prospector, to prospect the Merume River. We penetrated into the mountains and found some good prospect of diamonds. This we reported to Correia for further prospection.

On my return down river to Issano, the road junction on the Mazaruni, I received a message from Mr. Correia in Georgetown that he wanted to see me, so I travelled to town. This was the first time I had been home for three years and I was shown many changes in Kitty by my niece. She said she was afraid I had made up my mind to live in the bush.

Mr. Correia and Mr. Krakowsky, the Directors of the Morabisci Mining Company, wanted me to join the firm and cut a road from the Mazaruni river into the mines some eight miles inside. I agreed to the proposition, as I was tired after three years wandering.

CHAPTER XV
Bush Roads, Prospecting for Columbite and a Return 'Home': 1951-1956

I employed six Akawoi Amerindians who lived on the islands just off the shore from Issano Landing on the Mazaruni River to begin the task of cutting prospection lines to locate and follow the high land from the river to the Morabisci Mines where Mr. Robello, an old prospector long before my time, had found the mineral columbite. Morabisci Creek, which lay up stream from Issano about four miles on the left bank of the Mazaruni, formed one of the boundaries of the Morabisci Mining Concession. I chose a spot in the belly of the bay, about two miles below Bow Falls on the left bank of the river, to be my landing and shipping point for further operations. Here I built a leaf camp for the Amerindians and one for myself, which would house any stores shipped here.

From this point, I cut tracing lines to locate any high land penetrating into the bush. I was lucky to pick up a broken laterite ridge running north from the river. The lands to the east and the west were low lying, proving very difficult for the men who were droughing the loads on their backs to the mines, who at times had to wade through mud and water up to their knees. This was the reason I had been asked to locate a suitable route to build a road as early as possible. I was able to locate and cut an eight mile track from the river to the camp site in the mines. The Amerindians did the forward line work, underbushing the track twenty feet wide. I had to employ a further hundred labourers to fell trees, stump out the larger trees by their roots and junk and clear the fallen trees.

The quantity of greenheart and other hardwood trees in this area was surprising, including cedar trees measuring some six feet in diameter. These trees came in very handy in my building operation, both in housing and especially in the building of greenheart bridges. These proved essential, for though I had located the one and only piece of high land on which to build my road, this ridge proved to be broken in nineteen places. I employed four gangs of Afro-Guyanese sawmen to supply me with greenheart planks three and a half inches thick and fifteen feet long for these bridges and six men squaring piles and beams for the supports. Even then there were places where piles could not be driven into the earth, but had to rest on the granite rocks in the creek bed. At one spot, near a swamp which was too wide to bridge, I had to cut some huge hardwood trees, junking them to a length of eighteen feet with a diameter of a least two and a half feet. These acted as a corduroy spaced eight feet apart, on which I nailed two parallel lengths of greenheart planks spaced six feet apart, over which vehicles could cross the swamp.

The area was overrun by game of all kinds, wild hogs often running through the men's camp. Once, I was greatly amused to see the men, armed only with wood clubs, running down a hog. One blow on its snout will lay it helpless. The Amerindians loved to eat these wild hogs. They would build a barbricut (four or six hardwood forks are driven into the ground, on which cross woods are placed, on which to rest the meat) then a fire is built underneath and the meat covered with leaves. This drying process usually takes a whole day or night, but on this occasion, they could not bear to wait so long. I saw them jumping in and out of their hammocks and heard then chattering and laughing throughout the night as they cut slices from the meat to eat. Next day they could not work as they were constantly running into the bush to ease their bowels. There was also a supply of deer which my huntsmen occasionally brought in, labba, and birds such as the powis and the maam, whose breast is so thick with meat, the blade of a table knife will sink to the handle. The egg of this bird is a brilliant sky blue. Of course, along with this quantity of game, there were inevitably jaguars and pumas to prey on them. Their presence was the possible explanation of why an Englishman, who came into the Morabisci Creek prospecting for gold with a small party, was lost never to be seen again. He left his camp with his men one morning, but turned back as he said he had forgotten his spectacles. He told his men he was just going back to the camp to collect them and would return. He was never seen again. All that was found was one of a pair of rubber-top boots in the mud of the creek flat. We notified the police at Issano Landing who came to scour the area on foot and "Art" Williams patrolled the surrounding area with his plane. The search went on for a week without any results. The police discovered a skull, but it was too old to be that of the missing man.

One of the Amerindians with me had a narrow escape from death when he met up with a puma in the line. He was armed only with a cutlass. He just managed to dodge behind a tree and every time the puma attacked, he chopped at it with his cutlass and guarded himself behind the tree. Both combatants scored damage on each other and the puma, finding itself wounded and unable to get at the man, eventually slunk into the bush. The Amerindian managed to crawl back into camp with his left arm and shoulder lacerated by the puma's claws. I immediately dispatched him to the landing to be sent down river to the dispenser at Issano where he was treated.

About five miles from the river, I encountered the first ironstone or laterite ridge running in an east to west direction. I remember whilst I was climbing this ridge with a load weighing about one hundred pounds in my warashi, I was struck by cramp in my thigh muscles. I cried out in pain and could not move. An Afro-Guyanese drougher who was close behind me told me to throw down my load, then he came to my assistance, taking some ordinary baking flour from out of his bag. He briskly rubbed my muscles with the flour and in no time I got relief from the bound up muscles. This was the first time I had come across this remedy, and in later years I have been able to give assistance to others by this method.

One afternoon I was walking on this ridge when I saw my Amerindian huntsman picking up kop-kop ants, a clumsy insect with an exceptionally long abdomen. He was dragging them across his bare stomach so that he received a series of stings which formed a blister the size of a saucer. I asked him why he was punishing himself like this. He told me it was a powerful beena or charm for the successful hunting of powis and accouri. I have known other Amerindians to use certain leaves which they rub on their skins before they go out to hunt for deer, bush cow or wild hog. Another time, I saw an Amerindian catching, as it seemed to me from a distance, empty air with his hands. Drawing near, I saw he was catching flying ants and eating them. He said they tasted just like nuts.

The track we cut out on the first ridge proved to be too steep for vehicular traffic so later, when I received my heavy equipment, I built a road similar to one I had seen at Box Hill in Surrey, England. This formed a huge S, and covering the whole width of the ridge, cut down the gradient from 1 in 4 to 1 in 7 feet. The second ridge, although rising to about the same height of three to four hundred feet, proved to be more gentle in gradient. This second ridge supplied me with tons of loose ironstone gravel, which I later used in construction. As we cut through this ridge, I found we were blocked in one spot by a wall of laterite rock, and not having any heavy equipment to break through, I had to use pick axes and mattocks. To get through this wall faster, I paid the men up to five dollars a cubic foot. On the completion of this road track in six weeks, I requested a team of carpenters be sent in to construct nineteen bridges of varying lengths and heights, all built of greenheart. I then put my men to building bush camps for the labourers and the staff.

I had a visit from two Government surveyors, Cole and Edgehill, who had been sent in to check on the gradients of the road. They wanted to know where I had studied. I told them I had studied in the bush, where a pork-knocker or tributor has to study, invent, and contrive to get by. A lot was common sense, but one had to be able to read the land.

By this time we were able to start extracting the columbite. First, four gangs of six men each were set on to strip the top soil from the columbite gravel. This was washed in a tom and settling box in the same way as one washes for diamonds. Columbite is black, similar to ironstone, but much heavier and, like diamonds, it centres in a battel and sieve. Then an engineer came in to set up a device to mine the gravel. This comprised a steel bucket with teeth which was attached to a long wire cable, passed through blocks tied to the three huge mora trees and operated by a winch. This bucket scraped up the gravel from the creek bed, up the greenheart ramp we had built and into a washer, then passed to a vibrator to recover the columbite. This first creek we started operations on was later named "Young Creek" after me.

Not long after, Mr. Hatowski, an American who was backing this venture, brought down some highly paid engineers to set up a million dollar recovery plant. I had strongly advised against this as I knew from my prospecting that there was not sufficient mineral to supply a large plant, as the deposits were in small creek beds scattered over a wide area. I told him that roads would have to be built to connect the creeks, and loaders and trucks purchased, but he told me that as long as the material was there, his principal was to get it out as fast as possible. The construction went ahead. Over the years, there have been numerous mining companies that, having found some gold, have then imported expensive machinery without first prospecting thoroughly. As a result, a lot of valuable machinery has been left to rust in the interior. Guyana is made up of one of the older crusts of the earth and its precious minerals and deposits of gold are found in small pockets and not in large deposits as in other countries.

With the Amerindians, I then spent some time in cutting open new concession lines for the company on the borders of the large Morabisci Creek. Working in this area, we collected any amount of sawarri nuts, which are similar in taste to Brazil nuts. They are enticing to eat, but as they are very rich in oil, too many will loosen the bowels. One time during a lunch break, one of the boys went to wash his white enamel plate in the creek water. We heard the sound of teeth "kat-tang" on the plate. The boys said it was a haimara fish. I at once swung out a baited line and even before the hook could properly land in the water, it disappeared in a swirl. Feeling the tug on my line, I let the fish run and then struck. Oh boy! What a fight to land him, measuring all of four feet and weighing at least forty pounds!

After spending two years here, I appealed to the Directors for a raise in my wages as I was doing the brunt of the work. The engineers were drawing down $1,000 per month, and all expenses paid. I was only receiving $300.00 and having to bear all my expenses. My appeal was turned down, so I resigned my post and returned to Georgetown. (Before the year was out, I heard that the Americans had closed down operations, for the central plant they had built, instead of recovering the mineral, was passing it through the tailings and, as I had predicted, there was insufficient mineral to compensate for the huge outlay.) Back in Georgetown, the Lands & Mines Department again sent for me. The Commissioner informed me that there were two young American Geologists from the American Union Carbide Co. who wanted to travel to Iron Mountain, which was situated between the Berbice and Demerara Rivers and adjacent to the old cattle trail. Would I be able to work along with them and guide them to wherever they decided to prospect?

I met the Americans, two very nice gentleman, at the Tower Hotel. They explained their wants and where they wanted to go. The arrangements for hiring men and purchasing food and tools was left to me. I took on ten men as we would have to drough in our food and equipment some eight or nine miles from the Berbice river to the cattle trail. The Geological Survey boat had been put at our disposal for transportation from New Amsterdam in Berbice to Rock Point and back. I built two camps at the line junction with the cattle trail from where we had to walk at least two miles every day to and from Iron Mountain. The men were set on to take iron ore samples from the sides and the bottom of the dug pits.

I discovered some large fresh water lakes or ponds on top of the mountain. There were signs of tapirs having bathed there, for they have to seek water when they want to stool. Large jaguars evidently roamed the cattle trail, their huge paw marks being clearly defined in the white sand. One night one gave voice in the vicinity of our camp. The following night, one of my men slung his hammock on the ridge pole of the camp frame. He was making sure no tiger was going to eat him.

When we had finished collecting samples, the men had to carry them the eight miles back to the river. Many of them suffered from sore backs as the rocks, although in canvas warashis, rubbed on their backs. On our return to town these samples were shipped to the USA.

I then booked passages for everyone on the steamer travelling to Bartica in Essequibo county, and our food and tools were also freighted along with us. On arrival at "Stampa" we disembarked into a large bateau sent from the Mission at Saxacalli to meet us. We crossed to the left bank of the river and were put up at the Mission school for the night. The following morning, guides were provided to show us the area in Blue Mountain where we carried out the same kind of work we had performed at Iron Mountain, then our party returned to Georgetown. The Americans told me that the ore found at Blue Mountain carried a higher percentage of iron than that from Iron Mountain.

At a later date, I was asked to escort a Canadian Mining Engineer, Jim Millar, from Edmonton, Alberta, Canada. I hired more or less the same men I had taken on my previous trip, to go back to Iron Mountain and Wamara Mountain to collect iron ore samples. We travelled by steamer from Georgetown to MacKenzie City on the Demerara River. There a power truck was hired and we travelled overland along the cattle trail. We spent ten days at this location. On our return journey, the power wagon broke down on the cattle trail and the driver and one of the men had to walk on to MacKenzie for the broken part. The rest of us had no time to cut a camp frame before night fell, so I told the men to spread a tarpaulin in the centre of the cattle trail. They cut wood and built a fire on which we heated some water for coffee. I slung my hammock between two trees at the edge of the trail. Jim Millar found a place in the power wagon. When sundown came, a heavy mist descended on us and, being in white sand country, the cold set in. The men did not rest well as we were camped in the middle of jaguar country, and they sat around the fire telling tales about bush life which Jim was very interested to hear. At 2:00 p.m. the following day our driver returned in a jeep, and repairs were done to our power wagon. We left for MacKenzie, arriving there the same evening. I put the men in a hotel after I had freighted the samples and tools on board the river steamer. The following day I travelled with Jim Millar on the B.G. Airways Gruman plane to Mabaruma in the North West Region. We left the men in the city until my return. All this was in 1956.

At Mabaruma, I visited John Learmond, the District Commissioner, with whom I had played football in my younger years. I introduced Jim who told him the purpose of his visit. John kindly arranged to provide an Amerindian guide and a vehicle to transport us as far as possible to our destination at Hosororo Hills to take more iron ore samples.

Later the same day, I contacted a white-haired old Afro-Guyanese gentleman who had known my father when he was alive, and who had planted all the rubber trees in the compound and surrounding area. As I entered the house, Mr. Broomes said: "Son of the soil, you have returned home", for he recognised me immediately as David Young's son. This was some forty-five years after my fathers' death. I asked to be shown my father's grave. Mr. Broomes could not move from his chair, as he was partly paralysed from a

stroke, but he kindly sent his younger daughter to show me the spot. I found
the grave to have been badly disturbed. The railings and chain which had
been around the grave had been removed. Only the headboard with my father's name and the date of his death in 1911 remained, but I met a number
of people who had known and worked with my father. Jim took two colour
photographs of me at the grave. I made a resolution to return and have the
grave cleaned up and rebuilt, as my father had been one of the original pioneers of this far corner of Guyana.

After we finished our work at Hosororo Hills, Jim decided to travel back
to Georgetown by the coastal steamer because freighting his samples by air
would have been too expensive. Our journey was something to remember.
Leaving Mabaruma at Coomaka Landing in the afternoon, we steamed through
the Mora Passage and encountered the Atlantic waves. They really showed
us what they could do with the small vessel, which rolled heavily being broadside to the waves, the Captain's bridge nearly kissing the wave tops. The
cargo deck and the second class accommodation had to be vacated as the
waves were washing through these lower decks. No meals could be cooked
or served and hardly anyone could sleep. Everyone was in the first-class
salon. Some hot coffee and biscuits were produced which everyone shared.
At dawn the next day, I noticed the change from brown water to deep sea
green as the Captain had to swing out and back again to enter the Pomeroon
River where some cargo had to be picked up. We eventually arrived in
Georgetown, much worn out by the rough passage and very hungry.

On Jim's return to his hotel, he received a cablegram requesting him to
return to Canada immediately as both his mother and father had been involved in a car accident. Jim asked me to close up everything, pay off the
men and all the outstanding accounts, put the samples in storage and post
all receipts to him in Canada. He cabled money to me through the Royal
Bank of Canada to fulfil his commitments. I later received a letter from him,
asking after the men who had worked with him. In this letter he proposed a
trip by corial down the Amazon River from its source and, by creek jumping, down to Rio de Janeiro, Brazil. This would have been a splendid trip,
but it never materialised.

It was not long before I was again summoned by the Commissioner of
Lands and Mines who introduced me to Colonel Stubbs, a retired American
army man who hailed from Louisiana, U.S.A. I was to venture once again into
the interior, this time up the Berbice River in search of precious minerals.

CHAPTER XVI
Diamond and Gold Prospecting up the Berbice River – 1956

I organised a crew of ten men, including my nephew Johnny and his friend Henry Leung. The others were seasoned bush men who had worked on both gold and diamond prospecting. I arranged to have two balahoos (flat bottomed boats) built at Tacama, Berbice River by a Mr. Alphonso. These would be powered by two 12 HP Archimedes outboard motors. Rations, baggages and tools were freighted by transport and harbours train to Rosignol and across the river to New Amsterdam. The men and I travelled by the same train and boarded the river steamer where we tied our hammocks on the upper deck. The steamer loosed off at 7:00 p.m. and travelled up river the whole night, stopping occasionally at homesteads, timber grant landings and small saw mills to discharge cargo and disembark passengers. The steamer eventually arrived the next afternoon at Ebini cattle station, where the Government was importing purebred bulls to improve the local stock.

We arrived at Tacama late in the afternoon. Mr. Alphonso had our balahoos ready, the outboard engines, fuel and oils all prepared and a supply of kerosene oil for our lamps. We set out early the following morning as I wanted to reach our destination soon. Our progress was slow because the cargo taxed the two boats and the tide was against us, so I decided to make an early camp as the previous night none of us had slept well.

At Kibilibiri River mouth, we were hailed by some river people so I put ashore and was invited to partake of some "parakari" drink made from cassava root. I enquired if we might get a lodging for the night and was shown to a vacant leaf hut. These people were engaged in timber work and told us about the hardships and the shortage of cash they suffered. They wanted to know how far we were going and for what reason. I told them to club together to purchase a tractor and approach the Government for a cash loan to be paid back on the sale of their timber. I do not know if they took my hint. The following day we proceeded up river to Kwakwani, the Bauxite town, where we went ashore to purchase some items and some liquid refreshments. Mr. Alphonso from Tacama had told me to contact Mr. Jardine, a small shop owner living on the opposite shore to Kwakwani, so after leaving Kwakwani, I went over the river and introduced myself to Mr. Jardine, who kindly offered me the hospitality of his shop where the men and I could sleep. Mr. Jardine introduced his wife and two teenage daughters, ages 16 and 18 years, who were most kind and attentive to us during our short stay. I explained to Mr. Jardine the purpose of our trip and asked him if he would accompany us to direct us through the rapids and their channels and the points where I would have to haul my boats over the falls. He readily agreed, adding that his wife would also travel with him as she was a boviander or river person who could handle a steering paddle or an engine.

Arriving at Marlissa, the first of a series of rapids, I followed Jardine's boat, slowing down to negotiate a narrow channel between two rocks, then increasing the speed of the motor to contend with the increased current of the upper stream. The boats were fighting against the strong current of the upper stream and the problems caused by the varying depths of the stream. We eventually met Big Itabru Falls after passing through the "Gate", a narrow passage between two large rocks. The pool at the gate is very deep because of the heavy volume of water being forced through this narrow opening in the rainy season. The force of the current can be estimated by the size of a huge gravel bank which has been formed on the down river side of this pool. At this point, Jardine advised me to pitch camp in the bay on the upper side of the "Gate" and discharge our cargo in preparation for hauling the boats over the rocks of the falls the following morning. I also decided to stow half of our food above high water mark and collect it on my return trip. I wanted to travel light for our first venture through this range of falls. The approach to the Itabru Falls lies in a wide basin with a reddish glazed formation of rocks alongside the river on one side, and a beautiful white sand beach in a cove on the other side. Through a barrier of rocks some fifty feet in height, the river tumbles in a mass of white water fifty to sixty feet wide with a large black rock in the centre of the fallout. Once a boat captain tried to run this fall in high water, but hit the rock in the fall out and all hands were drowned. The fall is most picturesque seen in the setting sun, showing the red rocks, white water, green vegetation, with a blue sky backdrop. Later, when I took up painting, I endeavoured to capture this scene in oils.

I fell asleep in my hammock with the sound of the falls acting as a lullaby. I was up early next morning and had a bath in the river. After some hot coffee and pancakes, I stripped down to a pair of swim trunks. The men had cut a series of hardwood rollers, two or three inches in diameter and ten feet long on which the boat would be hauled over the falls. The cargo was carried over the top of the falls from the camp site on the beach. It took us about one hour of heaving and hauling on bow and stern ropes before our boats were refloated in the upper side of the falls. We jumped into the boats and brought them over above the falls to be reloaded, then proceeded to Little Itabru, a very fast and powerful stream, where our engines and the men were taxed to the limit to get the boat to surmount this rapid. We were allowed a short breather before we met our next rapids, known as Umbrella Falls. Rounding a bend in the river, I could see only boiling white water and black rocks and a narrow part of the river, through which the water was racing over a rock bar. I decided to put our cargo ashore on the river bank. Some of the men who could not swim too well were dispatched with this cargo around the falls to await us at their top. Big Itabru was a gentleman compared to these raging waters. We had to battle the water itself, stepping from rock to rock wading and swimming to haul on the ropes. When the boats eventually reached the rock bar, there was only one very narrow opening we could safely go through. The boats had to be practically lifted over this barrier; we could never have managed it with cargo in the boat. After reloading the boats, we steamed up to Winters Falls where the boats had to be discharged and hauled over again. These falls did not have the turbulence of Umbrella Falls. We proceeded beyond Winters Falls to Long Liquor Rapids, very shallow and fast. Again we had to get out and lighten the boat, the force of the water pulling on our legs. We then had to steam up Lindo Rapids to the mouth of Lindo Creek. This was my destination, being the boundary of our concession which extended from this point to ten miles down river to Marlissa Rapids. Here I decided to build my base camp.

I dispatched half of my crew back to Big Itabru to bring back the balance of our food in one of the boats. The men returned the same day to report that the river had risen above the high water mark and damaged our flour, biscuits and a bag of sugar. This was a flash flood caused by heavy rains in the nearby mountains. I had to send down a skeleton crew to Kwakwani to purchase some more food. In the meantime, the balance of the men and I erected a frame house, beating balamanie bark from the trees that we felled to make its walls and flooring and then build a roof from turru palm leaves.

This was a diamondiferous area, so I prospected the upper region of Lindo Creek, where there were splendid indications, good gravel, but very poor results. I cut my concession lines one mile due west from Lindo Creek mouth, then north to the upper tributaries of the Kamwatta Creek, then across the river from Kamwatta for 7 miles until I reached the upper Kurunduni Creek on the right bank of the river. At this point, the waters were still deep and darkly flowing, indicating the presence of kaolin clay.

After leaving Lindo Creek, we went down river to Winters Falls, where I did some skin diving in the deep basin at the foot of the falls, and the men, using bars to tumble the large rocks on the river bank, unearthed some lovely indications as large as a finger nail. When we washed the gravel from under these rocks, our reward in diamonds amounted to far more than all our alluvial work in Lindo Creek, so I pitched a temporary tarpaulin camp. Cow flies of a good size played havoc with our bare skins. Whilst we were at Winter Falls, Colonel Stubbs paid us a surprise visit. Accompanied by an American, Mr. Vanderkogel, an expert on aqualung diving, he had brought two rubber suits with face masks and flippers and air tanks. He then instructed us in their correct use. Henry Leung, John, my nephew, and I quickly mastered these aqualungs. The basin at the foot of Winters Falls was a good place to dive, being some twenty feet deep. When I dived to the bottom of this basin I discovered it to be formed of conglomerate rock. Puncturing this with my bar, I discovered real diamond gravel underneath. I suggested to Col. Stubbs that he buy a suction pump to bring up this gravel. The alluvial workings in this area had proved to be very rich in the early days, so why should not the river bed, which was the settling bowl for the surrounding hills and creeks, prove even more rich? I plotted a rough map of my findings which I gave to Col Stubbs.

Whilst we were camped at Big Itabru Falls, Ivan Wade, an associate of mine who was also a diver, came to tell me that he had had the misfortune of having his boat and all his apparatus, including his suction pump, sink near Christmas Falls, up river from us. He asked for help to transport his men, rations and another boat to the spot where his boat had sunk. The following day, we steamed up river with some of my men and some of Wade's men for nearly the whole day, meeting numerous rapids but none dangerous. That night we slept in Wade's camp, which was situated on a small island. The next day everyone worked to recover Wade's pumps and boat from the bottom of the river.

I then took my men to view Christmas Falls. These falls stretch the width of the river in the shape of a horse shoe, water emerging from all points between the rocks and the surrounding forest. It has a drop of approximately fifteen feet and because the water was not high, one could walk on the rocks out to the main channel. There is an old portage on the left bank of the river. The early explorer Schomberg was supposed to have erected a brass plaque on one of the larger trees to mark the date and name of one of his men who drowned here. I dropped back down to Wade's camp. He thanked me and said he could get along without any further assistance, so my party returned down river to Lindo Creek.

There, the creek by our camp provided a constant supply of haimara fish. The men would set spring rods at night before retiring to their hammocks, but once a rod flew and they heard a commotion in the water, the fish was soon off the hook and into the pot. I got to know Colonel Stubbs quite well. He told me about his family in Louisiana and said that I should accompany him back home there, though we put this off for a later date. Unfortunately, he died on a visit back home. His son came out to carry on the work, but had to close down operations soon after.

Whilst at Lindo Creek, I also received an invitation to visit Mr. Bleakley, a Government Geologist who was working in the area towards the source of the Demerara river. I dropped down river to his riverside camp from where Edwards, his boat man, carried me to the walking line on which Bleakley and his other geologists were working. The next day, I followed the geologists over laterite rock which was oozing water, in some places a foot deep. We continued walking through this water to climb a sandstone mountain about 1,000 feet high from which two black water tributaries emerged. At the top I found myself on a flat tableland of rock with dwarfed trees and shrubs. This then was the source of the Demerara River. There was a grand view all around. From the southern tip I could clearly see the Makari Mountain peak rising above us. Looking beyond, the mighty Essequibo could be seen as a distant silver streak. Further south, the Pakaraima Mountains, the source of the Berbice River, could be seen. About thirty miles beyond Makari Mountains, where the Essequibo and Berbice rivers come to their closest point, there is a trail from Rattlesnake river, a tributary of the Berbice River, over to the Essequibo river, coming out about two miles above Rapu Falls in the still waters approaching Apoteri. This trail between the two main rivers is about fourteen miles long.

Between the Makari Mountain and the Demerara river-head there is a conglomerate formation where some men were recovering diamonds. To the north east from the Demerara river-head was a view of Parish Peak, on the right bank of the Berbice river, a real loner rising some 1,000 feet above the surrounding forest. If you travel up the Berbice River and are in the vicinity of this peak, it seems to be always looking down into your boat. After completing my work in the Berbice river, I submitted a copy of the plan I had drawn up for Col. Stubbs to the Lands and Mines Department.

CHAPTER XVII
Cutting a Line for the Mahdia-Potaro Road – 1957-59

It was in 1957 when Mr. Jimmy Bamford, Commissioner for the Interior, sent for me on my return from the Berbice River. He asked if I would undertake the job of cutting a line from Karasabai Savannah on the Brazilian frontier to Mahdia-Potaro, as the government proposed building a road to Lethem on the Brazilian frontier. I was shown maps of the area and told I would find Amerindian trails to assist me. I accepted the offer. I was asked how long I thought it would take me to cut this line. I said about three months with six men and myself. Little did I know that I was opening the door to three years NOT three months of fatiguing labour, of walking for miles everyday, climbing hills and mountains, fording creeks and swamps and being nearly eaten alive by mosquitoes and sand flies. I was, though, compensated by seeing with my own eyes the rugged beauty of this part of our interior.

I collected stores, tarpaulins, tools and camping equipment and also a supply of kerosene oil for my lamps. I then purchased rations for six men for three months. I decided to carry my nephew, John Roth, who was with me in the Berbice river and an Afro-Guyanese, Fred Allen (a mechanic) who was an old bushman. The other four men I decided to hire when I arrived in the Rupununi Savannah. John, Fred and I flew from Atkinson Field by a Dakota plane to Good Hope Landing strip, which was on the land of Mr. Gorinsky's cattle ranch. I was invited to stay at the ranch house.

Learning of my intended trip over the mountain into Karasabai Savannah, he said there was a trail which followed the mountain foot to Karasabai, but in the rainy season this area was flooded from the mountain foot right out to the Ireng River. Mr. Gorinsky kindly contacted a young American who had his own plane and was then working diamonds in a tributary of the Ireng River. This man, Mr. Hart, kindly agreed to fly our cargo and two men to Karasabai. It took him five trips in all. I accompanied him on the last trip into Karasabai. Sitting up front in the small plane, I had a beautiful clear view of the Ireng river (the boundary to Brazil) and the large areas of savannah lands bordered by the mountains into which I was now to penetrate. I was met at Karasabai Air Strip by the School teacher, a Mr. Albert, an Amerindian, who originated from the North-West region. This gentleman kindly offered me the use of his house until I was ready to push off into the bush. On learning I wanted four Amerindians to accompany me, he sent for the head man or captain of the village. I told the captain that the rate of pay was $3.25 per day and that I would supply his boys with food. He recommended some sturdy young men – these were Macusi Amerindians – who seemed to know the surrounding country. Mr. Albert advised me to leave behind the rice I had brought, and take farine and cassava bread in its place, which would be lighter to carry and was the staple diet of the Amerindians.

The view from the mission school to the north and north east was of a wall of jagged mountain ranges; to the south east there were more mountains, cutting off the view to Good Hope Ranch. I did some pencil and crayon sketches of these views. Mr. Albert showed me over the mission grounds, proudly displaying the produce from his kitchen garden. Some of his pupils were digging out clay, mixing it with grass, then putting it into moulds. This was compressed, then baked in the sun to form bricks from which to construct adobe walls two feet thick for their houses. This thickness was needed to keep out the intense heat from the savannah in the dry season and the cold in the rainy season. Most of the savannah houses had roofs made from the ité palm, which will last for at least twenty years before they need rethatching. The more modern school buildings are roofed with sheets of corrugated iron, which is unbearably hot in the dry season.

I began my reconnaissance by driving in my zero post at the end of the air strip. From this point, I took various compass bearings and paced measurements. I followed an Amerindian trail from the mission, passing behind the first range of hills, which were sparsely covered with grass and dotted with clumps of bush, then continuing along the right bank of the Jauri river to the last savannah some ten miles from the mission. There I made camp at a lovely spot where crystal clear waters were tumbling over rocks. There was a wonderful all round view of the mountains from a high rocky hill behind our camp, I saw to the south east a range of mountain peaks, which the Amerindians said were at the head waters of the Burro-Burro river and, further to the south, Tiger Pond Savannah perched high on a mountain shoulder. From the savannah, there was an Amerindian trail over the mountain to Annai which is on the cattle trail and in the north savannah. Whilst camped there, some Amerindians came to poison fish with sticks from the hiari vine. The savannah Amerindians depend on fish, as other game in the grass lands is scarce.

One of my Macusi Amerindians knew a fishing trail which followed the right bank of the Jauri River into the mountain. I had to deviate from this

trail at a good many points to get a better grade for my road and there were
other spots where huge granite boulders came right down to the stream. Crossing a spur of the Kawarieng Mountain which forms the watershed between
the Takutu and Jauri Rivers, I had to cut through some wild bamboo no thicker
than my finger but with curved thorns on the joints. My men had to hold the
bamboo, then cut and release the branch or it would spring right back like
coiled barbed wire. The only creature which seemed to love this bush was
the tapir, for the thorns did little damage to its thick hide. I noted that the
soil along this route would be wonderful for planting – a red sandy clay.
Descending further, I found a dark grey or black sandy soil at the mountain
foot and continuing to the right bank of the Takutu, an upper tributary of the
Siparuni River. It was here I moved our camp, near to the site of an old
fishing camp. At this point, there was a decided lift in the formation of the
river going up into the Ariwa Mountain. The water was clear and swift and
very cold, whereas downstream it was a chocolate colour, deep, and spread
over a wide flat area.

My route to Mahdia lay to the northeast across the head waters of the
Siparuni River, but little did I know that this was a vast drainage basin for
the streams descending from the surrounding mountains. I had the men fell
two large trees upstream so they interlaced across the river to form a bridge
over which the men had to drough all our equipment because of the speed of
the water and the dangerously uncertain footing. Whilst we were in this area,
the men cut into what one calls nature's field, an area of approximately one
and a half acres with banana trees of all varieties intermingled with papaw
trees. Of course, all work stopped, whilst the men gorged themselves on the
fruit. I ate two very sweet pawpaws. The men cut down three bunches of the
red buck banana to boil as a vegetable. I returned to camp and decided to
cut on a north-easterly bearing, but found myself entering low-lying and
swampy lands. This was a heavily forested area through which no road could
be built as it would lie under flood level in the rainy season. The rains started
a little after we arrived there and on seeing the level of the water rising so
steadily, we had to beat a hasty retreat to high ground. I decided to fell a
good-sized silverballi tree from which I hoped we might be able to construct
a corial sufficiently large to hold our tarpaulin, tools, and some food. The
balance of the food I cached on a high platform to await our return.

On our way down the Takutu, I checked the meanderings of the stream
with my compass, making rough measurements with markings from point to
point. A thin rope towed behind the corial and attached to a float was used
as a measure. As the float met the mark, I put down the distance. Of course,

this was not an accurate survey but it gave us an idea of the distance we had covered. Some bends in the river swung right back parallel to the upper stream, at times measuring at least half a mile with only a distance of twenty feet between the streams. The areas on both banks were low lying with an occasional bump arising out of the swamp. There was no continuous high land. The water was dark brown, nearly black; some areas were so wide one was liable to stray from the right stream. We overnighted in two campsites on our way downstream. At its junction with the Siparuni River, we left the Takatu top and crossed over to the left bank of the larger stream, where the water was more turbulent. We built a leaf camp at this junction of the two rivers on a bank about fifteen feet above the water level.

From there we cut north for about one mile to where the land started to lift and there were signs of laterite and granite rock floats and weathered surface formations. We continued north for a short distance before swinging east to follow a laterite ridge, then back north following the high lands. We were penetrating hardwood forests that towered above us. At one point, we encountered a group of large quarta or spider monkeys with their red faces and red bottoms. They were annoyed with us for invading their domain and, screaming at us, they pelted us with broken branches and the large fruit they were feeding on. We had to beat a hasty retreat.

After covering a distance roughly five miles from the river, we again contacted a laterite hill which rose steeply, so I cut north-east to bypass it, only to find ourselves in flat low lands, eventually coming out back to the left bank of the lower Siparuni River. We had to retrace our steps to the foot of the steep laterite hill, which rose three hundred feet to a flat, forest-covered plateau. We continued north for about half a mile only to drop down steeply to a wide expanse of water. We traced this body of water upstream for about half a mile when I heard the thunder of falling water. This proved to be the Ireng Creek coming out of the Akorabi Mountain range. The men and I crossed this large body of water. I, being on the short side, was up to my chin in water. We started to mount the high land on the other side, thinking we had at last cleared the Siparuni tributaries, leaving the way open to Mahdia - Potaro.

I had moved our camp from the river to the southern side of this high laterite hill, to be nearer to our point of investigation. Rain had begun to fall continually after we moved camp. Every day the men and I returned to camp with our clothes soaking wet. There was no sun to dry them, only a smoky fire and this did not dry the clothes either. I used to go and jump into the cold creek water for a bath every morning and then get into my damp clothes.

Cutting feeler lines to the north-west from this camp, I came across some old gold claims which still had claim boards on the trees. The claim owners had been Harry and Dayton. These men had taken out quite a lot of gold from these claims but had abandoned them when the pay gravel went too deep.

Investigating the large expanse of water to the north, I climbed the mountain foot of red laterite clay, which was very slippery in this rainy weather. At points I had to deviate from my line to avoid large granite rocks. When we were about half way up, we came across a beautiful small waterfall descending from a height of about twenty-five feet. We all got under this fall, clothes and everything, for a refresher. We continued our climb but noticing the gradient was getting near perpendicular, I strained to climb to a vantage point above our miniature fall. I stood on a rock promontory and could see clearly my back trail from the river. I picked out the ridge where the monkeys had chased us and, in the near foreground, the high hill on the other side of which was our camp. To my right and left and directly behind me this escarpment rose to a height of 2,000 feet. The wall directly off the river rose to 800 feet in height, barring any further progress on my part. I took the opportunity to make some pencil sketches of the view I had from this point.

An incident occurred here which taught my nephew John a lesson he would never forget. I had repeatedly warned him not to wear ordinary yachting shoes in the jungle. It was only that morning he heeded my warning and donned a pair of rubber-top boots. As we were retracing our steps along the track parallel to the creek, the thumping of our steps must have disturbed a labaria (carpet) snake which struck at John's leg, ripping the upper portion of his rubber boots with its poison fangs. The Macusi Amerindian next in line killed the snake, which measured 4 feet. This species of carpet labaria, because of its markings, blends with the dead leaves on the ground. I explained to John, who had turned as white as a sheet, how this incident demonstrated the necessity for taking precautions in this raw jungle. Had he continued to wear shoes instead of the boots, the snake would have bitten him and being seventy to eighty miles from the mission, without the necessary antidote or serum, I would have had to bury him right there, as a bite from these labaria, if not properly attended, will kill a man in forty-eight hours.

Not being able to find a route to Mahdia, I decided to return to Karasabai. The Macusis were happy to learn they were going home. I'd had to control the food issued to them on a day to day basis because after the first two weeks, food issued to them to cover that period had been consumed in one week. Checking the stores, I found we were running short of food. We made a forced two day walk in one day, arriving back at our riverside camp late in the afternoon to find the river water had risen some fifteen feet to the top of the bank, owing to the constant rain, but our boat though floating high was firmly tied. We slept there that night and I awoke the men early to prepare coffee and bakes. We packed our canoe and departed back up the Takatu, leaving at 5:00 a.m. just when day was dawning over the treetops.

Because of the flooded condition of the river, we had to paddle the whole day against the current and it was not until 6:00 p.m. that we found a piece of land on which we could spread our tarpaulin to rest. We had to be content with a cup of farine and sugar water as there was no place to make a fire to prepare a cooked meal. We had passed our downstream camp frames submerged with only the ridgepoles showing. We had to follow the flow of running water because in this vast expanse of water one went easily astray. We were, though, able to cut down the distance of our journey, as we cut directly across the narrow pieces of land, being able to take a direct line cutting out all the twists and turns we had encountered on our down trip. It was a cup of farine and water again instead of coffee and bakes in the morning, but we pushed ahead upstream the next day to arrive at the mountain foot at 2:00 p.m. There I told the men to unpack our reserve stock of food and prepare a hot meal. They erected our tarpaulin tent, and slung our hammocks. Every man was hungry and tired from the constant paddling upstream, so we all went to sleep early. We made another forced march to cover the thirty odd miles back to Karasabai Mission. The water reached to my chin on the last crossing before reaching the Mission. Mr. Albert was much relieved by our arrival. He had feared for our safety and it was true that had the rain continued to fall, we would not have been able to get back to the Mission without building another boat.

After thanking Mr. Albert for his co-operation, I took my nephew John and an Amerindian guide to travel to Good-Hope overland. We had to walk through water in places on the savannah before we reached the swiftly flowing Ireng River. Our guide hailed a shop on the Brazilian shore whose owner responded kindly by taking us across in his boat. We then continued walking downstream on the high savannah in Brazil until we met a narrow crossing, a little above Good Hope. There our guide had to take John over first and then come back for me, as the corial could barely hold two people. Then we followed an old cattle track to Mr. Gorinsky's ranch house, which I was glad to reach and be invited to spend the night at, as I was wet to the skin and tired.

That evening, I sat down and gave Mr. Gorinsky a rundown of our trip into the Siparuni head. Mr. Gorinsky and others in the area doubted that they would ever see a road built from the coast through to the savannahs. I asked him to contact Mr. Hart, the American pilot who had flown us into Karasabai, to return to fly out my men and equipment back to Good Hope. I also requested that he contact Mr. Bamford, Commissioner for the Interior, reporting that I had completed my reconnaissance, and requesting he send a plane and $1,000.00 with the pilot so I could pay off my men. I spent three days at the ranch house preparing my report and maps of the area we had penetrated. The Gorinskys' maid took such an interest in me that one night she climbed through my bedroom window, but being so worn out I was not prepared to have any sport with her. The plane eventually arrived and on completion of my business, I departed for Georgetown, first touching down at Lethem. From there to Atkinson Field was another hour's flying. I handed in my reports and maps to Mr. Bamford the following day.

CHAPTER XVIII
Reconnaissance Work: Mahdia-Lethem – 1958

I was recalled two days later and introduced to the Director of Public Works and some senior officers from the Roads Division. I gave them a verbal description of my reconnaissance, describing the rock wall formation, which barred the route to Mahdia. I was transferred from the Interior Department to the Survey branch of the Roads Division and told to continue my reconnaissance from Mahdia - Potaro to Lethem - Rupununi.

I selected my nephew who had been on my previous trip from Karasabai, two Afro-Guyanese from the island of St. Lucia – both seasoned bush men, two Carib Amerindians from the Pomeroon river and an Akawaio Amerindian from Georgetown, who would be my camp attendant. I collected my equipment from the Public Works compound and advanced the men some money to purchase food.

We travelled from Georgetown to Bartica by river steamer. At Bartica, we joined the Transport & Harbours Bush bus to travel to Mahdia. There were no proper seats, only a canvas seat in an iron frame for the first class passengers; the other passengers were mixed up with the cargo, bruised and sore from the bumps and jerking of the bus. Arriving after dark, I had trouble finding accommodation, but I was lucky to discover a friend who had a shop. We had met in the Mazaruni River when I had been working diamonds.

The following day after I had sorted out our equipment and rations, we walked ten miles to a camp on the North fork. With us were two Patamona Amerindians I had taken on at Mahdia who were familiar with the local bush. We followed the right bank of the North fork which tumbled down from the mountains in a series of rapids and small falls. On a natural ledge of a high hill bordering the stream on our right, to its junction with the Konawaruk River, there was a government line up the left bank to the source, enabling prospectors an entry into the upper reaches of the Potaro river above Kaieteur Falls. I had to construct a high bush wood bridge fifteen feet in height and sixty feet in length over which we had to drough our equipment and food. Flash floods coming down from the Kurungiku Mountains caused the water to rise as much as ten feet and its current could be very destructive. We continued cutting a line to the south over some very cut-up and hilly lands, until we reached the lower Haimaraparu Creek. We crossed and traced this creek on its right bank to a quartz and gravel hill where we built our first camp.

The men caught some good-sized haimara fish in the bay near our camp. This proved a pleasant change to the shop food. This creek swung sharply to the west to its source in the Glendor Mountains so we continued cutting to the south. Within half a mile, we met a laterite hill which rose steeply to about 300 feet above the creek, on top of which I discovered a laterite rock formation, covered with light scrub bush and hardwood trees amongst which I noted a number of purpleheart trees growing to a height of well over a hundred feet. We continued over this rock-strewn terrain until we met another small creek, its clear water coming out of the rock. This I named Tom-Iron Creek because the men discovered a discarded iron. We built a temporary camp there. The men discovered hiari vines growing here, so I named this rock formation Hiari Hill.

A spur of Glendor Mountain barred our way to the south. The men cut a line across it so we could transport our equipment and supplies over it, to another clear-water stream coming out of the mountain. We built another camp on a laterite spur from the mountain, because the land at the mountain foot was low and swampy with numerous manicole and turru palms. I found the spur on which we had built our camp, when traced to the east, eventually led back to Tom-Iron Creek – a detour of some five to six miles. There were areas on this spur where spring water was bubbling through the laterite. This reminded me of the headwaters of the Demerara river, which was said to originate from swamp, but proved to be from water running through and over the laterite formation. Resuming the south line, I noticed the land changing to a light brown sandy-clay soil, on which growing reefs of greenheart trees rose to a height of eighty feet to the first branch, intermingled with wamara and purpleheart, silverballi and crabwood. This undulating land stretched for approximately five miles before descending gradually to the low flats of the North Muruwa Creek, which in the rainy season is a wide stream, overrunning its banks in many places. I could picture this whole area and three miles beyond to the mother creek "Big Muruwa", as a vast agricultural area. It has wonderful rich land for producing ground provisions which the Amerindians from Mahdia later took advantage of, as they were following closely in our footsteps. These Potamonas were nomads, planting a field, than moving on to another area to plant again. At the time they calculate their provisions would be ripe, they return to harvest, often combining this with a fishing trip.

At Big Muruwa, I built a more substantial camp. The senior surveyor and two others along with a government dispenser came to check on my road gradients. They congratulated me on the cleanliness and the layout of the facilities of my camp. The men reaped a harvest of haimara fish from the blackwater creek, which they smoked before we moved on. The senior surveyor was surprised to see me lifting my share of 100 pounds in my warashi. I told them in my crew each man has to share his responsibilities, his load and sometimes his food. We were far from home and we had to help each other. Continuing south from Big Muruwa, we ran into difficulties, for I found myself in a swamp up to my armpits. We had to retrace our steps and cut further to the south-west. This swamp area was named Nibbi Creek because of the amount of nibbi vines growing from the trees in the area. These vines are used for the plaiting of warashi baskets and even hats.

On a south-west bearing, we started to meet large granite boulders on low lying lands, the drainage area of the Kurungiku Mountains. We continued on this bearing until we emerged on the left bank of the Tiperu river at the foot of this mountain, where it passes over a range of rapids formed by a gap between the mountains. From a vantage point at the foot of the Kurungiku Mountain, I could clearly see a long range of mountains barring our progress. I picked out a high peak, which I presumed was part of the escarpment I had seen in 1957, the previous year. I pointed this out to the Government surveyor and told him that if this was the case, no road could pass there. I was instructed to verify this fact. I built a round bushwood bridge, strung from trees in the river, twelve feet above the water, over which the men had to drough our rations and other belongings. The men named this bridge Princess Margaret Bridge as the Princess was then in the colony. We continued to cut a line following the mountain foot over low undulating land and through medium bush. The land was of a grey sandy substance, good for agriculture. We crossed over a spur from this mountain leading to a hill of quartz rock. I located another small creek flowing to the south west. Here we pitched our tarpaulin tent as I guessed we were some twelve miles from Tiperu river.

Next morning, we cut south and met a next laterite spur from the mountain. I climbed a solitary peak rising some three to four hundred feet. I had to drag myself up by the roots of the shrubs growing there and dig my toes into rock crevices to gain the top, emerging on to a flat rocky summit of about ten feet by thirty feet and bare of vegetation. I was rewarded by a magnificent view of the entire range of mountains from the Tiperu river and stretching in an unbroken line to the west. I saw what looked to be a large body of water or a lake at the mountain foot and looked for a possible point to scale the mountain. When we had crossed the quartz rock spur, I could clearly see the escarpment at the top. I took out my notebook and made a sketch of the entire scene. Then we descended from the peak and cut towards the large body of water I had seen. We penetrated once again a dead bush, similar to what I had experienced at the foot of Peiama Falls in the Mazaruni River, silent and gloomy, no sound of a bird or any animal movement. We came out onto a large expanse of inky-black water overshadowed by large trees, unmoved by the slightest ripple. It had an eerie effect on us. We continued to follow the shore of this water until we heard the sound of falling water and discovered that it came through a narrow gateway of tumbled rocks on the mountain. This later proved to be another tributary of the Tiperu River. I noted a lot of crystallised quartz and other gravel between the rocks. I thought that prospecting this untouched area could turn up a pay of gold or diamonds.

The next day, the men and I cut a zig-zag path from the quartz spur, through vine-entangled bush where many fallen trees (as if a fire had swept through the area) covered the slope. We then followed a water lead into the escarpment wall, through which we clambered. This was some 1,500 feet above the forest floor. We descended for about 1,000 feet to find ourselves in an open valley of the Upper Tiperu River, its tributaries descending from the mountain wall which rose up in front of us. This was unspoiled nature, not a sign of any cuttings to mar its beauty. The forest opened in front of us in park-like glades. We mounted this slope of sandy loam until we was about half way up, and here we started to meet laterite gravel, very small, on the slope. We returned to camp at this point.

The following day I left a man in camp to prepare our evening meal. Two men were instructed to open and clear the line we had cut. The other men accompanied me to penetrate beyond the point we had stopped at the previous day. We must have penetrated another half mile or more before I perceived what looked to be an old cut away or farm as the bush had lightened up considerably. Pushing on to investigate, I nearly had a fatal accident as I found myself standing on the brink of a sheer precipice. I had to grab two trees to halt my progress. I was gazing into the vast valley of the upper Siparuni River. Directly in front of us the sheer wall dropped to a depth of 700 to 800 feet before it descended in slopes to the river flats. What a stupendous sight it was to gaze into the upper and lower Siparuni River. I immediately picked out the laterite hills I had cut over the previous year after leaving the Takatu. I also picked out the course of the Ireng Creek. We cut a tracing line following the face of the escarpment in a southerly direction. At certain points on the top of this mountain, it was four or five hundred feet wide and at other points a mere knife's edge. It was made up of laterite gravel and exposed granite rocks. We continued for a distance of approximately a mile and a half before I heard the roar of falling water, which proved to be the Ireng Creek head. It was most exhilarating to be on top of this mountain, breathing the pure air. The breeze was very strong and had a dampness to it as we were up in the clouds at 2,500 feet. I wrote a report, which I sent out to the main survey camp. The outcome was that a plane was chartered from British Guiana Airways to examine the escarpment wall. There were some folks in Georgetown who still felt there was a pass but my reconnaissance proved them wrong. I did not have a camera with me, but being fond of drawing, I made sketches at every opportunity, trying to capture the beauty I had witnessed and for future reference. We returned to Tiperu River and followed the right bank out to the Siparuni River. The lower Tiperu was made up of a number of small falls and rapids in which haimara fish swarmed.

A boat (minus an outboard engine) was dispatched from Pacutau Falls for us, to paddle some thirty miles up the Siparuni River as far as "S" Falls. We had to make an overnight camp at the Ireng Creek mouth. It was a dismal spot, the numerous vines making it hard to set up our tarpaulin tent. I was glad to leave there and proceed to just below "S" Falls. We erected a leaf camp there. I started an east line and met a laterite ridge running north and south, paralleling the Siparuni River. We crossed this to descend into the Marepowta Creek, a tributary of the lower Burro-Burro River. As we were cutting this line, when the men met the first large black-water creek, it was so silent and the water so forbidding they were afraid to cross, fearing anacondas or pirai fish in the water. I decided to lead the way, taking off my yachting boots, the better to swim, placing my prismatic compass in my hat and my bush knife in my belt. I told the men to jump into the creek when I did, to shout and make as much splashing in the water as they could. I plunged overboard, the men following. I often wondered what the reaction must have been of the creatures in the bush. We later felled two trees to interlace across the creek to form a bridge. On the second day of cutting, at the highest point of this ridge, one of the Afro-Guyanese and I saw a shadowy form slinking in and out of the trees to our front. Edwin said it was a jaguar. The animal seemed unafraid of us and would not move from our vicinity. I called to George, an Amerindian from the Pomeroon river to bring my gun. I only had B.B. shot in my cartridge but a well placed shot had been known to kill. I told the men to stay where they were. I crept forward, always keeping my eyes on the area where the cat was lurking. When near enough, I threw a piece of dry wood towards the spot where it was. Its reaction was to raise its head to peer through the trees at me. I raised my gun and shot what proved to be a large mountain lion or puma. The men discovered partly devoured carcasses of animals which the cat had covered with dry leaves. This was its larder, the reason for its reluctance to move from the area. I told Edwin to skin the animal and carry the pelt into camp.

I marked a large tree in the centre of the ridge on my east-west line, so that the main survey party following from Pacutau could pick up my trail. We followed this laterite ridge two miles to the south where I cut a next east-west line. On the west we met the source of the first black-water creek we had crossed and to the east another tributary of the Burro-Burro River. I had been instructed to cut south-east toward Surama, but on descending the laterite ridge, I met a reef of white sand, which we crossed to descend into lands below flood level. I saw clearly the water marks on the trees, some ten and twelve feet above the land. The land, a white clay or silt, was eroded to a depth of four or five feet in twisting channels and was covered with a growth of wild lily bush which grew to a height of four feet. The undersides of these lily leaves were infested by hordes of miburi ticks, very minute. When the men and I were cutting through this lily bush, we had to scrape each other's skin with a knife after bathing in the afternoon, to get rid of the ticks.

The first white water creek in this lily bush was so clear I could see to the bottom – and what a sight! It seemed as if hundreds of fish were swimming about, the haimara predominant. I cut three lines into this flat, but could locate no ridge of high land so I cut following a red sandy clay ridge to the southwest. This ridge also was flourishing with beautiful, straight greenheart trees. This hill descended into the flat watershed of the Sipariparu Creek. The other throw of the watershed descended into the Takatu River flats (1957 survey). This watershed was swampy and covered by palm trees. This we crossed to the foothills of the mountain on the far side.

On these reconnaissance surveys, I had no assistance from Aerial Survey maps, but had to cut blindly into the bush depending on the feel of the land. I had been supplied with a pair of powerful binoculars. When in doubt I had the men select a tall tree with convenient bush ropes for climbing which I used as observation posts, from where I could view the surrounding country and pick out the most likely route to follow. I took my compass bearings from up there and passed it down to my line leader. From one of these tree-tops, I could see across the Takatu River to where it joined the Siparuni and the mountain range from where I had turned back in 1957. I managed to capture these scenes on my sketchpad. We crossed a mountain spur from the Sipariparu to drop down into the Marinarukeng Creek, its source being in the Varonglar Mountain which towered above us on the right bank of this creek. We made a camp at the mouth of the Marinarukeng Creek. Here again Edwin proved the waters held haimara, for when he dropped his hook into the water, I saw a flurry of water when the hook was snatched by a large four-foot haimara.

The Burro-Burro River, from its junction with the lower Siparuni River to its head waters some thirty-six miles up in the mountains and about twenty five miles wide, and encompassing all its tributaries, covers an area of some 700 to 800 square miles which could become a giant fishing reserve. The Burro-Burro from the mountain foot forms a natural basin.

From the mouth of the Marinarukeng, we followed a ridge mounting gradually to the source of this creek where it swings east up into the Varonglar Mountain. I could see Watamong Mountain to my left on an easterly bearing. We climbed over the gorge of the Marinarukeng and sided the mountain on the western slope to find ourselves looking down into a deep shadowed valley formed by the towering Wurutipu Mountain. This is on the right bank of the Burro-Burro river, rising to a height of 1,000 feet. We descended at a point where two of the main streams met. This I named Two Mouth. The following day we moved camp from Marinarukeng Creek, arriving late in the afternoon at Two Mouth. Because of the height of the mountain walls around this deep valley, night set in sooner and the men only had time to plant four posts on a sand bank, put up two beams and a ridge pole and erect the tarpaulin tent. It proved to be the coldest spot I had experienced for a number of years. I had on all my clothes, a rice bag spread in my hammock and a blanket, yet the cold penetrated from the sand right through to my back, making sleep impossible. I was glad when I heard one of my Patamona Amerindians ask his partner the time. His reply was that it was two in the morning. The other exclaimed, "Rass man, leh we put on some hot coffee". We all got out of our hammocks to gather around the fire and told bush stories until dawn.

As we were opening the bush to build a better camp on firm ground, Peter Miller, one of my fastest droughers, came into camp with a letter from the main Survey Party, informing me this would be the last ration run as the main party was closing camp and returning to Georgetown. I would now be on my own. When I reached the Annai savannah, I should radio Georgetown for a plane to pick us up. Peter Miller left at midday, saying he wanted to reach back to Pacutau before night, a tough journey for one day.

From Two Mouth, we followed a central spur of red sandy clay, which was really a spur from Wurutipu Mountain. When we emerged to the top we cut south, following the hog-back crossing on a saddle which dropped steeply on either side, to mount again on this hog-back, the end of which cut away abruptly. I found myself gazing into a deep gorge – the waters flowing to the east. To the west I could see the main stream of the upper Burro-Burro river wedged between towering walls of rock. At this point of the southern wall of the Wurutipu mountain, our passage was barred by a good-sized waterfall descending from the mountain to the upper Burro-Burro river where it curves from the west to north, a mile or two above Two Mouth.

We returned to follow my east-west line descending on the red sandy clay hill to a wide but shallow rocky stream. I traced the left bank, twisting and turning between large granite boulders, to its source on the eastern shoulder of Wurutipu Mountain. We descended to the Burro-Burro river flat on a more gradual slope, on the right bank of this stream. I felt this could easily be a gateway across the eastern shoulder of the Wurutipu to the savannah lands beyond. I did some sketches from the slope of Wurutipu. We continued our east line on the right bank of the Burro-Burro River and camped by a small water fall. The terrain in front and down stream opened like a funnel, the hills swinging to the north and to the south. The main stream of the Burro-Burro River swinging to the northeast was shallow with large gravel banks. The vegetation also changed from high forest to low entangled vine bush and wild bamboo clumps, through which we cut to emerge into what looked like a small savannah, but proved to be a dry swamp.

I took stock of our rations and found them low. We would have to make some speed to reach Surama before the food gave out. I checked the compiled map of the colony and measured off the distance of seven miles to the cattle trail. I told the men that four of them would bring forward our load in their warashis whilst the rest of us would forge ahead to open the walking line. The weather was exceedingly dry and there was no water to drink until we burst out from the forest to find ourselves on the left bank of a large black water creek, the Taramu, an upper tributary of the Burro-Burro. We crossed over to the other side, it was fifty feet wide and five feet deep. We again met an area of dry swamp on which we opened the tarpaulin to sleep the night, hoping that no rattlesnakes visited us as this was their country. There was no wood to cut to make a camp frame.

The following morning I was getting anxious, as I knew we had covered a distance of more than seven miles and should have reached the Cattle Trail. Continuing southeast, our route lay over flat lands cracked by the sun. At one watercourse, we stopped to drink. The water was rank with electric eels, dirty and muddy. After passing this flat creek, the land started to lift again

in a succession of small hills and, late one afternoon, we reached the summit of a laterite rock hill with pools of spring water flowing from the honey-
comb rocks. I told the men to camp here for the night. George, an Amerindian from the Pomeroon River, was sent out to hunt for some meat. We heard
three shots fired one after another. He had met with a huge jaguar and been
so frightened he had fired the shots to scare it and he himself had taken off
at top speed in the opposite direction. Being in the area of the cattle trail,
one is apt to meet these cats hunting stray cattle.

Knowing we must be near the cattle trail, I took my gun, torchlight and
my bush knife and descended to the foot of this laterite hill. I was rewarded
to find old bush cuttings, probably made by balata bleeders who penetrate
these areas. I knew at once we were on the right trail. I returned to the men
in camp just as night was setting in and informed them of my find. I told
them that at dawn the next morning I would divide the party and trace the
hill foot to see if we could pick up a trail. I took one of the Amerindians with
me and within a quarter of a mile we emerged into the wide cattle trail. My
companion was so excited he fired off four loads to signal the other men. I
followed the trail to the left, which descended to the Kuiparu Creek, crossing the trail. The creek was forty feet wide and shallow. On the other side
was a cattle corral with lemon trees growing and a vaquero's logie. We rested
here for a few minutes when an Afro-Guyanese man approached us from the
north. He said he had walked from Tacama on the Berbice River and was
walking to Lethem on the Brazilian border, a distance of some 200 miles.
He informed me I had sixteen miles to travel before we met Surama savannah to the south. I passed a concrete marker on the trail dated 1920 marked
with the name of Edwin Haynes, the man who had cut the cattle trail from
the Berbice River to the Rupununi Savannah. It was the same gentleman
who had taken me up to the Potaro River head in 1925.

The following morning, I told the men to cook the last of our food, leave
all heavy iron pots on the laterite hill and just carry the government equipment and the hammocks and clothes in their warashis. We left the hill while
it was still dark under the trees, travelling over laterite and white clay soils,
crossing dry creek beds, until we met the Surama River some five hours
after we had started. The men rested here to drink some water, then pushed
on again. We emerged from the forest into high grasslands and islands of
trees. The heat of the sun on the grass penetrated my yachting boots and I
was like a "cat on hot bricks" running from island to island of trees to cool
my feet. About two and a half miles from the Surama Creek, we met the first
Amerindian houses. The first man I met proved to be an Amerindian from

the North West Region, who recognised me as a Young, for he had known my late father. I laid my distress to him. We were completely out of food and I and my men were very tired, having walked from "S" Falls in the Siparuni River over the Burro-Burro Mountains. He made us welcome, placing us in a new house he had just finished. He and his wife brought us farine, corn, salted beef and smoked fish and vegetables from his farm plus coffee, sugar and cows milk. The men quickly prepared a meal and put up their hammocks. In the late afternoon, whilst lying in my hammock, I heard a low moaning sound gradually increasing to a higher pitch which lasted for about twenty minutes. I had heard a similar sound, as if coming from the mountain, whilst we were camped at our last camp in the Burro-Burro valley. Mr. Rufino explained it was the hot air rising from the savannah in the late afternoon and the cold air rushing in.

I rested here for three days as both my ankles were swollen due to the forced march along the drought-hardened earth for thirteen miles along the cattle train and the hot savannah grass. Mr. Rufino had dug a water hole ten feet deep from which he drew water for cooking and washing purposes. My men and I walked back along the trail to a small water lead, where we bathed and washed our clothes. I arranged with Mr. Rufino to supply me with two pack bullocks to transport our baggage and equipment as far as the bush ends at Woweta Savannah. Rufino also kindly supplied me with a horse. He advised we start early so as to reach Woweta Savannah early to get into Annai before the heat of the sun intensified. Our party left at 3:00 a.m. in brilliant moonlight and we made our way through five miles of bush to reach Woweta Savannah at daylight, but there was no jeep there from Mr. Brasche to meet us. The equipment was unloaded from the bullocks, which returned to Surama. The men immediately started to walk to Annai, I riding the horse. I arrived at Mr. Brasche's Ranch house at 9:30 a.m. Mr. Brasche was in the process of repairing his jeep. Vivian Brasche said he would send his sons to collect my equipment at Waweta Savannah. In the meantime, I must be a guest at his house. His daughter Florrie showed me to my bedroom overlooking the savannah lands to the "Basin", with a view of the Kwatamung Mountains in the background. My men were lodged in a logie near the house and made comfortable. Mrs. Brasche and her daughter prepared and served lunch, ranch style, in the dining room. Mr. Brasche informed me messages had been received from Georgetown Public Works headquarters enquiring about me, fearing I was lost as I was long overdue. I spent three days here preparing my report and maps before I sent for a plane from Georgetown.

CHAPTER XIX

From Annai Along the Cattle Trail – 1958

On my return the next year, I was accompanied by an American, Mr. Cheetam, advisor to the Guyana Government on roads, and the senior surveyor. A land rover was put at my disposal in which we drove west along the Cattle Trail as far as Mora river crossing, pointing out on our way the route I proposed for the intended road. Mr. Cheetam stressed the necessity of good gradients. He said it was better to add miles to the length of the road if that ensured proper gradients.

The following day, my men arrived by another plane, bringing my equipment and rations. I asked Mr. Brasche at Annai for a piece of land on which I had been instructed to erect a ration store and a dispensary. I left Annai guided by a Macusi Amerindian whom Mr. Brasche had recommended, who seemed to know this area like the palm of his hand. He explained to me that the Savannah Amerindians used these trails to penetrate to the Taramu River on fishing trips. The Amerindians were like the tapir, following the less tedious course, usually along the contours of the land. I crossed some very rocky terrain to drop down into a large tributary on the right bank of the Taramu River. This stream came off the mountain in a series of falls; at one of these falls a tree was leaning dangerously over the falling water on which a beautiful purple orchid was growing. I had one of the Amerindians climb the tree and collect it. At the stream's junction with the main river, I found the river very shallow with large gravel banks and about three times wider than the lower river when I had crossed it the previous year. I built a camp on the high right bank of the Taramu River. Clearing the site, the men killed two good sized labaria snakes. As the weather was dry, I instructed the men to burn the area to chase away any more snakes that might be lurking there. The men damn near burned down the camp! Everyone had to take up tree branches to beat out the flames near our tarpaulin tents.

After crossing the Taramu, we mounted a spur on the left bank, having to detour in two places to cut around deep gorges formed by streams descending from Wurutipu Mountains. We built an intermediate camp on a spur from the mountain. From there I climbed to a vantage point on an exposed rock wall on the southern side where I had a view of Mawreen Mountain to the north of Surama Savannah where it slopes down to the Taramu River. I made some sketches from this point. I named this peak, Easter Mountain, as it was Easter 1959 we spent there. I eventually found my 1958 reconnaissance line on the eastern slope of Wurutipu Mountain. I decided to scale Wurutipu Mountain at this point. This proved to be a rough and tiring job. I only managed to climb to a height of about 800 feet, clambering over loose rocks between which spring water was penetrating. The sparse vegetation had wild orchids blooming on them. Most of the rocks were moss-covered with ferns growing in between. I managed to sketch the distant Annai savannah and trace the course of the Taramu River to where it originated in the mountains to the southwest. I climbed around the mountain to the north, overlooking the falls thundering down into the upper Burro-Burro River, showing the upper river nestling between towering mountain walls and jagged peaks at its source. Wurutipu Mountain seems to be the main spring from which the surrounding creeks are formed.

I returned to Taramu Camp having joined together my two survey lines. In cutting from Taramu River towards Annai, we had to contend with a large patch of wild bamboo to enable us to keep to the gradients I wanted to follow. It took the men a full week to cut through to my line from Annai. I had to send out one of my men who had the misfortune to slip and fall on his cutlass opening a nasty wound in the palm of his hand which required stitching. I took this opportunity to send out some of the men to the ration store to bring in fresh supplies. We moved camp from Taramu to a small clear-water stream and continued the tracing to Mora River. Knowing the width of this stream in the rainy season, I endeavoured to cut around the head, but found myself on a rocky plateau and swinging away from my route. I returned to camp – which the men had foolishly erected in the Mora river flat. They told me the adjoining savannah had no suitable wood to use to erect a camp frame. We had to make a sudden move at 4:00 a.m. as the men discovered the water was rising below our hammocks. Rain must have fallen in the mountain. The men had to place our provisions on trees above the water level and await daylight. Then they had to build an aerial bridge which went from tree to tree and pass out our equipment to the higher savannahs. The water in the riverbed had risen to a depth of five feet and across an expanse of at least 500 feet.

Continuing our reconnaissance, we had to follow the Old Cattle Trail which skirted the foot of the hills, bordering the mountain, until we met Toka Creek which was fifty feet wide with high banks. The village of Toka was on the right bank, comprising of some twenty houses and a school. Here I met Cyril

Davis, whom I had last seen in 1937 whilst I was with the New York Zoological Expedition. He kindly invited me to sling my hammock in his house. I was welcomed by his wife and his buxom sixteen year old daughter, Diane, who was still attending school.

I selected a piece of land 500 feet from Mr. Davis' house where I had another store erected. Mr. Davis brought Mr. Persaud's sons, who were the village carpenters, to help in the construction. The flooring was four feet off the ground, there were sawn boards for the walls and the floor and the roof was of ité palm leaves. Cyril carried two donkeys up Tirke Mountain at the head of Toka Creek where the men cut down the palms and the leaves were loaded on the donkeys. In my walk up Tirke Mountain, I noticed the plateau was similar to that of the Mora River head and could very well be of the same formation. Cyril told me that the lower creek had been a flourishing ité palm swamp but generation after generation had been cutting down the palms to roof their houses, so now they had to go into the mountain for roofing materials. Later, I walked with Cyril to the Benoni Creek, some four miles to the west of his homestead, where he showed me the deep crossing which I later had to bridge. I crossed over and climbed Benoni Mountain on the right bank of the stream, rising some 500 feet, grass sloped and free of trees. I looked to the south across miles of rolling savannah lands to the faint blue tinge of the Kanaku Mountain. On the left bank of the Benoni, I climbed a higher hill, some 750 feet from whose summit I sketched the trail I had followed, showing Toka Village in the foreground and Makrapan Mountain, a distant blue with the silvery streak of the Rupununi river. To the west I sketched a view of Mureiro pond and beyond Gorinsky's Ranch at Good Hope, with the mountains over in Brazil showing a faint blue.

The population of Toka Village comprised about fifty souls, men, women and children. There were two main families: the Davis and Persaud families intermarrying with a few outsiders. Whenever the rain fell in the mountains, the Toka Creek was flooded. This was the time for the boys and the young women to frolic in the cold waters. Diane invited me to accompany her to join her friends for a swim. On my arrival at the creek, I was astonished to see the lovely Persaud girls wearing only flimsy panties, their breasts exposed unashamedly, for they were amongst family. Diane peeled off her dress, leaving her practically naked, then teased me to follow her into the water. I felt rather self-conscious. Eventually both boys and girls mobbed me and pulled me into the water. There was much intimate play and laughter. It reminded me of the Phagwah Festival on sugar estates where, on the first day, it was the custom for people to wet each other with water. I remembered returning from my work in the field and crossing the middle walk trench in my bateau, when some of the girls from my weeding gang upset the boat, plunging me into the water. I had to join in the sport of ducking whoever I caught. Now in Toka, on our way back to the house, Diane took me on a short cut through the bush. She was walking in front of me, her wet dress plastered to her body, with every swelling pronounced. She stopped and turned, pressing her wet body to mine, inviting me to sample the balance of her beauty. I found this was no sixteen year old schoolgirl but a woman in passion who seemed to know all the arts of love making. I had been helping Diane with her lessons at night after dinner, but this experience in the bush put a strain on me in the house and I decided I ought to move from her father's house to the newly completed store building, which was isolated from any other building. Diane made it her business to visit me either early in the morning or late in the evening. I soon put a stop to this, as I did not want any trouble with her family. The Persaud girls must have learned of our intimacy, for two of the older girls started to find excuses to hang around my house wearing only the briefest of clothing. These girls evidently did not find anything wrong in sampling a little outside sex.

Mr. Davis showed me the highest point of the savannah after crossing Benoni Creek, the swamps to my left or south and to the north, the mountains bordering the Cattle trail. We skirted two large ponds of fresh water on this high land before we encountered a high wire fence, which Davis explained was the quarantine fence, used in the prevention of the spread of foot and mouth disease.

After completing our work in this area, we moved camp from Toka Village to Mr. Gorinsky's outstation where there was a pond of fresh water, some cattle corals, and a large, two-roomed adobe house with a corrugated iron roof. There the caboura flies gave us a lot of trouble during our working day, every bite drawing blood. When these disappeared at sundown, it was the only chance we had to bathe. Then I saw the huge candle flies dashing here and there as if searching us out, for shortly after, I could distinctly hear a loud hum as the mosquitoes arose in swarms from their hiding places. We had to shut the door and the windows against this invasion. The heat nearly cooked us in this enclosed atmosphere.

These were open grasslands, and we had to use red cotton cloth torn into strips to mark the route we took. However, when we reached Meritizeiro, Elmo Hart's cattle ranch, he warned me about using this red cloth we were using because he had a bad zebu bull. He had sent his house boy one morning to see his father at Pirara ranch, which was only a short distance from

Meritizeiro, but the boy had not returned until dusk. Elmo's bull had chased him and he'd had to take refuge in a clump of thorn bush where he had lain the whole day with the bull patrolling outside. These cattle respect only horsemen, but nothing walking on foot. My men were warned always to have a convenient tree nearby in case the bull came at them. We stayed a few days at Meritizeiro, where Elmo kindly accommodated me in the house he had recently built. The men were lodged with the vaqueros working on the ranch. I also met Mr. Hart Sr. We recalled the time in 1937 when our American Scientific Expedition had spent the night at his ranch at Pirara.

From Meritizeiro, we again contacted the existing cattle trail, which had swung back to the south from Good Hope. We cut across this trail and, following my compass bearings, we emerged on the Astro Fix, which I had been instructed to look for at Sunnyside, on the left bank of the Ireng River, the Brazilian frontier. We moved camp from Meritizeiro to the Good Hope Police Station. There I met Corporal Bobb with his constable, Ronald McDonald, son of Andrew McDonald, who had been with me on my trip through Brazil with the Zoological Expedition in 1937. Ronald was married to a Georgetown girl. They resided in a cottage in the compound.

An incident occurred here when some of my men crossed over into Brazilian territory and paid a visit to the Airport at Normandia, approximately three miles from the river. The same day I accompanied Constable McDonald visiting some Brazilian families he wanted to invite to a fiesta. But not finding the folks at home, Ronald took me to see Normandia Airport. There, I found my men in custody. They had purchased some liquor and, being under its influence, had (it was alleged) molested some Brazilian girls. I was fortunate to have Constable McDonald with me to act as an interpreter. We were introduced to the Sergeant-in-Charge of the outpost who told McDonald in Portuguese that the incident had been reported to his senior officer at Boa Vista, who was sending a plane that afternoon to collect the prisoners. McDonald explained that I was the officer in charge of the men, who had just completed a survey from Annai to the frontier. Señor Young would guarantee the removal of his men back to Guyana where they would be punished. The Sergeant said he would have to await a call from Boa Vista at 2:00 p.m. before he could put forward my request. In the meantime, I was invited to lunch with Ronald at the Sergeant's house. Confirmation was received at 2:30 p.m. that permission was granted to Señor Young to escort the prisoners back to Guyana, providing Señor Young would give his word that the men would not return to Brazilian territory. Ronald thanked the Sergeant on my behalf for his co-operation in preventing an international incident and his kindness in entertaining us so well. I also bade farewell to his wife and daughter. When we got back, I reported the incident to Corporal Bobb at Good Hope Police Station and explained the great help Constable McDonald had given me.

The next morning, I accompanied Ronald to a Brazilian trading store where I purchased a beautiful hammock for $35.00. I bid farewell to Mr. & Mrs. Gorinsky. The plane came for my party the following day and I returned to Georgetown.

Almost immediately I was asked by the Chief Engineer of roads, Mr. Jennings, and the senior surveyor, to accompany them from Bartica to the place identified on the maps as 113 miles, the old Consolidated Goldfields compound and, from here onwards to 124 miles, to which I travelled by Land Rover. I had been instructed to send ahead to Mahdia the men who had been with me in the Rupununi, with a month's supply of food. My task was to locate a high road from 119 miles, where the Eagle Mountain braces the road from the east and then rises to the west in the Ebini Mountains, tracing back to Mahdia a tract of land above flood level. We were lucky to cut through some nasty rope-bush to find ourselves on a natural laterite shelf with open forest. This shelf varied from 100 feet to 500 feet in width. Nearing the lower Mahdia Creek, the surface changed to large weathered laterite rocks and gravel. This natural roadway was only cut at one point, a gap forty feet wide, through which the gold dredge had worked its way, then it continued to within two hundred feet of the Mahdia Creek where it swung north-west, bracing the high laterite hill which forms the Government compound at 112 miles.

I spent the night at the Government Rest House on this hill to be awakened at dawn by the calling of the hanakwa birds, a constant "hanakwa-hanakwa". I had been an early riser since my sugar estate days and as I stood on my front steps to admire the brightness of the morning star, I watched the deep shadows disappearing from the surrounding forest, and the mists melting before the coming day. An orange glow was followed by a faint tinge of blue, a reflection cast on the ever-changing clouds that floated by, sweeping aside the vapour to smooth the entrance of the rising sun. A rose colour bloomed on the eastern slope of Ebini Mountain which rose some 2,000 feet from the dark forests, and wisps of cloud grew shell pink and turned to silver; then a glory of red and gold painted itself on the mountain escarpment. Up the wide valley of the Mahdia Creek was the towering Eagle Mountain, 2,300 feet high, whose head was shrouded in clouds.

Early morning finds the mountain slopes and the valley a deep grey-green colour, heavy white clouds of vapour arising from the deep gullies and waterways. As the sun rises, the colour changes to a bluish haze and as the sun moves in its descent to the west, the deeper purples and blue greens are seen in a haze, as if looking through a veil. Not until late in the afternoon do the clear cut features emerge in a darker green – an ever-changing picture throughout the day and a beautiful scene to capture on canvas. The natural formation of these mountains forms a narrow gateway into the deeper forest lands to the south, which I had followed to the Brazilian frontier.

On the completion of my task at 112 miles, I travelled to 72 mile compound. There I put up in the small rest house and my men in the labourers' logie. Our task here was to trace a more narrow bridge crossing, as the existing greenheart wooden bridge spanning the Ikurubisci Creek was 1500 feet long and very costly to maintain. My men traced the lower reaches of this creek but found it widening into low lands and swamp. I chatted with the school teacher and some of the Amerindian children, asking them if they knew of a narrow part of the creek. They suggested I go to see an Amerindian by the name of Joseph, who resided on the left bank of the creek near the existing bridge. He, hearing that I wanted to see him, and what I was looking for, told me that on his hunting trips in the creek flats, he had seen possible places, but higher up the creek, near the 73 mile post. Guided by Joseph and one of his sons, I and some of the men were led to a hundred feet crossing about one mile upstream from the existing bridge. Even better, there was a ridge on both banks with a foundation of laterite rock. The men felled a tree to act as a bridge, then Joseph took us along the ridge of white sand to the north. We crossed a small ravine, a tributary of the Ikurubisci Creek, then mounted a rocky laterite flat hill, beyond which we crossed white sand again to emerge on the existing road to 72 miles in the area of the 70 mile bridge. This line from 70 mile bridge across the Ikurubisci Creek proved to be a mile shorter. With Joseph's help we had found a shorter crossing for a new bridge and a shorter road on a less steep gradient.

Before we left, Joseph invited us to partake of some casiri and paiwari drink at his house. As we joined the transport bus the following morning we found all the Amerindians had come to bid me goodbye.

Back in Georgetown, I reported to Public Works (Roads Division) head office and submitted my plans and my findings at both Mahdia and 72 mile. The following year, 1960, I was sent back to the Rupununi to cut out some of the twists and turns on my line and to cut down on some of my gradients. To my mind the most difficult one was the climb from the Burro-Burro river and over the shoulder of Wurutipu Mountain, but I felt this could be surmounted by grading the contours which formed a ledge with a 1 in 10 gradient. In the Rupununi I went to visit old friends, but found Cyril Davis was

away from home on a visit to Brazil. I paid my respects to Mr. Persaud and
his family and to Cyril's wife and daughter Diane, who informed me that the
next time I left, she wanted to travel to town with me.

Whilst my party was camped at Toka Village, I was ordered to report back
to Georgetown with all my personal belongings. The Toka families were very
disappointed to hear the news, as all my men had to travel back to Annai
where they were to join the main survey team. Back in town, I was informed
that the Chief Engineer wanted to see me. He offered me a new job working
on the realignment and construction of a portion of the existing Bartica-Potaro
Road, from 8 mile to 22 mile. He told me he had asked me to do this job
because of the quality of my reports on the reconnaissance surveys I had
undertaken and their descriptions of the soils, rocks and forests on the routes
I had followed. They had a level of detail no other surveyor had ever submitted, which enabled the routes to be identified very exactly.

Matthew French Young
1905-1996

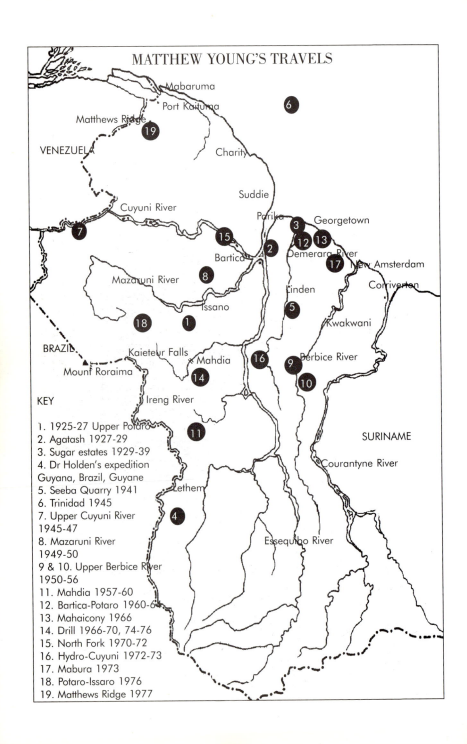

MATTHEW YOUNG'S TRAVELS

Mabaruma
Port Kaituma
Matthews Ridge
(19)
VENEZUELA
Cuyuni River
(7)
Mazaruni River
Bartica
(15)
(8)
Issano
(18)
(1)
BRAZIL
Kaieteur Falls
× Mahdia
Mount Roraima
▲
(14)
Ireng River

(6)
Charity
Suddie
Parika
Georgetown
(3)
(12)(13)
(2)
Demerara River
(17)
New Amsterdam
Corriverton
Linden
(5)
Kwakwani
(16)
Berbice River
(9)
(10)

SURINAME

Lethem
(11)
Courantyne River

(4)
Essequibo River

KEY

1. 1925-27 Upper Potaro
2. Agatash 1927-29
3. Sugar estates 1929-39
4. Dr Holden's expedition
Guyana, Brazil, Guyane
5. Seeba Quarry 1941
6. Trinidad 1945
7. Upper Cuyuni River
1945-47
8. Mazaruni River
1949-50
9 & 10. Upper Berbice River
1950-56
11. Mahdia 1957-60
12. Bartica-Potaro 1960-6
13. Mahaicony 1966
14. Drill 1966-70, 74-76
15. North Fork 1970-72
16. Hydro-Cuyuni 1972-73
17. Mabura 1973
18. Potaro-Issaro 1976
19. Matthews Ridge 1977

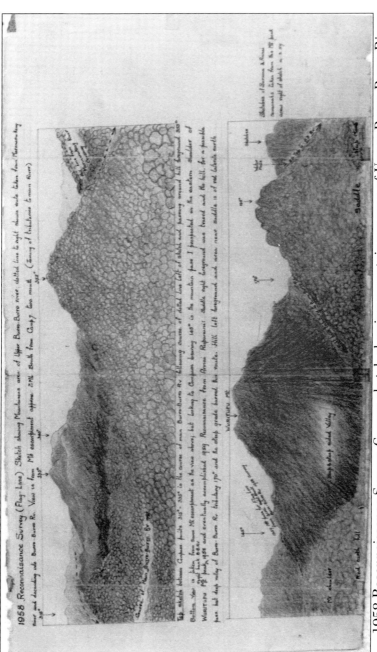

1958 Reconnaissance Survey. Crayon sketch showing mountainous area of Upper Burro–Burro River

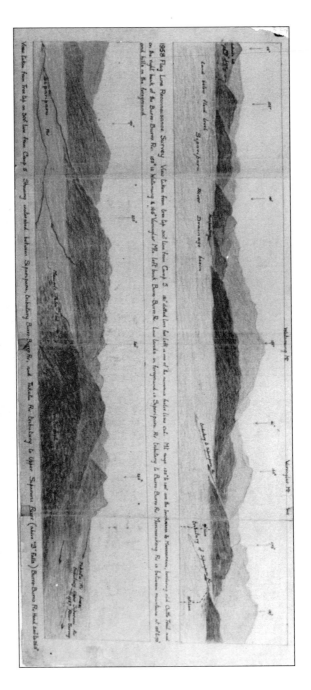

Crayon sketches from 1958 Survey in Mountainous area of Burro-Burro River

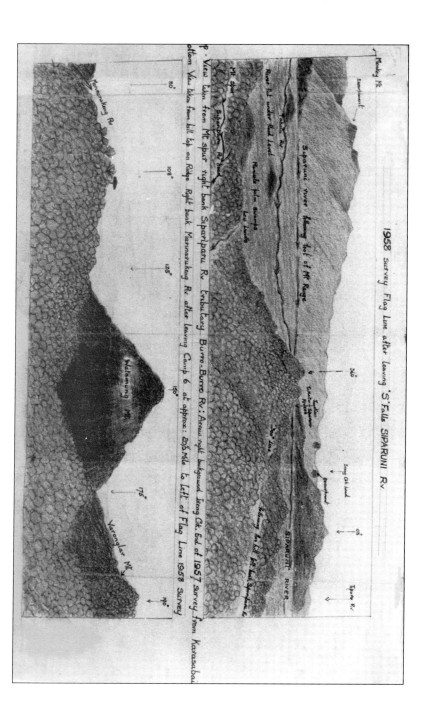

1958 Survey. Flag Line after leaving "S" Falls SIPARUNI Rv.

Top. View taken from Mt spur right bank Siparipanu Rv. tributary Burro Burro Rv: Arrow right background Iong Ck. End of 1957 survey from Karasabai

Bottom. View taken from hill top on Ridge right bank Maranaukang Rv. after leaving Camp 6 at approx: 20½ Mile to Left of Flag Line 1958 Survey

AMERINDIAN PORTRAITS BY MATTHEW FRENCH YOUNG

Wai-Wai Amerindian

Amerindian Beauty

Amerindian Mother and Child

LANDSCAPES BY MATTHEW FRENCH YOUNG

Interior Rapids

Interior Scene

Hinterland Scene

Matthew French Young and his grand-daughter
Mrs Karen Caballero

CHAPTER XX
Road Construction Bartica-Potaro 1960-64 and 'Retirement'
from Public Service

I joined Engineer Ramsamouge at 4 mile compound – on the Bartica-Potaro road in May 1960. I was allocated a two-room aluminium house with kitchen and bathroom attached and a camp attendant to cook and wash for me. The compound was situated on a hill at a bend in the road. There was a small clear-water creek at the base of the hill across the road. I was surprised at the number of awara palm trees growing in this area. When their ripe seeds drop to the ground they are collected and sold in the market. They are also a favourite food of akuri and labba. The office was situated at another compound a mile from my living quarters. Here the stores were kept and the gasoline and oils for the equipment working on the road.

Work was already in operation when I took charge, at 9 mile section, where two caterpillar D/7 and D/6 bulldozers were cutting through a white sand hill to a depth of fourteen feet and pushing the material into a gully one hundred and twenty feet wide by forty feet deep. When the afternoon rains fell, the drainage from the two hill slopes met on the fill and tore away the white sand shoulders. The engineer proposed laying a hollow concrete tube to drain the embankment, but I told him that as long as there was no support to throw the water off the fill, he would find the concrete tube washed down into the gully if there was rain during the night. This proved to be the case when we arrived at the site next morning. I asked the engineer to allow me to put my bush knowledge to the test. I put twenty axemen on the felling and cutting of twenty feet lengths of hardwoods four to six inches in diameter and posts seven feet long by six inches in diameter. I instructed my Amerindian gang to locate and fell some turru palm trees and plait the leaves into bundles. At the same time, I asked them to cut a good amount of hardwood pickets, five feet in length and two inches thick.

I started my operation by having the shovelmen dig a drain right across the base of the fill from hill foot to hill foot, two feet by two feet. The hardwood posts were then planted ten feet apart to a depth of four feet, leaving three feet above ground level. The twenty foot beams were then laid in the drain, bracing against the inside of the posts. The Amerindians then took the turru palm leaves, split them and laid them head to tail and forced them between the beam and the embankment. The hardwood pickets were then driven in at an angle of 45 degrees to hold the leaves pressed down on the beams, leaving one foot exposed and spaced at eight and ten feet intervals. Then the white sand from the fill was pulled down to cover the leaves and the beam. This was repeated until the beams met to the top of the posts. A platform three feet wide was left before another row of posts were planted ten feet apart across the fill. The same operation was carried out thirty feet up from the bottom of the spoil hill. I then dispatched some of my Amerindians to cut young bamboo canes in two foot lengths at the points where the 'eyes' were full. I had the men plant these in the same way as I knew cane tops were planted on sugar estates, on the road shoulder and at the top of the embankments. The rain and the sun did the balance, for when the buds burst out and the bamboo caught root, nothing short of an earthquake could move the embankment. (I first learned this bamboo work on the sea defences on the first sugar estate I worked. I had also used the same principal in building stop-offs in creeks when I was working gold.)

At 8 mile section, there was a low flat through which a small creek crossed the road. The engineer had got the bulldozers cut and fill this flat with dirt available nearby, but it had only turned into a mass of mud in which trucks and machines got bogged down. I put a stop to this and had a fifteen cubic yards scraper cut, load, transport, and dump white sand from the hill to the beginning of the fill. As the area of white sand grew it pushed the mud away. The scraper continued to dump and at the same time compact the white sand, so that the trucks could dump and return without fear of being bogged down. I then placed two concrete culverts across the fill to take off the creek water. When these two tasks were completed, I had the D/8 Cat tractor clear areas I had prospected for sand clay deposits and where I had decided the road should be widened and realigned.

Sadly, I had one fatality when my D/6 Cat operator – Drayton – was engaged in throwing down a large greenheart tree by cutting around the roots with the blade of the machine. Usually when the roots are weakened sufficiently, the operator raises his machine blade and pushes the tree down. On this day, his assistant saw the tree swaying and tried to signal Drayton by shouting and waving a piece of white cloth, but Drayton was so engrossed in the operation he did not take notice. The tree fell right across his machine, pinning him to the control levers. I measured the diameter of the tree. It was twenty-four inches. Greenheart is one our heaviest woods. I had to call a power saw operator to cut the tree so that the men could lift out Drayton's body and convey it home. His body was like a limp rag doll, for the weight of the tree must have broken every bone in his body. Because of this fatality, the work of clearing the forest for the realignment, cutting and filling of the designated roadway was given out on contract from 12 mile to 22 mile.

A surveyor was on hand with his crew to check the levels, at all times. When he was satisfied with the gradients, the Bedford 7 ton trucks were put to loading and dumping sand-clay on the surface, twenty-four feet wide and six inches thick. This was spread and compacted by a large caterpillar grader, then further compacted with a vibratory roller. Only on the hill slopes did I do any stone surfacing. At 8, 9, 10 mile, two and a half inch stone was spread and compacted, then treated with colas; twenty four hours after, one and a half inch stone was laid. This was sealed with hot bitumen and dusted over with white sand.

There were times when the engineer requested a certain quantity of sand-clay spreading to be done each day. It was fun to see the drivers racing to the pit to have their lorries loaded by a diesel three cubic yard shovel and then back on the road to dump their loads. There were times when I had to drive a lorry because a driver was absent. At one time, when the Engineer was absent in town, I encouraged the men to do a little more than their daily hours, by bribing them with a ride out to Bartica after they had completed their day's task. On the engineer's return some days after, he was surprised at the amount of work I had completed. I worked under the supervision of five different engineers to whom I was grateful for instruction in the art of road construction. When the 22 mile mark was reached, the construction came to a halt. The engineer returned to Georgetown and the maintenance of the road was handed over to the Interior District Superintendent, who resided at 72 miles compound on the Bartica - Potaro road.

It was during the last engineer's term of office that I removed the aluminium compound house from 4 mile to the 17 mile section. I cleared one area for my house and a larger area across the road where I erected an aluminium house for a dispenser. Then I supervised the building of four logies on posts, fifty feet by twenty feet by twelve feet, for the labourers and the lorry drivers. During this time, work was going ahead to fill the gap between two laterite hills. It was approximately 500 feet but not as deep as the 9 mile fill. When completed, I cut some four foot posts, six inches thick, painting them black and white to show the slight curve of the fill. They were not a foolproof safety measure. One day, one of my drivers must have taken on too much liquor, or had a late night at Bartica, for he drove his lorry loaded with sand clay into these posts, uprooting them, and then ran off the road onto the embankment and turned turtle. Had his lorry rolled over ten feet before it did, the driver might have been killed as he missed a tree stump five feet high on the embankment. This would have punctured his cab and pinned him inside.

It was at this time, 1962, that the country had a general strike. All transportation ceased and the only contact I had with Georgetown was by listening to the radio. I learned that there was unrest in Georgetown, stores were being set on fire, there was wholesale looting, people were being killed and British troops had landed to quell the disorder. I and many of my men wasted no time in packing up and leaving for the city, for at a time like this a man should be with his family. I was lucky to board the last stone boat travelling to Georgetown.

On the boat, taking the turn at Parika, I could see in the distance leaping flames from the city against the night sky. Entering the Demerara rivermouth, all I could see was smoke and flames in the business and waterfront areas. The Captain had to steam through this smoke and tie up at a wharf where there was no fire. After landing, we could find no transportation, so I and some of the other passengers, including some of my men, decided to walk home. We were stopped by a detachment of British soldiers who wanted to know where we had come from and where we were going. They searched our baggage. I spoke for the men, explaining that we worked in the interior and had just arrived by steamer to be near our families. We were allowed to proceed.

On my arrival home, I found the place in darkness. No one answered my knock so I whistled my favourite call. Only then did my wife open the door to fall into my arms and burst out crying. The family were all fully clothed and their bags packed. My wife explained that matters were so uncertain in the city, one never knew when the house might go up in flames. Next morning, I drove around town and saw plate glass from store windows strewn on the pavements and the road. Police and military patrols were all about, guarding areas still smouldering with fire.

When order was restored, I travelled back to my location at 17 mile, Bartica Road to continue with the road maintenance work. Observing the rate at which the maintenance men worked (they were employed on a daily basis), I was thoroughly disgusted by the waste of time in an eight hour day. I spent a day working at sifting and loading inch and a half stone to see what could reasonably be expected. Then I checked on how long it took to load a lorry with sand clay and how long it took to spread a square yard. I worked out a figure for these jobs and gave out future work on a piecework basis. At first, the men said it could not pay. When eventually they got into their stride,

they earned more and were able to go home earlier and were happily satisfied. I gained nearly 100% in production.

One day after I had started this scheme, the new District Superintendent
drove through my area on his way to Bartica. Not seeing any labour on the
road at 3:00 p.m., he drove back to my house at 17 miles wanting to know
where the labourers were. I told him how I had reorganised the work and
that the men had finished what they had been allotted for the day. The Superintendent told me I had no right to do this as it was against regulations
and that he was going to report me to the Chief Engineer of Roads in
Georgetown. When I reported to the Chief Engineer in town, I explained the
matter as I saw it, leaving out rules and regulations. I asked him if he would
prefer that I put the men back on a daily rate with the men labouring five
hours for eight hours pay. The Chief Engineer gave me the OK to proceed
with my idea. He said he would inform the Superintendent of his ruling. I
had, on numerous occasions, written letters to the Superintendent to draw
his attention to the condition of my lorry tyres. He informed me there was no
money to purchase new tyres. It so happened that a front tyre burst on my
three-ton Bedford tent lorry. The lorry turned over, a porter and the driver
were both injured, and I suffered some cuts on my arm. A passing lorry rescued us and we were treated at Bartica Hospital and returned to 17 mile
compound where I met the Superintendent, who immediately suspended my
driver without proper investigation. I immediately wrote a letter to the Director of Public Works and explained that the Department and NOT the driver
was responsible for the accident, as I had on file copies of letters I had written to the Superintendent, complaining of the condition of my lorry tyres.
My driver was reinstated and I thought it was funny about there being no
money, as the Superintendent had claimed, because I received a full shipment of tyres on the next steamer arriving from Georgetown. Matters came
to a head between the Superintendent and I when he demanded to know
why I was still employing my driver after he had suspended him. I did not
bother to explain that the driver had been reinstated by the Department. I
lost my temper and gave the Superintendent a good cussing and threatened
that the next time he interfered with my men and my work, I would take
matters into my own hands. Of course, my action led to another report to the
Chief Engineer in Georgetown and an enquiry was held. I was held to be
guilty of insubordination, and being 60 years old and due for retirement, I
was asked to resign. This was in 1964.

CHAPTER XXI

Coconut, Rice Cultivation and Painting: Plantation Park – 1966-70

On my return home, my wife told me I should take a couple of months rest, for when I did take stock of my life I realised I had been working on different jobs for the past thirty-nine years without any holiday, for as soon as I finished one job, I was requested to do the next.

On a visit to my niece at Plantation Leonora, a sugar estate on the west coast of Demerara, she requested I do a large painting for one of the walls of her spacious house. I had not painted a picture in my life, but she said since I could do such good pencil sketches, I must be able to paint. Back at home, I found a piece of three-ply board, thirty inches by twenty-four inches, which I first covered with a coat of white enamel paint. As I waited for this to dry, I drew on my memories of the numerous scenes of beauty I had witnessed in my travels in the interior. I decided on a scene from the Berbice river where the mountain sloped down into the river. I painted a brilliant sunset behind the mountain, the reds and yellows reflected in the clouds and in the river. In the foreground I painted three palm trees, black against the sunset. This picture, when hung in her house, created quite a stir and a demand from her friends for me to paint more scenes. I changed from plyboard to tentest, using the rough side to create a canvas effect. I took some ideas from the pencil sketches in my survey note books; after one has lived in the jungles for over twenty years, one can never forget the colours.

There was a demand for paintings of our highest waterfall, Kaieteur, with its drop of 741 feet, Mt. Roraima on the Brazilian-Venezuelan apex to Guyana, savannah grass lands, scenes from the various roads on which I had worked, river scenes and waterfalls and mountain landscapes. I was advised to put twenty-two of my paintings on exhibition in the Museum building. Customers immediately snapped these up. I painted some scenes of the city – the tree-lined Main street, Stabroek Market, St. George's Cathedral, the largest wooden building in the world – but my really good paintings were of the interior which I had come to know so well. A Roman Catholic priest who purchased a scene of Mora rapids with some Indians streaking the turbulent waters in their corial said that he bought the painting as the movement of the waters looked so realistic. Another of my scenes, that of the logging operations at Winiperu Landing in the Essequibo River, was purchased by the Venezuelan Ambassador and presented to President Leoni, and it now hangs in the Presidential Palace in Caracas. Other paintings have reached England, Canada and Africa. On the occasion of our Independence celebrations, the Prime Minister requested I paint local scenes for all government departments. Four of my paintings were purchased by a gentleman from McKenzie to hang in their Community Centre. An Englishman with whom I had worked gold at Tamakay Mines Mazaruni River who subsequently became an R.A. wrote me a very nice letter pointing out how I could improve my work of a picture of a creek scene by adding trees hanging over the water to cast a dark shadow on the already brown waters. He said this scene was an enticement to cast his fishing line in the shadows and pull out a haimara.

Eventually I started to paint on canvas with oils I received from my niece in the United States. Proper canvas could not be purchased locally and the paints and correct brushes were so expensive. I have continued painting over the years whenever I had leisure time, though there were times when I did not put a brush to canvas for at least a year. I did much travelling in the countryside and up the coastal creeks. After six months, I started to feel a yearning for the bush again. I was offered a job managing a coconut estate on the Mahaicony Creek. It was an open air life which appealed to me. The salary was not large but I looked on it as a pension. I was to occupy a large bungalow built on twelve foot brick pillars. It had three large bedrooms, a large living room, kitchen and store room, a large bathroom and toilet and a small private office. The whole building was mosquito-proofed. Lights were supplied by a Petter diesel engine, and water was pumped up into the house by a semi-rotary pump for bathing and cooking purposes. The few pieces of furniture were antiques made of mahogany wood. The proprietor, Mr. Sankar, an Indo-Guyanese businessman, asked me to estimate the money I would require to put the estate in order for the coming year.

I inspected the entire estate – Park North and South sections and the outlying section of Huntley further up the coast and two sections across the Creek. When I presented my figures to the proprietor, he nearly had a fit. He said this was an estimate for Booker Bros., the largest owners of sugar estates and not for him. I asked him if he wanted a flourishing coconut cultivation or just pasture land.

There was no proper drainage in any one of the sections, Stagnant water was killing the young plants; grass and bush were choking up the trees. I started on drainage in the northern section of Park, digging drains and canals. I used the mud from the drains to mould up all the coconut trees. This work was called mulching on sugar estates. Inlet kokers from the Mahaicony Creek were opened at high tide to swell the water in the four foot trenches and canals, into which the coconut pickers threw the coconuts they had picked. When the tide fell, the nuts floated down to the roadside or the factory area where they were counted and transported by tractor-trailer to the compound. At the end of each week, these nuts were distributed between some fifteen women from the surrounding neighbourhood who were regularly employed to cut open the husks and dig out the flesh. During the dry weather, this flesh was put on the concrete drying floors until it turned a nut brown or the finished product: copra. During the rainy seasons, the ovens in the factory were used to dry the flesh on trays of wire mesh – a temperature gauge was used to prevent the crisping of the coconut flesh. Then the copra was bagged off and weighed – each bag containing from 150lbs. to 180lbs. The copra was shipped to the oil mills in the city for which we were paid fourteen and a half cents per pound.

Due to the lack of proper administration, there had been a general decline in the drainage and cultivation, consequently a drop in the number and quality of nuts recovered. Weeding of the cultivation had only been done once a year, but I pressed that this be done at least twice yearly. I rebuilt approximately five hundred feet of creek dam, where the waters from the creek was undermining the embankment. The proprietor had estimated a cost of $5,500.00 for this repair. I rebuilt the dam using the same principle as I had on the Bartica-Potaro Road at 9 mile section, but instead of using greenheart materials, I used coconut trees and the leaves from the coconut palm, using greenheart piling and pickets only to brace the dam. When completed, it had only cost $2,000.00, a saving of $3,500.00. For the whole of 1966, I barely reaped 1,000,000 nuts. These were of a poor quality and when sold to the local copra makers, only fetched $28.00 per thousand.

I also suffered a setback in expenses when the cultivation was attacked by worms. Insecticides had to be purchased and sprayed between the branches by a hand-pump with a long hose attached to a long bamboo. Boys and girls were employed during this season and coconut pickers were paid extra for catching the little brown and yellow butterflies that laid their eggs on the coconut leaves. The evidence of nests with hatched worms was seeing two or three leaves stuck together on a branch; these were cut from the branch and tied in bundles. I paid ten cents for a nest, fifteen for a butterfly. Then there were the pupas found hanging from the bole of the trees or the branches; also the rhinoceros beetle which bores into the centre of palm, into the heart, killing the tree. Then there were the borer worms, about four to six inches long, which have soft white bodies but powerful cutting jaws, that eat under the lowest branch. Young coconut plants were a prey to the large black beetle which bores into the root of the plant, killing it. This was why I pressed for a cleaner cultivation so that any outbreak of pest infestation or disease could easily be detected and checked before it spread. In my office I kept empty jam bottles with pupas or cocoons showing the life-cycle of the butterflies and the hatching of worms. This reminded me to have my cultivation inspected.

The manager of a neighbouring estate, a Scotsman, who had been an overseer at Plantation Uitvlugt when I was at Tuschen, asked me to go with him to call on the Minister for Agriculture to demand a higher price for our copra. We were advised to form an association of all coconut estate proprietors and approach the government as a body. It started well, but on getting no encouragement from the government, members dropped out. Today the government has to import cooking oil, whereas the country, with its thousands of acres of bearing coconut palms, could have supplied sufficient oil for our needs and had enough to export to the Caribbean islands. The following year, I reaped 1,000,000 nuts by the half year, of a better quality, which brought a higher price. This proved that a better drained and a cleaner cultivation paid off.

However, in 1967, I resigned from Plantation Park to join the Fraser family, the proprietors of Plantation Drill. At Plantation Drill, which was made up of five sections of land, I met with the same problems I had encountered at Plantation Park. I explained to the proprietors that it would take a small fortune to put the estate back on its feet. I was going to take it section by section, making each section pay for itself before moving on.

I experienced a serious setback in the first few weeks I took over as Manager. At 3:00 a.m., Rutherford, the pig-minder, rapped my door to report that thieves had broken open the pens and stolen 101 young pigs. I had instructed Rutherford to pen all the pigs as I wanted to check all the stock on New Year's day. The local police were called in but proved of little help in recovering any pigs. Rutherford had his two sons sleeping with him, as well as two guard dogs, yet he claimed he had heard nothing. I later learned these young pigs were sold to individuals down the coast and as far up river as Hyde Park and that the whole thing had been engineered by Rutherford and others. He was dismissed.

The back yard of the proprietor's house was used to rear feathered stock, Pekin and Moscovy ducks, turkeys, chickens and pigeons. Fruit trees abounded on the premises, mangoes, pawpaw, custard apple, sapodilla, soursop, sweet oranges, grapefruit, lemons and lime. This produce was collected every weekend and shipped to the city on Sundays. There was also a beautiful garden of flowers of all kinds. I checked sixty-five head of cattle – milking cows and steers, with one old zebu bull which was inbreeding the young cows. Plantation Drill had boasted a herd exceeding two hundred head but during the 1962 disturbances, cattle thieves had gone into the pasture at night, killed and skinned animals and sold the carcasses to the local butchers. I instructed my men to round up the herd from the pastures every afternoon and place them in the paddocks at the rear of the cow pens and adjacent to my house. My check on the remaining pigs amounted to 189 large sows, boars, and piglets. I purchased two young boars from the Government breeding station. The whole herd comprised pure whites. Every two weeks, I shipped four large pigs, approximately 185 to 195lbs. each, to the city by the estate land rover. There were also ten heads of horses, small in stature due to inbreeding. I purchased a mare with some good blood in her, putting her to stud with an English stallion from a neighbouring estate.

I took in a five acre patch, drained and fenced the area, then planted hybrid corn, pumpkin, watermelons, eschallot and a variety of greens for the local markets, but as fast as I could plant, there were thieves who timed my operations and in many cases, reaped before I could. I had two rangers (special constables) who patrolled these gardens as well as the coconut cultivation. I had to dispense with the services of one as he was working hand in glove with the thieves.

I had a D/4 Caterpillar tractor of ancient vintage, three tractors and numerous ploughs to deal with my rice cultivation. The yield per acre was very poor when I took over as manager – only eight bags of paddy per acre. I told the proprietors it was better to graze cattle on this acreage. I brought up the use of chemical fertilisers with them, but was told Plantation Drill had the best land in the area. I visited rice farmers in the Mahaicony Creek and up and down the coast. Most of them were using fertilisers of some kind. I tried putting some sulphate of ammonia on a ten acre field of rice plants already two feet high. I was rewarded by reaping sixteen bags of paddy per acre. The following year, I shied various types of seed, using different fertilisers. I noted these in my field notebook for comparison on reaping. This crop gave splendid results.

Planting and reaping were the busiest times for the men and I, working up to midnight to bring in the crop. Rice forms the principal food of nearly one third of the whole human race and it sports more varieties than any other known grass. It has been cultivated in India and China from time immemorial and it is known under as many as one thousand three hundred different names. Two thousand eight hundred years before the birth of Christ, there was established in China a ceremonial ordinance by which the Emperor Chin Nung and his successors themselves sowed the rice whilst the seeds of four plants were sown by the Princess of the Royal House. Regard a rice field and consider that this plant was being sown by man nearly five thousand years ago.

Although most varieties of rice must have plenty of water in order to thrive, there are some varieties known as "hill rice" which can do with very little water. This variety is cultivated in our upland savannahs. Hill seed taken from Venezuela and planted on the river flats of Arakaka and Barima flourished so abundantly that the weight and dimensions of the grain weighed the plant down to the ground. The frequently repeated statement that Indian settlers introduced rice growing in Guyana is not in accordance with historical fact, as it was not until 1865 that the Indo-Guyanese began to grow rice here on a commercial scale. A hundred and fifteen years before that date, Storm Van Gravesande, the great Dutch Governor of Essequibo and the founder of Demerara, in a dispatch written to the States General in Holland, from Fort Island 19th June 1750, stated, "The English Colony in Carolina derives most of its revenue and support from the cultivation of rice. The soil in our colonies produces rice of a much better colour and size than that of Carolina. In Carolina, the crop takes a year to grow. Five months only are required in Essequibo." It was undoubtedly Van Gravesande who first saw the possibilities of rice cultivation as a means of providing food for the slaves and by 1800 it was well known that the runaways or "Bush Negroes" commonly grew it in the neighbourhood of their hiding places. Today, production in Guyana can be said to top 250,000 tons.

In my own cultivation, I enlarged the concrete drying floor near my house enabling me to dry more paddy. I re-measured the rice lands and calculated their proper acreage. Some tenants paying for ten acres found themselves having to pay more and some less.

I occupied a two bedroom cottage, with a living room and kitchen attached. I later added an upstairs office. The building was adjacent to the cow pen and paddy bond. I enclosed a small area behind my house in which I planted my kitchen garden, cucumbers, squash, pumpkins, sweet potatoes, cassava, bora beans, peppers and ochro. I had more than enough for my needs and to share with others. I kept leghorn and Plymouth Rock and Rhode Island Red hens to supply me with fresh eggs. I received one gallon of fresh milk from the cow pens every morning. I had to dispense with one cow-minder as he was adulterating the milk so much that, when tested, the instrument hit the bottom of the can instead of remaining buoyant. He was selling milk to make money on the side and filling up with water to replace the deficit.

The proprietors, who visited every week to bring the money to pay the labourers, treated me more as one of the family. I spent four happy years there. The work was more interesting and the general atmosphere was more genial than when I was at Plantation Park where I was always criticised for spending too much money. I had never received a pat on the back for all the improvements I had done at Park, whereas I had not been six months at Plantation Drill when I was commended for the general appearance of the estate. The proprietors admitted that it was only during my term of office that the estate showed any profit.

CHAPTER XXII
Recalled to Government Service: Self-Help Project, Mahdia, 1970-71

It was in June 1970 when two senior government officers came to see me at Plantation Drill. They were from the Ministry of Works and Communications. They informed me that Mr. Burnham, the Prime Minister, had requested my return to duty, as it was I who had cut the trail from Mahdia - Potaro to the Brazilian boundary. The Government had decided to build this road by self-help. They wanted me to join the project as the senior camp manager. I told them I would have to consider this proposal, for it was this same Roads Department which had called on me to retire and now some six years later, which wanted me back again. I was invited to attend a meeting with the Minister, the Superintendent of the Interior, auditors, engineers and supply officers. I later met the Chief Engineer of Roads and told him that the only way I would resign my job as manager of Plantation Drill was if I was offered a higher salary, with allowances, and a contract for five years. The Engineer said he could not give me a contract but could assure me of constant employment as the Government had dedicated itself to opening the interior. He knew my capabilities and would be glad to have me back. I notified the proprietors of Plantation Drill, giving them notice of my resignation. They were not too pleased about my abrupt departure, and neither was my wife, as she looked on Plantation Drill as a country residence.

It was mid-July 1970 when I was appointed to take charge of Camp No. 1 at 114 mile Bartica-Potaro Road and was flown into Mahdia air strip along with the Minister in charge of Works and Communication, engineers, health officers and others who were inspecting the camp buildings and other facilities being built. There was much to be done to complete this camp before the contingent of overseas volunteers arrived.

The road to Camp No. 2, some ten miles further on to the south, was eighteen inches deep in mud because of the recent rains. This road would have to be filled in with white sand and laterite rock at a later date, to enable trucks to move in to complete the camp buildings. In the meantime, all personnel would be staying at Camp No. 1. Water was pumped from a small creek below the hill into a 400 gallon galvanised iron tank suspended on a trestle 30 feet above the creek. The water was fed by gravity into the camp. There were two diesel engines (Lister) to supply electricity to the huts and the freezing units of the mess hall, and for the radio transmitters. The main building was the mess hall, one hundred feet long, twenty feet wide and twelve feet high, with a storeroom attached. There was one hut eighty feet long, twenty feet wide and twelve feet high already erected for male volunteers. All camp frames were made from bush round-wood with walls of tentest board and roofed with corrugated aluminium sheets. My camp manager's hut also housed the Government Information Services and the radio room. Extra carpenters and plumbers were engaged to erect more camps to accommodate one hundred and fifty volunteers who were students from the University of the West Indies and from England, Jamaica and Trinidad. Showers and latrines for both female and males were provided with running water.

On July 20, 1970 I welcomed twenty young women and ninety-five young men. This alone taxed my accommodation. White sand had to be brought in by lorries, dumped on the muddy hill slope, and spread to a thickness of ten inches on which a tarpaulin was laid. The area was covered with a roof of aluminium sheets resting on the camp frame. Sleeping bags were issued to the students. They had to put up with this rough accommodation until two more huts were completed. These students gave their huts appropriate names: "The Perfumed Garden" for the women; "Taj Mahal" for the men from Trinidad; "Hospital" the largest hut for Jamaicans and the Trinidadians; and, "V.I.P." for students from England. This hut was dubbed by the West Indian students: "Very Ignorant People".

There was a medical centre to deal with first aid injuries. Local doctors took it in turns to do their two weeks of self-help. When they were not available, certified nurses came. Of course, the number of patients increased when a nurse was in attendance. The Government Information Services set up a public address System by which I could speak to the volunteers. This was also used by the volunteers in their weekly concerts. The G.I.S. people also entertained the company by showing movie pictures thrice weekly. A library of fiction and other books was installed in my hut. Anyone could borrow and return when finished. The running of the mess was in the hands of the Guyana Defence Force – a sergeant and two corporals were the cooks. Food of every kind and of the highest quality was served at our tables. It was my duty as camp manager to welcome all incoming volunteers. This I did when everyone was gathered in the mess hall for their first meal. I told them that the Prime Minister had told me to draw up a set of rules and regulations for a smooth running of the Operation. These were the rules:

1. You will be awakened by the "Reveille" a bugle call at 5:00 a.m.
2. Breakfast will be served at 5:30 a.m.
3. You will be ready for work at 6:00 a.m.
4. Snacks will be served in the field at 10:00 a.m.
5. Work will cease at 2:00 p.m. when you return to camp.
6. Lunch will be served on your return.
7. Dinner will be served between 6:30 and 7:00 p.m.

I went on to say: "When in camp, your promptness at meals will be appreciated as your kitchen staff are volunteers too. Be properly dressed at all times when attending the mess hall. Wash your wares at the kitchen sink and dump your waste matter in the garbage cans provided. DO NOT and I mean DO NOT wash your wares other than at the kitchen sink or carry food into your huts as this encourages snakes. Please sweep out your camp huts and avoid littering the compound with paper and empty containers. Drinking water which has been treated with chloride of lime will be found in a 400 gallon tank outside the mess hall. Latrines for both male and female volunteers are provided, please use them, and NOT the bush area surrounding the camp as this would cause a serious health hazard. Remember our drinking water is pumped up from the creek. When lights are put out at 10:00 p.m., this is the time for sleep. I want no volunteer wandering around the compound after dark. Men's huts are out of bounds to female volunteers and more so, vice versa. I do not appreciate those people who try to make others aware of them by the use of unnecessary foul or abusive language. Leave this from where you came. Any uncalled for or noisy behaviour in your huts after lights are out is not permitted for if you do not wish to sleep, others may. Make sure your cigarettes are put out before sleeping, for remember the nearest Fire Brigade is 200 miles away. Entertainment – film shows – will be provided by the G.I.S. and impromptu concerts can be arranged by you yourselves. Women volunteers not employed on road work will assist in the kitchen, preparing and serving meals and also washing up. Their promptness to attend the kitchen when called upon will be appreciated. Should any other problems arise, please talk it over with me. In relation to meals, if there are any who, because of different religious beliefs and faiths do not eat certain meals, etc., I would be glad if these volunteers notify me or the sergeant or the corporal in charge of the kitchen immediately, so that other meals may be provided in time for them." I felt it was important that the volunteers were clear about the rules which were necessary for their safety and the orderly operation of the project.

Since these were mostly city people not used to the bush, I had to take special steps to keep the plentiful insect life at bay. My camp attendants would daily spray the huts after the volunteers left for work and the garbage cans, the areas around the kitchen, Mess Hall and the latrines with Baytex powder. My other duties included the keeping of proper books. This was set up by the Audit Department. A record was kept of all incoming foodstuffs, rum, cigarettes and their issue. A record of tools issued to volunteers and a receipt of all fuels and oils had to be kept, as did a list of the incoming volunteers.

The volunteers soon got to know my ways. When the constable failed on many occasions to blow the reveille on time, it was decided to tape it and play it over the public address system. When this failed, I had to revert to bidding the volunteers: "Good Morning, it's time to rise and shine. Get cracking". This last phrase stuck, and I was known henceforward as "Get Cracking Young". I used to take a plunge in the cold waters of the Mahdia Creek in the early hours and called upon the volunteers to do likewise. They bluntly told me they were not "fishes".

After breakfast, the volunteers were divided into various work groups by the project superintendent and put in the charge of leading hands from the Works Department. Volunteers worked with power-saw operators from the department who cut up the large bush wood, which they picked up to clear the realigned roadway. Many volunteers suffered minor injuries and were treated at the first aid station, and there was an occasional scare when they encountered the dreaded labaria snake.

Ministers of Government spearheaded each team arriving on the project, starting with the Prime Minister, who felled the first tree with an axe. His good wife learned to operate the power saw.

I had my trials as camp manager dealing with some of these students. They continually kicked over the traces, smuggling rum into their huts, smoking pot and of course disobeying the rule about not inviting the young women into the men's huts after lights were out. I spoke to them on several occasions, imploring them to fall into line and desist from making a noise, as others wanted to sleep. They told me that this was how they behaved at university. They promised to behave, but the moment my back was turned, they started again, even inventing rhyming calypsos about me, using all the high class words they knew to make them more effective. I could do nothing but "grin and bear it". However, after the first week, when some of their energy had been worked off, we got to understand each other, so much so that they honoured me by renaming Camp No. 1 as "Camp Young".

There were many amusing incidents, one of which was when a young woman interrupted my coffee to complain that one of the male students was stealing her panties from the line outside her hut. I left my coffee and went across to the radio room and, picking up the public address system, asked the young man who had taken the panties and bikini from the clothes line as a memento, to please return them immediately. Of course, my announcement was greeted by cheers. The gentleman did respond by returning the young woman's belongings. Another time, a group of pundits came in their own plane to do their stint of work. I had to issue four 5 lb. tins of ghee to them. They held their religious ceremonies to which all were invited. A good many volunteers later complained of a touch of dysentery after eating the dholl which was provided after the puja. One volunteer was heard to say to the cook: "Na cook da dholl again".

Later, a police outpost was opened at my camp, comprising one corporal and five policemen. Unfortunately, four of these were injured in a Land Rover accident and had to be flown to Georgetown Hospital. One was reported to be suffering from a fractured skull and injured spine and not expected to live. The police at the outpost brought a number of minor incidents to my attention which had to be nipped in the bud. Once knives were pulled out by youths in an argument in the Hospital Hut, and a male volunteer lurking in the vicinity of the women's hut after 10:00 p.m. was sent back to town, as were a small number of volunteers who were not prepared to work. A few internal incidents involving senior government officials were smoothed over.

At various times, no less than twenty-six foreign diplomats visited my camp. All congratulated me on its cleanliness. As something new, the "National Co-operative Road Project" attracted many distinguished visitors from foreign countries, newspaper correspondents and radio commentators from the Caribbean Islands, America and England, not excluding our own papers. The Prime Minister of Jamaica, Mr. Manley, came to do his share of work. Learning of my experiences over many years in the bush, he said I should write a book. One government official from Kenya, Mr. S. Awoor Tongoi, said this project was similar to his country's efforts to settle young men in the interior of his country. Whereas our volunteers were paid nothing, they paid theirs a minimum wage, though this is put aside until the area was cleared, then the young men were settled in and given the money they had worked for, to give them a start. Mr. Tongoi said the surrounding country and the soils were so similar to those in Africa that he felt at home. Journalists and members of the British High Commission came to see the work in progress, asking questions and taking pictures.

As the camp became more established, I received four pure white sows, one landrace and one duroc boar, four Holstein heifers and two Holstein bulls and two hundred broiler chicks. The pigs had to be housed in a portion of the chicken run as their pens had not as yet been built. The cattle were tied out to graze, but the first morning after, I found blood on their necks where vampire bats had been at work. I informed the Superintendent of the urgency of providing suitable housing for my stock, and based on my experiences of providing proper feed for this kind of stock during my stay at Plantation Drill, I ensured that proper feedstuffs were ordered from Georgetown. There were particular hazards arising from our situation in the bush. One day, the cow minder was nearly bitten by a carpet labaria snake when using a short sickle to cut grass for the cattle so I ordered a long scythe with which to cut the grass. On another occasion, when my wife was taking a walk to visit the pens, she encountered a five-foot fire snake, also known as the 'akuri matapee' snake due to its swiftness and the marking on the body which resemble the basket plaiting of the matapee, the Amerindians use for squeezing out the juice from the grated cassava root.

To increase the food supply at the camp, a swamp in the creek flat was excavated and pumped out, then refilled with water to raise tilapia fish. I had a chat with the pump operator who gave me some information about tilapia breeding. He told me that tilapia did not lay eggs, but vomited their young. How true this is, I do not know.

When you first arrived at Camp No. 1, what struck you was the scenic beauty, for facing the camp to the west were the towering Ebini Mountains, some 2000 feet high, forming part of the range going across to Konawaruk, Glendor and Kaieteur Falls. I was privileged to see the many changing faces of this mountain. In the early morning, after a night of rain, the mountain seems to be floating on a cloud of white vapour rising from the Mahdia Creek basin. One clear morning, I saw a single ray of sunshine cast by the rising sun falling on the eastern face, giving the rock formation a pink colouring. It seemed as if a window had been pushed up to allow this horizontal beam of sunlight out. In the heat of the day, a mauve light suffuses the mountains. With the setting sun, the colour changes to deep green, merging to dark grey. One evening there was a brilliant sunset. It seemed as if the clouds were on fire with reds and orange mixed with dark browns and black. I later tried to capture this effect on canvas, but having witnessed the real thing, I was not satisfied with my reproduction. During the rainy season, the different coloured blossoms and the many-hued leaves with their changing colours gave a brilliant setting to the mountain, rising behind in gigantic steps. I later

painted this mountain reflected in the water of the fish ponds. It turned out
to be an eye-catcher.

Guided by an Amerindian, Joseph Patrick, and accompanied by the Agricultural Officer, and against my wife's wishes for she said I was too old, I
followed an old Amerindian hunting line crossing over Mahdia Falls. We
skirted a large pond or lake, climbing onto a laterite ledge where I had crossed
my 1959 survey line, and three streams before we started to mount the laterite
slope. Our guide had to swing to the north to bypass some immense granite
boulders. We rested about three-quarters of a mile from the peak and
quenched our thirst from an ice-cold spring bubbling out of the rock. The
last quarter mile was practically perpendicular. This is where I felt my thigh
muscles knotting up and had to practically pull myself up with the help of
trees. At one point, I did not think that I could make it. I had to move very
slowly, constantly pounding my thigh and calf muscles. Old pork-knockers
say to take these climbs "Kiti-Kata" and you will "meet". I arrived at the
summit at 10:30 a.m., having left camp at 7:00 a.m. There were ground
kokerite palms growing on this high slope and many hardwood trees; also
exposed granite rocks and laterite. I sat perched on an immense granite rock.
There was a perpendicular drop below me of 700 to 800 feet. I made a pencil sketch showing the camp and Eagle Mountain in the background. I was
later to reproduce this scene on canvas with oil paints. It was purchased
and is now in England. We left the mountain top at 11:15 a.m. The descent
was nearly as difficult as the climb because of the steepness and the loose
laterite gravel. I again had to hold on to trees and shrubs to prevent me from
sliding down. Joseph shot a large red deer and packed it into camp where
we arrived back at 2:00 p.m.

Half an hour after my return I was seized with severe and very painful
cramps in both legs. The men had to massage them with Sloans Liniment. I
could eat no food but drank three cups of hot coffee. I gave Joseph food at
the mess hall, a dollar and some peppermints. I also told him to carry home
the deer as he had a family to feed. Later, I ventured to climb Eagle Mountain, 2,300 feet, situated in the vicinity of 119 mile section, where the Chief
Surveyor had informed me the Americans had a helicopter landing pad at
which point they had put down an Astro fix. He wanted me to locate it so
that our Surveyor could tie in our present road. A gold tributor who was working gold from the sugar quartz offered to show me the path as he was going
to meet his companion. I found the climb much easier than the Ebini Mt., as
previous gold companies who had operated here had cut a tractor road to
within half a mile of the summit. However, the last quarter of a mile was
similar in steepness to Ebini Mt.

From the summit, I had a beautiful view of the mountain near Mahdia airstrip, Mahdia village. To the north-east I could see a large body of water. This must have been the swamp I had passed on my way to Ebini. In the near foreground were two rocky spurs with precipitous sides plunging down into deep gullies leading to the road from the main mountain. I made a sketch of this view. We then followed the edge of the escarpment on a level piece of land until we came out in a secondary clearing about a quarter mile from our climb. The men I had with me managed, after much searching in the second growth and grass, to locate the Concrete Astro fix. From this elevated point, I could discern the vicinity of Tumatumari on the Potaro River. The Essequibo River could be seen as a silver streak in the far distance.

I also accompanied the Project Superintendent on an inspection of the proposed site for Camp No. 3 on the right bank of the Haimararaparu River. The camp ground was on a low hill. There was no scenic beauty there. Around the same time, two Canadian Mounted Police, Messrs. Ken Kramer and Harold McLaughlin, paid us a visit at Camp No. 1 to see something of our country and to get information as to what we were doing to open up the interior.

One unfortunate incident was to mar the closing days of such a happy camp. This occurred on 10 December 1970 when I had to investigate a report that a group of Afro-Guyanese from the militant Black cultural group ASCRIA were molesting a young Indo-Guyanese boy. When I called upon them to act as true volunteers and live together as friends, one strapping Afro-Guyanese with a full beard approached me and pointing his finger in my face said, "You ain't no boss man for me", and said that if they went out to Mahdia village to drink rum instead of working, it was no business of mine. I informed them that as long as they had come as volunteers and were living and eating in the compound, they came under my jurisdiction. If they did not like it, they could leave. Later an Inspector of Police, who had witnessed what occurred in the hut, advised me to get them out of the compound as they were threatening both the Indo-Guyanese boy and me, and other volunteers were saying they were not going to sleep under the same roof.

I, accompanied by a corporal and a police constable returned to the hut and informed the group that as they did not regard me as their camp manager, I was asking them to leave peacefully for Mahdia by lorry and they would stay under Police guard until a plane arrived to transport them to Georgetown. As they left, each one of this group of ten, stopped at my doorway to tell me what he thought of me and to state this was my last day as supervisor of this camp.

Both Camp No. 1 and No. 2 were shut down for the Christmas Holidays, leaving a skeleton crew to keep the place clean. The Ministry workers were allowed their vacation leave. I left a man in charge of the ration store with instructions to issue food for the men at Camp No. 2 but to get a receipt for all deliveries. The radio shack was left in operation so they could contact Georgetown if there was any emergency.

In January 1971, the project reopened. I had been instructed to take over the newly constructed Camp No. 3 at Haimaraparu, as I had more experience. Mr. Cambridge from Camp No. 2 would take over my duties at Camp No. 1; Camp No. 2 was closed down. I took an inventory of my stock, pigs and cattle, as well as the buildings in the compound. On checking my stores, I noted the amount of onions, potatoes, split peas and chowmein which had suffered from the humidity. They were either rotten or full of weevils or fungus and these items to be written off and deducted from my stock books. Before I left Camp No, 1, I had the carpenters extend the ration store and the hospital hut as well as the mess hall to accommodate more food and volunteers for 1971.

On the arrival of fresh volunteers to Camp No. 1, I gave the usual talk on the rules and regulations of the camp. I then introduced Mr. Cambridge, asking the volunteers to give him the same co-operation as I had received. I stayed for a while, for no doctors or nurses had arrived to take charge of the first-aid station and I had to attend to all the patients. Some of the volunteers dubbed me "Mr. Kill or Cure", though I had previously received written instructions from Dr. Egbert as to how to administer the liquid preparations, tablets, etc. I brought my ledgers and other books up to date and handed everything over to Mr. Cambridge.

CHAPTER XXIII
Hiamarapu Camp – 1971-72

I had a very difficult time in moving from Camp No. 1 to Camp No. 3, Haimaraparu Creek, as the rains had set in, making the road tracks slippery. The D/6 caterpillar tractor had to lend some assistance in towing me over some very treacherous spots. At Konawaruk River, I had to leave the bus and transfer to two tractor trailers.

On my arrival at Haimaraparu, I met a half built camp. I informed the project superintendent that the camp was far from ready to receive volunteers. There was no food, no firesides, no coal or gas and no cooks. But still the Superintendent forced the issue by sending in seventy-six volunteers. These people had it very rough, arriving in a trailer towed by a caterpillar D/6 tractor in the pouring rain. I had to serve them hot cocoa, bread and jam. At 4:30 a.m. the following morning, my attention was called to food items strewn on the kitchen floor by my camp porter and the electrician who had got up to prepare breakfast for the volunteers. I discovered a bent aluminium sheet forming a partition to the store room where someone had entered. A large footprint was discovered on top of a deep freeze where the man had stood to enter. Later on, one of the men discovered another set of food items hidden in the yard behind a fallen tree. Suspicion fell on one of the Government employees, as he had been in the mess hall very early. I asked him to stand on the deep freeze and his foot fitted the print exactly. I next examined his ration box which was fully stocked, whereas the other men's ration boxes were nearly empty. The matter was reported to the Superintendent who immediately transferred the man as his fellow employees complained that they had been missing food from their ration boxes.

Preparatory to moving in more equipment and supplies, a civil aviation pilot landed on Hiari Air Strip to test the runway. This was a continuous stretch of laterite rock. It was decided that the approaches had to be opened wider by a further clearance of trees and laterite gravel had to be excavated from nearby to be spread over the rock. Soldiers and civilians were engaged, with the assistance of power saws, to clear these trees. Heavy equipment arrived from Northfork – five lorries, a front-end loader and a bulldozer. Instructions were that they transport and spread laterite gravel at the turning ends of the runway. The work had to be finished in one day. I prepared breakfast for them at 6:30 a.m. and they continued up to 10:30 a.m. when the job was completed. I must say there was a high degree of co-operation between the workmen and the staff, for when there was any emergency, the men did not back off, but pushed day and night to complete the job. A good example of this was when we had to build another air strip ten miles further on, near Muruwa Creek. This strip, some 4,000 feet in length by 200 feet wide, was completed in record time. This was to accommodate larger planes.

I welcomed as volunteers twenty-one Amerindians from St. Francis Mission Mahaicony Creek – 18 males and 3 females. A few of them I knew from having timber dealings with them when I was manager of Plantation Drill. Soon after, Mr. Albert La Rose and thirty-five of his people arrived from Moruca Mission, Northwest District. He had been recruited at such short notice that he did not have time to purchase pots and pans, shirts, pants and yachting boots. I requested the supplies division of the Ministry of Works to forward these items which would be deducted from their wages. These Amerindians were to do two weeks self help. After this, they worked on a wage basis. They were utilised mostly in bridge building and the erection of camps.

The Deputy Prime-Minister spearheaded a group of Government officials for their week's work. When I pointed out the richness of the soil at Camp No. 3, Haimaraparu, he agreed to supply me with fifty citrus plants (orange, grapefruit, lemon and limes) and fifty coconut trees. When I passed through the camp grounds a year later the lime trees and others were burdened with fruit and the coconut palms were growing strongly. I was, though, very disappointed to learn from a nurse from the Public Hospital Georgetown that she only worked on an eight-hour basis and was not going into the field with the volunteers. Accidents, I explained to her, did not occur in camp but in the field where volunteers were working with tools.

Christian services were held in my office, attended by the project superintendent, police officers and, in the main, young women volunteers. There was so much feeling in the reading of the scriptures and the singing of hymns that the superintendent felt that this was a sure sign of God's presence. He would petition the Prime Minister to have the first town in the interior built here. This was ironical, for it was not three years later that all that remained of our efforts was a track through the second-growth bush, where nature had taken over. The government did not have the money or the machinery to complete such a gigantic task.

I had from the beginning argued against building a road in this area for, having cut the reconnaissance line over a decade earlier, I knew that there were too many rivers and mountains to negotiate to reach the savannah. There was a far better route through which I had walked in 1926 with the late Edwin Haynes, and this was in the watershed dividing the Essequibo River from the Demerara River.

Because of the heavy rains falling at the forward line, it was not safe to send volunteers by lorry to their work site. One lorry climbing a steep laterite clay hill had started to slide backwards and collided with a tree, throwing out all the volunteers. Fortunately, there were no serious injuries. Then, when the grader was climbing Hiari Hill, the gear had slipped and the heavy machine had run back down the hill and overturned. The operator had jumped clear but suffered a shoulder injury and had to be flown to town. On another occasion, the superintendent was descending this hill when the tractor trailer in which he was riding started to slip. The tractor operator, seeing disaster in front of him, jammed his steering wheels into the road embankment. The sudden stop threw the superintendent out, to land on his face and hands. He suffered some cuts and bruises. I had advised that a ledge be cut on the hillside following the contour of the hill to get a more gentle gradient but nothing was done.

In my weekly report, I pointed out that the added work of costing and accounting, plus the work of supervising the volunteers, stores, tools and fuels and also the receiving and posting away volunteers by flight sheets was getting too much for one man to carry. I was up at 4:30 a.m. and worked up to 9:00 p.m. every day, getting no slack time whatsoever. There were other incidents which added to this burden. Once the electrical freezer packed up. I was lucky that thirty-four women volunteers had just arrived at the camp. They cleaned and fried the fish, parboiled the meat and put it to smoke. The tainted meat I buried. I had to fall back on these same young women to prepare a daily menu when the cook, a corporal from the Defence Force, started a go-slow because I had remonstrated with him for not having the staffs' meals prepared on time. I had to contact the Defence Force Headquarters and ask for a replacement. Work also had to be found around the compound for the volunteers because of the constant heavy rains. Early in the morning around 2 or 3:00 a.m. I could hear the water coming off the mountains and by 8:00 a.m. the Haimaraparu Creek and creek flats were under water. On one occasion, two of my operators walking out to North Fork to receive their wages had to swim the Konawaruk River. The water had covered the bridge to a height of eight feet. These men ran a great risk, as the velocity of the rushing waters was terrific.

Finally there was some response to my reports when there was a midyear shutdown to give the Ministry workers a two week holiday. Mr. Cambridge and I were summoned to a meeting in the boardroom of the Ministry of Works and Hydraulics. Mr. Byass, Co-ordinator for the Self Help Road, Mr. Vandeyar, Personnel Officer, Mr. Kingston, Field Auditor, Mr. De Abreu, Public Service Finance, Mr. Westmass, Supplies Officer were in attendance. Mr. Byass said that Mr. Cambridge would continue to be in charge of volunteers and I would be in charge of all Government stores and accounts for employees of the Ministry. I would issue food for the volunteers on an internal stores requisition from Mr. Cambridge and also to the Ministry employees upon receipt of a ration form signed by the employee and countersigned by his supervising officer. I would receive the cargo from Georgetown with a price list plus freight and handling charges fixed by the finance department. This had to be exhibited in the store for information to customers. Mr. Kingston and Mr. De Abreu both stressed the necessity for proper books to be kept. A copy of the employee's total purchases had to be forwarded to North Fork office in time for deduction from the pay lists. Employees could not exceed their credit limit and no wages would be paid to an employee until his ration account had been cleared. Mr. Kingston suggested the employment of a stores assistant who could read and write to assist me with the stores and books, but the issue of stores was to be at my discretion and I was to be responsible for the ordering of all stores food and other stores, the necessary paper work for the keeping of fuels and oils and other materials arriving at the camp ground, and have responsibility for all plant, tools and machinery. I selected an Afro-Guyanese of good education as my assistant, but the Project Superintendent said he had more important work for this man but would give me another man later. This never materialised.

The Minister of Finance arrived with the first batch of volunteers after the resumption of the Project with G.D.F. Cooks and eighty-four volunteers, including my great-nephew, Michael and his friend. There was a shortage of sleeping bags. Some of the volunteers had to sleep on the bare boards of their bunks covered with a blanket. The camp manager from No. 2 took over the duties of handling the volunteers whilst I carried on checking and weighing all incoming cargo. The Audit Department had made it clear that I would have to bring forward all stock in hand and my receipts and issues from the beginning of the year (eight months work). Local purchase orders were to be forwarded from the city, so they could be entered in my daily goods-received book and my ledger. The backlog of bookkeeping kept me employed from 4:30 a.m. to 9:30 p.m. daily, as well as having to issue food for the mess hall and to Ministry employees working in the forward line.

I started on my accounts for the Ministry workers, but was stalled by the absence of any price lists from Georgetown. I had to force through much needed supplies for the construction of Camp No. 4, (piping for water, deep freezers, six-burner gas stoves and other essentials) where the Amerindian volunteers from Moruca and St. Francis missions were engaged in the erection of Camp frames and the building of log bridges. Incoming volunteers landed at Hiari Air Strip by the Twin-Otter plane, then proceeded via motor lorries to Camp No. 4 beyond North Muruwa River. These lorries were being constantly bogged down due to the rough roads.

A lot of my bookwork piled up as I had received no assistant. Then I was moved from Camp No. 3 Haimaraparu to Camp No. 4 on 13 September 1971. I immediately had to put my Amerindian labour onto extending the ration store and build a tool room. From the cold of the deep freezers where I had to take out rations early in the mornings to the heat of the ration store, I noted I was constantly getting colds. I found my whole body trembling from nervous exhaustion for I had had no rest since the resumption on 7 August.

I wrote out my resignation as camp manager to the Co-ordinator of the Self-HelpRoad Project, because of overwork and not having received an assistant as promised on my appointment in July. I returned to Georgetown where I was met by the Co-ordinator who conveyed me home. I informed him I was going to see a doctor the following day. I visited St. Joseph's Hospital and the doctor prescribed two weeks complete rest. I reported to the Co-ordinator the following day and handed in my resignation. He said he could not let a good man go and he would rectify the absence of an assistant immediately. Bill Foster, who really dealt with timber, was assigned to assist me in the stores and would in his spare time assist with the books. On my return to Camp No. 4, after a week's absence, I found that all the cargo which had been shipped up during my absence had not been checked and there were no records of what had arrived. I asked camp manager Cambridge why the cargo had not been checked, weighed and entered in the books. He bluntly told me that this was not his job.

The ending of the rains had brought some relief, though the outbreak of bush fires near the camp caused a new anxiety, but a bucket brigade formed by the volunteers quickly quenched the flames. As the camp became more established, my camp attendant, with the assistance of some of the volunteers, planted some catch crops near the camp. The soil was of a dark sandy loam. Anything planted there flourished. The greens produced were welcome in the kitchen. The usual kind of incidents occurred. Although volunteers had been told to use the bathrooms and not the creek for bathing, some of the more venturesome still persisted to use the creek until a couple of carpet labaria snakes were killed on the creek flat, deterring further bathing. Rum was being smuggled into camp by the lorry drivers from Mahdia Village, to be sold to the volunteers who created disturbances after lights were out in camp, giving camp manager Cambridge nightmares. Efforts by the Superintendent to stop this proved a failure. Who can stop a river from flowing? On another evening I was brought a message from the Superintendent by the driver of a land rover who had brought in a carpenter with a broken leg. A pontoon had sunk in the river with one of the two bulldozers being brought across the Muruwa river to commence clearing an area for an Air Strip. He requested I send four bottles of rum for the men working on the salvage operations. The men returned to camp at 10:30 p.m. after a successful salvage operation.

The return of heavy rains impeded progress on the Muruwa Air Strip. Machines were working around the clock trying to complete operations as early as possible to enable the strip to receive planes bringing in volunteers. Our operators and lorry drivers gave wholehearted support to this operation. One operator, Oscar Clarke, was constantly on the go. As soon as a machine or a vehicle became idle, Oscar jumped aboard and kept things moving. The Minister honoured him by naming the air strip after him. At 9:15 a.m. on 24 October 1971, the first plane touched down with sixty-one volunteers. I took some colour photographs of this operation and the view of Takwari Mountain rising some 1,310 feet to the east, over which the departing planes flew. To the west were the foothills of the Kurungiku Mountains rising to 2,000 feet and the headwaters of the Muruwa River.

I travelled from Camp No. 4 in company with the acting superintendent via a landrover to within two and a half miles of the Siparuni River, for the track the bulldozers were clearing was blocked by fallen trees. From this point, we walked to the river through the survey line and awaited the arrival of the heavy machines to clear a road to the river bank. On our way back to camp, the bulldozer operators told me they had shot a morabanna snake and that their machines had killed two bush masters, both deadly poisonous snakes. Five miles from Muruwa River crossing, our land rover was blocked by a large fallen tree. Not having the necessary tools to clear the tree from the road, the superintendent and I decided to walk, as it was a brilliant moonlit night, to get assistance from the labourers' camp. We covered the distance in an hour and a half. I dispatched two men with power saws and a tractor. We did not reach the Muruwa River crossing until 1:00 a.m. Two jeeps and a lorry had come to meet us, bringing hot coffee and biscuits. The staff at Camp No. 4 were standing by wondering at our delay. A pontoon built of roundbush wood, buoyed by empty oil drums, was used to cross our

landrover over the Muruwa river, for the steel pontoon which had sunk earlier had been transported to the Siparuni river crossing.

Later, the Superintendent with a crew of labourers and carpenters built a
flat bridge, 1,000 feet in length to cross this river. They cut hardwood blocks
to act as a foundation on which to lay greenheart and other hardwood timber
to form the bridge. I accompanied the Superintendent to witness the crossing of our heavy equipment over the newly completed causeway and bridge.
I was asked to take some colour photographs of the machines crossing over.
When the heaviest piece, the caterpillar front-end loader was on the bridge,
over the river itself, my heart was in my mouth. I was all tensed up until it
reached solid land again.

I took a break form my book work and took my assistant Bill Foster on a
trip to the forward line to meet up with the Army's spearhead from the
Siparuni River crossing. We had to travel by tractor trailer as the trail was
too rough for the land rover. After two tractors got stuck in different creek
and swamp crossings, we decided to walk and passed a D/7 bulldozer on
the hillside with a track slipped off on which the mechanics were working. I
met up with the spearhead of the army, but they still had over a mile to clear
to meet our section. I left at 4:00 p.m. on board a bulldozer which was returning to pull out the tractors stuck in the creeks.

We arrived at the operators' camp by the Siparuni river at 10:00 p.m.
Tractor operator McDonald gave me a hot cup of cocoa and a few biscuits
after which I promptly fell asleep in a bag hammock. The following morning, I felt as if someone had beaten me with a stick as I was stiff and sore.
The best tonic was a dip in the cold waters of the river. Bill and I again got a
lift to return to the forward line. We were determined to be in at the finish, despite our rugged trip the day before without food. From the site of the proposed
air strip five miles beyond Siparuni river, I pointed out to Bill the mountains
bordering Tepuru Creek on the upper left bank of the Siparuni where I had
walked to the top in my reconnaissance survey in 1958 and further on, from
the last laterite hill before descending to the Burro-Burro Creek flats, I
pointed out Watamung mountain on the left bank of the upper Burro-Burro
river. After meeting with the army engineers at the point of "shake hands", I
returned to Camp No. 4 at 10:10 p.m. very tired and glad to get into my cot.
Bill Foster, who was really a timber man, had been impressed with the stand
of timbers he had seen in the Siparuni and Muruwa areas.

This part of the country had caught my eye since I had traversed it on my
1958 survey. I knew of the vast areas of fresh fish in the tributaries of the
upper Burro-Burro river, the gold resources in the upper Siparuni river tribu-

taries, the timber stands on both sides of the river and, not least, the wonderful soil for agriculture which covers most of this area. I tried to encourage some of the younger volunteers, especially the Amerindians from the coastal creeks, to settle here.

Back in camp, I found the camp manager was getting some headaches from a set of the younger volunteers who were creating a lot of noise in their huts after lights were out. Some of these had to be sent back to Georgetown the hard way, by tractor trailer and under police escort. An altercation had also arisen between the camp manager and the Ministry paymaster about space to pay the labourers. He refused to give up his office so I called the paymaster and told him to use my office. I had some problems too. Three Potamona Amerindians, who had been employed at the camp, had taken goods from the stores and absconded, taking passage on a plane from Mahdia back home to Monkey Mountain mission. I had to contact the police outpost there for them to send a patrol to collect the money these Amerindians owed.

I was pleased to meet again Father Metcalfe, the flying priest and a former volunteer at "Camp Young", who flew into Muruwa Air Strip accompanied by a passenger. They were on their way to Lethem where Father Metcalfe was now stationed. He informed me that he flew from as far north as Velgrad down south to Isherton in the Southern Savannah (my base camp in 1937 with the New York Zoological Expedition). We spoke of the Melville and the Hart families who were now living in Brazil at Boa Vista. Father Metcalfe told me there were are as many as sixty-six landing strips in the interior of which Muruwa strip was the best. A Mr. Young from the Public Free Library in Georgetown and others were treated to a land rover trip from Camp No. 4 to Mahdia. They said it was a wonderful job we had done. They were shown some of my earlier survey sketches of my reconnaissance work with my notes. Mr. Young and a Miss Northy said these pictures of the road should be preserved as a historical record.

There were a few incidents such as when an old woman died whose corpse had to be flown to Georgetown, accompanied by a nurse and a policeman and two male volunteers, and when some of the Ministry employees cursed the camp manager when under the influence of liquor.

Ministry Audit officers, a Mr. Legall and a Mr. Duncan who arrived at Camp 4 to verify stock, said Georgetown had informed them that I now had a ledger clerk to assist me. A Mr. Bovell had indeed been sent from town but had been posted to North Fork Offices. I explained to the auditors I had been working fourteen hours a day since August without an assistant and the backlog of work on the books was too much for one man to close by yearend as I had other duties to attend to. The Project Superintendent made a nasty remark when he said that had I not been absent at the forward line for two days to witness the "shake hands" with the army, my books would have been up to date. I replied that had the two days in the forward line been multiplied many times, the period would still not have been long enough to close all the books and that if he had any conscience he would admit that I was at my desk as early as 4:30 a.m. to 10:00 p.m., as long as there was light to work by. Moreover, since the nurse's return to Georgetown with the dead woman, there had been no nurse or doctor at the first aid post and I had been obliged to act in their place.

I must mention that some middle-ranking managers, when in the presence of their superiors or strangers, seem to lose their equilibrium. When I remonstrated with the camp manager for taking items from the ration stores after the stock verifiers had completed taking stock, this man (no gentleman) gave me a first class abusing in front of the volunteers, using all the more coarse words from his vocabulary. If a business is to be run properly, rules had to be followed, especially with Government property and this was my responsibility.

I completed the accounts, shipped out all the perishable goods from my store and sent them, along with my books, to Georgetown. For months I had known no rest. When I finally returned home, my whole body was a mass of nerves. In early 1972 I was sent to North Fork to assist the stock verifier in handing over the stores to the army. I was then referred back to Roads Division. Mr. Rohlehr, Senior Surveyor, asked me if I knew about a railway survey in 1913 from Boa Vista, Brazil to Georgetown, British Guiana. I told him that I had heard about this from the late Edwin Haynes, then Government Surveyor.

CHAPTER XXIV
Road-building: Wismar-Mabura Hill – 1972

I was instructed to join Engineer Balbahadur and Road Superintendent George Todd in locating a road along the ridge dividing the Demerara and Essequibo Rivers from Wismar on the Demerara River to Mabura Mountain to enable the Forestry Department to penetrate the greenheart forests. My duties were similar to those I had been doing on the self-help road project: machinery, vehicles, tools, fuels and oils and the ordering of food for the men. I was later to assist the surveyor in locating the best route to follow.

I travelled by land rover from Georgetown to Wismar via MacKenzie Road, crossing the Demerara river bridge. I stopped at surveyor Sooklall's camp near the tributary of a creek. Here the two men I had with me filled plastic jerry cans with fresh water. It was hard going for the land rover as we had to follow a deeply rutted road of loose white sand to a point six miles from Wismar where we swung south along the ridge for two miles where we met Bishop's Camp. Here the men were instructed to open an area and erect four round-wood camp frames for tarpaulin tents.

I had assisted Mr. Todd in Georgetown in selecting the necessary machinery and lorries to work on this project. There was a D/7 caterpillar bulldozer to be used in clearing and a D/6 caterpillar bulldozer to cut and level the roadway. A bridge at 11 Mile section had to be reinforced with hardwood timbers to enable our heavy equipment to cross. This was at Powis Creek, the first of the many streams that we were to cross. I built a tarpaulin camp near the creek on the flat, but when the heavy rain fell, I found water running through the camp and we had to move to higher ground. I found there was a "catch cow" formation two feet below the sandy surface preventing the water from penetrating. I was exceedingly cold, camped on this sand, not helped by the crowing of the powis which used to wake me up in the mornings.

On my return to Georgetown to purchase some food and endeavouring to pack my ration box, I suffered a slipped disc in my lower back. I had to be assisted upstairs by my wife and daughter. I was treated by a physiotherapist but was still laid up for five days before reporting back to Roads Divi-

sion office. I collected two steel canisters in which to keep my books and
stationery, drew a cheque for $400.00 to advance ten new men to purchase
food for their employment on the project and visited the Public Works yard
where I selected an old chassis with a wooden body, used previously by the
community development. This I had converted to a trailer to house my office
on the road, thus saving the need to erect a camp office on every camp ground.

Surveyor Ross and a crew of men, guided by an Amerindian who lived
and worked in the area, were to spearhead our road construction. The ridge
we were to follow swung back and forth, sometimes near the one river and
then swinging heavily to the other. The surveyor was lucky to find an old
timber road sixteen and a half miles from our starting point. This acceler-
ated our progress a great deal until they had gone twenty-four and a half
miles at which point a line had to be traced through the forest to enable us
to keep on the ridge, emerging onto another timber road. Workmen were
kept busy trimming all the overhanging branches to allow free access to lorries and graders. All protruding tree stumps and roots had to be cut out with
axes and mattocks and deep holes refilled. Our route lay through white sand
country and light muri and dacama bush.

Camp No. 3 was located just within the 40 mile section on the right bank
of a tributary to Kwapanna Creek, a large black water, which discharged on
the right bank of the Essequibo River. I assisted the surveyor in trying to
locate a feasible ridge around the head of this creek, but after passing through
a manicole swamp, the land climbed to a high and rugged granite and laterite
peak on the ridge. The superintendent, Mr. Todd, decided to follow the timber trail and cross the main Kwapanna River at a spot where a timber mer-
chant had his compound at the foot of a steep white-sand hill. Before crossing, Mr. Todd had his bulldozers cut and push down white sand from the
nearby hills to cover the existing corduroy timbers to a depth of two feet and
compact it to prevent our equipment and vehicles from slipping off into the
soft creek flat. Our progress had been through scrub bush intermingled with
wallaba forests, but at 40 miles we were entering an area of greenheart forest. Meat for our pot was fairly plentiful with deer, labba, akuri, powis and
an occasional tapir and, of course, haimara fish. There were three or four
instances of our men and vehicles meeting pumas on the road leisurely crossing sometimes at midday but mostly in the late afternoons. Once an empty
timber trailer was in the 35-37 mile area, when the driver spotted a jaguar
on the road. He put his foot down on the accelerator and chased the jaguar
down the road, not giving it a chance to break for the bush, but my friend
the jaguar, finding the heat of the chase too near, swung in its tracks and

leapt onto the cab of the truck. The driver slammed up his window. He was greatly relieved when the jaguar, not getting any purchase on the engine hood, fell off and disappeared into the bush.

At the 42 miles section, we had to swing from Johnson's Road to Klautky's Road so as to follow the ridge. It was very interesting to note that as the texture of the soil changed, so did the forest. In the white sand areas were muri and dacama bush – a light growth, then on the same sand, miles of wallaba forest intermingled with soft woods of silverballi, simarupa and others. On the brown sand loam, hardwoods and greenheart grew in profusion. On the red laterite clay were many species of hardwoods, purpleheart, wamara, cockaralli and many others. In the softer creek flats, stretches of crabwood and white cedar grew. We experienced some difficulties between the 47 mile and 49 mile sections as we had to deal with some steep red clay hill slopes. When the rain fell, rubber-wheeled vehicles had to await a tractor to give them assistance in climbing or drivers had to walk to the nearby timber compound of Klautky and ask for assistance. Weathered laterite rock and gravel were found on this red clay. I had the bulldozer clear the forest at these spots and heap up the laterite material to use on the maintenance of the road at a later date. The bridges over both the Mariparu and the Mariappa Creeks had to be reinforced to take our heavy equipment. These two creeks are upstream of the Arisaru Mountain where our road route was diverted from west to east, passing over a shoulder of the Arisaru Mountain to the west and Tiger Hill to the east. Both were mostly iron ore or laterite formations.

I had to build a temporary camp at 48 mile section for there was a four hundred foot stretch of soft clay on the right bank of the Mariappa creek through which the vehicles had a hard time crossing. Lengths of hardwood timbers were laid side by side, three together, and pinned into place by hardwood pickets at spaces of two and a half feet, then a next set of three timbers were laid side by side and pinned. The entire four hundred feet was corduroyed lengthways, then the lorries were loaded with white sand which they dumped over this corduroy work to a thickness of two feet, which was compacted by heavy machinery. This formed a solid road on which vehicles could cross safely. Approaching the bridge at the 49 mile section, which was fifty-six feet long, the creek was only two feet deep, but the approach was of a catchcow clay, very hard and very slippery when wet. In this section, both day and night we encountered bush cows or tapirs feeding on the congo pump leaves, a favourite food for them.

During the time we were in this area, there was a crew of gold workers prospecting the Appaparu Creek which discharges into the Demerara River, but they found no favourable deposits and had to move on. On crossing this creek, we again encountered brown sand. The work crews used to encounter a jaguar taking his ease on the road way. At a later date, I found tracks of what seemed to have been a family reunion, for I saw the smaller pug marks from the cub along with the larger pug marks of the mother and father.

On leaving the brown sand, we again encountered white sand, the forest changing once again to muri and dacama bush. At this point in the 50 mile section, we had to leave Klautky's Road and swing to the west to follow the ridge. If followed, this would carry us out to the Demerara River some two and a half miles beyond this point. Mr. Ross, the surveyor, had been told by Mr. Klautky of an old track which passed through an area of fire-consumed bush to meet one of Klautky's roads crossing from the Demerara River to the Essequibo River. The D/7 cat. bulldozer had a good deal of work to do, not so much trees to push down but clearing fallen and burnt logs and acres of giant wild ferns. At one spot, the blade of the machine disturbed the slumbers of the giant anaconda snake amongst the ferns. The snake, twenty-seven feet in length, was quickly dispatched with a gun shot. Some time was spent here whilst the surveyors were tracking the ridge, as the area was a wide flat of white sand. Eventually the east-west road was located from river to river.

On crossing the east-west road, the ridge soil again changed back to brown sand with greenheart and other hardwood forests. The brown sand changed to a brown clay and then dipped suddenly into a gully. The other side formed a laterite formation of large boulders. The surveyors traced the line to surmount a high hill of loose black laterite gravel. The bulldozer was set to grading down the gravel from the hill slope and stockpiled at the hill foot. No road could follow the surveyor's line over the hill so I set my men on to following the contour of the hill, which proved to have nearly a level gradient, to connect to one of Mr. Van Long's concession lines for his timber grant. From the foot of the hill, the ridge followed a narrow course over honeycombed laterite rock through which water was springing. At 59 mile, I found a small lake at the top of the ridge. I collected some orchids from this area. At 57 miles I had taken the opportunity of climbing the laterite peak from where I had a clear view of the north of Arasaru Mountain; to the north-east, I saw the mountains dipping down into the river at Great Falls on the Demerara River. I caught a glimpse of Mabura Mountain to the south. I made some pencil sketches in my note book from this peak. The ironstone ridge where I stood continued north-west and then west to within six miles of the Essequibo River and Mr. Van Long's timber compound. The terrain on either side of the ridge dropped away steeply to ravines and creeks leading out to both rivers.

On leaving this laterite ridge, we met an area of white sandy silt which formed a quagmire for vehicles when the rain fell. It was also overshadowed by giant mora and purpleheart trees. Power saws were used to widen the road and to let the sunlight in. Then the lorries were loaded with laterite, gravel and rock to spread in the wheel tracks to enable the lorries to proceed more freely. We had to surface portions of this road from 61, 62, 63, 64 miles with corduroy covered with a heavy layer of white sand. This work could only be carried on in the dry weather when the lorries could manoeuvre without mishaps. What held things up was that as fast as this area was cleared, the timber grant owners used our roadway to haul out their timbers and, of course, make a terrible mess. Due to the constant breaking down of our lorries, this sanding work took a couple of months to complete.

At 63 miles section, there was some misunderstanding between the head office in Georgetown and our project superintendent George Todd. Those in Georgetown wanted to know the possibilities of driving a road from this point out to the Great Falls on the Demerara River. Surveyor Ross and his crew were engaged on this, thus slowing our progress to Mabura. I took it upon myself and a few of my men to continue the route to Mabura, tracing a line around the headwaters of the Sarabaru Creek which originates in the Mabura Mountain and discharges in the Demerara River. The watershed at this point of the tracing was very narrow, walking along it the gully heads could be seen to the right and to the left. At 65 mile, I cut a line between the Sarabaru head and the Yaya Creek, which throws its waters into the Essequibo River. I covered about a mile and a half, at which point there was a narrow fifty foot gateway leading up to Mabura Mountain, 950 feet high. The D/7 cat. bulldozer operator, Cyril Vieira, cleared a road up this slope for 4,525 feet, leaving 1,100 feet to reach the summit. Large granite boulders and deep gully heads crisscrossing this route barred his way any further. Then we cut a line from the summit of the climb north-west for a distance of half a mile to emerge onto a rock promontory, giving a wonderful view of our back road as far as Arasaru Mountain. Mabura had a sheet rock face to the west and the mountain itself has no pass, so we had to trace a sand ridge from 65 mile for a distance of two miles, then descend to Yaya Creek flat, which was approximately 740 feet wide. On the other side of the creek, the high lands came to within twenty feet of the creek edge.

A temporary camp was built on the left bank, on the other side of Yaya Creek. Mr. Todd then put on all the heavy machines to clear the greenheart forest on the white sand slopes, then they cut and pushed the white sand across the creek flat to form a causeway twenty feet wide and four feet thick with three hollow wood culverts. The creek flat was of a soft pumpkin-col-oured clay. Men with power saws cut the greenheart timbers for the bridge. The bridge was complete in two days on 13 July, 1972. Two forestry officers and three senior officers from the Ministry of Works paid a visit and agreed this was the end of Phase 1, opposite Great Falls.

During this period of four and a half months, I had to make several jour-neys to the city, leaving camp and travelling out to Wismar at night to get relief from the heat of the white sand during the day. I usually took coffee on the hill overlooking Wismar as dawn was breaking and reached town in time for when the office opened at the Ministry. I had to bring in all the outstand-ing orders for parts for our machinery and lorries as well as order rations for the men every month. Fuels and oils also had to be ordered and arrange-ments made for transportation into the project area. On my last visit to Georgetown on this first phase of the project, I had met the co-ordinator for the Self-Help Road who mentioned that he would like me to come back on the next project, as he felt the other camp manager was not capable enough, but I said that the hydro-power survey wanted me too in the Cuyuni River. He said he would lend me to the survey until he was ready for me.

Heavy rains during the period May-June gave us all a good beating, for on leaving camp in the morning, we never returned to it until 9 to 10:00 p.m., soaking wet and cold. I must say, though, that there was a wonderful relationship between George Todd and his men. They went all out to com-plete Phase 1 on time. All the time I worked along with Mr. George Todd, I felt I worked with a friend who did all in his power to make his men satisfied with the rough conditions under which we all worked. He was always with us through thick and thin.

I spent five days closing all books and accounts, making out a list of equip-ment and tools on hand at Mabura and making up the men's time sheets. Then camp broke up. Later, Mr. Todd met me at Roads Division head office and asked me to return to the project to assist with some more paper work, but I had to decline as I was already tied up in preparing equipment for my next job with the hydro-power survey in the Cuyuni River.

CHAPTER XXV
Hydropower Survey, Cuyuni River – 1972-73

On receiving my letter of transfer from the Wismar-Kuruduni Road Project, I was introduced to the Chief Engineer of the Cuyuni River Hydro-Power Project. The Field Engineer, a young Indo-Guyanese, Rahim by name, who had studied in Yugoslavia and spoke that language, and Mr. Lochan, Senior Surveyor, briefed me as to the location of camps, equipment and radio communication between the various locations of the other surveyors. I would be in charge of the base camp with the ordering of food for the men at Bartica, fuels and oils for transportation, medical supplies, camp and boats, equipment and radio transmitters. I employed a camp attendant and arranged for a transfer of a radio operator I had with me on the Wismar project. I posted my personal belongings with two canisters of books and other items I would require for the keeping of records. Then I went to take my leave of the Chief Engineer of Roads who mentioned that he had told Engineer Boodhoo to get me to lead the reconnaissance survey on the road to be built from the bauxite town of Kwakwani, on the right bank of the Berbice river, along the watershed of the Corentyne river to New river, a left bank tributary of the upper Corentyne river, the frontier to Dutch Guiana. But this would be at a later date.

I left Georgetown in late July in company with Mr. Rahim and our two camp attendants. Rain was falling heavily. The river steamer was packed like sardines, most of the passengers having to stand all the way up river to Bartica where we arrived at 4:00 p.m. Accommodation had been arranged for us at a hotel at Bartica. Surveyor Thompson informed me he felt we would require three more outboard engines for the amount of boats required for our river transportation. I ordered a drum of kerosene oil for camp use. I had to cool my heels at Bartica for two days, as a lorry belonging to our contractor Rafferty was under repair. Rafferty had the contract to transport our cargo from Bartica via the river to Camaria Falls foot – Cuyuni River – then by road around the falls, a four miles stretch. I left Bartica by speedboat for Camaria Falls, the passing scenery bringing back old memories.

At Camaria Falls foot, I met an Amerindian woman, very elderly with grey hair. She made herself known to me for she had assisted my sister in the house at Agatash Estate in 1927. Her name had been Esther Byroe. She was now Mrs. DeSouza, though her husband had died. She was now farming ten acres of land assisted by her son. She had aged terribly since I knew her as a young sixteen year old. She could not be more than fifty-six years of age but she looked at least seventy years. Rafferty's lorry had already transported two loads of our cargo over the falls road. The last trip would carry our party with our baggage. At the first piece of bad road where the lorry had to climb a steep bump, Rafferty asked us to get down from the lorry to allow the ancient motor to climb. Surveyor Thompson told me not to disembark and handed me a tray of eggs to hold. Halfway up the hill, the lorry gave a sudden jerk as it hit a deep hole, causing the eggs in the tray to break in my lap – the white and the yolks penetrating though my pants to my crotch. I was glad to arrive in camp where I could wash my pants and have a bath in the river. I spent my first night sleeping in my hammock under a tarpaulin tent. I met steersman Bertie Ansdale, and Bill Kramer who was on loan from the Geological Survey Department. It was in his boat that I travelled up river next day from Camaria to Matope Rock and Falls. Our entire load was carried over the rock and reloaded into Bertie Ansdale's boat which was much larger. Matope Rock still had an old logie in which travellers could store their cargo and sleep. Old Birdie Allicock, another steersman, informed me that when Sprostons were running the Interior River Service in the old days, they had a large compound in the bay at the foot of the falls. He mentioned that one Matthew French did a lot of construction work building the concrete causeway, over which the boats were now hauled, and general transportation for the firm. I told Allicock this Matthew French was my Godfather and I was named after him.

The boats left the rock at 10:30 a.m., having to steam through Simiri, Matusi, Tukeri and War Office Rapids. There were some very strong crosscurrents and fast streams. The steersman had to be twisting and turning between the ugly looking rocks and calling on the engineer to give full throttle on the engine when surmounting a bump. Passing Wariri Rapids, the captain called my attention to the old clearing for the gold mine camps. We then passed Aremu Creek mouth to enter a narrow hole in the bush which proved to be the passage up river. At this point, it called on all the skill of the steersman to turn practically at right angles in a fast running stream and surmount a hump of water before coming out into still water again. At Stop-Off, so called because in low water there is a bar of rocks across the river and boats had to swing at right angles going west, passing the upper end of Wurushima Island, then swing back after circling the rocks, to continue a mile or two through still waters to the foot of Tenamuth Falls. I must mention before proceeding any further that Aremu is one of the many gold mines that foreign companies have invested thousands of dollars in equipment and never worked the mine. There was a report that a bar of gold-bearing quartz traversed the creek a quarter mile from the mouth of the creek. At Tenamuth Falls, the entire load had to be discharged and carried over the rocks to the upper end of the falls, then the crew had to manhandle the boats through the falls with the assistance of ropes, a very tricky job, for if the bow is allowed to swing into the strong current, it will just sweep the boat against a rock and that would be the end of the boat.

We continued up river after reloading the boats through a long stretch of still water. The steersman took a left-hand channel through a narrow gap and had to climb a short but swift-flowing stream. At the top, the boat was slowed down to negotiate a shallow twisting channel between and over rocks, to once again emerge into deeper water. Here the boat swung across the river parallel to the top of the falls and up the left bank, then right around an island at the head of which we entered the area of scattered rocks forming Tajina Rapids. The boat slowed down and ran into our camp site. I did not appreciate the gloomy look of this camp ground. There was insufficient clearing around it and too many overhanging mora trees, not a safe or healthy look. I met Mr. Lochan (senior surveyor), Mr. Fredericks and Mr. Thompson, the other surveyors. Mr. Rahim, the engineer, and I shared a tent. I asked my radio operator to join me. Fernandes, my camp attendant, quickly put on some coffee and prepared a hot meal.

Mr. Lochan was carrying out dragging operations in the river above Tajina Rapids, prospecting for a landing pool for a plane. Surveyor Thompson left for Patwa Creek, on the left bank of the river opposite quartz stone, accompanied by Mr. Lochan. Mr. Thompson was to cut a line from the river inland to locate the ridge or watershed between the Pomeroon and Cuyuni Rivers. Engineer Rahim left for down river to contact Mr. Woon who was working on drilling operations in Surveyor Jessamy's area. Surveyor Fredericks and I travelled down river passing through Tajina and Paiyuka Rapids to the still water below which it was decided to locate the landing pool for the plane. I selected a high spot on the left bank of the river, just behind one of the islands, to be the site for our base camp. The men were instructed to build two fair-sized frames to make tarpaulin camps. Bertie Ansdale informed me he had discharged drums of fuel about half a mile below the spot I had selected for my camp. Paul, my radio operator, erected the aerial for our transmitting set. Call signs for contacting surveyors were as follows: Papa Romeo – Surveyor Thompson, Mike Foxtrot – Mr. Lochan, Charlie Romeo – Young's base camp, Kilo Mike – Mr. Woon, Lima Papa, Kamarang Camp, Mazaruni River.

I reported to Mr. Ramsahoye that the landing pool was approximately two and a half miles below Paiyuka Falls, lying in a north-east to south-west direction. I later marked the area with empty oil drums which I banded with red and white paint to show on the dark river water. These drums were tied with nylon ropes and anchored by a large rock.

I had my men clean up the camp site and fell some of the heavy over-hanging mora trees. They also cleared the bush from the river side and cleaned a boat landing and I had them build a floating ramp on which to discharge our cargo and on which fuel drums could be rolled up to the camp ground. After I had settled into the camp, I cut a hunting line behind it, discovering some highlands and flat hills running in an easterly and north-easterly direction. The river bank going upstream was very high and joined a large blackwater creek about a quarter mile up stream. There were signs of game in the forest and I discovered haimara fish in the creek. Two men from Bertie Ansdale's boat, Joseph Cornelius and his friend Paul Howard, came ashore to look for crabwood seeds with which to catch paku fish. They asked to borrow my gun and disappeared – for four days. I sent three men into the bush at 5:00 p.m. on the first evening of their failure to return. They shouted and beat the resounding mora tree spurs without result. I reported the matter to the Chief Engineer in Georgetown. I said I would continue the search the following day. I cut numerous lines penetrating into the bush from camp. I sent Bertie Ansdale down river as far as Tenamuth Falls with three men to cut a line three miles inland and to patrol the river bank. The men reported the area inland was low and full of swamps but there was no sign of the missing men.

The following day I took three men with me along my hunting line to the large Blackwater Creek to the north. From there we followed the course of this creek for approximately two and a half miles to the east where I discovered the creek broke up into numerous streams, some seeming to come into our creek and others going away. These, when followed through low and manicole swampland, led to another large blackwater creek flowing to the south. The men had continued beating mora tree spurs, blowing a bottle (the bottom of which had been knocked out) and shouting, listening for an answer. Rain had begun to fall heavily and the bush started to get dark. I instructed the men to turn back for we too might have strayed in these swamps. I returned to camp at 6:00 p.m. just when night was setting in, wet, tired and hungry. I radioed Georgetown to contact Bartica Police for assistance in our search. I received a message that the police were at Camaria Camp with Mr. Lochan and they would be reporting to me the following day.

I again went out with my men the next day to travel down river as far as Tenamuth Falls, there to penetrate the bush on a south-easterly line to try and locate some sign of the men. We returned to camp at 4:30 p.m. having had no success. Paul, my radio operator, informed me that the Co-ordinator for Surveys at Georgetown Head Office, had instructed I open a landing site one hundred feet by one hundred feet for a helicopter to land and assist in the search. Later the same evening, I received a radio message from Georgetown notifying me that the two missing men had found themselves twenty miles down river and were in Surveyor Jessamy's camp. It was the first time I had seen Bertie Ansdale laugh after four days of anxiety for his boys. Howard was like a son to him. The men had been absent for four days and three nights.

When Bill Kramer came down river in his boat, I took the opportunity to send for the two men at Jessamy's Landing. On their return, Cornelius informed me that after they left camp, they had shot a wild hog, following which had led them astray. They had slept in the bush that night and came out to the river at Jessamy's Landing the following day. I did not learn of this until two days later. There were some laughs on their return to camp. When asked to go out and look for crabwood seeds, they said, 'Never again.'

The first plane arrived and touched down on our landing pool at 12:15 p.m. on the 8 August 1972. Pilot Jardine said that there was plenty of room and the direction was right. I did though have make some changes to the drums which marked the pool. When the level of the river rose due to the heavy rains, the drums dragged their anchors and I had to lengthen the ropes and re-set their course.

Bertie Ansdale and I used to go fishing in the river at night below Paiyuka Falls. He caught a maripa catfish, then set a floating seine. Next morning, we returned for the fish which should have been in the seine, but there was no seine. Bertie assumed that a lau-lau, a giant skin fish had carried it away. I remembered that when I was on the Mazaruni river, I used to set a floating seine for fish to supply the camp. On two or three occasions I had found my seine torn. This had been caused by the water dog or otter, seizing the fish in the seine. I carried one man with me to fish in the large blackwater creek and returned home with three large haimara. Chief Engineer Ramashoye,

Field Engineer Rahim and Mr. Chappel, who was in charge of drilling operations, arrived by plane and spent the night at my camp. I contracted Kilo Mike by radio, notifying Mr. Woon that these men would be travelling into his location the next day to inspect his drilling operations on the ridge. The following morning I dispatched a small boat to Jessamy's Landing with these gentlemen.

At 4:30 p.m. I learned from Kilo-Mike, Mr. Woon, that only Mr. Chappel, a seasoned bush man had arrived at this location. There was no sign of either Mr. Ramsahoye or Mr. Rahim. Rain fell heavily during the night. The river level rising again. The next morning, I received a message from Mr. Woon to inform me Mr. Ramsahoye and Mr. Rahim had still not arrived at his location, but perhaps they had slept at Jessamy's camp. He was sending out some men to check on their whereabouts. At 3:20 p.m., Mr. Ramsahoye and Mr. Rahim arrived by boat from down river. They told me that having no guide to show them the trail to Mr. Woon's Camp, they had lost their way on meeting a junction of trails and were undecided which one to follow as it was late afternoon. They had decided to sleep in an old porkknockers camp with but a single old bag cot. They were very hungry as they had had no food since leaving my camp.

A meeting of all the surveyors operating in this project was held at my base camp. Mr. Ramsahoye informed them that they were to send in their daily progress reports to me and I would relay this information to him in Georgetown. Furthermore, their work crews had to submit their ration lists to me as well, earlier enough to give me time to compile the amount of food to order. Medical Kits would be made up at base camp for issue to all parties. I would also assign boats and engines to all locations and deal with the orders for fuels and oils. Radios would be assigned to each surveyor, the batteries would be recharged at base camp.

I was accompanied by Mr. Rahim on my first ration run to Bartica. Our journey down river to Camaria, which included a walk of three and three-quarter miles to the falls foot was not unusual, for as time went by, we learned we had to put up with a lot of inconvenience caused by Rafferty's transportation service. The boat trip from the falls foot and out to the mouth of the Cuyuni river where it joins the Mazaruni was very dangerous for small boats, especially because on this wide expanse of exposed water, a sudden squall of wind could swamp a boat.

On arrival at Bartica, I had to check with the Chinese store with regards to our supply of rations and hand in my order. In Bartica, Mr. Ragnauth, Officer in charge of Geological Survey stores and the Ministry Overseer in charge of fuels and oils proved to be of great assistance to me, especially in supplying a boat and tarpaulin to transport our cargo back to Camaria. However, I did have to travel to Georgetown to speed up the delivery of equipment and stores which had not yet arrived at Bartica. I left Bartica by plane but on arrival at Ogle Air Strip, I had no land rover awaiting me as ordered. The pilot of the plane, Mr. Jardine, kindly offered me a lift home. There, I had to sit on my back steps as my wife was out and I had to await her return. I spent eight days in town, collecting parts and other items requisitioned by the survey parties. I travelled back to base camp where I spent four days on my book work, then I had to travel back to Bartica as our rations had not arrived because of a breakdown with Rafferty's boat service.

Arriving at Camaria, I had to wait until Rafferty put his lorry together. Nearing half way back to camp on the portage road, our way was blocked by a broken down timber truck. I had to leave two men there to watch our cargo whilst I had to walk the balance of the way to Mr. Lochan's camp, arriving there at 7:30 p.m., practically having to feel my way at the last as night had set in. I lost another day there awaiting Rafferty and our cargo, though I spent an interesting night at Lochan's Camp where I was introduced to Mike Lochan's father and his small son. Mike's father was from Trinidad. I was more than surprised to learn of the number of bushmaster snakes that abounded there. He informed me that one of the remedies for drawing poison from someone who had been bitten was to make an X incision at the spot of the bite and put it close to a hot fire. The heat draws out the poison. I had a scare there, for on jumping out of my hammock at 4:00 a.m. to pass water outside the tent, I narrowly missed stepping on a four foot labaria snake. It was Mike's camp attendant who, on hearing the slithering of the snake on the tarpaulin carpet, shone his torch light, discovering the snake which he quickly killed with a stick. I told Mike he should make a wider clearing around his camp. The bush was too near, encouraging snakes.

CHAPTER XXVI
Hydro-Power Survey: Finding the Pomeroon Ridge – 1973

Whilst I was at Mike's camp, a radio message was received from Mr. Rahim in Georgetown that I was to go up river to Mr. Thompson's location to assist in finding the Pomeroon Ridge. I left Base Camp in company with Mr. Thompson and his assistant Ronald Persaud along with one of my men, Enos (a river man from Gold Hill Demerara River who was with me on the road to Mabura), and a week's ration for our stay to locate the ridge. Next morning, Enos and I packed our warashis with our rations, hammock, blanket and clothing. I had heard that Thompson's droughing line was a killer, but little did I visualise the difficulties of the long stretch of manicole swamp or I might not have started in carrying eighty pounds on my back.

This swamp was a half mile in length, but the time it took to negotiate walking on manicole tree trunks and stumps, plus slipping off the tree trunks into swamp water and rotten vegetation up to my waist, it seemed like ten miles. I was unfortunate to get a cramp in my right leg and had to abandon my warishi on a tree stump half a mile from camp. I was pleased to be greeted with hot tea and food on my arrival at Thompson's riverside camp, which was wet and overshadowed by large mora trees. I had to borrow a change of clothes as my own were left in my warishi. I went to the creek and stripped off my dirty clothes and had a good bath, washing off all the swamp muck. Enos and his partner arrived a little after me, but Surveyor Persaud and three of his men did not make it and returned to the main camp.

The walking line was flat to the river but rose up on steep red clay hills and intermediate swamps difficult to negotiate in the rainy season. Thompson's camp was situated off the main line on the right bank of a tributary of Patwa Creek which had clear and icy cold water, with a laterite gravel bottom. Enos went back to the line to bring back my warishi with my clothes and food, then we took a walk through the surveyor's line for four miles where we picked out a camp spot near a small, clear water creek. We underbushed an area large enough to build a small leaf camp. I felled two turru palm trees whose leaves would roof our camp. Enos shot a powis and a maam and picked up a good sized turtle on our return to Thompson's camp.

Next day, on our return to our new camp site, I overbalanced as I was crossing over a tree spanning a small creek and fell on my back. I lay there stunned for a moment. I had wrenched my right shoulder and got all my belongings wet, but I managed to crawl out with Enos' assistance. On our arrival at our camp, Enos lost no time in lighting a fire and putting on a pot of rice and fish caught in the creek and a pot of coffee. When we had eaten, we thatched our roof with the turru leaves then we cleaned out the creek, cleared the water holes and dug a garbage pit, just before the rain came down heavily. On unpacking my warashi, I discovered a pair of yachting boots was missing. I asked the surveyor's assistant, Sahoye, to check the creek where I had fallen. I was lucky for Sahoye found them the next day, tied up in some bush in the creek.

I spent the next nine days, accompanied by Enos, cutting feeler lines and following various ridge spurs in my endeavour to find the main ridge. They were days of sweat and fatigue, through rain, up steep, slippery hills, holding onto tree roots to reach the top, sliding down deep gullies to trace all the directions of the flows of water leads and creeks. A few miles from the river, we found a large blackwater creek flowing into the Pomeroon area. The following day I was joined by an Amerindian who had previously worked with the Geological Survey who had found the ridge at a different location. Enos and I showed him the end of our line and the ridge which the Amerindian confirmed was the correct ridge dividing the Cuyuni from the Pomeroon. I sent out a message to Surveyor Thompson and he in turn contacted Georgetown by radio. We were to build a fire and make plenty of smoke on Tuesday, 26 September, as a reconnaissance plane would be flying along the ridge from Camaria with the Co-ordinator and others to check on the location of the ridge.

We packed up and left this location for my base camp. I was very tired from constant walking, and having been living on fish broth and rice, bakes and coffee for the past two weeks. I again had a rough trip walking back along the survey line, having numerous falls over tree stumps. My Amerindian companion had to assist me with my load. After covering eleven and a half miles through the rain we reached the riverside camp at 3:30 p.m. Bill Kramer gave me a hot cup of coffee. I then boarded the boat en route to base camp. The throttle lever of our outboard engine broke after passing the first island and the men had to paddle the remaining distance assisted by the flow of the river. I arrived at base camp at 5:30 p.m. where I met Mr. Lochan and the Co-ordinator, Mr. Earle. I made a sketch map and explained to them the problems in tracing the ridge. Later, Surveyor Thompson reported that the ridge located proved to be a spur descending into a tributary of the Pomeroon River. He would be moving out for discussions.

I suffered pains in my back and my knee and had a slight fever from overexertion and spent the next three weeks in camp writing my reports and making up my books. The men were engaged in cleaning and burning bush in the camp grounds. I accidentally dropped my glasses in the fire. The frames were destroyed but I managed to retrieve the lenses which I forwarded to Georgetown for a new pair of frames.

Surveyor Jessamy reported he had met Mahazarally's timber road on the ridge, from where a road led out to the Supenaam river. Thompson's radio had gone dead and he had to report to me by letter. Assisted by the lowness of the river water, the men caught a number of packu fish, which were cut open, salted and smoked. When fresh supplies ran short, I sent two men to the blackwater creek for haimara fish. The men also went out at night to a spot where wild plums were falling to shoot the labba feeding on them. I bought some banana and plantain suckers from Bartica which I had the men plant in my base camp compound. I also brought in some cassava sticks which were also planted, and I had the men plant pumpkin, watermelons, pepper trees and many other beans and greens. I wanted to make our camp self-sufficient.

There were some characters in the camp, like "Doc" Yussuf, Rahim's camp attendant and Paul my radio operator who were both famous for talking in their sleep. Paul's job was to run the lighting plant and charge radio batteries when needed. He had on occasion to travel to town. Before leaving, he gave Yussuf all instructions about the lighting plant. One evening "Doc" said he had been trying to start the plant without success. I went over the method of starting it with him, asking him about the switching-on of the gasoline as I noted the lever was in the wrong position. "Doc" as good as told me I knew nothing. I had to light my gas lamp for camp use. At 3:00 a.m., whilst asleep in my hammock, I felt a presence over me. I awoke to find "Doc" leaning over my hammock watching me. He said he had been studying the starting of the plant, would I go with him to check if he or I was correct. I set the levers of the gas, etc. and at the first pull the motor started. "Doc" owned that he was wrong.

Some quiet nights the men used to hear a mournful whistle coming from the bush. Old bushmen will tell it is a snake, but if you are in the company of Amerindians, especially those living in the areas near the upper rivers or savannahs they would tell you it was a "kanaima" man, an outcast from his tribe or an avenger. There were other visitors. A large jaguar had been in our camp in the early hours for I saw the large pug marks in the mud and Bertie Ansdale had to kill an anaconda snake measuring some twelve feet which somehow had climbed into his boat. It was not a good sleeping companion, for Ansdale usually erected a tent over his boat every night and slept there.

In cutting a walking line up along the river bank, I was unfortunate to have a vein on my right hand stuck with a thorn from a small palm tree. The vein immediately started to swell and in no time my hand had swollen to twice its size and was exceedingly painful, giving me a high fever for three days. "Captain", one of our boatmen, prepared and put a poultice on the hand which drew out the poison, but I spent two or three sleepless nights before I got relief. Another day, I received a message from Jessamy and Craig, who were surveying on the ridge, complaining about bats. I told them what precautions to take and the remedy if bitten.

I had to travel to Bartica to arrange a programme for a visiting team of Yugoslav engineers dealing with the hydro power project. Mr. Lochan asked for the loan of my camp attendant to work along with the Yugoslav team on their visit. I took numerous colour snapshots of hills, mountains and rapids while on my trips up and down river. In my spare time at camp I went back to painting in oils on canvas various scenes, some from memory, of the beauty of this bush. Then I was again instructed to travel up river to Fish Creek and there follow an old geological line to the Pomeroon Ridge and cut back up river to contact Surveyor Thompson. I took three of my men, Enos, who had been with me on my first trip and De Jesus, Taj Paul, my radio operator, and the Amerindian from geological survey. I travelled by Captain Ansdale's boat. He dropped us off at the landing and agreed to return for us in four days time. I erected a small tarpaulin tent under which I and my men would spend the night. Rain began to fall heavily and water started to run through the camp. The men had to cut drains around the tent to take off the water. I got the men to fell two large trees over the creek and put up a hand rail so we could cross over safely with our loads. We then pushed forward to 7½ mile camp ground where we erected another tarpaulin tent. From this spot I could investigate the ridge which was a mile and a half further on.

The slope and the top of the ridge was made up of red laterite clay with a base of honeycombed laterite rock and boulders. The descent on either side was very steep and difficult to climb in the rainy weather. Our guide from the Geological Department started off from the hill top and after cutting a line for some time, I informed him he was cutting in a circle, so I cut west from the summit descending into a manicole swamp whose waters were flowing back to the Cuyuni River. We pushed forward and climbed a very steep hill beyond. Having the same laterite clay formation, we followed a ridge spur for one mile. I noted the amount of greenheart trees growing to well over one hundred feet high. We descended into yet another manicole swamp where water was flowing in two directions. I knew there must be a connecting saddle to the ridge we had left.

The following day, Emmanuel, the Geological Survey man, showed me their survey line descending the first hill on a 30° bearing, to lands bordering water flowing back into the Pomeroon. It was in this area I first came across the wild dog, often spoken of but rarely seen. There was a pair of them chasing a labba which ran across the line in front of me. These dogs were brown in colour and about the size of a small terrier with sharp pointed ears. I have covered the bush in all parts of the country but had never before encountered these dogs.

It was just below the height of the first hill that I discovered a saddle. We crossed from hill to hill continuing the cutting for a mile and a half, but found I was travelling in an easterly direction, whereas I was looking for a north-west bearing. We continued on this bearing until we descended into a fair-sized body of water flowing across the Geological Survey 30° line in the vicinity of their old 10 mile camp. I retraced my steps and cut on another spur going south which carried me into another, but larger manicole swamp. I split the party on the saddle, on a last trial to connect the right saddle to put us on the correct ridge. It was De Jesus and Emmanuel who cut on a narrow finger of the ridge for about a mile and a quarter miles before connecting to another saddle, but low, which connected to another hill on the ridge. This proved to be the ridge running in the right north-west bearing. Rain had been falling steadily. We returned to camp wet and tired, but satisfied our job was complete. I decided to return to base camp, as the men had run short of food. To continue cutting to meet Surveyor Thompson on the ridge would need a month's supply of rations. I had arranged for the river boat to return for us in four days time, but on reaching the river, we found no boat awaiting, probably because the river had risen with all the rain that we had been having.

We lost another day awaiting the boat. Not having any food for an extended stay, I sent three men to cut an up river line to Thompson's camp three and a half miles away. They returned at 12:15 p.m. paddling Capt. Kramer's boat. They told me they had to swim three creeks. At Thompson's camp they had found no-one there and no outboard engine. However, the fast flowing water helped our progress and we arrived back at base at 2:00 p.m. I found our radio antennae down, so I had two men climb the trees to re-erect it before I could send a message to Mr. Lochan at Matope. I reported that I had located the ridge, was preparing a written report and would enclose a sketch map of the area showing our tracing lines.

The rains had really set in, accompanied by high winds. During the night I heard a large tree fall at the landing. Next morning, I saw the fallen tree near the mechanic's tent. Rambarran the mechanic said he had run outside for safety. I had repeatedly warned the surveyors to clear all overhanging trees from around their camps, yet on two or three occasions, I had visited their camps to find them damp from overhanging trees. I was saddened but not surprised to see Surveyor Thompson arrive at 8:00 a.m. to inform me that a mora tree had fallen on his camp, killing Agostini James, his huntsman, smashing his body flat into the mud. He had to be buried at the same spot as his body could not be moved. I had to report this incident to the Head Office in Georgetown and to the police at Bartica. I also received a message from Georgetown that Engineer Rahim was to be transferred to the Mazaruni river. My camp attendant was to accompany him, as "Doc" Yussuf was not able to climb mountains. Two of my best men, Enos and De Jesus, were transferred to the soil technicians at Camaria.

Mr. Sewah Persaud, a timber grant owner, who now had a dredge operating below Aikawan Falls for gold and diamonds in the upper Cuyuni River, stopped in at my camp to ask for help as the shaft bearings on his outboard engine had broken. He wanted to borrow an engine. I told him to spend the night at my camp and I and Bertie Ansdale would run him up river in our boat the following morning. It took me five hours travelling to reach his camp at Aikawan as I had to tow his boat. Our engine consumed twenty gallons of gasoline, which Sewah gave us back. At Aikawan, I met Roy Metcalf, a New Zealander who was a geologist assisting Sewah Persaud in his operations and had been prospecting the river for eighteen months. He told me he had some photographs of the country taken from a satellite, which showed all the old river beds. Some were now two hundred feet above the present river levels. The old river courses seemed to have run at right angles to the present ones. We left his camp after taking lunch and arrived back at base camp at 6:00 p.m. On this trip up river, Bertie Ansdale told me the names of the various rapids, twisting and turning all over the river, the names of the creeks we passed, the locations of dry and full water channels and the location of old gold and diamond workings. I made a note of everything in a note book which I kept for such information.

I had to order more rations for the men to last up to 15 December, but those who were staying on as watchmen during the shutdown for the Christmas holidays would receive a month's supply. I was instructed to place boats at the most convenient points and arrange for all the M.T. fuel drums to be shipped down to Camaria en route to Bartica. I would leave a man in charge of the base camp with all stores and equipment. It was on my last return trip from Bartica with rations before the Christmas break that I had one of the thrills that one encounters when travelling the river in these remote areas. Two boats under Bill Kramer and Bertie Ansdale left Matope Rock at 4:20 p.m. loaded with drums of gasoline and rations for the men at Thompson's location at Patwa Creek. A violent thunderstorm caught us in the open river, when the boats were negotiating Wariri Rapids, turning day into night. I was in Ansdale's boat which was in the lead. There were times when looking back I could not see Bill Kramer's boat through the driving rain. We were steaming up Tenemuth Still Water, but the force of the winds caused waves to splash over the gunwales into the boat. The time and distance to reach the falls seemed endless. Everyone was sheltering from the driving rain except me as I was kept busy bailing out the water from the bailing hole. Eventually the boat entered Tenamuth back channel just as night was setting in. Bertie thought there might be sufficient water to steam up the rapids but he was out of luck. So Paul Howard, the bowman, had to leap from the boat onto a large rock at the falls foot to hold the bow, whilst the other men paid out the heavier warp rope. They had to pull the boat through these raging water as the engine could not work between these rocks, especially at night.

There was a nerve-wracking period of about twenty minutes when one or other of the men who was leading the rope would disappear into a hole between the rocks. As the rope slackened, the boat would swing out into the current. Then the Captain used some of the choicest words used on the river, wanting to know if they wanted the boat to capsize in the falls. I jumped out to give some assistance but had my legs swept from under me by the force of water, as I strained to hold on to the gunwale. Bertie, seeing my predicament, cursed me roundly and ordered me back into the boat. He said no one could see in the dark whether everyone was present or who was missing and the noise of the rushing waters made hearing even shouted instructions impossible. Eventually, one of the men produced a torch enabling us to see the bushes on the river bank. Howard, the bowman, and Cornelius, plunged from the boat over the rocks to tie the warp rope to a tree. Two or three times the boat nearly breached as it was so heavily laden, before the men eventually managed to haul it to still water to take a breather. Then we moved on with the engine at half speed, driving close to the bush on the left bank, sometimes shearing out to avoid rocks, until the boat again reached the deep water above the main falls. The wind did not improve matters. All of us were soaking wet from the rain and the falls. When we eventually arrived at base camp at 8:05 p.m., I stripped off my wet clothes and let the boys in camp give me a brisk rubdown and a hot cup of cocoa.

A few days later, I received a message from Surveyor Thompson to send Bertie Ansdale's boat to his landing as he was moving out all his equipment and men, as both he and his men were suffering from fatigue and unable to tie in his survey with Jessamy's. Engineer Rahim had notified me that I would be needed next year to close up the Cuyuni Survey. I told him I had only been loaned to the Hydro-Power Survey for three months, but my time was extended to close up operations.

The following year, January 1973, I returned to Hydro-Power in the Cuyuni river. Boats and fuels were requisitioned and sent to Camaria to be forwarded to Matope where Senior Surveyor Lochan was closing up his survey of that area. After this work was completed, I was instructed to collect all the Geological Survey boats and send them back down to the Camaria Falls location. I also was instructed to load up and post all government supplies back to Georgetown. Surveyor Thompson returned to Fish Creek in company with Craig to tie in his ridge survey with Jessamy's. I was instructed to report back to the Roads Division on the closing of this operation. My new project was on construction of the Mabura to Kurupukari Road.

CHAPTER XXVII
Work on the Mabura-Kurupukari Road and a Ministerial Safari – 1973

I resumed duty on the Mabura - Kurupukari road on the instruction of the
Chief Engineer of Roads, Mr. P. E. Phang, to carry out the same duties I had
been engaged in the previous year with Superintendent Todd. I was introduced to the new engineer for the project, a Afro-Guyanese, Tommy Smith,
who had informed Mr. Todd he did not need me, but on learning of the level
of responsibilities I had to shoulder and the quantity of books and accounts
I would have to write up, he quickly changed his mind. I employed Tage
Paul, who had been my radio operator on the Hydro-Power project, De Jesus
to be my stores assistant and "Doc" Yussuf as my camp attendant. I organised a Honda lighting plant and two LEC freezers for the camp. I checked
with Central Workshop for a few more lorries as I had heard that the Mabura
Project was very short on machinery.

I left Georgetown on 16 March 1973 at 4:00 p.m., travelling by a Bedford
7 ton lorry, loaded with equipment and stores. We stopped at Wismar for an
hour and a half to allow the men to eat and purchase food for the journey, as
we had sixty-seven miles to travel over rough bush roads before we arrived
at Yaya Creek Camp – which we did at 2:20 a.m. I tied my hammock and
quickly fell asleep in the engineer's tent. Sam, the engineer's camp attendant, gave me a cup of coffee early the next morning. I instructed De Jesus
and Tage Paul to discharge the stores, equipment and fuel. They then cut
bush wood frames to erect a camp on the left bank of the Yaya Creek over
the bridge, sufficiently large to accommodate the four of us, plus the rest of
the equipment, stores and rations when they arrived. I partitioned off an
office in which I built a table for my book work. I then left for the forward
line in company with Enos and McKenzie, both men who had served with
me before.

I went to check on the bridge approach at Seeballi Creek, Engineer Smith
joining me there. Enos and McKenzie, whose real trade was squaring shipping timbers, were instructed to fell and square greenheart timbers for the
bridge span of eighty feet – six 40 foot timbers to rest on a central foundation of greenheart supports. Murphy, the carpenter, and his men would con-

struct the bridge. On my return to camp, Engineer Smith asked me to take a stock of all tools, fuel, and equipment at Yaya Creek compound and as a regular duty, compile all the ration slips submitted by the men and order in bulk from the government Co-op shop, checking and pricing all requisitions. My assistant, De Jesus, would be given a special lorry to travel to town at the end of each month to collect the rations and any other outstanding stores. But Engineer Smith also requested that when I had brought all my books up to date, I would assist in spearheading the forward line in selecting the best possible gradients and cutting out all unnecessary curves, using the existing survey line as a base.

Workers with the help of a D/7 caterpillar tractor were busy clearing the wallaba forest over white sand country. They returned to Yaya Camp every evening, transported by lorry. When this broke down, I had to send a tractor and trailer and my land rover to bring them into camp.

Tage Paul had reported that the Honda generator was not producing sufficient power to illuminate the camp and that the "LEC" freezers were not working properly. Engineer Smith asked me to travel to Georgetown to get them repaired as fast as possible. There I also reported to the Chief Engineer of Roads and Engineer J. Joseph, telling them it was imperative I get some more lorries and another bulldozer if we were to achieve any real progress. I asked for the transfer of Bridgenarine, a lorry driver who had worked with me on the Bartica - Potaro Road in 1960, from the Garden-of-Eden project. Loaded with the Honda generator, the LEC freezers, Marconi radio transmitter, wet cell batteries and rations for the surveyors, the land rover unfortunately broke down at MacKenzie on our way back to camp. The repairs could not be completed that night, so I and the men had to spend the night in the land rover, being devoured by mosquitoes. I was glad when day dawned to allow me to get all the kinks out of my body. We returned to Yaya camp at 12:30 p.m. I had two hours rest, then I had to return to Wismar, a drive of 73 miles, to witness the payment of our employees. On my way out, I met the ration lorry coming in, so I returned to Yaya camp to put Yussuf in charge of the rations and carry out Browne, the lorry driver, and De Jesus to draw their wages. At Wismar Police Station, the paymaster informed me he had insufficient money to pay all my men so I instructed them to climb aboard the two lorries and we proceeded to Georgetown Head Office where I reported this matter to Engineer Joseph. Accounts branch were contacted and a cheque was sent to the bank for the money. After I had witnessed the payment of the men, I returned to Yaya camp at 10:30 p.m., having travelled 387 miles in one day. I was very tired and hungry, not having had time to grab a meal.

I pushed with the forward line work, opening another camp ground on the left bank of the Seeballi Creek. There the machines encountered a reef of greenheart and other hardwood trees growing on sand clay soil. A tractor trailer had to be used to spread white sand on the steep hill slope approaching Seeballi, for when wet, the hill slope proved a danger to rubber-wheeled vehicles, as there was a deep gully on either side of the saddle connecting the two hills. I found a beautiful stand of timber in this area and other hardwoods – purpleheart and silverballi – brown, yellow and silver species. The men got a good supply of haimara fish from the creek and the huntsman kept the camp supplied with deer, labba and wild hogs, mixed with powis and maam birds. Around the Seeballi camp area and in the upper reaches of the tributaries, I discovered old gold claims. I was later to learn that the Flemmings from the upper Demerara River were the claim holders. One Sigmund Croft had made a small fortune here. He died and no one had ever discovered the area of his strike.

At 77 mile, Enos, McKenzie and I discovered an old walking line branching off to the east. We followed this line for a distance of three miles crossing two fair-sized tributaries of the Seeballi flowing from a south-easterly direction, originating from the laterite hills – a continuation of the Mabura Range. I saw many outcrops of quartz on crossing the last stream. We started to ascend a gradual slope of near black honeycombed laterite rock on which grew hard scrub bush. After a quarter of a mile this line branched into two lines, so I turned back. I noted wild cashews dropping from a tree near the line and under it the tracks of a tapir. Enos told me that when the tapir fed on this fermented fruit, they had a tendency to get drunk and will lie down and sleep nearby. That night I sent out two men with a gun and a torch light to shoot this tapir, but they missed.

One night, I left camp at 1:00 a.m. with my huntsman to walk downstream on the left bank of the Seeballi Creek to shoot labba, which can be located by the red reflection of their eyes (the same as an alligator's; deer, tapir, and cats give a green reflection) in the beam of our torchlight. The huntsman led the way through a narrow twisting track on the slope of a laterite hill. I slipped on some laterite gravel and rolled down the slope, but fortunately, no damage was done. My huntsman nearly trod on a labba in the creek flat, which jumped away to hide from the probing beam of our torchlights. The huntsman caught the reflection of its eyes and collected it after it was shot. A little further downstream, approaching another hill, a branch stream joined the main creek on the other bank. Our torchlights caught the beam of a pair of green eyes, which proved to be those of a small jaguar which slunk into the bush on our approach. We returned to camp at 5:30 a.m. in time for coffee. Spring rods were also set with baited hooks at convenient spots on the creek bank to catch fish, but one had to be up early to retrieve the catch before an alligator or a water dog made off with it.

I received a message from the Chief Engineer of Roads to report to Mr. D'Abreu, Permanent Secretary of Finance, as state auditors were querying some items from my stores on the 1970-1971 Self-help Road Project. On reporting, I was asked by Mr. D'Abreu and Ray Singh, the Roads Division accountant, who had given permission for certain transactions and the pricing of goods supplied to the project. I informed told them that the Minister and the Project Co-ordinator were those who had given permission and that the Stores Clerk P.W.D. saw to the purchasing. As camp manager, I had only received whatever goods were shipped to me, and I had priced the goods according to the price lists I received from Georgetown, carrying out the instructions I received from the Co-ordinator. I reported this incident to the Field Auditor who had given me clearance on my books in March 1972. On my return to Seeballi Camp, Engineer Smith asked me to trace a ridge line between the Seeballi and Yaya Creeks out to the Essequibo River. I took Enos and McKenzie. We packed our warashis with two days' food and a change of clothes. A lorry dropped us off at the 69 mile pole. We cut on a bearing of 330 for 3,000 feet from the road to clear the headwaters of the Yaya Creek, then swung to 345 to 360 following a white sand ridge. We twisted and turned on this ridge for a distance, by pace measurement, of 11,750 feet. It seemed as if I had cut too far west from where I had begun for we were continually crossing the waters of the Seeballi Creek. I returned to camp for discussions with the Engineer and Surveyor Narayan. I informed them it would be easier to cut from Yaya Creek to contact the ridge lower down. I dropped down to Yaya Creek the following day with five men and followed a fishing line downstream to meet Nagasar Sawh's timber road at 11:10 a.m. at an old leaf camp. The men and I took our snack here, then leaving our warashis at the camp, we proceeded to follow Nagasar Sawh's road upstream.

It was a red sand clay ridge, bearing north-west and then west to contact the first tributary head. The road continued on this high ridge swinging south-west, then south, then south-east where operations had ceased. From this point, I continued cutting south for one mile where we met a branch of the Yaya. I traced this water upstream until we met the ridge again. We traced this ridge back to the logging road. We returned to the logging camp a distance of five miles, where we prepared a meal, had a good bath in the creek and slept the night. Those who did not have hammocks slept on the balamani bark floor. The leaf roof had large holes in it. It was lucky no rain fell.

We returned the following day (Holy Thursday), to where we had stopped tracing. It was decided some men would continue tracing, some would open the line, the balance would bring forward our loads. There was a disagreement between McKenzie and I as to which direction to proceed. He was for continuing south across the Yaya tributary. This I explained would not be following the ridge. McKenzie's line proved to be a failure as it met more tributaries of the Yaya. Further progress was curtailed as I was struck by an attack of vomiting and fever. I urged the men to continue, saying I would retrace my steps to camp with the assistance of one man. McKenzie was against this as the men did not have not sufficient food and would not be able to trace, cut and drough loads. We decided to close the trip and return to Yaya camp. I left at 9:30 a.m. to walk the twelve and a half miles out to the road. I had to stop repeatedly as my thigh muscles were knotting up. I reached the road at 2:00 p.m. and Bridgenarine collected us in his lorry at 7:00 p.m. and took us back to Seeballi Camp.

Good Friday, 20 April 1973, was spent in camp. Murphy had given me a rub down with Radian B liniment. I took two fever tablets and awoke without fever, but on getting out of my hammock, I could not bear any weight on my legs without suffering intense pain. I had pulled a muscle in my left leg and Murphy said I had 'narra' which had caused the vomiting. He gave me a massage and fixed the narra. I spent the day in my hammock, again getting fever. Tage Paul put a hot fomentation on my left leg and then rubbed me down with Radian B liniment. I got much relief from this and after a week I was able to go out again.

I pushed ahead with the forward line machines until we met the Ekuk Creek discharging into the Demerara River. This was white sand country, but carrying heavy stands of timber. Enos and McKenzie had already located a reef of greenheart trees to use as bridge timbers, but unluckily, most of the trees felled by the power saws proved to be hollow so they had to go further afield for suitable trees. I put on a gang of men to underbush the approach to the creek best suited for a bridge crossing and fell the trees in the alignment. The two caterpillar tractors, the D/7 and the D/6, were put on to open borrow pits in the white sand from the hill on either side of the road. This sand was then pushed down to the creek edge, building a causeway covering the tree stumps from a depth of between seven feet and two feet to the creek edge, some one hundred and fifty feet in length and thirty feet wide. The timbers for the bridge were then hauled to the spot, and the two machines crossed over to do a similar operation on the other bank, though this causeway was three hundred feet in length rising up on a white sand hill.

Four camp frames were erected to the right of the road, on the left bank of the Ekuk Creek, 86 miles from Wismar. The men moved up and made their camp here. The surveyors were left at Seeballi to bring forward the mile posts. Enos pointed out the high water mark on the trees in this creek flat and I advised Tommy Smith to raise the height of the bridge and install hollow wood culverts as I had done at Yaya Creek, but he insisted it was OK and it would take too long, for he wanted to push ahead with the clearing. I could foresee trouble here as the causeways formed a bottle neck. The rainy season had set in, slowing down all forward line work and the breakdown of both the D/7 and D/6 caterpillar tractors and the Leyland tractors put a stop to all work beyond Ekuk Creek. At approximately 1.4 miles beyond Ekuk Creek we encountered a stretch of clay lands, which in this weather proved a mess. There was no drainage, the D/7 and D/6 tractors having to cut drains towards the creek tributaries to drain the surface. This mud flat later had to be surfaced with white sand to enable traffic to pass freely. Engineer Smith was constantly going to Georgetown for medical attention. He told me the bush did not agree with him so I was shouldered with most of the responsibility. Beyond this half mile of mud flat, I encountered a laterite hill, which stretched to within a quarter mile of Ukaribi Creek. There were other problems I could foresee. Engineer George Joseph radioed me from Georgetown to inform me that river captain Henry had said he could convey out fuel in drums by river only as far as Itanami Falls. This would mean he would have to roll the drums over the rocks. I was rather sceptical about this operation as these oil drums could be easily punctured.

Because of the rainfall, I split my workforce, sending the carpenters to 10 mile area to rebuild the bridge. The TR/208L Adams operator was sent to haul the logs which Enos and McKenzie would prepare. On the completion of the bridge, the men would erect leaf camps at 10 mile, 40 mile and 67 mile compounds in place of the tarpaulin tents I had been using. On completing the repairs on the tractors, the operators were instructed to open up the width of the road across the mud flat to enable the sun and the wind to dry the surface. After sanding the road across the mud flat, both D/7 and D/6 tractors were engaged in forcing their way through the hardwood forest across a stretch of laterite hills to white sand, four miles beyond Ekuk Creek. Here both machines again broke down. I took a walk, accompanied by Surveyor Narayan, from Ekuk Creek to Ukaribi Creek some eight miles in front, to visit Surveyor Kissoon. Ukaribi Creek's name had been changed to Camoodie Creek after an incident in which the surveyor's camp attendant nearly lost his life. He had been sitting on a log across the creek, fishing, idly swinging his legs awaiting a bite on his hook. I surmised it was the shadow of his swinging legs which had drawn the attention of the anaconda for it raised it head out of the creek water to wrap the boy's legs in its coils. His cries drew the attention of a man in camp who rushed to the boy's assistance and cut off the snake's head with his cutlass. When pulled from the water, the snake measured seventeen feet. Had the man not been in camp, the boy would have lost his life.

Surveyor Kissoon had cut a line from the creek crossing out to the Essequibo River, a distance of half of a mile. I would later use this line as the location of my fuel dump. I erected a six foot triangular piece of white cloth at the creek mouth to attract the boat captain's attention, denoting the spot where he was to dump the fuel drums. Surveyor Kissoon had also scaled Akaiwanna Mountain, but on my examination, I found the gradient far too steep and difficult to clear, having deep benches with large granite rocks and laterite. I advised that he reconnoitre around the mountain, following the contour to seek a lesser gradient, even if we had to bridge some ravine heads. This was later done, making the road a little longer but less dangerous.

I had been instructed by the Chief Engineer of Roads at Head Office in Georgetown to pick out and open up all the beauty spots I encountered on the road for tourists. On the top of Akaiwanna Mountain, I looked at the untouched wilderness about me, the valley lying open in front, a half mile wide and a mile long, its level floor cut by the swinging course of the creek. As its head, the mountain wall rose steeply in huge broken steps, and a stream tumbled down it in rushes and falls as it drove from the upper reaches of rock. Along the valley sides trees climbed, dotted and vine-tangled, to cling to the enduring stone – on the near side against a high sharp ridge, on the opposite side against a vast rock buttress, towering to a tremendous peak. Between the ridge and the buttress, the valley entrance dropped abruptly into forests covering the downward slopes and divided by the deepening gorge of the creek as it sought the lower levels. Beyond, the ground rose again in ridge upon ridge to the high south-eastern mountain peaks, the source of the Akaiwanna Creek which discharged into the Essequibo River on its right bank into ten miles of turbulent water. On the other side of the mountain, I came across water falling into a deep and wide pool, the water icy cold, clear as crystal so that I could see the smallest stone some twelve feet below.

One mile before meeting Ukaribi Creek in the white sand area, I traced a line following a narrow twisting ridge three quarters of a mile out to the Essequibo River. From there I had a beautiful view of the rapids stretching four miles across the river to Tikwari Mountains. At this river spot, I found there was wonderful ground for agricultural purposes, having a rich black and brown sandy loam soil and a good supply of fresh water from the nearby water leads. The broad river rocks below formed a good place for bathing. I opened this line with the D/6 caterpillar tractor to use as a jeep road, and also cleared a good portion of the river front. I was later to learn a man had settled here to farm and raise chickens. I had suggested to the Interior Development Corp. that they should send in a lorry once a month to bring in would-be settlers and to carry out the farmers' produce. The idea was to encourage people to open up the interior by following our road. This request was never fulfilled.

I returned to Ukaribi Creek to set on a crew of men to place a ramp on either bank on which the caterpillar tractors could cross. Unfortunately, the steel snatch-block suspended from the branch of a large mora tree broke when it took the strain of the mora logs being lifted into place, so I had to finish the job with the assistance of the caterpillar tractors. I sent the larger machine, the D/7 caterpillar, across the creek to continue clearing the road. The D/6 was used to cut down the red clay hill, pushing the material down into the four hundred foot wide creek flat to form a causeway (in the same way as I had done at Yaya Creek) starting at a height of twenty-one feet to diminish at the creek's edge. This ramp was later surfaced with white sand from the ridge road. The crossing at this point was sixty feet from bank to bank, but the logs eventually spanning the creek were one hundred feet long with an average diameter of two feet. The depth of the water at this time was twelve feet, but in heavy rains the level of water would overflow its banks to a depth of twenty feet. We eventually reached Batwall Creek at the foot of the mountain. I had the machines clear a good camp site on the left bank. At this site, the men discovered there were some good sized haimara fish in the deep rocky pools. I had the men cut bush materials for the erection of four camp frames for tarpaulins.

Mr. George Todd, Senior Superintendent, who originally had started this road from Wismar, was transferred back to the project to replace Engineer Smith, who was always sickly in the bush. I returned to Ekuk Creek, as all workmen were required to travel out to Wismar to cast their votes for the national elections on 12 July to 14 July 1973.

There were heavy rains accompanied by thunder and lightning on the night of 13 July. Knowing what could happen when the creek waters rose, I called upon Enos to assist me in bringing in the Goodenough pump from the bridge at 3:00 a.m. in driving rain. Fearing the rush of water from the moufltains might bar traffic on the road, I dispatched the last of the men on a lorry at daybreak. I was left in camp alone except for De Jesus and the huntsman. By 8:15 a.m., on 14 July, Ekuk Creek River was a raging torrent of muddy water, rushing out, sweeping away trees and all the white sand of the built-up roadway and rising some three feet above the bridge and destroying two hundred and seventeen feet of white sand fill. I took three colour snapshots of this disaster and reported the matter to the engineers at Head Office in Georgetown. I sent De Jesus and Andries, the huntsman, to check on the fuel drums at Ukaribi Creek. De Jesus was to bring back the D/7 tractor and Andries the Leyland tractor, so I would have machines on hand to commence the rebuilding when the labourers returned from Wismar. De Jesus reported that there were a total of ninety-nine drums of fuel at the dump. I forwarded this information to Mr. Todd in Georgetown. De Jesus brought my attention to the fact that 25% of the fuel drums were only half-full and a good many of the others were more water than fuel, the result of rolling these drums over the Itanamie Falls on rocks.

The clearance of the road over the mountain to Louie Creek was eventually completed. I had to fill in two narrow ravines, put in a hollow wood culvert to take off the water and cut a detour following the contour of the mountain to enable the machines to drop down on a more gentle gradient to the mountain foot. Louie Creek crossing had a span of forty-eight feet over a depth of six feet of crystal clear water.

Enos and I, accompanied by another man from Surveyor Narayan's party, decided to visit Surveyor Kissoon's camp beyond Akaiwanna Creek. After crossing the mountain by tractor-trailer, we had to walk four miles through an old forestry survey line to Frenchman's Creek. On crossing this creek, I noted a reef of sandstone rocks crossing the track. We then swung east following the survey line to climb a high laterite hill where we saw a good stand of greenheart trees. Here the line swung back south-west, descending onto a white sand ridge which dropped off into the wide flats bordering Akaiwanna Creek. Rain from the mountains had swollen the waters three feet above the banks. The survey men, who were droughing in rations for Surveyor Kissoon, were held up there and were on the point of turning back. I urged them to locate the log bridge spanning the creek, which could not be seen but could be located by feel of the feet. A human chain was then formed, the men balancing themselves against the rushing waters to pass their warashi loads from hand to hand. I was the last to cross. The men had given me a long pole stick with which to balance myself, but the force of the water just swept the pole aside. I overbalanced and was swept downstream by the rushing water.

I had to do a little swimming and managed to crawl out some two hundred feet lower down.

Half a mile from the creek, we came to an abandoned camp site at the foot of a sand hill. We took some food and hot coffee before resuming our walk, continuing through a park-like forest of dacama and muri bush with clearings of white sand. A bush fire must have passed through this area some years before for there were remains of blackened tree trunks lying on the ground and broken tree stumps scattered over the landscape. We arrived at Kissoon's camp, ten miles from the creek, in record time, because of the falling rain and the heavy clouds. At least we had not been punished by the reflected heat from the white sand which we would have been if the sun had shone. After a bath in the creek, I was given a belated lunch by the camp attendant and some very welcome coffee. I slung my hammock, still a little damp from the road, and fell asleep. The following day we walked another six miles to where the survey line ended, the site of Kissoon's next camp. This walk was over open muri bush and wide open savannah-like land of white sand. The camp site was on a high ridge, with a beautiful panorama of the Akaiwanna Mountain range on its way up to the Kurundini River, a large tributary of the upper Demerara River. Water had been discovered on this high ridge one foot below the surface and I learnt that Mr. Kissoon and his men had encountered a few jaguars on it. Whilst there, Mr. Kissoon gave me a tracing of his work from Ukaribi over the mountain to his present location and we discussed the route he should take to reach Kurupukari. I returned to Ekuk Creek the following day. At Akaiwanna Creek crossing I noted the water had dropped six feet. At this point the crossing was sixty-two feet wide, the depth thirteen feet. On our way back, the reflected heat from the sand gave us a hard time until a shower of rain saved us.

We returned to Frenchman's Creek the following day to cut a deviation line to cut out the climb to the lone laterite hill, crossing lower down in the ravine and shortening the distance by a mile. I put on two of the machines to open a base camp at Frenchman's Creek where we could store all the machinery and stores at the end of the year's shut down. In the earlier years, gold had been discovered at the source of the creek by a French man, hence the name. Remnants of the machinery used were still to be seen between the second growth of bush. Progress was slow, the arrangements for paying wages not least causing considerable delay. To transport the men from Ekuk Creek 86 miles to Wismar, and allow time for the men to purchase more food and have a good time and return, took at least a week. Multiply this by the number of pay days and you have a staggering amount of hours lost.

There was also the continual delay in getting supplies sent from Georgetown, and the Project Superintendent sent me there in an attempt to speed up delivery of stores, parts for machines, oxygen and acetylene, fuels, oils and gasoline. I also checked on why lorries were detained for so long in the central workshop. I also brought Mr. Todd's attention to items (spares for vehicles) which had been charged to our Mabura Project for vehicles which had never been on it.

On my return I travelled by land rover in company with Minister Desmond Hoyte and Engineer Joseph. At Yaya Creek our progress was checked by erosion of the white sand ramp caused by flash floods from the mountain. We all had to collect pieces of driftwood and fill the gaps to allow the land rover to cross. This was the result of one of many instances of warnings I had brought to the notice of engineers building roads in the interior which had been ignored. One must be able to read the signs of the bush. Water levels, as shown on tree trunks is one important sign, but being able to estimate for the consequences of a mountain rush of water, swelling a river by as much as ten feet in an hour or two is another. I had experienced this in the upper Mazaruni River and in the rivers of the Rupununi savannahs and one has to calculate not only the volume but the velocity. It is surprising to see bush and small trees laid flat by these rushing waters.

On 14 November 1973, Minister of Works Desmond Hoyte, Minister of Mines and Forests, Jack, Minister of Economic Development, King, Parliamentary Secretary Wrights and Chief Hydraulics Officer, P. E. Allsopp, paid a visit to the forward line as far as Akaiwanna Mountain. They spent the night in my camp at Ekuk Creek. During our discussions, I mentioned to Minister Jack the deposit of oil shale I had discovered on the slope of the Akarai range of mountains bordering the Brazilian boundary in 1937, at the head of the Essequibo River. He said that I might be called upon at any time to show the location of this to the Geological Department. I told them too there was a vast drainage basin at this point, encompassing the headwaters of the Essequibo River and its large tributaries, the Kasaikaitu and the Kuyuwini, plus the head waters of the Takatu River which form the border to Brazil. In later years, oil was discovered in the Takatu Basin – so why not in the upper Essequibo Basin?

The caterpillar bulldozers had continued to penetrate through the forest to reach the old cattle trail two miles from Kurupukari and Mr. Allsopp and Engineer Joseph, accompanied by Mr. Todd, followed this rough road to walk out to Kurupukari on the right bank of the Essequibo River, 19 November 1973. The following day, a PX13 land rover driver, Mr. Loy, from the engineering department of Guyana Airways Corporation, paid a visit to my camp at Batwall Creek, accompanied by a Mr. Alleyne, on a hunting and fishing trip. I took the opportunity to travel to Kurupukari in their land rover. Captain Allicock, who was stationed at Jason's Camp on the other side of the river, carried us across the river. I took snapshots of the Kurupukari Falls and the compound on the left bank of the river. I checked the mileage from Kurupukari to Ekuk Creek. It was fifty-five and a half miles to the Wismar road junction plus six and a half miles to Wismar, making a total of 148 miles from Wismar to Kurupukari.

I moved from Ekuk Creek to Frenchman's Creek to supervise the installation of hollow wood culverts on the last laterite hills before reaching the cattle trail. Because of the time which would be wasted in travelling the 33 miles from Frenchman's Creek, I moved my tarpaulin tent to the hill overlooking the river at Kurupukari Landing. I had the men clear the old location of the police station, during which they killed three labaria snakes. I set fire to the underbrush before erecting my tent. There were numerous lime trees growing in the area and an avocado pear tree. My camp attendant planted the area around with greens.

On 26 November 1973, the first section of the Unifloat pontoon arrived at Kurupukari, other units arriving by trailers and lorries. I had the caterpillar front-end loader cut and fill the hill slope to the river and cut away the river embankment in preparation for the loading of machines and vehicles to cross the river on the Pontoon. Engineer Joseph asked me to paint the name "DESMOND, H." our Minister's name, on the side of the completed pontoon. Minister Hoyte sent a case of rum and a cartoon of cigarettes for the men on the completion of this phase of the road to Kurupukari Landing.

A channel was marked by floating oil drums below the Kurupukari Falls, as surveyed by Hydrographic Survey. This proved to be a little over a quarter mile distance from bank to bank of the river. However, the same thing happened here when the level of the water in the river rose as had happened on the Cuyuni river when I was on the hydro-power survey. Drums broke free of their moorings and were discovered away down river the following morning. The channel passing, just below the falls, had been known for years to the Amerindians living locally. The first pontoon bridge crossing was completed by the Hydrographic Survey, piloted by Andries, a local Amerindian. Two powerful Harbour Master outboard motors were mounted on the stern of the pontoon, the bow being allowed to move up or down as required.

After this, the machines were sent back from Kurupukari to open the cattle trail to a width of a hundred feet, leaving ten feet as a road shoulder, with a ditch of fifteen feet dug by the bulldozer blade and pushed up to the road centre on either side. This was done to allow the subterranean water penetrating through the white gravel resting on a hard black catch-cow to run off into the creeks. I then had to bridge two ité palm swamps which crossed this section. As he was cleaning up the swamps, the D/7 caterpillar operator, Murray, was scared out of his life when, lifting the blade, a fourteen foot anaconda appeared on it. Murray promptly dropped the blade again and yelled for murder. It was lucky I was in the vicinity. I encouraged Murray to get back on the machine and to work on my signals. I signalled to him to lift his blade easily to allow the snake to move. The moment the snake's head appeared above the swamp water, I grabbed hold of it, just below the head, then I signalled Murray to lift the blade completely from the snake. When it was free, I pulled it out of the swamp, the men scattering in all directions. These snakes are harmless as long as they do not have an anchor for their tail. They cannot wrap around anything and constrict it.

The other machines were sent back into the soft yellow clay area approaching the laterite hills near the cattle trail to widen the clearing to allow the sunlight to come in. Walking from these Siroppa laterite hills to Kurupukari Landing late one afternoon, in company with Enos and McKenzie who were squaring some greenheart timbers for the bridges, I encountered a pair of jaguars at the junction of the road and the trail. Others had seen them in this same vicinity. There was plenty of game in this area especially wild hogs and tapir.

From the Siroppa Hills to the laterite and granite hill at Kurupukari, there is a stretch of two miles, which in full rainy season is covered by four feet of water. If one looks at the map of this area, one can see a stretch of low-lying lands on the right bank of the Essequibo River, starting from Maam Creek and passing between Makari, Siroppa Hills and Kurupukari Landing. This forms a natural channel for flood water flowing down to Indian Island. This was definitely an old river bed; the rounded gravel the bulldozers exposed is only found in running water.

I was informed by the Superintendent of the Surama - Kurupukari project that the Minister, Mr. Desmond Hoyte would be travelling through the road from Georgetown to Lethem in the Rupununi with a "safari" of land rovers. The party, arriving on 11 December 1973, would sleep in Jason's Compound in huts especially built for them on the left bank of the Essequibo River. As I had been Camp Manager on the Mahdia - Annai Road Project in 1970-1971, I was asked to make the necessary arrangements for dinner and coffee on 11 December and prepare a lunch snack for the journey the following day. I dispatched a man and a land rover to Georgetown for food items, cutlery and wares, pots and pans. Requisitions would be forwarded to me at Kurupukari by lorries along with bottled refreshments. I arranged with the Amerindians residing there to supply me with some wild game and packu fish from the river on the day the visitors were to arrive.

Both Jason and Engineer Joseph had reported the bad condition of the road from Kurupukari to Surama. Joseph's land rover had got stuck in the mud and Jason was only able to travel through by tractor. Mr. Todd and I advised Jason and Joseph to call off the "safari", radio the minister and inform him of the condition of the road, but Jason said he was sure they could get through. I had ridden this trail from Surama to Kurupukari when driving cattle on horseback. I had been forced to swim my horse at certain spots. As long as rain was falling, I knew there would be no end of difficulties encountered. There were problems at the camp, too. The "LEC" freezers were taxed to the limit, having meat, fish and drinks to cool and ice to make. I had to give away an amount of packu fish and bush cow meat before it spoiled on my hands. I had to build ground firesides to accommodate the number of pots needed. Unluckily, rain began to fall on the morning of 11 December 1973, making the camp surroundings very muddy and the river embankments very dangerous for the loading of the steel-decked pontoon. I was in touch with Radio Demerara from the time they started the broadcast on the progress of the "safari" so was able to have everything in order for their arrival.

Minister Hoyte and five land rovers made the first crossing on the pontoon at 6:00 p.m. just as night was setting in. I met him at the landing and welcomed the party to the camp. Other participants in the safari arrived at my camp on the other shore and had to be ferried across the river by motor boats, as it was too risky to load vehicles on the pontoon in the dark. My men assisted the visitors in hanging their hammocks as many of them could not tie the ropes safely. Dinner was served volunteer style, queuing up with your plate, cup, knife, fork and spoons for roast and stewed meats, packu broth and fried packu, vegetables and rice, plus rum and sweet drinks. Rain still continued to fall steadily and some of the leaf roofs started to leak. I had to move the ladies continually until they found a dry spot. I was aroused from my sleep at 1:00 a.m. The lorry and jeep drivers had broached the liquor box and were having a jolly time. I had to chase them out of the kitchen to their various huts. The cook had to be up at 4:30 a.m. to prepare snacks for the party and they were disturbing him. Little did I know that he too had been imbibing some drinks. I had to be on his heels later to get the quantity of food prepared.

Visitors were getting up at 4:30 a.m. when I went down to the river to bathe. I warned them about kaimans and the haimaralli snake, whose bite is just as deadly as the bushmaster's, which had a habit of lurking near water spots where food is washed from utensils. Breakfast was served at 6:30 a.m. Rain continued to fall. Mr. Allsopp, Chief Hydraulics officer, gave a talk, advising that the vehicles move forward together so as to give assistance to any that got into difficulties. I joined the Chief Engineer's Chevrolet pick-up, riding on the baggage at the rear. Trouble started half a mile from the start when the army jeep got stuck at the first water lead. From here on there were a series of mishaps: bogging down or slipping off round wood bridges. The Chief Engineer was in constant touch by walkie-talkie radio with the last of the vehicles. At midday, a halt was called to gather all the vehicles and to take out the lunch parcels. To my shame, I discovered that the kitchen staff had been so drunk they had packed only bread in some parcels, fish and bread in others, but mostly the visitors had nothing to eat, including myself.

On resumption, radio communication was lost because some of the vehicles forged ahead and some left behind. Caterpillar tractors were standing by at the very worst spots to give assistance. At one time, a bulldozer was towing seven vehicles. The nylon tow ropes were constantly snapping in an area of soft black mud and rotten vegetation. After crossing Little Mocha Mocha Creek, the party stopped at No. 28 camp for hot coffee and sand-wiches prepared by the men working in that area. Leaving there at 1:00 a.m., the safari proceeded to cross Iwokrama Mountain foot. Exposed gran-ite rocks gave us a bad time and as night fell one could see the sparks struck from the rocks by the treads of the caterpillar machines. After passing over the mountain spur, we entered another stretch of swamplands. Jason's land rover, which was in the lead, got stuck. Our pick-up, going to its assistance, also got bogged down. The Minister's land-rover then tried to give some as-sistance with his front winch, but I advised against it as this type of swamp is like a suck sand: the more you rock the vehicle, the firmer it settles down.

No further progress could be made as at this point the D/7 caterpillar tractor had to go back to help those in difficulties at the rear. Rain contin-ued to drizzle. Everyone spent the balance of a miserable night cooped up in their vehicles. I rolled up in a bag and, covered by my rain coat, cat-napped until the red howlers awoke me at dawn. Caterpillar tractors ap-peared at day break, hauling the leading vehicles clear, the rest following, to Camp 38, where we all appreciated hot coffee from some of the workmen. I took the opportunity to strip off all my wet clothes and had an icy bath in a mountain torrent. The forest changed, leaving the hardwood trees for softwoods and palm trees, manicole and turru palms. The soil was white like silt; the terrain more or less flat. We were now on our way to Surama Savannah where we arrived at the compound at 12:30 p.m. From this savannah, one has a wonderful view of the surrounding mountains.

I met an old friend, Mr. Rufino and his family. These were the people who had given me a house to rest in and food to eat when I came out of the jungle on the 1958 Reconnaissance Survey. Lunch had been prepared for the party and a generous supply of beer was served. Mr. Phang's pick-up was sent back on the road to search for Mr. Lee's land-rover and two others that had not reported to Surama. Afterwards, we proceeded to Woweta Savannah situated in a depression of the surrounding savannah. In heavy rainy season, this area is covered by water. Approaching Annai, the savannah rises, and at Annai compound, amidst the tooting of horns, Minister Hoyte was greeted by the chairman of the community. We then paid a visit to the "Basin" and were given a roast beef and champagne welcome.

All this brought back memories of my previous trips, dating back as far as 1925, again in 1937 and in 1958/59 at the end of my road reconnaissance survey, and now in 1973. I had known many friends who had lived in this area. On leaving the "Basin", the safari had to cross a number of dry or near-dry creek beds. I explained to the Minister that had the rains fallen in the mountains on our journey, some of these waterways would have been impassable, for a near-dry creek bed can turn into a rushing torrent of muddy water two hundred feet wide. At Toka Village, the welcoming party had gone home as the safari had been expected the previous day. At Benoni Creek, a roundwood bridge had been constructed, three feet wide on either side for the wheels of the vehicles but with a gap between. There were some misgiving on the part of the drivers, but as soon as one crossed, the balance followed. From here on was a straight drive across the savannah to Good Hope Police Station, arriving at 7:00 p.m. Looking back over the savannah, I could see the head lights of the following vehicles blinking with the jerks on the rough track, looking like a host of candle flies. We then proceeded on the laterite road to Lethem. The last time I had traversed this road was August 1959.

On crossing the bridge at Pirara Creek, we passed Old Ben Hart's Ranch House. In 1937, I spent the night here as a guest with the American Scientific Expedition on its way through to Brazil. All I could see now were the walls of the house, which had been pitted by rifle bullets when the army put down the ranchers' uprising against the Government. We crossed the Manari

Creek bridge and bypassed the Orella Ranch House, arriving at Lethem
Government Compound at 9:00 p.m., amidst cheering crowds. I learned that
the residents of Lethem, visitors from across the river in Brazil and Amerindians from the outlying savannahs and mountain regions had been waiting
for the past twenty-four hours for our arrival. I recalled Superintendent Jason's
words to Minister Hoyte as we left Kurupukari. He had informed the Minister that this would be the shortest day of the safari, 12 December. It turned
out to be the longest as we did not arrive at Lethem until the following day,
13 December 1973.

Mr. Charlie Melville (who had been with me in 1937) and Peter Gorinsky
were at Lethem to greet us. It was Peter's father who had so kindly put me
up as a visitor on my reconnaissance surveys in 1957-1959. Mr. Gorinsky,
Senior, as Peter recalled, had told me in 1957 that neither he nor his grand-
children would ever see the completion of the road I was surveying. Peter
now said, "Look, you still have come through, sixteen years after your survey" and the idea of the road had been fulfilled. There were cocktail parties, dancing, and a dinner had been arranged as part of the reception. The
Minister opened a new motel. One of the owners was none other than Corporal Bobb who had been in charge of Good Hope Police Station in 1959 when
I finished my survey. He was now retired. I spent the night in a house belonging to the Superintendent of the Lethem Abattoir.

I joined a G.A.C. Caribou plane for Georgetown the following day, 14
December 1973 at 11:30 a.m. I had then to report back to the Mabura -
Kurupukari Project. I reported to Superintendent G. Todd at Frenchman's
Creek Camp. My Letts 1973 Diary had been left at Lethem. I was later in-
formed it had been given to Superintendent Jason. This he denied. I regret-
ted the loss as it contained a year's information on this project. I left French-
man's Creek on 22 December 1973 on my 69th birthday, arriving home in
Georgetown at 11:30 p.m.

CHAPTER XXVIII
Roadbuilding: Wismar to Kurupukari and a Second Retirement – 1974

In January 1974, I was invited to attend a senior officers' meeting with Hon. Minister D. Hoyte to outline the guidelines for the continuation of the Mabura-Kurupukari Road Project. I spent most of January in Georgetown collecting stores, parts, fuels and oils, purchasing and forwarding these to their destination, and sending rations for the men in the forward line by lorries. On 30 January, I was asked by the Minister to travel by land-rover to the junction of the Mabura Road where it connects to the cattle trail to meet an Indo-Guyanese gentleman, just returned from England, who wished to walk over the area from the upper Demerara River at Cannister Falls, to examine the possibilities of rearing sheep on a large scale. God help the sheep amongst the jaguars and pumas that roam this region as their own, I thought, if Mr. Singh decided to settle in this area.

I had my own plans for a development and had applied to Minister Hoyte for the piece of land adjacent to the new road, on both sides, and starting from the end of the white sand at a blackwater creek and ending at Kurupukari landing, encompassing some 1,000 acres. I was told to follow up my application by submitting a surveyor's plan of the area to the National Development and Agricultural Department. I filled out the application forms and paid a fee of five dollars. I later I was interviewed by Mr. Cumberbatch, an officer of the National Development and Agriculture Department who said the area I applied for – 1,000 acres – was too much for one man. I explained to him that this was a remote area. I planned on long term crops: a citrus and coconut plantation. I referred to my ownership of Agatash Estate, 1,700 acres, which I had purchased in 1927. I also explained to him I wanted to open a tourist camp for weekenders from Georgetown, for many visitors had told me it would be a good idea to erect some bush camps, putting in lighting plants, generated by the falls, and refrigerator units. Mr. Cumberbatch as good as told me I could not have the land because the Government had earmarked certain areas in the interior for land settlement and this was one. I was not pleased. For years I had been preaching the need to build roads into the interior so that farmers, loggers, and others could settle there. Here

I was, having been through all the privations of survey life, and having done most of the footwork for the present developments, being told by this youth I could not have the land. This episode still upsets me, now at the time of writing in 1980, when the Government has no money for further development and the essential services are not functioning as there is no foreign capital to import the necessary fuels, when no food other than on the black market is coming into the country and our people, instead of looking to settle in the interior, are emigrating "like rats from a sinking ship."

But life had to go on. I had a hard time travelling back to Frenchman's Creek Camp with lorry driver Nascimento. At 2.10 p.m. at 9 mile on Mabura Road, the diesel engine got an airlock. The driver had to walk out and catch a transport to Rockstone on the Essequibo River to collect parts. He returned at 5:30 p.m. We left there at 6:00 p.m. We were conveying the Flemming men who were returning to Seeballi to continue their gold operations. I dropped them off at 77 mile section at 11:20 p.m. Rain had begun to fall. After clearing Akaiwanna Mountain, the vehicle got an air lock again, two miles from Frenchman's Creek Camp. I decided to walk through the rain, losing the sole of one of my shoes, for they were not made for this type of work. I arrived into camp at 3:25 a.m. I borrowed some of George Todd's clothes as mine were still on the lorry.

Whilst I was in town, I had requisitioned a fuel tanker to transport fuel from Wismar and fill the empty drums at different locations. River transportation had not paid off as we had lost much of the fuel by leaking drums. I had to request that three-quarters of the drums be replaced as all the old ones were leaking. Superintendent Todd had also travelled to Georgetown to acquire some new Chevrolet lorries to replace the old Bedfords, which were constantly breaking down, but these Chevrolet trucks proved a failure as they could not pull a heavy load through white sand areas and their consumption of gasoline was enormous, consuming three or four gallons per mile, so Mr. Todd had to ship them back to Rockstone and receive in place some new Bedfords.

Maintenance work continued in the heavily forested areas, the machines opening the road to a width of eighty feet to allow the sun and the air to come in. Other soft spots had to be surfaced with white sand. Timbers were being cut and hauled to complete the Ukaribi (Camoodie Creek) bridge, Akaiwanna and the shorter bridges across the swamps on the cattle trail and the blackwater creek leading to Kurupukari landing. Whilst I was at Frenchman's Creek, three gentlemen arrived in a Suzuki land rover, one a Chinese man who claimed to have worked with the Frenchmen in the gold mine in the mountain. They had come to investigate the possibilities of reopening the gold mine. Then Mr. Todd moved me back to Kurupukari to push the forward line work, Mr. Bovell, the storekeeper from Surama, being transferred to Frenchman's Creek Camp to take over from me.

At Kurupukari, we were invaded by a group of tourists from Georgetown in three land-rovers. They had come to see the road and to hunt and fish. They agreed with my ideas about opening tourist camps. Members of the Motor Racing Association also arrived, on Honda and Kawasaki motor cycles and in a land-rover. The party in the three land-rovers made an attempt to go through to the savannah lands to Lethem but were turned back by the heavy rain fall and washouts in the road. During the visit of the Racing Association people, I carried them over the river to the Amerindian settlement. They took numerous snapshots and saw a tame black kibihi about the size of a small dog. Mr. Vieira invited these Amerindians to come back to Kurupukari that night for some drinks. They got so drunk, I had to get Enos' son to carry back the women and children by boat. One child was left behind as he had fallen asleep in a hammock. Another incident occurred with one of our survey party having too much to drink and picking up a cutlass to chop the huntsman, an Amerindian youth. I had to speak severely to this man and send him off to his camp. This noisy incident so frightened the Amerindian youth that he ran to hide in the bush near the river. I had to call and coax him out, then I took him to my camp to sleep in a cot until the next day.

There was a shutdown of operations for Easter, because the heavy rains were impeding progress. I stayed on at Kurupukari and had Enos and his son as watchmen at Frenchman's Creek Camp. On 22 April 1974, Superintendent Todd informed me that the Minister had given him four days to complete the surfacing by white sand of the mud areas approaching the cattle trail. He was then to leave Kurupukari and go back to 10 miles where he was to open a large compound. I had to ship back all stores and fuels and oils to 10 mile, just keeping on hand sufficient for my machines. One tractor-trailer was assigned to Surveyor Kissoon, to assist him in transporting his food and equipment on the road to Surama. I had to get the pontoon to transport fourteen horses across the river. These horses were en route to the Rupununi Savannah.

I received a visit from the District Commissioner for Upper Demerara River, Mr. Persaud. He spent two days at my camp as he was visiting the tributors in the area to check on their permits and gold claims. My next task was to go to Surama to collect all empty fuel drums. We stopped at 18 mile creek, which is deep and clear, with large granite rocks which form deep pools. I left the men to catch some haimara fish, whilst I went with one man to check on the higher reaches of this creek. We encountered a fair-sized jaguar which slunk into the bush on our approach. Mr. Bovell, storekeeper at Surama, had been instructed to travel back with a tractor-trailer to carry all the stores and equipment to be forwarded from Kurupukari to 10 mile compound. Because of the small size of the trailer, Bovell had to make three trips. I took an inventory of all the tools at Kurupukari and sent back all available machines to 10 mile.

Francis Ram and seven others arrived in a diesel powered land-rover P.I. 2903. They were on their way to Lethem. I told them of Mr. De Nobriga's mishap due to washouts on the Surama Road. Mr. Ram told me he had done this trip some years previously, by the old cattle trail from Tacama Berbice River, crossing at Cannister Falls on the upper Demerara River. When Mr. Ram returned some days later, he broke down at Mocha-Mocha Creek and my tractor had to haul his land-rover out to Kurupukari. Another visitor was Mr. Justine Pierre who arrived at Kurupukari to do some river prospecting for diamonds. Justine had been with me in 1937-1938 on the trip through Brazil with the New York Zoological Expedition. On 16 May 1974 I suffered a slipped disc at the landing. I suffered intense pain and could barely crawl back to my tent on the hill. I radioed Mr. Todd at 10 mile compound and reported the incident. I requested transportation out to Georgetown. Three engineers arrived in a hardtop land rover but I could neither bend nor sit down without suffering pain, although these men had offered to convey me out. I could not lie in my hammock, but had to crawl on my belly into a canvas cot. Then Mr. Todd sent a canvas-topped land-rover in which I had to stand up all the way out to 10 mile compound and although the driver was very careful, every little jerk caused me intense pain. We left at 8:15 a.m. and arrived at 10 mile compound at 6:00p.m. I was in intense pain when I arrived, having covered 131 miles of rough bush road in nine and three-quarter hours. I was given a plate of food and some hot coffee. I continued my journey to Georgetown in the surveyor's land rover, standing all the way.

Back in Georgetown, the doctor told me I had done more damage to my back muscles and ligaments by travelling those 216 miles over rough bush track than if I had laid down on my cot and rested for two weeks at Kurupukari. I was on my back for ten days, my wife having to spoon feed me, as it was very painful even to lift my head. The doctor visited every other day to give me treatments with a heat lamp. I was given 14 days' sick leave but had to extend it another eight days, which was deducted from my vacation leave. The doctor had to practically lift me off the bed and teach me to walk again. Whilst at home, Mr. George Todd visited me and informed me he was requesting a transfer back to Georgetown for family reasons.

On 12 June 1974, I returned to 10 miles where Mr. Todd introduced me to Superintendent De Rouche. No camp had been erected for me so I spent one night in Mr. Todd's camp and one night in the radio shack. Since I got off my bed in town, I suffered from a severe pain in my left hip, right down into the calf of my left leg. I could barely crawl along with the assistance of a stick. I returned to Georgetown for further treatment. I saw two doctors who injected my leg until I resembled a pin cushion. I swallowed any amount of pills without relief. My wife said it was time I gave up working in the interior as I would be entering my 70th year in December 1974. My family and the proprietors of Plantation Drill, Mahaicony, wished me to return and manage the estate again.

On my return to 10 mile, I had to visit the Mackenzie Hospital to take physiotherapy treatment. Mr. Wharton, who was in charge of this treatment, turned out to be one of the students from England who had worked as a volunteer on the Mahdia Self-Help Road. I reminded him of his hut, the V.I.P.s, about which he laughed. I tried to supervise as much of the forward line clearing from my land-rover, for I could not move freely on my leg, which continued to pain me. Rain began to fall again so I sent home for my oil paints, brushes and canvas to occupy my time in camp.

From information I'd been given, I travelled some of the old timber trails to locate deposits of laterite rock and gravel, and areas in front to locate sand clay. Whilst in this remote areas, I distinctly heard my name called. It had first happened when I was locating air strips for Major "Art" Williams in 1945. I was camped along with five other men in a tarpaulin tent on a laterite ridge. I recollect it was bright moonlight when I awoke. I sat in my hammock and lit a cigarette. I distinctly heard a voice calling "Matthew! Matthew!" I swung around to see who was calling, but saw no one other than the other men in camp. In 1948, whilst I was on my own, prospecting for gold in the Mazaruni River at Awarapari Creek, I distinctly heard the call "Matthew! Matthew!" and now here I was, cutting a rough line in the bush to try to check the extent of the sand-clay deposit, when I heard again, "Matthew! Matthew!", never more than twice. Thinking someone was calling me to go to where the machine was clearing the area to make a borrow pit, I asked the land-rover driver if he had followed me into the bush to call me. He had not.

I travelled to 40 mile, to my old camp ground. There I had to open a large compound on the white sand and locate a source of fresh water to pump into overhead tanks to supply the houses that were to be erected there. I received a radio message from Georgetown to proceed to the forward line on the way to Kurupukari to help search for a land-rover belonging to the Agricultural Department, which was long overdue. I took a lorry and driver, two porters and a power saw operator. After surmounting Akaiwanna Mountain, we discovered the missing vehicle at 106 mile. It had suffered a broken axle crossing the mountain. We hooked it to the lorry and set off. Late in the evening we encountered heavy mists, particularly in the cleared areas of white sand, and the lorry had to creep on some of the down slopes as the headlights showed the bush in front but not the road.

When day dawned, we were in the vicinity of 19 mile. The loose sand at 15 mile proved too much of a drag on the lorry with the broken land-rover. I told the men to leave the vehicle there and get back to camp. The grader, a far heavier machine, would be sent to tow it into camp. Whilst at 40 mile camp, my huntsman set out at night to shoot a tapir and narrowly missed being bitten by a large labaria snake. He was lucky to see the snake in the beam of his torch light and shot it. He was good bringing in powis, deer, labba, wild hogs and haimara fish. Unfortunately, he slipped and fell whilst fishing and slit open his wrist on a broken mora spur. I had to put seventeen stitches into his flesh. He took this operation without a murmur but another of the men at my camp, an Afro-Guyanese who had to take five stitches in his hand after he slipped and fell on his cutlass could have been heard howling with pain half a mile away.

I handed in my resignation to Superintendent De Rouche and Engineer Joseph and informed my Minister that due to the injury to my back and my subsequent disability in moving around, I felt it better if someone else could fill my place. I handed in all my camp equipment to the stores and got a clearance slip. I travelled to Rockstone so that my driver and camp attendant could draw their wages. I bade farewell to all my men and left 10 mile location on 30 August 1974 and travelled to Georgetown.

CHAPTER XXIX
A Return to Plantation Drill and a Year of Deaths – 1974-76

I reported to the proprietors of Plantation Drill at their Bel Air home in Georgetown on the same day as I left the road project. I informed them I had dropped off three greenheart beams I had brought from the bush to the estate for bridge building. I informed Mrs. R.G.Humphrey I would take over the duties as manager on the estate on 2 September. She told me Andrew Fraser, who would be leaving for Canada shortly, was still occupying my old house, so I would have to occupy the proprietor's two-storeyed house and the servants would be instructed to look after my meals and my general needs.

On 2 September 1974, I travelled the thirty-two miles from Georgetown by courtesy of the proprietor's car, driven by Alli. On my arrival, I did not meet Andrew, who had taken over from me in July 1970, so I handed a letter from Mrs. Humphrey to Sharon, his daughter, in which the proprietors had instructed him to hand over everything to me as from that day's date. My wife and I were shown to our bedroom by Stella McCalmont, the maid and Johanna Dalrymple, the cook. I met Andrew Simpson, the ranger whom I had left there in 1970, and told him my plans for taking an inventory.

The following day, on Andrew Fraser's return to the estate, I received the cash in hand, one "Unique" automatic pistol .32 and six bullets. I checked 156 head of cattle, 393 pigs and 5 horses. I checked with the cow minder to see if he was still keeping a daily tally of the milk production. I inspected the shallow well in the pig compound. I was informed by Andrew Fraser that the deep well in the main compound was running dry. He had to pump out the water for use in the cow pen. It had lost the force of its natural flow. I indicated that this job would be a priority matter, as water was essential for the cattle and for the adjoining gardens.

Now that I was once again moving around the estate to see things for myself, the reins of administration automatically fell back into my hands, but more than anything, I noted that the pain in my leg had disappeared. On a farm, one has to be continually on one's toes, up with the birds at dawn and to bed after sun down. One has to be prepared for emergencies of all kinds, not only with the livestock, but also one's cultivation, irrigation and drainage. A farmer's life is no bed of roses, for there are many disappointments to face: drought and floods, failure of crops, the stealing of produce, just to mention a few. One must have faith and patience and a belief in the Almighty. It is no use to take on a job of this kind unless you love the life. One must be interested in the work to make a success of it. I have been fortunate throughout my working life to be able to work mostly in the open air: farming, reconnaissance surveys, road construction, diamonds and gold. I may at times have suffered privations and near starvation, but the lure of the open spaces always drew me. The only indoor work that held me to my desk was drawing, mapping, and later in my retirement, oil painting on canvas.

I held a meeting with some farmers who were occupying part of the La Reasonable section of coconut cultivation for their kitchen gardens. I told them I would issue permits for those granted permission to plant, on the understanding no rent would be charged, but they would have to keep the area clean. I emphasised that they were to plant no long term plants (plantain or banana suckers) and warned them against stealing coconuts. I informed them that if our cattle penetrated the area and damaged their gardens, they were permitted to impound them. The fences were not in perfect condition as vandals had uprooted the posts and stolen the wire. I had, though, an instance of a farmer, who claimed to have a farm in the Sarah West section of our cultivation, chasing my boys who were grazing cattle, with a cutlass. Since Mr. Fraser had given all farmers in this section notice to quit the land some months previous to my return, I served a notice on this man warning that if he was found on the coconut cultivation without proper authority, he would be charged with trespassing. It seems this man went to the Regional Minister to complain, for I received a letter from Minister Salim requesting that I give the farmer time to reap his short term crop. I replied that I had been back on the estate five months, that he had been given sufficient time to reap those crops, but I acceded to the Minister's request.

I arranged with Girdharry, the cowminder, to take over the cottage in the compound, which had been empty for some time, to save him travelling from Enmore every morning and returning by bus at night. He could bring his wife who could plant the small garden there. The benefit of having him live there was that at any time I was absent he would act as a watchman. I was visited by the district assistant veterinary officer, Mr. Khan, to invite me to a seminar on livestock to be held in the Mahaicony Government School. He said he would be in to see my cattle and pigs to check for an exhibition at Sophia. I contacted Mr. Ramlall at Mahaica to find out if he had a good stallion for sale, as I wanted to get one to serve the five mares I had. Ramlall had some good bloodlines from an English thoroughbred which he had imported some years before. He told me that he had sold his two stallions to Mr. Geoffrey Fraser at Bushy Park estate so I had to borrow one from Mr. Fraser.

A Mr. Frank Allen, Barrister at Law, paid a visit to inspect his beehives and extract some combs for honey. We found, unfortunately, that due to the spraying of insecticides on the coconut cultivation and the rice crops, many bees were dead in the fields. It was when I was manager there in 1968-1970 that Mr. Allen had approached the proprietors to allow him to keep some beehives on the estate. I later joined with him and supplied two hives of my own, as well as subscribing financially. We occasionally imported one or two queens from the U.S.A. At a later date, Mr. Allen got other people interested and a company was formed. An expansion programme was put forward to purchase land at Parika and Mahaicony on which to set up new hives and to build an extraction house. There was a growing market for honey and its by-products locally and abroad, though not without its cost. I had some painful experiences, receiving numerous stings, whilst Mr. Allen was schooling me in the care of bees. In later years, I was to introduce beekeeping to the residents at Mahdia in the Potaro District and at Matthews Ridge in the Northwest Region.

I purchased 276 feet of six foot chain-link fencing to keep cattle from breaking into my garden and planted this area with a few three-years coconut plants, plantain and banana suckers, cassava, sweet potatoes, tomatoes, corn, pepper and eschallot. I had some grapefruit trees already bearing. This area had been an old cattle paddock – the soil was of a brown sandy loam. I got some wonderful returns from this garden.

Nearly two months after my arrival on the estate Mr. and Mrs. Andrew Fraser and their children left the estate on 27 October 1974 for Canada. I immediately put on some men to cobweb and wipe out the house in preparation for painting. They also cleaned out the bottom house in which was stored a lot of junk. I had the carpenter make some shelves with intermediate divisions (bins) in which I had one of the men sort bolts and nuts of all sizes. A 'tall boy' was built, the top section for storing parts for tractors and bulldozers, the middle section for nails of various sizes; the bottom, other stores. A padlocked cupboard held tools for the vehicles and other equipment. Lubrication oils and gasoline were kept under lock and key in this store room. Tar, white lime and field tools were stored in the open room near the door. I had the men break down an old gasoline bond and fowl pen behind the proprietor's house, preserving the best materials to build an office next to the storeroom. I had the floor of the storeroom and the office cemented. Half inch wire mesh was nailed around the sides above the walls, instead of windows. All unserviceable items were thrown into a hole which was later filled in with earth. Old engines and water pump were stored in the old donkey stables. I then filled in and cemented the area of the old copra bond, to make extended storage space for paddy reaped from the fields. I had the carpenter lay the greenheart beams I had brought from the bush across the side-line trench and leading to the front entrance of the proprietor's house and plank off the bridge.

I received sixteen gallons of paint (pink, blue, green, white) and one gallon of turpentine on 5 November 1974. Painting commenced the following day and was completed by the 12th. I ordered Aquatite with which to stop the leaks in the roof. This was then painted red. The men were all amateur painters so there was a general clean up of floors and windows.

Shortly after my arrival on the estate, I had received a letter from the Permanent Secretary of Finance, Mr. De Abreu, asking me to call in to see him at the earliest opportunity to discuss a matter to my interest. Mr. De Abreu told me that Minister Desmond Hoyte had asked the Government that some reward be granted to me for services rendered to the country during my life time. The matter of a State pension would be discussed at Cabinet as would be the issue of some award for services rendered to my Country. The Government also wanted me to give an exhibition of my paintings and an account of my pioneering work.

I travelled to Georgetown to visit the Manager of the Guyana Water Authority to get some expert advice on the reactivation of our deep well. On my return to the estate, I wrote a letter to the Ministry of Works requesting the purchase of a corrugated 4ft. diameter tube to act as a koker, and a letter to the Ministry of Transport and Harbours Department offering to purchase some old railway rails to act as bridge bearers on bridges I intended to build across the riceland canals. I visited some of the outlying coconut cultivations and found they had been badly neglected, allowing heavy bush and wild trees to the diameter of four to six inches to grow between the coconut trees. One section especially was noted for the size of its nuts. There the fences had been removed, leaving the area open to thieves. To safeguard against these heavy losses, I knew that a clear view of the area had to be maintained for the benefit for the rangers. However, due to the size of the trees, the mechanical weeder would have been of no use, so I gave out the clearing of the area to axe and cutlass men. The general maintenance work was repairs to wire fencing, collecting and transporting coconuts from field to bond, weed-

ing compounds, collecting and transporting pig feed, weeding sections of
the coconut cultivation, cleaning drainage trenches and checking the sale
of coconuts and pigs weekly.

Dr. Fraser, chairman of the company, paid periodic visits and gave me
advice. He said I should feed the cows 2% urea to 98% of molasses. Dr.
Fox, veterinary officer, assisted with sick pigs and cattle. Mr. Pooran, rice
board officer in the district, came in for discussions on rice.

I travelled to the Rice Development Corporation at Burma to order 3,000
rice bags for my autumn crop. Mr. Reynolds, field mechanic, said it would
cost me $16.50 per hour to have a rice combine travel from Burma to Drill
Estate. He said he would travel to Plantation Drill to check on my rice during the week. Because of the dry weather, the rice ripened faster than I an-
ticipated. Mr. Reynolds contacted me early the next day to inform me he
had a Massey-Ferguson Combine at Perth Village. If I took it now, it would
save me paying transportation from Burma. I immediately contacted workmen from Fairfield to report the next day for reaping operations. I started
reaping on 6 October and finished on 27 October bringing in 4,959 bags of
paddy. The charge for reaping is $2.00 per bag regardless of the weight,
which is why proprietors hold out for the larger bags which can take 140
pounds of paddy. Lately, though, the bags supplied from Burma can barely
hold 120 pounds and they are so rotten they will tear if pressed.

There was constant dissatisfaction from farmers on the grading of paddy
at the Government's Burma Mills. My first shipment was awarded "C" and
extra "D". My next shipment was downgraded to substandard at $11.00 per
bag. When I informed my Chairman, Dr. Fraser, of this he instructed me to
ship some of the substandard to him at East Lothian Mills where he produced No. 1 Rice. I took a sample of this rice and showed the Manager of
Burma Mills that this was the rice produced from the paddy he had designated substandard. I therefore shipped the balance of my crop to East Lothian, where I received not only a higher grade in rice, but benefited by
receiving the side products.

There was an unfortunate accident when my foreman, Singh, getting off
the tractor-trailer by his home was hit by a motor car, smashing his legs. He
was taken to the Georgetown Hospital where he lost one leg and spent a
couple of months recuperating. On 30 November 1974, I received a new-
land rover, though I could not get another diesel and had to be content with
a gasoline motor. It was grey in colour with a cream hard top and no ventila-
tion. I had to dispense with the glass windows in the rear doors so as to
allow free passage of air. This was after one of the pigs being driven to town

died on the way and the other was only saved by the driver turning back to the estate. Then Baba Tangayan, the gardener from the proprietor's garden, reported sick and was taken to the Georgetown Hospital on 2 January 1975 where he died two days later. The same week, Stephen, my carpenter, had to be rushed to Mahaicony Cottage Hospital suffering from alcoholic poisoning. I had long been warning this man about his drinking and had threatened to dismiss him, but I saw it was a waste of time. I was to suffer another shock when I learned of the death of one of the proprietors, Miss Winnie Fraser, a most dedicated gardener. She was buried the following day and I was asked to be one of the pall bearers. Baba Tangayan's funeral was also well attended by all the villagers and his fellow workers. I met his son from Canada and his daughters. A wreath made from his own garden flowers was arranged by the maid and cook from the proprietor's and a card affixed: "Rest in peace thou good and faithful servant". The day after Miss Winnie was buried, I learned of the death of the cook, Johanna Dalrymple, who was at the Georgetown Hospital. It was exceedingly bad luck for the estate: three deaths within two weeks. Stella, the maid, was now afraid to stop at Drill House alone as the estate boys said they saw Baba's ghost in the yard. I told her the boys were only joking to make her nervous.

I moved from Drill House into my own house after Christmas. It still smelled of paint. I noted how bare the walls were without any pictures. At a later date, I painted 15 scenes from the interior. One four foot by two foot painting of Kaieteur Falls was greatly admired by the Chairman, Dr. Fraser who said *that* resembled a real Kaieteur. Electrical wiring was renewed in all the houses and the Electric Corporation men connected our lines to their main line.

Ploughing for the spring rice crop began early November 1974 and the first seed paddy was shied on 13 January 1975. I informed the proprietors of my intention to have a dragline dig out our main drainage trenches which had been badly silted up. Now that the Government had decided to dig out Bellamy Canal, the main drainage trench which drew off the water from all the estates adjoining Drill, I saw a chance of improving our drainage. I also arranged to renew the main koker from Drill main drainage trench to Bellamy Canal. I started reaping the spring crop from four fields in Davis section, recovering some 1520 bags of paddy from fifty acres, the highest yield per acre I recovered since I have been on the estate. No sooner was the spring crop harvested, I had the tractors ploughing lands for the autumn crop on fields I had selected. We shied N.79 seed paddy on 20 May 1975 onto fields that had been ploughed. By then the dry weather had been broken by heavy rains. I selected some of the Hybrid "S" seed paddy recovered from my spring crop in the Davis section to replant in my autumn crop.

Plantation Drill and the adjoining estates had to await the rains before planting as there was no irrigation water to assist. This problem had been put before the previous Minister for Agriculture who promised to help, but up to the time I left the estate, Government had made no move to assist. I had pointed out that the lands between Mahaicony and Mahaica carried a waterway from the upper Mahaica Creek which brought water right down to the coast lands and that during the time of the early Dutch occupancy this had been used to ship the slave-grown cotton from the backlands, in punts to the coast. This old canal was silted up, barely discernible. If the government really wanted to help the rice farmers, this old canal, if opened up even to half of its width, could supply the coast lands with fresh water. Instead, they decided to cut a canal parallel to the road from Mahaica Creek to bring in water, but what happens when the dry weather sets in? Where would they get the fresh water for the land? Then the creeks push down NO fresh water and, on the other hand, salt water comes in with the tides.

The Government "bee" expert dropped in for a visit to inspect our bee-hives, along with a friend from Holland. Seeing my oil paintings in the house, he asked which university I had studied at. I said the interior was my tutor, but otherwise I had taught myself. He said I had a gift from God. That same month, May, I travelled to Georgetown to attend a ceremony at Guyana House at which President Chung pinned the Medal of Service on my jacket for outstanding service to Guyana in Interior Development. Dr. Fraser, our Chairman, received a higher award for his services in the veterinary field. The proprietors were greatly pleased that there were two honours for persons from the estate.

Heavy rains fell during the months of May-June. I had to order two cage-wheels to assist the tractors in the mud of the rice fields. The preparation of all lands available was going ahead to plant for the autumn crop. The weather was not the only cause of problems. One afternoon, the cowminder reported to me the poultry boy had drank some malathion from a bottle. I ran over to the proprietors yard and found Mohammed in the gardener's potting room lying on the floor. I put him in the land-rover and rushed him to Mahaicony Cottage Hospital where the nurses pumped out his stomach. It seemed that the ranger had remonstrated with Mohammed over something to do with his work and this was how the boy had reacted. Then my pig-minder, Rutherford, was sent to the Georgetown Hospital by the G.M.O., Dr. Harricharran, where he died on 21 July 1975. The estate seemed to be suffering from a jinx, for this was the fourth death in six months. Then Carpenter Stephen was apprehended by the ranger with seven coconuts in a bag on his way home. He begged my pardon and said it would not happen again. However, I was made to understand this was a regular practice on his part to sell the coconuts and take the money to buy rum. I told Stephen that if he wanted a few nuts, all he had to do was to ask me and I would have given them to him, as he was an employee of the estate. On another occasion, I gave the ranger my gun to patrol the boundary adjoining the next estate where thieves were rampant. The ranger got up in a tree, but when he saw the thief with a bag of coconuts, he fired over the man's head, instead of at the legs. The thief dropped the bag of nuts and ran.

Wisi-wisi ducks were swarming on to the rice fields to eat the paddy seed so I invited Mr. Gonsalves from Mahaicony and Mr. Machado from Belfield to come with their guns for the sport of shooting them. I also did some night hunting for labba in company with Machado who was very fond of the sport. My doberman bitch gave birth to eleven pups under my front steps. I had to move them to the kennel. A week later, I missed "Shaney" and called several times but she did not appear. I sent out a search party and the men found her with her right front paw wrapped with barbed wire. Dr. Fox, the veterinary officer, was called in to look at the dog as she was getting a fever. He said it was nothing and the dog must have caught a chill. He prescribed no medicine and said the dog would be OK in a couple of days. The next morning when I went to visit "Shaney" I found her stretched out as stiff as a board – dead. She left seven pups which my wife had to feed with a nursing bottle. I had the men dig a grave on a high spot in the front paddock near the road. I cried like a child as I felt the loss very much. She was a good companion and watch dog. I received a letter from the Secretary of the company with her regrets. The night watchman and the men in the yard also missed her very much. When Shaney heard me get up in the morning, she would run up the steps to hit the back door with her paws, creating a noise until I let her in for her milk.

I had to bid farewell to my daughter Dianna, her husband Ronald, and my granddaughter Karen as they left on 10 July 1975 to take up residence in Canada. I did though receive a surprise visit from my niece Margaret who now lived in the island of Antigua with her children. She slept at my house with her one daughter, the other two children were staying with Geoffrey Fraser at the next estate. Margaret spent her birthday, August 1, with me. They were very interested in my photo album. Margaret had to leave as she was flying back to Antigua, but said that the children would return to spend some time in Guyana. Charmain, the eldest girl of eleven years, took over my kitchen and, putting out Sheila, my cook, made ham & eggs and toast. She was foot and foot with me all over the estate and travelled in the trailer with the men to collect coconuts from the field. She was a real tomboy, climbing all the fruit trees in the yard.

I strained my back in the yard helping the men lift a trailer off its wheels. I kept forgetting that I suffered from a slipped disc. I had to travel to town to visit a physiotherapist. The doctor said it was better I keep moving around than if I lay down in bed. I visited the G.M.O. of the district who gave me an injection and some pills, but got very little relief. I eventually had to travel back to town, on my wife's insistence that I saw an American doctor who gave me a series of twelve heat lamp treatments which did away with all the pain in my back and legs, after all the months of seeing various doctors.

I returned to the estate to reap a bumper autumn crop, recovering 7,057 bags of paddy, an average of 30 bags per acre. The proprietors gave a bonus to their employees and raised the wages of some of the more worthy employees on my recommendation. I began the ploughing for the 1976 spring crop at the end of October.

I learned of the death of my brother-in-law from heart failure whilst I was reading in bed on 30 November 1975. I woke my wife to tell her. It seemed as if this year was full of deaths of people who were close to me and those that had worked with me. On 22 December 1975, I celebrated my 70th birthday, and my wife and I travelled to Pln. Leonora to spend Christmas with my niece.

In the new year I returned to my other love when I was commissioned by Mr. George Fraser to paint a picture of his estate, Bushy Park from the road, showing the coconut cultivation with the manager's house, the water tanks, poultry pens, pig pens. On presenting this to Mr. Fraser, he said it seemed as if I had not left out one coconut tree. Dr. Fraser's daughter Judy purchased a river scene of the upper Essequibo river to carry back to Australia. I received a visit from my eldest daughter, Mavis, from England and one grand daughter. On their return to England they took three paintings, one a self-portrait.

That year, the May-June rains set in before I completed reaping the spring crop. I lost thirty-eight acres of paddy due to high water in the fields, the paddy lying down in the water and growing again. When I started to shy seed paddy on the fields prepared for the autumn crop, I had to pump water continuously from the rice fields due to heavy rains. Some fields had to be shied with seed paddy twice, only to lose them to high water. I lost two of the fillies born to my mares and suffered the loss of some of my cattle. I reported to head office my losses in the rice fields and amongst my livestock. Nineteen seventy-six seemed to have started off as badly as the previous year which had ended in so many deaths. I applied for a month's leave to travel to Canada to visit my daughter. I left on 17 July 1976 but had to return on 14 August to reap my autumn rice crop.

Then I received a letter from the Minister for Economic Development requesting I take charge of the renovation of the Bartica - Potaro Road. I was offered a salary with allowances, plus a free house, amounting to more than twice what I was receiving as manager of Plantation Drill. I broached the subject with the proprietors of the estate who said that I knew the state of the finances of the company. They could not afford to pay me that salary, neither could I look for a pension from the estate. They knew I was a good man or else the Government would not have recalled me and then again they knew of the love I had for the interior. They said they would miss me very much but that they would not stand in the way of such an offer. I took stock of my livestock, made up my reports on the rice cultivation and handed over all my books and figures to the Secretary of the company. The couple of years I spent there had been like a second home and I was sorry to leave.

CHAPTER XXX

Return to Government Service: Road Maintenance Potaro and Mazaruni –
1976-77

I was once again to work in an area which I had traversed some years previously. The Hon. Minister for Economic Development informed me that cabinet had approved my appointment as Superintendent of Roads in the Potaro-Mazaruni area. I would be working under the Maintenance Engineer for Roads in the Interior. I was informed that the road from 93 miles to 114 miles had deteriorated badly due to bad drainage and had numerous large pot holes.

The Superintendent in charge of Ministry Equipment would check on available road equipment and let me know what I could acquire elsewhere. On learning there was no refrigerator in the house at 111 mile compound, Mahdia, I ordered a kerosene refrigerator as there was no electricity in that area. I was given a small Diahatsu jeep. I hired Claude King, a driver-mechanic, to drive this vehicle. I also purchased some four gallon plastic jerry cans to carry kerosene oil for the refrigerator and gasoline for the jeep. I also purchased some 20 gauge cartridges for my gun for I knew from experience the amount of game to be had in that region. My food and personal belongings were packed in the tray of a German lorry driven by one J. Baptiste who would be travelling to Mahdia in my company. I collected mails and letters of introduction from the Maintenance Engineer.

I left Georgetown on 7 October 1976 travelling via the highway to Linden (Mackenzie), crossing the bridge spanning the Demerara river to Wismar, west along the Rockstone Road, passing the Mabura Road Junction at 6 mile, and out to the river at Rockstone Ministry Compound, then north and down river to Sherima where our vehicles were ferried over the river below the Sherima Rapids by a motor powered pontoon to the left bank. The river below this crossing is wide and smooth. At the Ministries compound on the left bank, I met an old friend, John, who used to be my camp labourer at Camp "Young" Self-Help Road Project 1970. He was now operating the lighting plant at this compound. I noted the quantity of machinery and vehicles in this compound. I visited the radio operator, Allicock, who had also been at 114 mile Camp "Young" during the road project. We proceeded on the

Sherima road to 19 miles Bartica-Potaro Road Junction (I had prospected this area for sand clay deposits in 1960-64), then we swung north to Bartica passing through very familiar scenery. I noted the bamboo I had planted at the 9 mile fill in 1960 growing thickly and holding the road shoulder. I saw with my own eyes the deterioration of the road surface where only colas had been sprayed on the sand clay surface, exposing the original white sand base. The only surface standing up was the stone work I had done at the 10 mile and 8 mile hill slopes. I arrived at Bartica where I met a number of old acquaintances, then I went to see the new District Superintendent, Mr. Chung. I arranged to borrow eight drums of dieselene to carry to 114 miles. I overnighted in CD Persaud's *Hotel Modern*, where I had spent many nights en route to various parts of the interior. I left Bartica the following day at midday. After passing 22 mile, we entered the one track bush road, passing through the cool wallaba forest, eventually arriving at 72 miles compound at 7:30 p.m. I handed in some mails to Ramsaroop, the D.S.I.. I was tired and hungry from travelling but was not even offered a cup of tea and had to sleep hungry in the Rest House.

The following day I travelled to 111 miles compound, Mahdia, where I met Sonny Persaud, who was the overseer, and his wife. I handed Sonny the letter from the Maintenance Engineer, instructing Sonny to handover everything to me. Mrs. Persaud was very kind in inviting me to partake of a meal and some coffee. I then went to the Rest House in the 112 mile compound where my driver King and I would stay until I could occupy my house when Sonny moved out. There were three bedrooms and one large bedroom to accommodate seven beds, a bathroom and water closet and a kitchen with an old oil-burning stove. Because of the dry weather the district was experiencing, there was no water in the wooden vat, therefore no water could be pumped into the Rest House tank to take a shower. I told King to drive me to Water Dog Creek at 114 miles, just beyond the airport, where we took a bath in the cool clear waters of the creek. I filled two containers with fresh water for our cooking purposes.

The following day I drove to Apanachi on the Issano Road to meet Oscar Clarke who had been with the Road Project at Muruwa 1971, to see if he could activate a D/7 caterpillar bulldozer which I could use at 114 mile. Clarke was now working with the Upper Mazaruni Road Project and held a foreman's position. I then travelled back to 72 mile compound where I found J. Baptiste's German lorry in the workshop. He said a tree stump had jammed the cab by the side of the road. I found the grader operator Barnwell parked in the compound and instructed him to leave immediately for 111 mile compound. He was to grade all the rough spots on his way in.

The only tractor trailer driver, Benjamin, and two labourers were engaged in loading water from the 109 mile creek into two 400 gallon tanks with buckets to transport to 112 Mile Compound. This was a constant operation as there had been no rainfall for weeks. I was later to borrow a Honda pump from one of the St. Lucian storekeepers to pump this water from the creek, so instead of eight or nine trips to 112 mile, I could get double the quantity in a much shorter time. The next day I inspected all the Government buildings with Sonny Persaud, the laterite quarry at 114 mile with road foreman Hunte and the maintenance work being done on the road. I went through all the paper work with Sonny Persaud before signing the takeover. Sonny informed me that when he took over from his predecessor, there had been no proper check taken or inventory. I had to report this matter to the D.S.I. I took a physical check of stores, yards and buildings at 111 mile with the assistance of road foreman Hunte and E. Baird, Amerindian foreman. On 14 October 1976, Sonny Persaud and his wife left for Bartica in my jeep, King driving. Persaud was on transfer to the Essequibo Coast, but he left his belongings in the house. I took on an Amerindian, Mario Francis, from Paramakotoi Village over the mountain to be my huntsman. He would use my 20 gauge single-barrel gun, receiving four cartridges every morning he went hunting. All meat was to be brought to me so that foreman Hunte could share it between my workmen. I also hired four Amerindians from Campbelltown, a settlement within the Mahdia area. I instructed foreman Hunte to use these men in the underbushing of the 114 mile laterite deposit as I wanted to excavate laterite boulders for road repairs.

I had no machinery to use on excavation so I had to put a gang of six men to prise up the rocks with crow bars. To get them out, they had to smash these rocks with sledge hammers to a size that could be handled to load into the lorry. These men were paid at a higher rate than the ordinary labourers. I ordered some post-hole borers with which I could prospect for sand clay deposits. The area aback of the laterite quarry was further investigated. I found a number of 40ft x 4ft x 4ft shafts that had been sunk by McBain & Co., gold prospectors. This gave me an idea of the extent of the laterite deposit lying available for road work for a number of years to come.

Grader operator Barnwell was again requested to return to the Toolsie Persaud Timber grant to do some more grading. I met the District Administration Officer, Mr. Neville Williams and the People's National Congress Chairman, Mr. Springer, with whom I worked very smoothly for the time I was engaged in my work there.

The Ministry carpenters from 72 Miles were presently engaged in building an armoury under the police station in 112 Mile compound. I checked with my carpenter for materials required for the Kangaruma Rest House and tressel for the overhead water tank. Two empty oil drums and a connecting pipe would be required for the cooling system of the power plant at the rest house. On my last visit to Kangaruma, I had met Smith and his wife who were now the caretakers for the rest house. Smith had been my compound labourer at 17 mile on the Bartica road in 1962. He had quite a nice kitchen garden planted. I had also visited the nearby camp of Mr. Leslie Armstrong situated on the bank of the Potaro river. I met Meadows, a retired carpenter from Bartica Ministry, who was now minding chickens and ducks and planting a small patch for Mr. Armstrong, the warden.

I received a great boost on the arrival of a caterpillar, two and half cubic feet front-end loader with an operator, Atkins, and serviceman, Collins, who were accompanied by the Mechanical Superintendent Stevens. This machine did the clearing of the laterite quarry, digging out of rocks and stock piling and loading lorries with laterite gravel and rocks. I concentrated on repairs to the road from 112 mile compound out to 103 mile hill slopes. These spots were later covered with white sand, the rolling traffic compacting the laterite. Deep holes were surfaced with the broken laterite sweepings from the quarry. As this work progressed, the road shoulders were also cleared, especially at the approaches of dangerous turns.

Benjamin's tractor was put to hauling out wallaba poles from the bush to the roadside. These poles were to be planted in and around the 112 mile compound for the extension of electric lighting. My jeep broke down on the Issano road with driver King. The jeep had to be loaded onto a German lorry and shipped to Georgetown for repairs. King went too as he said he had received a telegram from his wife, who was ill. That was the last I saw of my jeep and driver. Thereafter, I had to rely on the lorries for transportation from point to point. On R. Moore's return from Bartica with fuel, I took the opportunity to travel out to 72 miles to meet with the D.S.I. and to bring in cement and sawn boards. On our return journey, as the lorry climbed the steep hill at 101 miles, its wheel rode over a large rock in the road and the jerk ejected the men in back along with the cement and boards through the back gate of the tray. At the top of the hill, I glanced through the rear window of the cab to see only an empty tray. I instructed Moore to turn back immediately but owing to the narrowness of the road, he had to travel for nearly a mile before he could turn the lorry. When the headlights of the lorry picked up the men and materials on the road, the men were lying in various positions between the bags of cement and tarpaulin. Moore exclaimed: "Oh God! Skipper, them boys dead!" but on jumping down from the cab to investigate, I saw the men were playing possum and laughing at our concern.

Some of them were bruised but had no serious injury. I left all the materials where they, as there would be no other traffic that night and returned to 111 mile. The following morning, I sent back the lorry to reload and bring in the materials. Whilst I was at Mahdia, District Commissioner N. Williams had asked me to relay a message to Police Sergeant Sparman to return to 72 miles and collect him in the police land-rover. The Sergeant refused to comply with this request, which amounted to gross insubordination. Police in these faraway places are left on one station too long. They feel they are the cocks of the roost.

I took a physical check of items in the stores hut at 111 mile, with Richard Hunte (foreman), Schroeder (acting stores clerk), Johnson (greaser on the grader) and Rollux (quarry worker). I wrote up the issues from Schroeder's issue book. It was no work of art for there were numerous mistakes, and I discovered that when Schroeder was under the influence of liquor, he forgot to write up his issues. Consequently, I had trouble in balancing my stock especially the fuel on-hand. I handed the keys of the store to Richard Hunte with the instruction to only issue fuel and stores in the mornings from 7:00 to 8:00 a.m. All unserviceable stores were to be itemised and forwarded to Central Stores at 72 miles compound. I wrote to the D.S.I. about the items required for the completion of the mines officer's house in 112 mile compound and forwarded a list of unserviceable items.

The Amerindian labourers were instructed to underbush the area behind the rest house to the south and north of the cottage hospital opening the area from the height of the hill to the foot to allow light and cool air to penetrate. I received my kero oil refrigerator by lorry but not having access to my house at 111 mile, I let the men place it in the rest house. I had to be on my feet for three days, living on sandwiches and coffee to push on the road repairs before the grader left for Bartica. I cooked dinner on my return to the rest house at night. On one occasion, I made a curry from some wild meat, but not having any electric light, I had to use a smoky oil lantern. On dishing out the curry onto the plate of rice, I discovered cockroaches that had been cooked in the curry. That was the end of my dinner. I requisitioned a Coleman pressure lamp from 72 mile stores.

Father Parrott, a Roman Catholic priest who had been occupying a room in the rest house, departed for Georgetown and Mr. Daniels, a Paramakotoi Amerindian, took over as Agricultural Field Assistant and occupied the Agricultural Officer's house. I sketched a scene of the 112 mile compound, showing all the buildings, with the Eagle and Ebini Mountains as a background. I later put this on canvas with oil paints. I did a number of other bush scenes whilst I was here at 112 mile and 111 mile house.

Rain commenced to fall on 8 November, the first after a long spell of dry weather, and I learnt that the Regional Minister had instructed the District Superintendent of the Interior to send my grader to Bartica to prepare a sports complex for upcoming sports. He felt this was more important than the work I had to do. This machine had to travel 107 miles to 4 mile compound where the operator, Barnwell, said he was idle for thirteen days when it could have been engaged on constructive work in my area. I wrote a letter to the Hon. Minister for Economic Development complaining of the high-handedness of some senior officers in procuring machines without finding out if they were otherwise engaged. The Regional Minister was reprimanded and told only to borrow my machines in cases of emergency.

Mario Francis, my huntsman, who had been supplying us regularly with fresh meat and fish, was unfortunate to be bitten by a bushmaster snake as he was pursuing a flock of wild hogs. He shot the snake, then returned home to lie down in his hammock. It was another Amerindian who reported this to me. I sent a lorry to Campbelltown to bring Mario to the cottage hospital where, luckily, the charge nurse had just received a new set of anti-venom shots which she promptly injected into Mario at 7:00 p.m. Another injection followed at 9:00 p.m. and the third at 3:00 a.m. the next morning. I sent for the plane and forwarded him to the Public Hospital, Georgetown, where he spent a couple of months before he fully recovered.

Painters arrived to paint the armoury under the police station. The Sub-Regional Chairman of the P.N.C., Mr. Springer, called upon me to assist with the preparations for the P.N.C. Conference to be held at the Community Centre. My lorries had to travel to the Guyana Defence Force compound on the riverside at Tumatumari to load and transport canvas cots and mattresses to Mahdia. I met the Regional Minister at the District Administrator's house and he told me I should get four more lorries shortly. I said I would believe it when the lorries arrived. He said Minister Hoyte thought everything was going well with my work, but it was the Maintenance Engineer who was the stumbling block to my getting the equipment required. I had to travel back to Tumatumari to return the cots and mattresses at the end of the conference. I took this opportunity to inspect the laterite deposit at Tumatumari on which the school was built. There had been suggestions that the school be removed to the right bank of the river so that the laterite hill could be worked for material for the road. I had a chat with the schoolmaster, who requested I do some repairs to the school.

I had occasion to write to Minister Hoyte on the urgency of acquiring more lorries for transporting road materials. One load of rock transported from 114 mile quarry to the point of operations took an hour and a half, then there was a wait of near three hours before the workmen received another load. This meant, with only one lorry available, that the labourers had to spend their time weeding the road shoulders, before they sat down idle. There was too the problem that the German lorries we were getting could not stand up to the rigours of travelling over these rough bush roads. They were nothing compared to the Bedford lorries which the Engineers said we could not get. On my return from Tumatumari, I received a report that Baptiste, driving his lorry whilst under the influence of liquor, had run off the road at 113 miles, and a man had been thrown from the tray and had to be sent to the cottage hospital with a suspected fracture of his hip, and that when Baptiste had returned to 111 mile compound, he had swerved in the business area and damaged the ramp leading to C.P. Fraites store and run into a garden next door. I called on Baptiste and his porter to write out a statement. Baptiste claimed his steering was out of order. This would be checked by the mechanics. I also had to deal with the front-end operator and his serviceman who, I had noted, for the past three paydays had travelled to the city without permission, leaving the machine idle until their return after a week. I called them in and warned them of the consequences if they continue to leave their location.

I met Jo Young, a young Scotsman who used to be forest manager for the Winiperu Logging Operations, who was now operating a suction pump in the Potaro River prospecting for gold in the vicinity of 103 mile bridge. He said he was getting some good returns, and the only drawback was the delay in getting a regular supply of fuel over the road from Bartica. I told him I was experiencing the same difficulty. Sometimes my road work was held up for a week or more awaiting fuel. I had requested a storage tank be put down at 111 mile compound, but nothing ever materialised. Delay in dealing with fallen trees, the result of heavy rains and wind squalls, was another stumbling block to improving the journeys vehicles made, especially on the Issano Road, along which the weekly transport buses had to travel with their cargo for upriver shops. I had to send out for power saws and a crew of men and it was sometimes four days before an obstruction was cleared.

A survey team arrived at Mahdia and were flown by helicopter from Mahdia airstrip to the top of Eagle Mountain, to the same landing pad I had discovered in 1970, which the U.S.A. had built during World War II for their helicopters. They used a brilliant light at night which I could see from the rest house. They told me this light was used to measure distances from mountain to mountain.

I was called upon by a family of St. Lucian islanders to convey a dead body to the burial ground as the police had refused to assist, although it was the police's responsibility to see the dead properly buried.

I planted some hybrid corn I had brought from Plantation Drill on the hill slope behind the rest house, but owing to the poor quality of the soil, they came to nothing, but the ordinary kitchen greens flourished. I also installed two beehives in the garden compound of the Commissioner's house. Some of the beeswax frames I had taken from two hives belonging to a man living at 109 mile. He had sold his house and asked me to take over the two hives where the bees were swarming. I had to don a net over my hat and shoulders and using rubber gloves, I took out four frames from each hive and replaced new frames between the working ones. I opened a new hive and transferred some of the working frames along with some new frames. I took two new hives with only six frames and set them up at 112 mile compound. I recovered seven pints of honey from the combs I took out. Bees if properly looked after, could be the basis of a viable small industry in Guyana. Unfortunately, because of the invasion of African bees from Brazil, many areas were lost. Some bee farmers had to run for their lives and some hives had to go up in smoke to prevent danger to neighbours.

I had to write a detailed report to the Hon. Minister for Economic Development on the work I had done during the two months I had been there and a copy was forwarded to the Maintenance Engineer. I also prepared a report on all buildings and materials for Mr. Ramsaroop, the District Superintendent of the Interior as he was handing over to Mr. Basil Chung who was to take over in 1977. I closed the quarry work, leaving approximately 86 cubic yards of laterite boulders on hand. I had estimated we would require another 600 cubic yards to complete filling the bad spots between 93 mile and 112 mile, especially as some pot holes can take two 5 cubic yards lorryloads of stone. I reported that I would require a D/7 caterpillar tractor to make borrow pits to get out sand clay and white sand for road surfacing and fills.

I arranged with foreman Hunte to place three eight-hour watchmen at 111 mile compound to safeguard the stores, machinery in the yard and the house. There was a general shut down of operations throughout the Interior Ministry to allow the employees to take their Christmas Holidays. I left on the 13th December and reported to the Georgetown office. I asked the Chief Engineer Roads, Mr. Phang, for a Motorola transmitting set for Mahdia, but it seemed that the Upper Mazaruni Project had them all.

CHAPTER XXXI
More Roads: Tumatumari and Mahdia – 1977

On the 3 January 1977, before my return to the Potaro-Mazaruni Maintenance Program, I was called to a meeting with the Hon. Minister for Economic Development, Mr. Desmond Hoyte and the Maintenance Engineer
and the Permanent Secretary for the Ministry. The Minister told the Engineer he was not at all satisfied with the action taken to supply me with the
necessary equipment to maintain the roads in this area. He also asked why
Sonny Persaud's belongings were still in the 111 Mile Compound house preventing me from moving in. He hoped the Engineer and the Permanent Secretary would have these matters settled quickly. Two days after there was a
meeting in the Maintenance Engineer's office. Present were Mr. Welles, Tech.
Engineer, Mr. Ramsaroop, outgoing District Superintendent Interior, Mr. B.
Chung, the new D.A.I. Permanent Secretary and me. My responsibilities
would be to maintain 154 miles of roadway: 19 miles to 114 Mile Potaro,
Tumatumari Road from 92 miles to Potaro River, Issano Road from 74 Mile
Junction to Mazaruni River, Kangaruma Road from 104 Mile Junction to the
Potaro River. From 19 Mile to 07 Mile would be supervised by the Upper
Mazaruni Road Project and from 07 Mile to Bartica would be under the
Ministry of Works and Transport. It was agreed to appoint three overseers
and four road foremen, but this never materialised.

On 8 January 1977, I left Georgetown by plane and was met at the Bartica
air strip by R. Moore with his lorry. I borrowed eight drums of dieselene
from Regional Development at Bartica, then met Mr. Chung, the new District Superintendent Interior. I asked that Pat Legall, stock verifier, be sent
in to my location to check my stores at 111 Miles compound. I travelled on
to 72 Miles M.W.T. Compound and met the Amerindian office staff comprising Amerindians from the surrounding area who were doing a first class job
running the office. When I reached the rest house at 112 Mile compound, I
met with Father Parrott and Bishop Benedict Singh of the Roman Catholic
Church. They were there to open the new church building. I was unfortunate to be taken with dysentery and could not attend the opening ceremony,
but I had the chance to tell the Bishop something of my travels in the hinterland. He also glanced through my book of memoirs and said I should put it

in book form as there were a lot of people who did not know the bush and would find it interesting reading. Weather conditions prevented a plane landing at Mahdia air strip when the Bishop was due to return to the city so I organised a local land-rover to convey him to Georgetown by road.

On the morning of 16 January 1977, an English couple were discovered sleeping in a pup tent in the 112 Mile compound by Dispenser Beharry. They had arrived during the night and could not locate the rest house. Mr. Beharry invited them into his house for coffee. I was later introduced to Mr. Denis Clayton and Miss Kathleen Whitford. I arranged for them to occupy a room next to mine in the rest house for the time they would spend at Mahdia. They were on holiday from England and wanted to see and learn as much as possible of Guyana before they continued their South American tour. They accompanied me on my trips to various points, such as Tumatumari Compound which was occupied by the Guyana National Service. I introduced them to the senior officers who escorted Kathleen and Denis to the Falls which by then were harnessed to produce hydroelectric power for the settlement. Kathleen took numerous pictures of the compound and the rushing waters of the falls and also made notes on all she learned. The G.N.S. Compound was on the high left bank of the Potaro river overlooking the falls from which there were beautiful views of the river. They also toured the workshops in which G.N.S. recruits were learning various trades.

I took a lorry and a party of Amerindians as far as 124 Miles. En route, I had the men trim all overhanging trees and weed out all bridge approaches so that I could examine the timbers and the planks. I found a few of the bridge timbers rotted and a good many of the planks missing. These would have to be replaced before any heavy traffic could pass. The situation at the Guyana National Service compound at 124 Miles was the same, but I also found the machinery parked in the compound overgrown with high grass and bush. I noticed that unoccupied buildings were being eaten by wood ants. I wondered what these National Servicemen did with themselves during the day, for they evidently took no pride in their surroundings.

Back at Mahdia 112 Mile, I had to put on two men to bail out the cesspit at the rest house; I moved to Kangaruma rest house for two days to get away from the stench. On my return, I again had to park all my heavy equipment because of a shortage of fuel. This caused me to lose not days but weeks of progress. On numerous occasions, I had to borrow drums of dieselene from the shop keepers at 111 Mile Mahdia just to keep some lorry on the road for general transportation. I inspected an old spring of water at the base of 112 Mile compound hill, which I understood the B.G. Consolidated Gold Company had harnessed to supply fresh water to the houses in 112 Mile compound. I reported this matter to Tech. Engineer Willis who said he would investigate future possibilities, but nothing was ever done. However, a new diesel power plant was installed in the 112 Mile power house to replace one that had been damaged by lightning during a storm on the night of 21 November 1976. The residents had been without electrical power for nearly three months.

On the 2nd of February 1977, Mr. Ramsaroop, the D.S.I. handed over officially to Mr. Basil Chung. I showed Mr. Chung the cramped quarters I had been occupying since my arrival at Mahdia. There was no room in which to do my office work and no space to unpack my personal belongings. Since my arrival at Mahdia I had been living out of suitcases and boxes. On 7 February, Mr. Sonny Persaud arrived with a Ministry lorry to collect all his personal belongings from the house in 111 Mile Compound. After his departure, I inspected the house and discovered not one piece of furniture left. My terms of appointment stipulated that I would be supplied with a furnished house. I immediately notified the new D.S.I. Mr. Chung who authorised me to travel to Georgetown to get a permit from the Maintenance Engineer with which to purchase furniture and a refrigerator from Booker Bros..

On my return journey, I was accompanied by Ronald Beharry, our dispenser. Because of the Mashramani or Republic Day celebrations we could find no accommodation at any of the Bartica hotels, so Ronald contacted a prison officer who said he could provide us with sleeping accommodation at his house in the Prisons Compound on the left bank of the Mazaruni River. Ronald and I had to travel from Bartica by the prison launch, across the wide Mazaruni river to the prison. Our friend provided us with dinner which he cooked himself and offered us a liquor made from sourie fruit. He said he picked and washed the fruit, sliced it in half lengthways and dropped it in a bucket. This was then covered with sugar and allowed to sit for a couple of days. The fruit gives off a juice which the sugar soaks up, then the syrup was poured off. It makes a wonderful liqueur. Ronald and I had to share one bed.

The next day we crossed back to Bartica, then returned to the rest house at 112 Mile. I put on some of my men to cobweb and scrub the floor and shelves in 111 Mile house and then move my belongings there from 112 Mile. It took six men to handle the refrigerator and the heavier furniture up the long front steps of the 111 Mile house. I arranged the furniture to my liking. The following day I had a house warming, serving cook-up rice, souse and drinks to Neville Williams, the District Administrator, Dispenser and

Mrs. Beharry, the Postmaster, the Police N.C.O. and my road foreman, Richard Hunte and his girl friend. A priest was called upon to bless the house.

I had been asked to upgrade the road from 45 Mile Compound to 72 Mile
Compound. I had one lorry, one grader, and one front-end loader. These were
dispatched to 72 Mile Compound en route to 45 Mile. Because of the heavy
rains falling on the way from 111 Miles to 72 Mile, the men were cold and
hungry so an overnight stop was made there. Then the D.S.I. requested that
my lorry proceed to Bartica to carry out pay-sheets. Baptiste, having four
drums of fuel on board his lorry, dumped the drums at 45 Mile Compound
on his way out of Bartica. On his return journey, he found someone had removed the drums. He reported this to me so I called in the police at the 72
Mile outpost who returned to 45 Mile compound where the imprints of tractor wheels were seen at the spot Baptiste had dumped the drums. The missing drums prevented any work on the road as this was the only fuel I had in
the area. The following day, en route back to 111 Mile, Baptiste saw the
drums on the approach to the 103 Mile suspension bridge. The watchman
informed me it was McDonald who had dropped the drums there and said
he would be back to collect them. I knew McDonald as the man working at
the river with suction pumps. I had my men load the drums in the lorry and
then lodged them at the Mahdia Police Station as evidence. When the police contacted McDonald, his explanation was that he was trying to assist
me by bringing in the four drums. Why then had he left them at 103 Mile
instead of bringing them to 111 Mile Compound? We had our own brush
with the police when Sergeant Sparman reported to me that Kanhai, one of
my lorry drivers, had driven in such a reckless manner as to knock down a
woman. The D.O.A., Mr. Williams, had to take away the lorry keys from
Kanhai.

Rain continued to fall heavily. I noted the leaves were changing colour
and the trees blossoming. This was unusual since this did not usually happen until the May-June season. I prepared and forwarded to 72 Mile office
my first quarterly report on road progress. All this paperwork really called
for a clerical assistant to check labour and make up timesheets. I mentioned
this matter at a meeting with the two outgoing and incoming District Super-
intendents but nothing had come of it.

At 104 Mile, there was a piece of roadway which the T.H.D. passenger
and cargo lorries said was very dangerous, especially at night. I had to widen
it by driving down hardwood bush posts fourteen feet in length with eight
inch diameter. I then laid an inner layer of beams secured by pickets driven
in between at a 45 degree angle; plaited palm leaves were laid inside to

prevent the fill of white sand from running out. This fill was compacted and surfaced with laterite boulders and sweepings from the laterite quarry. The completed job was twenty feet wide. At other danger spots I had two of my men cut five foot by four inch bush wood posts. These were peeled and painted with black and white circular rings. These "dumb policemen" were planted on the borders of fill-ins and on dangerous curves. Civil Aviation came to ask for help in improving the Mahdia air strip. I lent them men to assist in the survey. They wanted to swing the direction so as to add more length to the runway. I informed them that they would have to contact the Guyana National Service at Tumatumari as they had all the necessary equipment for clearing and bulldozing. I had no machinery of that kind.

I received a report that the lorries I had sent to 72 Miles for repairs were being utilised by the staff at 72 Miles and driven all about. I had to travel to 72 Miles and remonstrate with the foreman in the garage, telling him that no one was allowed to take them out until repairs were completed and then they should be returned to their location. I had to send back my grader and the operator to 72 Mile compound as the operator proved very uncooperative, not wanting to work hard on maintenance for the few months he was allotted to my location. He spent more time on the neighbouring timber grants than on road maintenance. I also received a complaint from Mario Francis, my Amerindian huntsman that my camp attendant, Cecil Persaud, was selling the wild meat he had shot. I queried Persaud about this allegation but he denied the charge. This was not the first time complaints had been lodged against Persaud, especially when he was under the influence of liquor. I eventually had to dispense with his services for he was always sleeping out and sporting with his friends. I returned one day to find my house locked, no food prepared and no camp attendant. I wrote out his immediate dismissal. I also had to speak to a lorry driver and the tractor operator about drinking and driving, and issued warning letters to both men that continuance would result in suspension.

I met Rafferty, an old friend from 1973, when he was doing our river and lorry transportation for the Hydro-Power Survey. He was working at the B.G. Consolidated power plant at 112 Mile compound, setting up a gas plant, burning ordinary bush wood, extracting the tar and producing cooking gas. His effort were marred by insufficient money from Government. My lorries and the tractor-trailer were engaged at times in loading and transporting wood to the gas plant. One of the men working on the high thirty foot frame had the misfortune to fall in the elevator. I had to send him to the Cottage Hospital.

On 6 April 1977, I learned of the death of Jimmy Wallace, a Scotsman and a personal friend. He had been a sugar estate overseer at Plantation Uitvlugt when I was an overseer at Plantation Tushen, both Booker Bros. sugar estates. We had met again when he was managing a coconut and rice estate at Letter "T" Mahaicony and I was manager of Plantation Park coconut estate, and later when he was in charge of the Lamaha Water conservancy. His death came as a shock, for the last time I had seen Jimmy, he was bursting with health, but cancer is a funny business for I understand that it was this he died of. I later received a cable from my niece in Jamaica on 18 April notifying me of the death of my last remaining brother who died in England (Kent) where he had been residing since his retirement from Bookers Sugar Estates in 1964. C.D. Young was two years older than I.

I received a letter from Mr. Chung, the District Superintendent Interior, informing me of his intention to visit Kaieteur Falls, setting off from Kangaruma, and inviting me to travel with him. On the 9th of April I travelled by lorry to Kangaruma where I spent the night to await the arrival of Mr. Chung the following morning. All the baggage and food was loaded into a boat at the river landing, then we pushed off. The outboard engine failed to start, but after many crankings we got a start and proceeded on our way up river. We arrived at Amatuk Falls at 2:15 p.m. where our cargo had to be discharged and carried over the falls to another boat beyond the falls, where it was reloaded with the assistance of some porkknockers. At Waratuk Falls the same exercise was carried out, only the portage was much shorter. The boat in which we travelled the remaining distance was leaking badly and the seams had to be caulked with cloth and a man kept continually at bailing. I had brought my Kodak Instamatic camera with some colour films. I took some snapshots of the scenery bordering the river and the mountainous rock walls that formed the Kaieteur Gorge.

Our party arrived at Tukeit landing at 5:45 p.m. Captain Roy and his wife, both elderly Afro-Guyanese, welcomed us and showed us to our rooms. The cargo boat was discharged and our baggage and food brought into the rest house. After dinner, which we ate by gas lamp light, we retired to our cots as the next day we would make an early start to climb the escarpment. The last time I had been here was in the drought of 1926, fifty-one years ago, when all the forest was on fire and the water in the river was low exposing all the rocks and sandbanks.

Next morning, after breakfast, we left the rest house at 7:15 a.m. I lead the way along a wide track through the hardwood forest. There were two women and a child in our party. We reached the plateau at 9:15 a.m. The climb was very easy (not like when I had climbed it in 1925-1926). Bridges had been built across the streams and stones on the walking line smoothed off. There were a few places where we had to clamber over some large rocks and at one point we had to edge past a wall of porous rock from which water was running to join the small streams. I walked through the scrub bush to the police outpost on the Kaieteur landing strip, where planes arrived with cargo for the miners' bush shops and occasionally with tourists to view the Falls. I walked back to the edge of the escarpment to meet the rest of the party. I led them by another path bordering the edge of the gorge and eventually emerging to a point where we had a wonderful view of the direct drop of the falls and the deep chasm below. The party took a number of snapshots backing the falls and of the falls itself, then we visited the rest house in which most of the furniture was handmade by Amerindians. I met Mr. Armstrong, the Warden for the district, who informed me he would be travelling down river to Kangaruma with us. I left the rest house and walked across the plateau for a distance of a mile and a half where I met some miners at a shop owned by John Wade, an old friend. His brother treated us to cool drinks. Our party left at 2:30 p.m. to return to Tukeit Landing where we arrived at 5:30 p.m., very thirsty and tired.

I peeled off my clothes and took a cold bath in the river. After dinner, we sat out in the gallery facing the river and took our drinks, then retired to bed. No mosquito nets were required here. We left Tukeit at 9:10 a.m. the following morning. Mr. Blaize, our captain, had cleaned his spark plugs and at the first pull our engine started. We stopped at a small clearing where we landed to pick some oversized lemons which peeled just like tangerines and were partly sweet and not sour like the common lemon. We arrived at Kangaruma at 2:35 p.m. to find my lorry awaiting our arrival. The entire party travelled to 111 Mile Compound where they spent the night, travelling back to 72 Miles the next day.

I found a letter from Kathleen Whitford from England saying what a wonderful time she had at Mahdia with me, and there was also a letter from Bishop Benedict Singh, thanking me for my kindness to himself and Father Parrott. He mentioned how he had enjoyed listening to my experiences in the bush and invited me to visit him at the R.C. Cathedral.

On 1 May 1977, I prepared to move my entire operation to 84 Mile Logie. The front-end loader was to be operated by one of my quarry workers since at the last payday both Atkins and Collins had left for Georgetown carrying the key for the machine and had not returned. I was supplied with another key by the mechanic who arrived from Georgetown to service the machine.

A D/6 caterpillar tractor and two German lorries driven by Baptiste and Kanhai were to transport the men and their rations to 84 Mile Logie. I carried a tarpaulin which I erected for my tent. I was to upgrade this portion of the road, draining pools of water and filling deep holes in the 83 Mile section. I located an area of sand clay which I had the D/6 caterpillar tractor clear, cut and heap the material for loading by the front-end loader into the lorries. This was dumped in the low spots, the fill gradually pushing off the water into drains cut by the D/6 tractor. This material was spread and compacted by the front end loader and the D/6 caterpillar bulldozer. We moved forward patching and filling bad spots to the 31 Mile section. There the logie had fallen off its blocks. There was insufficient room for the entire party so I moved into a labourers' hut on the Winiperu road on the other side of the Ikurubisci Creek. I took Baptiste with me so I could move with his lorry from the creek to 31 Mile. He would wake me in the mornings banging his pots and pans preparing the breakfast. Some of the Amerindians accompanied me and built a tarpaulin tent opposite my hut. It was a good spot. Mario Francis really hit the jackpot, finding many wild hogs in the area and the creek supplied haimara fish. The large blackwater creek was also very handy for an early morning bath and for the washing of our clothes.

I had a visit from one Toti Adams who came in a jeep with a companion to hunt. I allowed them to accompany Mario, my huntsman, and they returned with five wild hogs. Leaving one with me, they returned to town, promising me to return again. On each visit, I could expect some fresh bread and other luxuries.

I cut a line from the Winiperu sand-clay pit through the bush to emerge at the 33 Mile section. The bulldozer opened up this line to form a road through which I could transport sand-clay in the lorries to 38/39 Mile sections to surface the road and fill low spots. The entire length of this new road was 1,425 ft. by 10 ft. wide, twisting and turning between the oversized trees. At the Winiperu sand-clay pit I discovered a layer of fine coarse gravel, white in colour, resting on a bed of red gravel, a little more coarse. I took a sample because I thought it would be good for road surfacing if found in sufficient quantities.

The heavy rains had really set in, this being the beginning of the May-June rainy season. One of the lorry drivers reported a washout where a gully head and nearly half the road had disappeared into the gully. I set on the D/6 caterpillar bulldozer to push down the bush towards the gully head and then cut a diversion road two hundred feet from the gully. At a later date, I would have to build a pall-off at the gully head with heavy timbers. Matters were not improved when I lost a lorry in an accident when one of my drivers was using the Winiperu Road to bypass a section of bad road on the road we were resurfacing and, unexpectedly, a timber truck appeared, causing my driver to take to the bush at the road side but not quickly enough to avoid damage to the lorry which had to be towed to 31 Mile Compound to await repairs. Winiperu Road had been built specifically for transporting large timbers. When the powerful Camel trucks were hauling a heavy load of greenheart timbers, sometimes as many as five or seven depending on the size, and measuring some sixty to eighty feet in length, there was no way these machines could not stop in a short space. Rain continued to fall steadily and since sand-clay work could not be carried on in such weather, I decided to close operations in this area and return to 111 Mile Compound.

Whilst back there, I made a crayon sketch of the Road House with the Ikurubisci Creek in the back ground, and then the visit of two Amerindian families to their husbands at my camp ground encouraged me to further drawing work. Anne Theresa, Stanley Simon's daughter, a sturdily built girl of fifteen or sixteen years was always paying my house a visit in company with her young brother and sister. I met her by the creek washing her clothes and taking a bath. I made a pencil sketch of her in her birthday suit. I later put this on canvas with oil paints and my wife, on a visit to Mahdia, took the painting and sent it to Canada to our granddaughter.

I moved back my party to 111 Miles but stopped in at 72 Miles to hold discussions with Mr. Chung about subsistence claims for the men and me for the period we had been away from base. Mr. Chung rejected these saying that the area from 19 Miles to 114 Miles was our location. I had to carry this matter to a higher authority to get what was due the men.

At the end of May, I accompanied Mr. Chung to Georgetown to purchase some food stuff and returned to Mahdia on 4 June in time for the Prime Minister's visit to the area. Two helicopters flew in the Prime Minister and party at 2:30 to 3:00 p.m. Residents of Mahdia gathered in Mr. Gravesande's dance hall at 4:00 p.m. The Prime Minister said that he only had a short time to spend so we had to state our names and business quickly. I spoke on behalf of my men and our road equipment. The P.M. promised to give us more and better lorries. He further stated that if the men were due a subsistence allowance for their term on the bush roads, this must be paid as he had the money for so doing. The P.M. visited Rafferty's Gas Plant and said this plant could supply the whole country with the much needed cooking gas. At the dance hall, the local school teacher appeared before the P.M. very much under the influence of liquor and the P.M. said he would see the Education

Minister and have him transferred immediately. The Prime Minister left by
helicopter, not being able to visit 72 Mile as planned, as night was setting in
and the weather was bad. He mentioned in Gravesande's Hall that he remembered my appointment to the Bartica - Potaro Road by the Cabinet the
previous year, and that I was a man they greatly respected and appreciated
and that I was known throughout the country. The P.M. said he could recall
when I used to awake him at 4:30 a.m. and tell him the Volunteers were to
go jump in the Creek and they would get a cup of capadula tea and he had
said, "I ain't no fish to go jumping into the creek at that hour". This was in
1970 on the Self-Help Project to build a road to the savannah at Annai *en
route* to Brazil.

One outcome of the P.M.'s visit was that the Georgetown Water Authority
Engineer, Persaud, arrived by plane to look into the possibilities of a pure
water supply for Mahdia. He found that the spring behind the school in a
gully at the foot of the 112 Mile Compound hill, which I had previously investigated, could produce 2,500 gallons of water every three hours. He also
visited Mahdia's main creek and the Mahadianna Creek (Waterdog), a tributary coming from Eagle Mountain at the end of the air strip. Engineer Persaud
said he would compile his notes and send in a report, but he admitted that it
would be a very expensive job, and knowing that our government did not
have that kind of money, we could kiss goodbye to a pure water supply. Back
working on the road, I put the D/6 caterpillar bulldozer to clearing the area
around and to the east of 111 Mile Compound from the road to the laterite
hill, for I saw a possibility of cutting a road up to the height of the hill, to
pass the St. Lucian shopkeepers' business area.

Angie Willie, a woman who had been appointed "Touchau" or Headman
of the Amerindian settlement adjacent to Mahdia, paid me a visit and asked
me to visit them and help her pick out a spot for the erection of a "Benab",
a general meeting house. The Prime Minister had asked me to use my bulldozer to clear a spot for her. I ended up by clearing all the bush from and
around the settlement. This settlement was on a high level plateau surrounded
on three sides by running water. The D/6 caterpillar bulldozer was then put
to clearing the area from 112 Mile Compound in front of the church, then
the operator cut down the high road shoulder leading down the hill and widened the road, to allow a good view for vehicles as the old road was very
narrow and steep, with a sharp turn. There had been one or two accidents
involving lorries and land-rovers meeting on this road. I traced a road from
behind my house to connect with the crossroad from 112 Mile Compound
leading east through the Islanders settlement. I opened this area with the D/

6 caterpillar too, as it gave the residents a shorter walk to the shopping area on the lower road. I had my men underbush the laterite hill slope behind my house and burn the bush to plant a few orange trees and a kitchen garden. I also had them clean out the small creek at the foot of the hill to make a bathing pool and so save the vat water for house use. On the creek flat, I planted eddoes. A tarpaulin camp was set up at 103 Mile suspension bridge for the carpenters to repair the cross-planks and point the metal bridge. I condemned the bridge at 107 Mile and put down a metal culvert encased in compacted white sand, reinforced by new greenheart timbers, then surfaced with laterite rock. From this bridge, I opened a new road to cut out the "S" bend. Working in this area, I met Hamilton, a farmer and coal burner, who told me a story of a pork-knocker who had stopped and helped himself to some young corn from Hamilton's farms, evidently thinking no one was in the area. When Hamilton approached the man with his gun and asked him who had given him permission to pick and eat his corn, the young man said he was hungry and so had helped himself. Hamilton told the man he must eat every scrap of the corn, cob and all, or else he would shoot him and carry him to the police. The poor man ate everything.

Another 'outcome' of the P.M.'s visit was the arrival from Georgetown of Richard Collins, a young Englishman who had been on the trip to Kaieteur, who came from the Town Planning Office to look into the feasibility of a housing scheme for Mahdia. This was on the Prime Minister's instructions. I told him to find a good water supply first, then he could look into a housing project.

CHAPTER XXXII
Mahdia Settlement: A Piaiman at Work

I walked along the Pamela Road from 112 Mile Police station to the Potaro river, a distance of seven miles. I was accompanied on this walk by three Amerindians from Mahdia settlement. This road had been built by the British Guiana Consolidated Gold Company to bring in machinery and stores from the Potaro River. I noted the remnants of three bridges which I hoped to renew. There was a stretch of six and three quarter miles of laterite deposits which could maintain the roads for years to come with the abundant monkey pot trees growing in the area to supply bridge timbers. I later put my Amerindian workers to felling these trees which were hauled to spot by the D/6 caterpillar tractor. I planned to build timber bridges of the same kind as they have on wood grants. I had the men place the timbers across the creek on the high laterite banks. The D/6 operator was instructed to clear Pamela Road from 112 Mile Compound right out to the Potaro River. This was completed in two days with the operator and his assistant working late into the night.

One of Baird's sons was taken with a sickness which no doctor seemed able to cure, so a piaiman was called in. These piaimen possessed an intimate knowledge of the medicinal value of our forest plants and were also good ventriloquists. I noticed a newly built benab of palm leaves near Baird's house, the type used by the piaimen for their seances. In an adjoining hut, I met "Old Steel", a wizened little old Amerindian with greying hair, who enjoyed the reputation of being the cleverest or strongest piaiman in the district. Shortly after dusk, the sick boy was taken into the benab, where he was made to sit down on a tortoise shell. The piaiman, after closing the opening of the benab with palm leaves, sat on another shell opposite the boy. The rest of us sat outside the benab in a circle. Aromatic smoke now began to seep through the leaves to the accompaniment of the rhythmic shaking of a large gourd rattle. This is a *sine-qua-non* of the piaiman and is very strong medicine, no female being allowed even to look at it. Presently the piaiman's voice was heard in a droning sing-song, which continued for ten minutes, then another voice was heard, certainly not the patient's. A lively conversation, which sounded like question and answer, continued between the two voices. Presently the second voice became silent and yet a third strange voice was heard, deep and gruff, talking to the piaiman. This seance continued for nearly half an hour after which the piaiman emerged from the benab and the patient was carried back to his father's house. "Old Steel" now told the mother that he had spoken to the spirits of the camoodie (anaconda) and tiger, these being the strange voices we had heard from outside. The spirits had told him that they had been asked to "punish" the lad by an Amerindian girl to whom he had been unfaithful. Asked whether they meant to kill him, they replied that this was not their intention, which was only to "punish him bad". If the piaiman took the steps necessary in such a case, they would trouble the lad no more.

"Old Steel" told this in a manner of fact way, as if he were describing a hunting trip seriously, without any suspicion of joking. He finally added that he would depart at dawn to get the necessary medicine with which he would return in three days. Meanwhile the patient was not to move out of his hammock. True to his word, the piaiman returned on the third day and spent the night brewing a concoction from the various leaves and vines he had brought with him. This the lad had to drink regularly after his meals and his mother was certain that from the very first dose, the lad's improvement began. Within two months, the young man was himself again. Baird later brought me eight pieces of handicraft work he had plaited himself and a large jaguar skin which his son-in-law had shot. I paid him $100.00 for this beautiful skin and $8.00 for the eight pieces of handicraft. One of his younger daughters wanted to travel to Georgetown to learn typewriting. I told her she should get a letter from Mr. Williams, introducing her to a school in Georgetown. She could stay at the Amerindian Hostel.

At the end of August 1977, I had a request from Mr. Isaacs, the acting District Administrative Officer, for transportation for farmers who Dr. Reid, Deputy Prime Minister, had sent into the area North Fork to Konawaruk. This was the area bordering the North Fork river through which I had cut a road on the side of the hill in the 1971 Self-Help Project. A lorry was dispatched for these farmers. They had tarpaulins, lanterns, gas lamps, tools, etc. and sufficient food for two weeks. The balance of food was stored at Mr. Isaacs' house in 112 Mile Compound. These so-called farmers used to come out every two weeks for more food, until Mr. Isaacs found out they were selling the food to residents in the Mahdia area to get cash to buy rum. As to farming, these men did not turn over any soil to plant, nor do any cleaning of the land. They were having a good time at the Government's expense. This reminded me of the land settlement scheme the Prime Minister had

opened at 114 Mile Self-Help Road Camp. There I had been instructed to
leave all six camp huts intact. When I queried the officer in charge of this
scheme, as to what type of people he was going to get to settle, he only said
he had people. I left a stock of two Holstein bulls and seven cows, a good
number of pure white pigs and a few doroc pigs, and about 1,500 chickens.
Each settler was to have taken a piece of land and cleared it. After planting
and building a shack on his land, he was to have received either one head of
livestock or some chickens, but the type of people who did settle here killed
and sold the stock, and imported a jukebox and rum. The police had to be
called in on numerous occasions to settle disputes and there was no work
done on the actual settlement. I have known, too, of other areas in the country in which the government had tried to assist young people but these young
people preferred the town life, not willing to sacrifice their time or efforts to
make something of themselves. I remember that in 1970 some Indo-Guyanese
came to Camp Young from the Corentyne Coast and seeing the available
lands surrounding the camp, asked me how much land they could get if they
settled in the area. I said they could get as much as they could beneficially
occupy. I knew that rural Indo-Guyanese loved the land and made good farmers but these people seemed to be out of favour with the government.

I had a visit from Miss Sandra Flynn and Miss Susan Gorwyn to my house
in 111 Mile Compound. They were visitors to the area and were staying at
Nixon's House in 112 Mile. Susan called back later to ask me to escort her
to the Amerindian Settlement to meet the people at Campbelltown. I was
recalled to my house as I learned the paymaster had arrived. Susan, who
was on a visit from England, accompanied me to witness the payment to my
labourers and the fact that the men received no subsistence allowances for
the month they had been on the road in May. She came back to the house at
8:00 p.m. accompanied by Sandra Flynn and Paul Shaw, who was teaching
at the University of Guyana. I learned that Sandra was a teacher in
Georgetown and that she knew Mother Assumpta Tang, a Carmelite Nun who
had been at my camp on the Self-Help road Project but was now living at
Isherton in the Rupununi Savannahs, in charge of a school.

Another visitor was Mr. Joe Young who arrived from the Potaro River. He
said he had to attend court, and spent the night at my house. He had walked
the distance from Issano Mazaruni River where he was now working gold by
suction pump in the Morabisci Creek. He reported fallen trees throughout
the length of the Issano Road at 51 Mile. My wife arrived from Georgetown
by plane accompanied by Gaston Tamerell, a French chef, who had cooked
for me previously when I was at Morabisci Mining Co. He would be my new
camp attendant as I had dispensed with Cecil Persaud. Then Mr. Chung, the

District Superintendent Interior, arrived with the Maintenance Engineer Persaud on a road inspection. The Engineer held a meeting under my house with the men employed in my section of the road. J. Baptiste, the Union representative, brought up the matter of the nonpayment of our subsistence allowance. Engineer Persaud ruled that Mr. Chung should pay the subsistence claims for I showed him an administrative circular which I had in my files dealing with the matter. Mr. Persaud praised me for the condition of the road from 103 mile to 112 mile. A month later I was informed by Mr. Chung that all subsistence claims had been signed and were ready for payment, and he also told me that Mario Francis' 'Not present' pay sheet had finally been recovered. This was the result of carelessness on the part of 72 miles office staff, Francis having to wait a long period for his wages, which his snake bite prevented him from receiving.

I had the carpenters ripping boards and planks to build an office under my house as I did not like the men tramping in and out of my house. I had the painters paint the stores hut in and out. Heavy rain squalls with high winds threw down trees across the roads into Kangaruma and the Issano Road. Foreman Hunte and the entire gang were sent in with power saws and axes to clear the roads. But I was then instructed to keep all bridge (103 mile) materials in my compound and not at the road side by the bridge. This would entail a loss of time, for every morning the carpenters would have to select the materials they required and have them loaded and transported by lorry to 103 mile. The D.S.I., Mr. Chung, said he had no money to pay for subsistence for carpenters living at the bridge site. This move on the D.S.I.'s part retarded progress on bridge repairs as many days were lost owing to the condition of the lorries, for they were always breaking down.

The St. Lucians (islanders) celebrated their National Day 'La Rose' on 29 August, 1977, with a parade through the village. A cook-up with an all night dance at Nixon's Hall completed the day. I took out some colour snapshots. Our relationship with the villagers was always good. One time I was asked to allow my carpenters to build a coffin for a dead person in the village. They used materials from my compound to put it together, and of course, the Big Bottle of Rum was passed as fast as the nails were driven in.

There was a shortage of water at the hospital due to a spell of dry weather so I sent a radio message to the D.S.I. at 72 mile to return my tractor and trailer so that I might transport water from the creek. I received no reply. People could be seen with buckets walking from their houses down the steep hill to Mahdia Creek and struggling back up the hill again with their buckets full of water, a most fatiguing operation.

Mr. Isaacs, the acting Administrative Officer for the district, informed me a team of inquiry was coming to look into the Administration. He asked me to draw up a list of requirements for the area.

Meantime, I had developed severe pains in my left shoulder, so I booked a plane passage for my wife and me to return to the city to seek medical attention. I had received an urgent message to meet the specialist Engineer at 72 miles, but I had no transportation to travel there as all my lorries were parked in the compound awaiting repairs, so I left for Georgetown without knowing what this was about. At home in Georgetown, on 14 September 1977, I received a letter from Engineer Persaud, which he had sent by his land rover driver Bradford, notifying me that my services as Superintendent of Roads would no longer be required as from 15 October 1977. I visited Engineer Persaud at his office by the Sea Wall at Rabbit Walk. He informed me that the Government was cutting down on all sections due to lack of money. I made an appointment with my Minister, Hon. D Hoyte to whom I showed my letter of retrenchment. He said he would speak to another department – Sea Defences - and would notify me later. To complete a bad period, I lost my wallet containing my ID Card, my gun license and other papers to a pick-pocket in Stabroek Market.

I returned to Mahdia on 21 September 1977. Mr. Isaacs had heard of my retrenchment and came to see me about a trip to Issano but I had to decline as I had too much to do to square up on my work and hand over everything intact to my successor. I continued on some oil paintings I had started and some men from Mahdia village came to view them. I carried out a stocktaking exercise assisted by Overseer Chandler and Foreman Hunte. I made out a duplicate copy which the others signed before I forwarded it to 72 mile office. Mr. Butters, a timekeeper and checker, would be taking over duties from me. I prepared and forwarded my third quarterly report through Mr. Chung the D.S.I. for Engineer Persaud.

Before I left, we received a second-hand Lister engine and generator which I had the men store under my house. I arranged to have Garnett, the mechanic, put it in working order so as to supply electricity to 111 mile compound. Out of the blue, Atkins, who had been the operator for the caterpillar front-end loader, returned to 111 mile compound after a prolonged absence and without any explanation so I sent him back to the District Superintendent at 72 mile compound as I had no further use for a man who could leave his job without permission or any explanation and carry away the key of the machine.

Richard Hunte's girl friend killed a labaria snake near her back steps so I took the precaution of having the D/6 cat. bulldozer push back the bush and trees, two hundred feet from the area of the three cottages. Foreman Hunte cast hollow concrete blocks to build a wall around the office under my house and I had the men put down a sand-crete floor in the office. I had the bulldozer open the area in front of my house to make adequate space for vehicles and machines to park. Mechanics from 72 mile workshop had been busy trying to repair all the vehicles parked in my yard but there was the usual shortage of parts, and even if the vehicles were put in order, the constant shortage of fuel meant that they were never really beneficial to my work.

Mr. Chung, the D.S.I., came to see me to talk about a draft a personnel plan for 1978. I showed him a copy I had of a District Road Organization maintenance plan which I had been given when I joined the Roads Department in 1960. He did not know about this and asked the clerk in charge at 72 miles to get a copy for him. I told the D.S.I. that I would not be requiring my copy as I would be leaving the area shortly. The clerk in charge said there were some audit queries about 1975 Stores so I told him I had only taken over on 4 October 1976. The clerk further wanted to know if the residents at 112 mile compound paid electric light bills. I said that as far as I knew they did not.

The last work I did in this area was to survey the areas I had cleared at the Amerindian settlement, the 112 mile compound and the area cleared by the bulldozer. I drew a map of the area from 112 mile compound showing the connecting road to Campbelltown and Republic Area leading through the St. Lucian Settlement to contact the main road at 111 mile. I also tied in the last road opened on the laterite hill spur leading to the descent into my compound. This plan could be used as a reference for my successor. There was a heavy rainstorm accompanied by deafening peals of thunder and vivid flashes of lightning. One explosion of thunder and a vivid flash of lightning just outside my house made me jump out of my chair. This seemed to be a parting gesture from the weather.

Mr. Chung brought retrenchment notices for some of the men. I was sorry to see them go as they were very good workers. I took an inventory of everything in my house and handed over to my successor, Mr. Butters. Dispenser Beharry and his wife came to bid me farewell. Richard Hunte, my foreman, took my parting very hard. Rain continued to fall heavily on my way home.

Back in Georgetown on 15 October 1977, I reported to the Maintenance Engineer and handed in my final reports and mails. The following day I met the Hon. Minister D. Hoyte who said he had told the Engineer that he wanted to see me. Though I had seen the Engineer only the day before, it seemed strange he had not told me anything.

CHAPTER XXXIII
Matthews Ridge, Northwest District – 1977

On 16 October 1977, at my meeting with the Hon. Minister for Economic Development, Mr. Desmond Hoyte, I told him if the Government had no more use for my services, I would be emigrating to Canada to join my children. Mr. Hoyte said no, he could not let a good man go. He wanted me to travel to Matthews Ridge, Northwest District to assist with the roads on a contract basis. I was offered a five year contract but only agreed to a three year term. I told the Minister that I would only accept this appointment if there was a guarantee that I would be in complete charge of my section without interference from party members, as I was at Mahdia. I requested that I be sent on a tour of inspection to check on the condition of the roads and the availability of machines and lorries at Matthews Ridge and the outlying sections.

I travelled from Georgetown by plane on 22 October 1977. I was met at the Matthews Ridge Airport by the Chief Executive Officer Mr. Gregory Gaskin. We travelled by land-rover two miles to the Administration Office situated on a high hill overlooking the industrial site and Pakera village, with a backdrop of high hills forming part of the Blue Mountain range. I was introduced to the Permanent Secretary, Mr. Bob Wyatt, (whom I had known when he was at the Ministry of Works and Transport and I was at Mahdia Potaro District), and other members of the office staff. I was given accommodation at the Senior Rest House at Hill 2 on the Ridge for the time I was at this location. I heard that the Minister for Works and Transport Mr. Steve Narine was holidaying on the Ridge, so after dinner I went across to Guyana House (reserved for ministers and visiting dignitaries) to visit him and have a talk on roads in general. I brought up a question of why so many different projects were started without having the money to complete even one. Would it not be better to complete one before starting another? That night, Mr. and Mrs. Gaskin visited me at the Senior Rest House at 9:00 p.m., after I had retired to bed, to invite me over for dinner at 8:00 p.m. the following night at their bungalow. There was no mosquito net to cover my bed. The mosquitoes made sleep impossible for the three nights I spent there.

The following morning, I walked a mile and a quarter down the ridge road to the industrial site comprising the railways yards, garages, main stores building, power house, train station, electrical workshop, the mechanical and buildings workshops and the lumber yard. The C.E.O. introduced me to Vincent Lewis a middle-aged man from St. Lucia, who was to be my road foreman. I queried him about road equipment. He informed me that there were no lorries and no earth moving equipment on the road. I had noticed some pieces of equipment in the yards and in the area adjacent to the yards which apparently had not been in operation for the past two years as they did not have the parts to repair them. I travelled by land-rover 7 miles to Papaya, the Guyana National Service Centre. On approaching the Papaya saw mill, three miles from the ridge, I noticed the wreckage of a large trailer at the base of a steep hill. Lewis informed me that the Mac truck hauling the trailer up the hill with a heavy load, had got into difficulties and run back down the hill, causing an accident in which several men were injured and one hospitalised with a broken leg. Lewis said that a diversion road had been started, but had run into difficulties and had been abandoned due to the presence of granite rocks. I noticed the surface of the dirt road to have numerous potholes and exposed granite rocks, and although the terrain was hilly, the roads lacked proper drainage.

I visited the air strip lying in an east-west direction, which originally was built over a low drainage area. A 700-foot long hollow wood culvert had been laid underneath the strip to drain a pond formed by the water coming off the hills to the north. Lewis said that it looked as if parts of the underground culvert had started to rot, causing a blockage in the drainage. This really called for a renewal of the culvert and if this was to be done I said I would recommend laying two and a half feet diameter concrete pipes of the kind made at Makouria stone depot on the left bank of the Essequibo River below Bartica.

I then travelled thirty-six miles out to Port Kaituma in company with the Assistant Regional Development Officer, Jim Holder, who was returning to Mabaruma by speed boat. The road surface from the ridge to Arakaka, some 18 miles, was in fair condition, made up of clay and sand clay soils. The drainage was good except for a stretch at 15 miles where there was an overflow from the hills in the rainy season running over the road. Beyond the Barima River bridge, there was one mile of road under flood level. A sharp 'U' turn at the bridge resulted in a back up of flood waters causing the road to be submerged under three feet of water. I proposed that either a canal be cut at the beginning of the high land to take off at least 25% of the flood waters from the upper to the lower reaches of the river, or that the road be built up with rocks transported from the stone quarry two and a half miles from Kaituma. The suggestion was made to excavate a canal on both sides of the road and raise the level with this earth, but I argued that this would not stand up to traffic in the rainy season. There had to be a solid stone foundation or nothing. There were also many twists and turns in the road between 14 mile and the Barima bridge which could be realigned to make a straighter road with less blind and dangerous turns. I travelled one mile beyond Port Kaituma to the pump station which takes its water from the Kaituma River and pumps it into the overhead tanks in the Kaituma Staff Compound. I also inspected the Kaituma waterside and stelling, where boats are discharged. At a meeting with Mr. Gregory Gaskin I handed in my reports and recommendations based on my inspection.

It was decided that I would take up my duties on 15 November 1977. I would receive the same salary I had received at Mahdia plus my duty allowance. I would be supplied with a furnished house which the C.E.O. said he would have painted. On 26 October 1977, I left Matthews Ridge at 5:45 p.m. after a heavy thunder storm and arrived home at 7:30 p.m. very tired, as the mosquitoes had given little or no sleep on the Ridge.

Back in Georgetown on 27 October, I visited my old friends, the Chief Engineer of Roads, and other Engineers who might be in a position to help me acquire some road equipment for Matthews Ridge. There were some projects that were stalled with machinery to spare, but no money to carry them on. I also contacted the Upper Mazaruni Road Project (U.M.R.P.) Engineer to assist me with concrete pipes for culverts only to be informed they were not casting them any more. On 1 November 1977, I submitted a full report on my findings at Matthews Ridge to Hon. Minister Mr. D Hoyte. I informed him there was not one piece of working equipment at Matthews Ridge, nor were there any dump trucks to transport road materials. The Minister asked me when I would be able to take up my duties at the Ridge. I said it was no use my going if I did not have the necessary equipment to work with. It was only 'He' who could accelerate the acquisition of the necessary machines. Engineer Joseph of the Roads Division informed me that the U.M.R.P. had #800 Colas. As Trinidad had stopped exporting this material, it would have been hard for me to acquire it anywhere else.

I had requested money from the Minister to purchase parts for a Grader Model 112 and a fuel pump for a Barford front-end loader and was able to acquire a Massey Ferguson Tractor Model 1105 from the Upper Mazaruni Road Project and two trailers from the Ministry of Works and Transport from their depot at Crane, West Coast Demerara. I met the Regional Minister for the North West Region and told him I was awaiting my letter of appointment from the C.E.O. Matthews Ridge. He said he would look into it as I could not do anything constructive without authority.

Minister Hoyte arranged with the Guyana National Service (G.N.S.) Motor Vessel *Jaimito* to ship my equipment to Port Kaituma. I was to have been assisted with more equipment from Civil Aviation, Mabaruma, but the director said he had received instructions from Cabinet to proceed with construction of his strip at Mabaruma. He was sorry he could not assist me. I again visited the Minister of Works and Transport who eventually gave me two German lorries from the Crane Compound. These had to be checked at the M.W.T.R. workshop at Kingston before they were eventually shipped to me. Minister Hoyte instructed me to send a radio message to the C.E.O. on 13 December 1977 at Matthews Ridge informing him my equipment would be arriving via the G.N.S. boat *Jaimito*. I later learned that Capt. Benn had off-loaded my equipment at Kaituma. No one knew anything about it so Benn had carried the tractor and two trailers to Coomacka Landing for the Mabaruma Project. I did not receive it until three months later.

On 29 December 1977 I received my letter of appointment which stated I would commence my duties as from 1 January 1978. I showed the letter to Minister Hoyte who said he would rectify this mistake as he knew I had been on duty since 1 November 1977 trying to locate and acquire equipment for the Ridge. On 7 January 1978, I returned to Matthews Ridge in company with Mr. Gaskin, the C.E.O.. I was assigned the same room at the Senior Rest House on Hill 2 of the Ridge. Mr. Gaskin informed me my house was not ready for there was no refrigerator or electric stove. I attended a meeting at the Administrative Office for all supervisors where I was introduced to the other men on the supervisory staff. The C.E.O. introduced the Land Development Officer and the Regional Minister for the Matarkai Region. I informed him the Hon. Minister for Economic Development had said I would be allotted furnished quarters and as long as I had to put up in the rest house, I would claim a subsistence allowance.

Later, Mr. Gaskin presided over a seminar on utilities, roads, pure water supply, railroads, the electric power plant, electrical workshop, mechanical workshop, buildings, saw mills and garage. A budget was drawn up and each utility would have to work within the amount allotted to it. A system of accounting, leadership, authority and welfare was to be observed. The C.E.O. said that the Land Officer should take an example from me as I was on my job everyday. Mr. Gaskin asked me to take over as manager of utilities until he could appoint a suitable man.

From the start, I had opposition from the supervisor of the mechanical workshop who refused to give me the information I required. He went so far as to say he had seen no written appointment on my being the manager for utilities. He felt he was a power and, being a confidant of the Regional Minister and a party member, felt he could do no wrong. But every rope has an end, and when he bluntly refused to co-operate with the administration, he was transferred to Georgetown. This business of what some of the men understood by party membership could be a problem. On one occasion, my road foreman got out of line, giving me a first class cussing in front of all the labourers. He had been drinking liquor when I remonstrated with him. He informed me he was a party member and I could not do anything to him. His case was tried by the Personnel Officer and a member of his Union. He was found guilty of insubordination. I suspended him from duty for two weeks.

I appointed Vincent La Cruz, an Amerindian, who was a diesel mechanic, as supervisor of all mechanical work in the Industrial site. I asked La Cruz to select the best of the Barford lorries lying rusting in the dump site and try to build one complete lorry. I asked him to give me a list of parts required to put the grader and the front-end loader on the road. La Cruz was also in charge of the railroad engines. He had some good men under him.

I inspected the Barford roller and found the machine had been cannibalised, the engine taken out and other parts missing. I told the mechanics to loose off the front roller and the two large rear wheels. I had the welder make a tow bar so that the David Browne tractor could pull it to compact spots on the road and to roll the air strip. A Manitowac motor shovel lying on the flat was repaired and put to load manganese fines into tractor trailers and lorries for spreading on road surfaces. I made a thorough inspection of the dump site which the men dubbed "Guyana Gajraj", where I saw where millions of dollars had been thrown down the drain. Lorries, land-rovers, graders, and other pieces of equipment just cast aside without any attempt to repair. At that period, the Matarkai Agricultural Project had money to spend. I was to learn from the farmers and other residents of the waste that went on. I walked from the yards six miles to the foot of Blue Mountain. I was shown areas that had been planted with fruits and garden produce, only to have it rot on the airfield or at the riverside at Port Kaituma awaiting on the promised transportation to the outside markets. I saw acres of citrus fruit being taken over by bush as there was not sufficient money to reactivate the scheme. From what I saw, I thought that the Port Kaituma - Arakaka area was best suited to farming, the soils being more suitable. Efforts had been made to revive agriculture, but the farmers were reluctant to try again and there was too much overhead expenditure for the Government to make it pay.

Because I had no equipment to start with, I instructed my road foreman to have the road gang, some twelve men, fill pot holes with available road side stone. On the top and bottom roads of the ridge they were also to weed road shoulders and clean drains. Foreman Schultz at Port Kaituma was simi-

larly engaged. He made a request for road tools. I told Lewis to make an
inventory of all road tools on hand and to make a list of tools required for
both gangs, i.e. wheelbarrows, spades, both long and short handled, shovels, cutlasses, axes, sledge hammers, crowbars and pinching bars. The inventory revealed the need to put forward an urgent requisition for road tools
for my road gangs – six men at Kaituma, six men for the Pakera section and
six men for the Ridge gang. I was later to learn that when other sections
wanted some work done, they used to borrow my men. I put a stop to this, as
the expenditure was charged against my section. Any other division requiring assistance would have to make a request for the number of men and
time they were required for this amount would be charged against their section. The constant request for my road gang was a set back to my maintenance work so I asked the C.E.O. to set up a separate jobbing gang.

I had a visit from John Campbell, an all rounder, operating heavy equipment and driving land-rovers and lorries. He informed me he had been working with the late African Manganese Company and could give me some indications where the company had mined the richest ore. He mentioned that
when the company had closed their operations and handed over everything
to the Government, the equipment, trains and workshop had been in good
order. He said it was poor maintenance on the part of the Government that
had allowed the machinery to deteriorate, and then there was the lack of
money to purchase new parts. I also had a visit from Alpheus John, an Amerindian who used to work with me in the Berbice River in 1956, when I
was engaged by the St. Francis Metals Co. prospecting for precious minerals and diamonds. He informed me that Lewis, my road foreman, was using
some of the men from my road gang to work his own farm and Matakai (the
word MATARKAI was made up from the different sections: Matthews Ridge,
Arakaka, Kaituma) was paying these men. When I called up Lewis and questioned him about the men working on his farm, he bluntly denied the charge.
It was not long after this that I learned- the men mentioned were related to
Lewis' wife. I had to dispense with their services.

The local people – Afro-Guyanese – have a saying: "Bush got ears" and
I learned from the 'grass roots' that people had heard the Minister (Regional)
and a union official say they did not know why Young and Edwards (a surveyor) had been appointed to Matarkai as there were men who had been
there for years and should have been appointed. The union was to have called
a strike in protest but nothing occurred.

Finally, my first pieces of road equipment arrived on 16 March 1978,
although I had shipped them from Georgetown in December 1977. I planned
to start road maintenance at Matthews Ridge and work out to Arakaka and

continue to Port Kaituma – thirty-six miles of roadway. Then I had five miles of road from the Ridge to the Papaya Training Centre and two and a half miles of Ridge roads. I had to locate and stockpile materials for road repairs, and I was not lucky enough to find any deposits of laterite rock as I had at Mahdia - Potaro and had to revert to using the overburden and residue from the manganese mines. I did though locate some quartz stone hills at 6-7 miles and at 19 miles from the Ridge. I managed to find some shale from an old quarry at Pakera over the railway line two and a half miles from Kaituma, though these rocks would have to be blasted. I examined the old crusher, which needed some new jaws and an engine to power it. I planned to put this in operation as soon as I could get sufficient funds (La Cruz was working on an engine in the workshop). I used the manganese fines to surface the main roads from the Ridge leading to the Matthews Ridge Airport and the Pakera Village and Hospital, but it would have been a waste of time and material to spread them on the steep ridge roads as the heavy rains just washed them away. On the hill slopes I had to use a coarser grain and seal the surface with #800 colas.

Two miles west of the administration office was the Matthews Ridge Airport. There I began work on the drainage where a 700 foot hollow wood culvert lying under the landing strip had gone rotten. I had to excavate an eight foot by three foot canal parallel to the airport to draw off an overflow of water from the pond and pass the water through another culvert further to the west. The creek leading into the pond further to the north-west in the hills was cleaned and the water diverted to flow through another culvert a quarter of a mile to the west and passing under the road to Papaya. The mouth of the culvert had to be dug out for a distance of approximately 150 feet by 10 feet by 18 inches deep as the stream bed had silted up over the years.

I also examined and replaced rotted hollow wood culverts throughout the forty-one miles of roadway. I would have preferred to have used cement culverts, but as I have mentioned, these were no longer being made. The drainage of the industrial area proved another problem. When the original site had been planned, the Manganese Company had put down six feet diameter heavy galvanised pipes in the foundations to take off the rush of water from the steep hills of the ridge. The drainage water flowed through into the flats beyond and discharged into a creek. Over the years, silt had built up in the drainage basin, blocking the tailing. Consequently the pipes under the foundation had silted up too. When I examined the drainage, there was only an eighteen inch exit from the pipe, consequently, when there was a heavy rainfall, the area was flooded. Men with pickaxes and shovels were set on to try and clear the exits, but this was useless work unless the tailings could be cleared to form a draught. I had planned to use an excavator with a bucket but this machine was sent down river to Morawhanna where the government was doing some new empoldering of lands. I tried to clear the tailings out in the flats, but the D/7 caterpillar bulldozer got bogged down so this venture proved a failure. Pakera Village, which lies in the valley between the hills, also suffered from bad drainage. The small four foot drains had, over the years, been overgrown with vegetation – and the residents had used them as garbage dumps. The exit into the small creek needed digging. The problem was the money needed to employ a steady maintenance gang. This was the problem with the entire project.

Another maintenance task was to examine, and often replace, bridge timbers. I had to completely rebuild a bridge at 12 mile from Port Kaituma which had burned down when someone setting fire to the road-shoulder grass in dry weather. To save twenty miles of travelling everyday from the Ridge, I was instructed by the Chief Executive Officer to travel to Port Kaituma and put up at the Government Rest House where I would be nearer my operational work. I travelled out to Port Kaituma by the morning train. There, I left my baggage at the rest house, then visited the Administration Office where I spoke with the clerk in charge. Then I visited the wharf at the riverside where I met my road gang supervisor, Schultz. I told him I would be staying at the rest house to push the building of the bridge at 12 mile and that I wanted him and his men to travel to 12 mile by the morning train and return by the afternoon train. Returning to the rest house for lunch at 1:00 p.m., I was told by the woman caretaker, an Afro-Guyanese, that I could not get accommodation there as the Regional Minister had told her to reserve all accommodation for Party members who would be attending a Seminar.

So I, a Senior Officer at Matarkai was to be debarred from doing my official duties by the ruling of the Regional Minister! I just got as mad as hell and said the Minister and his Party members would have to build the bridge at 12 mile, for if I could not get accommodation I was returning to Matthews Ridge. I caught the afternoon train and returned to my house on the Ridge. The following morning, the Regional Minister sent for me and asked what had happened at Kaituma. I told him that I was sure that he knew, for I was certain that the caretaker at the rest house, who was a Party member, must have telephoned him to inform him what I had said in anger. The Minister said the woman had phoned him and he asked me to return to Kaituma as there was now adequate room at the rest house since some of the Party members had made other arrangements for accommodation. I told the Minister I

would do my work from Matthews Ridge which meant that though I would
lose time in travel, I would be free from interference from Party members. I
wrote a duplicate letter to the Chief Executive Officer reporting this incident. I had met with Party interference with my road equipment whilst operating at Mahdia in the Potaro Region, but the Minister there had received a
letter from the Hon. Minister of Economic Development telling him not to
interfere with my equipment unless there was an emergency. Politics seemed
to have ruled this region for too long. I saw from the beginning that there
was constant tug of war between the Chief Executive Office of Matarkai and
Party members, from the Regional Minister and the Regional Development
Officer down to the labourers in the yard. The Chief Executive Officer had
been trained for the post that he filled and had the ability to push development, but there was always some Party undercurrent working against him.
Not only was this Chief Executive Officer plagued by party interference, but
his successor, too, threatened to resign if the party did not keep out of his
jurisdiction. He said he only needed my assistance to get his work done.

I brought this situation to the attention of the Hon. Minister of Economic
Development when I visited him in Georgetown. I further wrote a duplicate
letter to the Chief Executive Officer, with the original to the Minister in
Georgetown, recommending a change in the Regional Minister and his assistant, the Regional Development Officer. There were numerous party semi-
nars, public meetings, sports, dances and a lot of talk on party policies, but
no development. I was gratified to learn later that these two officers had
been transferred to other regions. The wheels of God grind slowly but they
grind exceedingly well.

I held the post as C.E.O. for the interval between the departure of Major
Gaskin and the appointment of Colonel Morgan. I had a taste of Party med-
dling and antagonism, but I made a firm stand and was finally able to start
making some road improvements after I received some heavy equipment on
loan from Land Development Division. I cut a road from a point dividing
Administration Hill on Hill 1. The bulldozer had to clear a track and then
using his blade, cut into the hill, pushing the dirt out to the outside slope
following the contour, and gradually descending in a 1 in 10 gradient, passing the foot of the washing plant, crossing the existing road leading into the
industrial site and the railway lines, to join the main road at the Cassava
Mill three-quarters of a mile from the start. The C.E.O. had requested this
road as he wanted it to pass the industrial site, to put it under more security.

CHAPTER XXXIV

New Roads for Baramita, Amerindian Middens and the
Jonestown Tragedy – 1978

I had been shown a track through the bush from the Guyana House on Hill 2, passing though second-growth bush, which I understood had previously been planted with corn, but was now lying idle, through then about half a mile of virgin forest to a small waterfall formed by the waters of Arakaka Paru Creek descending from the ridge adjacent to the east of our ridge. I later had my D/7 caterpillar open a road three quarters of a mile in length and approximately thirty feet wide. There was a steep descent from Guyana House which I later eased off by a zigzag ascent up the 500 foot slope. This road proved a drawing card for visitors and the inhabitants of the village, so much so the Chief Executive Officer appointed me to be in charge of tourism. I was asked to cut bridle paths to any places in the bush adjacent to the main road where people could have picnics and go fishing. ·

I also did some improvements on the top and bottom roads of the main ridge leading to the staff compounds, opening up blind and narrow turns. At one point on the bottom road, I had to cut into the high road-shoulder for a distance of fifteen feet and push the dirt into a gully at the narrowest part of the turn. I reinforced the outside shoulder with a three tier pall of hardwood posts and beams, between which I planted bamboo to hold the loose material of the fill. I had done a similar job at 9 mile Bartica - Potaro Road on a deep white sand fill and at 104 mile Mahdia Road on the Potaro Road. When the bamboo grew, the roots held the loose material in place. As I have mentioned before, I had learned this type of work when working gold and diamonds where I had to use my own initiative, also on the coastal sugar estates where bamboo was used to hold the foreshore from erosion from the tides. This type of roadwork is termed cribbing when reinforced concrete is used.

At the same time, I cut a detour at the steep hill on the approach to the Papaya Saw Mill, tracing a line on a lower level, trying to steer clear of the dolerite rock formation that had curtailed a previous effort to lower the gradient. I opened this new road a quarter mile in length and 150 feet wide. I had to contend with the rock formation for a distance of 700 feet, but it was loose rock and not bedrock. I had to install two hollow wooden culverts forty-two feet in length to take off the water from the high hill and pass it under the road to the lower flats. This new road proved easier for traffic. I also cut and sided Tiger Hill to lessen the 1 in 4 gradient which had caused undue difficulties in the rainy season as the base material was a hard laterite clay and very slippery. This cut also filled the two gullies approaching the hill, allowing me to get a straighter road on a less gradient. I had to open about two miles of tractor road into the farm areas at 6 mile and at the Minab farms adjacent to the village. There was an existing road from the airport going two and a half miles south to Blue Mountain. There were two timber bridges which had rotted and had to be renewed before it could be opened to traffic. The Mounted Police outpost lay three quarters of a mile from the airport and comprised three cottages and a barn. The police had one stallion, eleven brood mares and seven other head of horses. Horses were bred there for replacements to the Georgetown branch. I had to use my D/7 bulldozer to excavate a pond of water for the house. There were only two policemen stationed there. Walking every day from Hill 2 on the ridge down to the Administration Offices, the industrial site and other areas, meant I was covering some 7 to 8 miles every day and I found my body was losing too much salt. I lost eleven pounds in the first few months I was there. I asked the dispenser at Pakera Hospital to give me some salt tablets. He also X-rayed my right foot and found my big toe had an old fracture which had been causing me pain after I had walked any distance.

On the visit of the Minister of Economic Development, I requested I be given a land-rover so as I could supervise the widespread areas. I had to travel to the city and pick out a damaged land-rover from the Ministry of Works and Transport Yard. The workshop had it repaired, costing me a little over two thousand dollars. It was shipped to Port Kaituma via Mabaruma. It was held up there for some seven and a half months. I received it minus its new tyres and the mileage gauge registering 51,925 miles. It seems as if the Ministry at Mabaruma had done over 7,000 miles monthly. I had waited for 13 months between requesting and receiving my land-rover. I had also waited five and a half months before my letter of appointment was finally given to me with all the correct clauses included on a three year contract. I had to wait for two and a half months before I eventually moved into my own house and seventeen more months before I received an electric stove and a refrigerator. This was too much like Mahdia - Potaro when I had to wait five months before I could move into my own house at 111 mile compound.

I was asked to open a road from three and quarter miles beyond Papaya Training Centre to Baramita on the left bank of the Barama River. This settlement was only accessible by plane other than walking the Amerindian Trail. The logging foreman, Smart, had gone to cut block lines from Tassawinni Creek to Whanna River and estimate the quantity of timber available for saw mill operations. It had been intended to move the saw mill from Papaya, as it was really too far to transport logs there from the surrounding areas. Smart recommended we use Massey-Ferguson tractors with winches to haul out the logs, load the logs on timber trailers, which would have to be constructed, and cut and build a main haul-road to bring out the logs. I had to rebuild a bridge across the Tassawinni Creek using purpleheart logs felled in the vicinity. The saw mill supplied me with the necessary planks to finish the job. I took two Amerindians and walked the line to Whanna River, a distance of two and a quarter miles. I later surveyed the line and had my D/ 7 and D/8 bulldozers clear the forest 200 feet wide while axemen or power saws cut down the trees in the area of the proposed saw mill site. I had my Amerindian foreman and three other men trace a line forward from Whanna River on the route to Baramita. I later walked this line, a distance of five and a quarter miles, plus the two and a quarter miles from Tasawini. Not having walked such a distance over such rough conditions, climbing steep hills and surmounting fallen trees for some time, my thigh muscles rebelled. I started to get cramps and had to rest repeatedly, arriving into my foreman's 'bhuttoo', a leaf camp, at 4:00 p.m., just as the bush was getting dark. I changed into dry clothes and hung out my other clothes to air. I had to get Harold, one of the Amerindians, to rub my thigh and leg muscles briskly with ordinary baking flour. This, as before, proved a fast remedy for cramps.

Rain fell heavily during the night and my other clothes got soaking wet. On my return journey out to Whanna river, I took a leisurely walk in order not to put any strain on my muscles. I took note of the various species of timber and their approximate number. I also noted dolerite rock outcrops, quartz, and some signs of laterite over the hills I crossed. The land toward the last creek, Warapa, which the Amerindians said was only about three miles from Baramita, rises in elevation. It was in these remote areas, near the rivers and creeks especially in this north-west region, but also stretching throughout the coastlands, where an ancient people lived and had their being, signs of which were to be seen in their shell mounds and kitchen middens. This I know from the things I found in these mounds when I dug into them: stone axes and other tools with which the people cut down the trees and made their dugouts and canoes; bone-scrapers and smoothers with which they made their weapons of the chase; fragments of their bowls and basins and yes, even the marrow bones of their enemies whom they had eaten.

Of course, these are not all actual mounds. Some, especially in the cane fields of the sugar estates and on the east coast savannahs are so flat as to be almost imperceptible to the eye.

The shell mounds are found only near the coast and consist of millions of small striped shells, like the shells of snails of a species still found in the lower reaches of many of our rivers. Mixed with these shells are the bones of many animals, fish and human beings, bone tools, pieces of pots, but not so many stone axes or other tools of like material. It is believed that the shells were brought to these spots by generations of the people who lived there and used them for food. Almost invariably these shell mounds are found close to the rivers and creeks and were undoubtedly refuse from the homes of water-loving people. One of the most famous of the shell mounds is at Waramuri Mission on the Moruca River. This mound is about twenty-five feet wide at its base. It has been excavated to its full length and depth. Right through, from top to bottom, were found traces of these people's residence there, so it may be imagined how many years they must have lived on this one spot to form such a big rubbish heap.

The kitchen-middens, found generally but not always on hills, contain no shells but a much greater proportion of pottery, stone axes, flint arrowheads and often complete skeletons. The North West District is literally studded with these interesting memorials of a race long vanished and they extend right down the coast to Skeldon and southward to the Rupununi. The pottery made by these ancient people was quite different to that made by the present day Amerindians as is proven by the fragments found. Their pots and bowls were decorated with crude carvings and embellished with knobs and handles of fantastic shape, caricatures of alligators and tortoise heads being very common. Of greatest interest is an incised flat vase found at Mabaruma in the North West District. This specimen is said to be the only complete one of its type known, belonging to a culture that flourished around the Orinoco river mouth at the time the Europeans first arrived there.

Of greatest interest too are the stone beads from Karapa Creek midden on the Mahaica Creek. Quartz is one of the hardest of stones, yet these ancient people not only fashioned beads of it but also drilled the holes in them even though they had no metal. How was this done? Fortunately this art was still practised within recent times by certain tribes in the Amazon to the south of us, and a traveller has actually witnessed the manufacture of quartz beads. They were drilled with the mid-rib of the leaf of the ité palm. Of course, hundreds and probably thousands of leaves had to be used to drill a single bead and the traveller learned that it required three generations to drill one bead. Thus, if a young man began to drill the hole through the one inch long bead, he worked on it off and on until he became an old man and died, but the hole would not yet be half through, so his son went on with the work until he too die of old age. It was the grandson who in middle age or late life finally completed the hole. In my travels to the headwaters of our rivers and in the open north and south savannahs, I have witnessed rock carvings of ships and figures of men and animals. There are also caves in which these ancient people recorded their lives in paintings, on the walls. At Plantation Park, the coconut estate on the Mahaicony river where I had been manager, I located a heap of sea shells which I used to surface some of my roads, little realising it might have been one of the shell mounds of these ancient people.

On my return to Matthews Ridge from the bush, I made a plan of my survey of the road from Tassawinni Creek to Warapa Creek and also submitted a written report on the timber and road materials I had seen in that area. I had to submit monthly reports to the Chief Executive Officer of the work I had completed on the roads and elsewhere, also the cost. Every three months, I submitted a quarterly report and half-yearly report for the Matarkai Board Meeting. At times, my field work caught up with my paper work, making it necessary to work late into the night to complete my reports.

It was at the end of my first year as Superintendent of Roads at Matarkai Development Authority that an incident occurred that shocked the entire world. I have, during my years of travel in this vast interior of Guyana, seen the beauty and vast possibilities that lie there and termed it 'God's own country'. Food is abundant for those that do not shirk to labour. The climate is ideal for crops. The rivers and creeks produce fish and the forests game. This beautiful and blessed land of ours was jarred out of its tranquillity on Saturday, 18 November 1978 when news was brought to me at my house at Matthews Ridge at 6:00 p.m. of an incident at the Peoples' Temple Jonestown where five visiting Americans had been shot and killed and many more wounded at the Port Kaituma Airstrip.

Following this, on the same day, Reverend Jim Jones, the head of the Peoples' Temple religious cult, had called on all his followers to commit mass suicide, fearing reprisals from our soldiers as the result of the shooting incident. Many were inhumanely poisoned or shot down. However, we did not learn of this shocking waste of human lives – men, women and little children – until later. At my location at Matthews Ridge, some 36 miles inland from Port Kaituma, I was acting as Chief Executive Officer, as my C.E.O., Major Gaskin, was in Georgetown. The Regional Minister and his Regional

Development Officer were on a visit to Moruca, an outlying district. I phoned
Mr. Thomas, the Senior Officer at Kaituma, and he appealed to me to send
police or soldiers to safeguard the residents there who feared for their lives.

I phoned Major Gaskin, our C.E.O. in Georgetown. Inspector Benjamin
of the Matthews Ridge Police and Major Benn of the Guyana National Service Training Centre at Papaya were alerted. I placed all my land-rovers on
stand by and arranged with the dispatcher to have the train crew on standby,
ready to transport troops. Major Gaskin phoned from Georgetown informing
me he would arrive at 10:30 p.m. with Guyana Defence Force soldiers that
same night.

All the women and children residing on the two hill compounds at
Matthews Ridge congregated at my house, as they were afraid to stay in their
own homes, fearing some of the Americans from the Peoples' Temple would
penetrate the bush to shoot them. I had my hands full calming the mothers
of the little children. Mattresses, blankets and pillows were spread on the
floor of my living room where they huddled together for companionship. I
rang the garage and instructed the dispatcher to send all the land-rovers to
the Matthews Ridge Airport two miles out and stand by to switch on their
headlights to guide the incoming planes. At 10:30 p.m. on the dot, we heard
the droning of the first plane. I had all my house lights switched on to act as
a guide to the pilot of the plane, and all the women and children ran out of
the house to see the plane circle the airport about four times before landing.
Another plane landed ten minutes later. There was a marked relief in the
women knowing that the soldiers had arrived. Shortly after, Maj. Gaskin arrived, accompanied by some of his staff, and was surprised to see my house
full of women and children. I gave him and his lieutenant some hot coffee,
after which he left for the administration office carrying his secretary to take
phone calls from Georgetown and relay them to Port Kaituma. He informed
me he would leave for Kaituma at 3:00 a.m. on Sunday with the train and
some land-rovers. At 4:00 a.m., Major Johnson of the Guyana Defence Force
and four others arrived by another plane. He was accompanied by a member of the American Embassy in Georgetown who had come to get the names
of the American dead and wounded. Major Johnson contacted a G.D.F. lieutenant at Port Kaituma who informed him that one congressman, a photog-
rapher and three newsmen were dead and four others wounded.

Major Gaskin, who was with the first detachment of troops, entered
Jonestown at dawn on Sunday, 19 November 1978 whilst the jungle was still
shrouded with heavy mist. The soldiers moved silently through the forest to
penetrate the area surrounding Jonestown little knowing what to expect. They

were met by a silence so profound, for on entering the town itself they found not one living soul.

Major Gaskin phoned me. He could not describe the scene, it was so pitiful. Men and women had died clasped in each other's arms, family groups of mothers and children. Most who died there were next to the auditorium. Others were found in the cottages or the surrounding forest.

Three monkeys, a macaw, a dog and a cat were the only living things found in this dead town.

The Peoples' Temple Agricultural Project, situated some three miles along the Port Kaituma - Matthews Ridge Road and extending some three and a half miles inside from the main road, had been a thriving agricultural community of approximately twelve hundred inhabitants who had cut from the virgin forest an area of approximately 2,500 acres. They had erected a small saw mill which supplied the materials to build their homes, hospital, stores, workshops and bonds. The whole area surrounding this town of about fifty buildings was planted on both sides of the access road from the main gate and extending beyond with cassava, plantains, bananas, citrus and other fruit trees, and with a wealth of various ground provisions. They had sunk their own well from which they pumped water to supply the whole town, piping it to individual houses. One mile outside of town they had erected a cassava mill. In this area were the livestock: pigs, cattle, horses and poultry. In Jonestown, there was a mechanics shop, a machine shop and a welding unit. They repaired or turned out spares for their machinery. Their stores, both hardware and groceries and dry goods, were well stocked. The doctor's house, hospital and dispensary were equipped with the most up-to-date medical equipment, thousand of dollars worth of drugs that were unobtainable in our Georgetown Hospital and a library of thousands of books, mostly on Socialism. There were two lorries, three tractors and trailers, a caterpillar D/6 bulldozer, a combination Hi-mac and front-end loader, ploughs and other farm equipment and a generating plant.

I had the privilege of visiting Jonestown twice on 12 June and on 16 June 1978. Johnny Jones, the adopted son of Reverend Jones, and Lee Ingram, who were lodging at the Matthews Ridge Rest House when I too was there earlier in the year, had invited me to give them some pointers on road construction and maintenance and on the erection of a water tower and the type of fruit trees to use for preserves. I had been served lunch in the auditorium where the meeting was held. Everything I ate had been grown on the farm. At the end of the meeting, Johnny introduced me to his dad, Jim Jones, who had arrived towards the end of the meeting.

Five of the members gave me a guided tour of the town. Next to the kitchen was the dispensary and bakery, then the laundry equipped with five washing machines, then a boiler to heat water. Beyond this we came to the smoke house where they cured their own hams, then the herb hut where three women were preparing jams and jellies, fruit syrup and preserves. I visited the Junior Citizens, little babies both black and white, under the care of young women. The youngsters were in their play pens, the older kids were in the compound area. Johnny told me that all the furniture and toys were made right there. I saw some beautiful rugs and mats made from odds and ends by the more elderly women. There was a natural blending of colours and design that caught the eye. I must say from the moment I entered the main gate to travel into Jonestown, I was met by waving hands and smiling faces. There were white and black Americans, Japanese, Chinese, Indians and many others.

I was struck by the movement of the people. I saw no instructors in the fields or elsewhere. It was like a large beehive of activity. There was no lost moment and everyone seemed to know where to go and what to do. I asked one black woman if they were all Americans, she said NO! They were all Guyanese now. Johnny told me that they did not use money there. If a man or a woman wanted new pants or a shirt or a pair of boots, they would have to turn in the old ones before they were issued with the new. No one was allowed to smoke or drink any alcoholic beverages but visitors were treated to the best. I met men there who had owned their own businesses in the States, who had sold out to come here in this deep jungle to start a new and peaceful life, to get away from all the conflicts of modern living.

On my departure, I stood and looked around me to witness what these people had accomplished in the four years they had been there. I was amazed and said to myself that this would be a good example for our own co-operatives to follow, dedicating themselves to make Guyana self-sufficient.

Five months later, I was to witness something that I could not have believed possible. In that area of smiling faces I found only death and the stench of rotting bodies, piled on top of one another awaiting removal by the American helicopters engaged in that air lift.

Why this mass suicide, why this waste of human lives, why had they thrown away all they had accomplished? Why? This was the mystery. How could one understand the influence of one man over his fellow men and women to do such an inhuman act? Only a madman could have gone so far as to murder little children.

This tragedy put Guyana on the map of the world.

CHAPTER XXXV
The Stench of Death at Jonestown – 1978-79

On 25 November 1978, Major Gaskin asked me to accompany him to Jonestown. We left the ridge at 4:15 a.m. driving through heavy ground mists, arriving at Port Kaituma 6:05 a.m. I saw ten men sleeping on the floor of the Administration Office. Major Gaskin contacted Georgetown and spoke to Colonel Singh at the Guyana Defence Force Headquarters and Hon. Minister Desmond Hoyte.

There were seven foreign correspondents there who requested transportation back to the city. Foreign correspondent Mr. Reynolds spoke to the BBC at 7:00 a.m., reporting that the airlift of the dead bodies was still in operation but that it should be completed that day.

Major Gaskin and I left Kaituma by the same land-rover at 8:00 a.m. We met over one hundred people trekking along the road with baskets and bags on their way to loot at Jonestown. Major Gaskin, who had armed himself with a rifle, spoke to them and advised them to turn back as the soldiers had received instructions to shoot anyone found looting. The whole area was under martial law. We stopped at the gap leading to the Cassava Mill where seven men were loaded down with loot. One man tried to get away, not stopping on the command from the major. He dropped his load and made an abrupt stop though when Major Gaskin fired a shot over his head. These men were all placed under armed arrest in the hands of the soldiers.

Proceeding for another mile and a half, we approached the entrance to the town. I was met with the stench of death, of rotting bodies. The operation of preparing the dead bodies for shipment by helicopter to Timehri Airport was in the hands of U.S.A. soldiers. Major Gaskin asked me to accompany him to take notes and to meet Major Johnson G.D.F, who was presently in charge of Jonestown.

On passing downwind from the area where the dead were piled, the stench overpowered me so much I vomited up all my coffee. Major Johnson, Major Gaskin and I took a walk to the helicopter pad where the bodies were being loaded onto the helicopters. There was not a lost moment. Helicopters were constantly on the move, coming in, bringing fruit juices and beverages and fresh clothing for the Americans who were engaged in this air lift. I was introduced to four American colonels who told me their men were specially trained to handle the dead. They handled them like slabs of meat, hauling the bodies from the tractor trailer and placing the bodies in green plastic bags to be loaded onto the helicopters. I was more than ready to move from that area, for although I had been supplied with a respirator, I could still smell the stench and my stomach was rebelling.

The cottages I examined looked as if a cyclone had passed through, for clothing, sheets, blankets, cushions, mats and furniture were all tumbled up together, the result of the army searching for survivors. In one cottage I came across seven men pushing clothing into suit cases. I asked them if they worked here and they said no, so I signalled Major Gaskin who came with his rifle and chased them out. One man trying to get out of the front door with a bag and told to halt did not stop and drop his bag until he heard the click of the cocked rifle.

Major Johnson informed us there was a library where we might pick up some reading matter. We entered a long tarpaulin-covered tent, which seemed to have been the school, for it housed some twenty wooden cupboards filled with thousands of books, mostly on Socialism. Passing through this tent, I came across a long table the end of which was covered with used syringes and small bottles of injection liquids. White tablets were scattered over the table and floor.

It was from here the doctor and his assistants had used the poison on the followers of Jim Jones.

Leaving this tarpaulin tent and approaching the main auditorium, an open building, I was again hit by the overpowering stench of dead bodies. Radios, tape recorders and valuable electrical equipment was strewn all over the floor of the auditorium, the people's meeting place. When I had visited this building and had discussions and lunch on 16 June 1978 it had been full of smiling faces. Now as I looked at the gruesome sight of all these bodies, I could hardly believe my eyes. I was later told there were 925 dead.

I was instructed to return on Monday 27 November 1978 with a team of men to secure all movable objects and put them in one building. I was approached by a tall American soldier of some rank who enquired what I was doing there. I told him I was a government officer there to secure everything. He said that was good, as there were thousands of dollars worth of equipment lying around and thousands of dollars worth of drugs.

I left Jonestown in company with Major Gaskin at 1:30 p.m. by land rover. We stopped at Kaituma for some beers to wash the stink from our throats.

The sandwiches and a flask of coffee I had prepared before leaving Matthews Ridge had to be thrown away as both had been contaminated by the stench. We arrived at Matthews Ridge at 5:00 p.m., hungry, thirsty, and dirty. I stepped into my bath, dropping all my clothes to soak in a tub of hot water, soap powder and disinfectant.

On my return to Jonestown, I was met by armed police who escorted me to see Major Johnson who informed me a Mr. Simon had been appointed by the Ministry of Regional Development to take charge. One of my men, a mechanic, nearly got himself into trouble when I was leaving. The police searched my land rover. They found a tin box of rusted tools which my man claimed were his, but under threat of arrest admitted he had picked up in the compound. On 29 November 1978, I was again sent back to Jonestown by helicopter with seven Peoples Militia to assist the G.D.F soldiers. These seven Militia personnel were made to empty their bags – some of them were women – to ensure security. Thousands of dollars were discovered hidden in feed bags in the cassava mill and in some of the cottages in the Jonestown compound by the Criminal Investigation Department in the first search. Later, men cleaning up the compound came across other caches of money. Despite the security, some of the traders and individuals at Kaituma reaped a harvest in loot. The C.E.O. sent a message to those concerned that if they were found with loot in their houses, they would be immediately dismissed from their employment with the Matakai Authority.

On Thursday, 30 November 1978 at 8.30 a.m., I had to shut down my power plant, because, although I had managed to get a load of 756 gallons of dieselene, the incident at Jonestown and the use the local and armed forces had made of Matthews Ridge had meant that I'd had to keep on the electrical power for twenty-four hours a day for six days.

My involvement with the aftermath of Jonestown continued. The Agricultural Officer from Port Kaituma had taken charge of the livestock at the Jonestown farm (he was also in charge of intensive farming at Port Kaituma) and my heavy machines were involved in clearing and ploughing lands in that area for a few months. The state also had a farm six miles from the Ridge and when it came to the time to clean up and plant, the office staff and employees of the industrial area were called upon to give a week's labour. I too did my stint of weeding and clearing. I was attached to the old men's gang. There was a piece of land adjacent to the farm and near the road where I felt we could put in a crop of rice. I mentioned this fact to the Minister, suggesting we could erect a plank stop-off in the Creek that bordered the land. Water could be cut in to irrigate the land when the paddy seed was sown. The land was ploughed but it was found that it was not level enough to retain water. To level it would have entailed too much labour and time and I did not have the necessary equipment to do that, although I had received a number of bags of seed paddy to plant. The C.E.O decided to plant black-eye peas instead. This labour was undertaken by the office staff and employees from the industrial site, though to reap this crop, Amerindian labour was engaged to assist the office staff. An area adjacent to Pakera Village was also utilised to plant black-eye peas. Ground provisions from the Kaituma farm was shipped by train to supply the ration store at Pakera Village where we all did most of our weekly shopping. The following year, the ration store was taken over by the Guyana Pharmaceutical Corporation. The people were then able to get more of a varied stock and a more regular supply.

There were other incidents in this region which fortunately our Pakera Hospital was able to deal with. The hospital, which lay due east and approximately two miles from the administration offices, had been built on a vantage point on a hill overlooking the village. There was one dispenser, 'Doc' Hope, in charge, with a staff of one matron and about 20 to 24 beds, an x-ray unit, a maternity ward and a dispensing room plus the kitchens. 'Doc' Hope proved his ability on more than one occasion in emergencies. A land-rover coming from Papaya ran off an embankment parallel to the airport and plummeted twenty feet, landing with a crash on its bonnet. There were eight men in the vehicle. Luckily there was no death, but a lot of injuries. At another time, a Venezuelan Guardia National Army plane crashed on landing at the Matthews Ridge Airport. After seeing the plane circling a number times, I phoned the garage to send two land-rovers to guide the plane in with their headlights, as I thought it was one of our planes. I was informed at 9:30 p.m. that seven of the passengers had been assisted out of the crashed plane by personnel from Matthews Ridge, but unfortunately three soldiers had been trapped in the burning plane. These men's bodies were recovered the following day, just charred remains. I arrived at the hospital to find Matthews Ridge residents flocking inside. The police had to remove them to allow 'Doc' Hope and his assistants to move around more freely. There were four bed patients and three walking. The pilot of the plane had his right leg broken in two places and he was also cut and bruised. The mechanic also suffered a broken leg and the co-pilot and one other were also cut and bruised. The pilot, an army major who spoke a few words of English, explained to me that on touching down, his left side engine had cut out, causing the plane to swerve to the left of the strip, run off a broken part of the embankment, turn turtle and catch fire. The police, on questioning the men, found they were returning from St. Helena on the Brazilian border and travelling to Cuidad Bolivar when the pilot found he was low on fuel. He had contacted Timehri Airport who instructed him to land at Matthews Ridge Airport. Miss. Jaime our District Co-op. Officer was called upon to translate as she could speak Spanish and Mr. Owen, our new Regional Development Officer, contacted his brother in Georgetown to notify all Ministries, the Venezuelan Consulate and the Security Forces. On Saturday, 21 July 1979, a Guyana Airways Corporation twin Otter plane landed bringing two doctors, Dr. Mootoo and Dr. Charles, the Civil Aviation Inspector, a police contingent, personnel from the Government Information Services and photographers. Major Chan-a-Sue, the pilot, took all the injured on board and returned to Georgetown, to return later for the balance of the party.

On Sunday 22 July 1979 I noticed from my house on the Ridge some plane movements at the Airport. I sent my land-rover to investigate and report. My driver came back saying there were two Venezuelan aircraft on the strip. I travelled to the airport and met Captain Van Cooten of the Guyana National Service and a policeman. I saw a small helicopter marked Y.B. MTC-11 parked near the crashed plane and a Beechcraft twin engine plane with markings GN 742T, GUARDIA NATIONAL, and a Venezuelan army plane, parked near the G.A.C. office. I met Colonel (GN) Emiles Espinsia Topia, Major Anbal Drismendi Murray, TK (Medical), and MD David Arana. I chatted with them and understood that they had been instructed by the Venezuelan Consul in Georgetown to fly from Tumerero Venezuela Air Base to Matthews Ridge to collect the dead and parts from the crashed plane; but Colonel Joe Singh of the Guyana Defence Force Border Command had ruled they move nothing but the dead bodies. I sketched a picture of the crashed plane which I later put on canvas with oil paints. Markings on the crashed plane were GN 7953.

On 28 August 1979 I received a visit from Colonel Jesus Maria Duin Medina, a Military Attaché at the Venezuelan Embassy Georgetown. He was lodged at Guyana House for two days and had come to thank the people and the hospital personnel for their help on the night of the crash. When asked what he could do to show his gratitude, 'Doc' Hope asked for a supply of linens etc. for the hospital, but I mentioned that it would be better if he gave us a portable lighting plant to serve the hospital in emergencies such as the last one, then the hospital would not have to depend on the Matarkai turbines. I presented Colonel Medina with the oil painting of the plane. He later wrote me to the effect that he had presented my oil painting to the

Fuerzas Armadas de Cooperacion (F.A.C.) and it would be kept at the Historical Panel - of the Force Aviation Unit – Remembrance.

On 13 December 1978, the inquest into the shooting and mass suicide at Jonestown - Port Kaituma was opened in the administration building 'Court Room'. Dr. Leslie Mootoo and crime chief 'Skip' Roberts attended. One of the chief witnesses, Odel Roberts, an African-American, who had been a member of the cult, told all that he had seen from his hiding place under the senior citizen's house. He told how Jim Jones had ordered all the babies to be brought up first, then the adults, both men and women, were lined up to take the poisoned beverage. The guards were the last to take their share. It was during this hearing that I learned what had really been going on behind all those smiling faces, how members of the cult had been beaten and starved, how some of them must have gone through hell because they had wanted to leave, but were prevented by the guards. Jim Jones hád not wanted the outside world to learn of what really went on in the cult. This was why the Congressman and others had been shot down at the Kaituma Air Strip.

I learned later from the C.E.O.'s secretary that Johnnie Jones had telephoned the administrative office asking to speak with me, as he had something important to tell me. Unfortunately I was out on the road and did not get the message. This was only the day before the massacre.

In another part of the Matarkai region was the Burnham's Agricultural Institute, situated on the right bank of the Barama River in the Arakaka area. I was asked to give a speech at its graduation event. When I visited the Institute (Mr. Daw was the Principal in charge with an assistant) I learnt that young men and women who wanted to study agriculture were recruited from various parts of the country and sent to this remote area. They were housed and fed at the Institute and taught the preparation of soils, the planting of a variety of crops, the care of livestock. I noticed that most of the land was of a sandy loam texture and that of the lower or river lands was mostly clay. These students spent some months here then on receiving their diplomas, left to branch out into the country to spread their experience. There were about six buildings which housed the students, their mess hall and classrooms, then outside were the pens for the pigs and stables for the cattle. They had a Ford tractor and trailer to do their transportation. There was a ration store and a power plant to supply electricity.

When I gave my address I told them how I had grown up in the County of Kent, a farming community in England, and how boys from the slums of London had been brought in to Feegans Farms two and a half miles from where I was attending school, and that they lived and worked under the same kind of conditions as they experienced at the Institute. I told them how on receiving their diplomas, the boys from the slums had been shipped to Canada – and asked who were the millionaires of Canada today.

I told them that a farmer's life was full of ups and downs and plenty of disappointments and that a farmer must have faith in himself. On the completion of my address, I quoted Kipling's immortal poem 'If'. The students were so struck with the words that the principal asked that I give him the poem, so that each one of them could receive a copy.

'IF'

If you can keep your head when all about you
Are losing theirs and blaming it on you;
If you can trust yourself when all men doubt you,
But make allowance for their doubting too;
If you can wait and not be tired by waiting,
Or, being lied about, don't deal in lies,
Or, being hated, don't give way to hating,
And yet don't look too good, nor talk too wise;

If you can dream – and not make dreams your master;
If you can think – and not make thoughts your aim;
If you can meet with triumph and disaster
And treat those two impostors just the same;
If you can bear to hear the truth you've spoken
Twisted by knaves to make a trap for fools,
Or watch the things you gave your life to broken,
And stoop and build 'em up with worn-out tools;

If you can make one heap of all your winnings
And risk it on one turn of pitch-and-toss,
And lose, and start again at your beginnings
And never breathe a word about your loss;
If you can force your heart and nerve and sinew
To serve your turn long after they are gone,
And so hold on when there is nothing in you
Except the Will that say to them: 'Hold on';

If you can talk with crowds and keep your virtue,
Or walk with Kings – nor lose the common touch;
If neither foes nor loving friends can hurt you;
If all men count with you, but none too much;

If you can fill the unforgiving minute
With sixty seconds' worth of distance run –
Yours is the Earth and everything that's in it,
And – which is more – you'll be a Man my son!

This was not my only involvement with our country's attempts to instill agricultural skills in our young people. The Guyana National Service training centre was situated some five miles from Matthews Ridge. It was here that youths from all walks of life, both male and female, were trained as pioneers and received a basic agricultural education. Fresh batches of volunteers were constantly coming and going.

My equipment was constantly involved with this movement, in the transportation of rations by lorry and assisting in cutting and levelling playing fields and clearing lands for planting. Of course, I was obliged to charge them for the hire of the heavy machines and the lorries. The Papaya settlement received their electrical power from Matthews Ridge power plant and sometimes, due to the unavailability of dieselene which caused shutdowns in the plant, Papaya was left without electricity, causing a great loss in their food – beef, pork, chicken sometimes having to be dumped. Captain, later Major Van Cooten, whom I had first met when he was at the Tumatumari Youth Camp on the Potaro River, and I got on very well together. I did my utmost in assisting the smooth running of his operations at Papaya. He, in return, assisted me with periodical supplies of fuel when Matthews Ridge ran short. His pioneers played a great backup role in the Jonestown affair. I attended a passing out parade when the Prime Minister addressed them. Their officers could be very proud of the men's showing on the parade ground.

At a later date I was asked to address them and open the annual intercompany athletic championships at Papaya. My address was based on the theme of trees.

'Some of you must have heard the old-timers speaking about the bush in the early days and were afraid to come into it, but I can tell you from my personal experiences, covering some thirty years of my life, of the beauty and peace one experiences in the bush. With the beauty, though, there also lies the danger of falling trees, caused by high winds which only two short years ago caused the death of so many young pioneers at this location when a tree broke and fell on them.

In the interior, you always clear your camp site one hundred feet from the surrounding bush. I have seen an Amerindian huntsman buried when a circular wind blew down some mora trees under which he had built his camp. If you are walking in the forest and a storm blows up, stand still and watch overhead. If a tree is falling towards you, run to it, never turn your back, for the falling tree will bring down other trees and you will be liable to be killed or seriously injured.

'Look around you. What do you see but trees? Purpleheart, mora, crabwood, kabukalli, simarupa and many other species, which God created growing together. Why then cannot mankind follow nature's example to live and work together?

'Guyana has 83,000 square miles of land, most of which is virgin forest. There are thousands of acres of agricultural lands waiting to be farmed, plus all the diamonds and gold that is there in our country. Papaya is but a drop in an ocean of possibilities. Taking it step by step, and led by your able and seasoned officers, I am sure you can make your contribution on the scoreboard of success. The sports you are about to engage in form a sound footing for leadership. Guyana has been blessed with great men and women in the past and you young people, I hope, will be better men and women in the future.'

As the sports drew to a close, dark clouds appeared overhead, accompanied by strong circular winds which blew off some of the aluminium sheet roofing of the shelters. This was followed by a heavy downfall of rain. This seemed to emphasise the talk I had just given to the pioneers on the subject trees.

CHAPTER XXXVI
Matthews Ridge – 1979-80: A Country in Collapse

Wastage of money through damage and neglect of equipment was not the only failing at Matarkai. Mr. Jimmy Smith, Government Livestock Officer, who also resided on the ridge, had cattle grazing on approximately three square miles of land between the Arakaka River and another creek. He also raised sheep and goats. On his transfer from Matthews Ridge to the East Coast of Demerara, most of the cattle were shipped out leaving just sufficient head to supply Matarkai with a supply of fresh beef. The cattle were slaughtered and the carcasses shipped into the ration store at Pakera Village. On the handing over of this herd to Matarkai, I made it my duty to call for a check on the numbers of bulls, oxen, cows, etc. as I had done at Plantation Drill, Mahaicony when I was manager. When the Regional Minister heard I was making this check, he sent for me and informed me than these cattle were none of my business. Soon after this I was informed that cattle thieves were slaughtering the cattle and selling the meat to the local butchers. A raid was carried out on a house at Arakaka, where a quantity of beef was found and two men were apprehended by the police. This did not stop the disappearance of an occasional sheep or goat. Human cattle thieves were not the only reason for losses. Jimmy Smith had suffered a severe loss when a jaguar entered the sheep pen one night and destroyed seven head of sheep, jaguars eating only a part of a sheep. Jimmy sat out for two nights with a companion to try and shoot the intruder, but the jaguar was smarter and never returned to the kill.

The herd was eventually put under the responsibility of Mr. Daw, the Principal of Burnham's Agricultural Institute at Arakaka. My land-rover driver, Peters, informed me he had seen two jaguars early one morning on the road near our tennis court on Hill 1. I examined the road shoulder and saw the pug marks. Mr. Pestano, our Health Officer, whose house was adjacent to the tennis court, said the jaguars had gone so far as to peep into his living room windows. I sent to the police for a 12-gauge shot gun and a few cartridges but these cats, sensing a gun, disappeared from our vicinity only to be seen on the road leading to the Arakaka Paru Creek. I used to hear their hunting cry from across the deep valley at night. There were smaller cats around that were more welcome. One day, I noticed a stray cat hanging around my house, so I enticed her on to my back veranda with a saucer of milk. I had noticed a rat was stealing bread from my kitchen table, so I tried to lock the cat in the house but she bored through the mosquito mesh at the windows. Nevertheless the cat's even temporary presence seemed enough to send Mr. Rat elsewhere.

Life was difficult due to the constant shortage of fuel oil for the power house, with the result that we often had no current to boil water or to cook on our stoves. I used to have to gather wood and build a fire under my house to prepare a meal. This, though, was time consuming, and because I had to be up early, and spend most of the day on the road and in the Administration Offices, I though it best to employ a woman to cook and clean my house. The first two women proved to be undependable, many days not reporting for work. The third proved the best, for she was clean and could cook and bake bread. She lived with her aunt on Hill 1. I eventually took my meals at a restaurant in the village, but on receiving my own stove and refrigerator, I had the woman continue to cook.

A Civil Aviation team of two men, Mr. Bellety and Mr. Mingo, flew into Matthews Ridge requesting assistance to reactivate the Beacon at Pakera, which had been out of operation for sometime. Grass fires had burned some of the poles supporting the electric wires from the main line. I called in Hiles, my electrician, who informed me that it would require twenty foot poles so I set on some men to fell the trees at 6 Miles and transport them to the spot. They also weeded the Beacon compound, repaired the barbed wire fencing and rebuilt a gate which local cattle had broken down. I had the men dig holes and erect the poles. Mr. Bellety, seeing some of the paintings in my house, placed an order for an Amerindian head. This I delivered to him on his next visit.

I had to visit the scene of a rail derailment two and a half miles from the ridge. The locomotives were constantly jumping the rails due to the lack of sleepers and poor maintenance. The crew on maintenance had been cut by half because of insufficient funds to keep on a full crew. At the scene, six rail lengths had been disturbed by the locomotive in jumping the line. At my request for sleepers from Papaya Saw Mills, Mr. Gonsalves said his men had not been on the job since the last pay day. I went to Papaya to investigate and met a fellow called Glasgow, an employee from the Mill, under the influence of liquor. When I asked him why he and the others were not on the job, he told me he was not working, he was drinking now, so I told him to continue drinking as I was suspending him from duty as well as the other four men. I wrote a letter notifying the Union of my decision. I later transferred two of the men to the maintenance crew on the rail tracks and three I dismissed. I had to form a new crew to work the saw mill from men in my road gang until I could replace them with a good crew. This makeshift crew produced sufficient sleepers to enable the maintenance crew to put the locomotive back on the rails. The absenteeism after pay days cost the authority a lot of wasted man hours. The supervisors on the industrial site themselves set a bad example, for they invariably checked in for work then disappeared back to the village where, on two or three occasions, I had seen them in the rumshops drinking during working hours. I threatened instant dismissal if at any future date anyone was caught. My road gang suffered most as they were mostly Amerindians and could not hold their liquor. Later I found that Lewis, my road foreman, sold them rum to profit himself. I gave him a severe warning pointing out that if no labour turned out to work I would have no need of a foreman. The situation of absenteeism and slackness on the job grew so bad that Regional Minister Durant took it upon himself to shut down operations at the ridge from 15 December 1978 to 15 January 1979. This should have been the Chief Executive Officer's decision, but Major Gregory Gaskin was in Georgetown. Peters, my land-rover driver, called for me at my house with a message from the Minister, stating that he wanted to address everyone on the industrial site.

Before everyone could assemble, the Regional Minister left at 4:00 p.m. by a helicopter for Georgetown, leaving Regional Development Officer Wyatt to explain this decision to the labourers and the staff. The Public Service Union and the G.A.W.U. both condemned this action by the Minister. They said the men should have been given at least a week's notice. Wyatt tried to explain matters to the labourers, but there was a loud clamouring for their money. Wyatt asked me to appoint a maintenance road gang, but I said it was no use putting men on the road without assistance from machines. These were out of action awaiting repairs, and further more there was no fuel.

The results of this crisis affected all operations in the area. Major Van Cooten of the Guyana National Service wrote to Metarkai saying that thousands of dollars worth of food at the GNS farm would be destroyed unless they were supplied with electrical current. I instructed Vincent La Cruz, my diesel foreman, to drain all the fuel from the heavy equipment in the area in order to assist the G.N.S.. Major Van Cooten also sent three drums of fuel. I also phoned Mr. James at Mabaruma to ship four drums to Kaituma by the launch *Damon*. On receipt of this fuel, the power plant was switched on at 6:00 p.m. and off at 9:00 p.m. Minister Durant, Minister Mingo and Wyatt the R.D.O., requested lights be kept on until 10:30 p.m. as they were entertaining in the village. I said I could not do this as I had to conserve fuel for more important services. Of course this decision put me in the bad books of the Minister, but I felt that if I was to do a proper job and stick to my decisions, I had at times to tread on a few toes. I received a report that men were stealing dieselene from the reserve tanks in the power house. I had to speak seriously to the watchmen on duty, who were invariably involved. Their excuse was that there were insufficient lights in the yards and they could not see anything.

At Port Kaituma, I was informed by Mr. Duke, Captain of the launch *Damon*, of an unidentified plane that had come in with brilliant lights and circled the area, dimming its lights in the operation, and then swiftly left in a burst of speed with blazing lights. Other residents noticed this plane on three occasions between the hours of 8:30 p.m and 9:00 p.m. I reported this incident to the Ministry of Home Affairs through Major Benn of the G.N.S. Some people said it was a U.F.O.

Colonel Morgan and I took stock of items in the stores. There were some motors and other machinery we discovered in cases that the storekeeper had not even known about. La Cruz and his mechanics were instructed to examine all of the equipment lying in the yard adjacent to the railway lines and the river. Some were repaired right there, some shipped into Matthews Ridge and the balance left as scrap metal. La Cruz had to find a Ford engine to replace the motor at the Kaituma pump, which had to be overhauled.

My road gang for the Matthews Ridge section was slashed by fourteen men, leaving me with six, and the Port Kaituma section was reduced by four, leaving only two. How I could possibly maintain 40 miles of roadway with eight men, I did not know, especially as the men would take up more time travelling from point to point, unless I could find transportation for them, than doing actual maintenance work. The launch *Damon* was beached for repairs to its bottom, but on examination, it was found that not only was the planking rotten, but structural timbers too. It would cost a lot of money to practically rebuild it, money we did not have. The beaching of this launch put a strain on transportation for those passengers travelling downriver to Morawhanna to catch the steamer for Georgetown and for the hucksters travelling from the coast to barter their produce upriver.

An arrangement was made with a fishing trawler to visit Port Kaituma every two weeks to bring in a catch of fresh fish which would be then moved by train to Matthews Ridge ration store. This made a great change from the constant diet of chicken and beef every day. Some of the local business men, though, made a point of trying to corner the market by purchasing all the fish, then turning around and selling it at a huge profit.

I was introduced to a two-man Korean team who I was made to understand were there to instruct us in the art of terracing. I wanted to know why the Government would waste time and money on a project such as terracing in a country with so many square miles of available lands for agriculture. I knew terracing was done in China and Japan where there was a lack of flat lands to farm. What made this worse was that I had to put one of my D/7 caterpillar tractors and a crew of men to work under the Korean supervision. This was in the area of the State farm situated six miles from the ridge. The men were transported almost every day from the ridge to the farm. There were times when fuel was unavailable and the Koreans had to sit and wait until the vehicles were rolling again. The soil at 6 mile farm was of a red sandy-clay, which when rain fell proved difficult to farm. I knew from my own experience in farming, that when the top or sweet soil is cut away, the subsoil will take some time to be treated by the elements before any successful planting can be done. In the Paramakotai Mountain area, the Amerindians laughed at the efforts of the Government Agriculture Department who were sent in there to prepare lands for the Amerindians to plant. The bulldozers simply pushed away all the sweet top soil on which the cassava plants were supposed to flourish, and the Amerindians looked elsewhere to plant where the top soil had not been disturbed. I have cleared land with heavy equipment, but only of the bush, being careful not to disturb the top soil. Men with axes and saws were then put on to cut up the bush, heap and burn it, before planting. The Korean effort lasted for three and a half months when the heavy rainfall curtailed the movement of the heavy machines. Regional Minister Durant presented two purpleheart ornaments to these two Koreans and also sent a letter of appreciation to the leader of the North Korean people, Kim Il Sung. Up to the time of my leaving Matthews Ridge, in June 1980, that land had never been planted.

The ridge and Pakera Village had constant blackouts due to the constant short supply of dieselene. The hours, if any, that the power plant worked were limited to say, 6:00 a.m. to 8:00 a.m. and then shut down until 4:00 p.m. to work until 6:00 p.m. in the afternoon. This only allowed two hours to prepare breakfast and dinner. Then there was a blackout for the rest of the night. Not having lights to read or write by, I had to lie on my bed until sleep caught up with me. Many mornings I woke at 3:00 a.m. to take a cup of coffee from my thermos flask, then lie in my chair smoking my pipe to await the dawn. Then one of the Merlin engines at the plant caught fire, and when examined by the electrician, Mr. Hiles, it was found that the generator wires were burned and the whole component would have to be shipped to Georgetown for rewiring. Two Merlin engines were already standing by, awaiting much needed parts so this left us with only one engine. Consequently, every Wednesday morning, when this engine had to be serviced, we did not have current even to prepare coffee, and since the pumps on the ridge and in the village were only in operation when there was current, I obtained an oil drum, had it washed out and set it underneath a gutter so the rain could fill it. I bathed with this water which was icy-cold in the morning.

I had suffered a slipped disk in 1966 and there were times when it attacked me whenever I bent down or received a jerk when travelling in the land-rover. I found myself laid up with one such incident. The doctors had advised I lie on my back on a stiff bed or board and take as much rest as possible, but I was constantly disturbed by the telephone – the railroad, the garage, mechanic shop, Port Kaituma and Papaya National Service, wanting me to make decisions or asking for orders. This was after the Regional Minister had told me his Regional Development Officer would carry out the duties of C.E.O. when Major Gaskin was not there. For the two days I was laid up with my back, I had to depend on my neighbours to assist me in preparing my meals. During the time I was on the ridge, I did not complain of ill health, though I did suffer from constant sneezing caused by the dust from the manganese fines. At one time I had suffered for two weeks with hard boils erupting on the back of my shoulders and upper arms and had to poultice them. Other than that, I enjoyed splendid health.

In January of 1979, whilst I was in Georgetown acquiring some four German lorries for Matthews Ridge, I received two telephone calls from Matthews Ridge informing me that the Regional Minister had called a public meeting in the School Hall of Pakera Village and had slandered both Major Gaskin and myself to the people, telling them he did not feel it necessary to have either of us back at Matthews Ridge. I informed my Minister, the Hon. D. Hoyte and he made it his business to visit the ridge to investigate. On his return, he instructed me to carry on my duties there. I later met the Regional Minister when he came to Georgetown. He informed me that Major Gaskin had left the ridge without informing the employees about their wages and salaries. I replied that he had done the same on 14 December 1978 when he closed operations on 15 December and had flown away by helicopter, not waiting to explain his decision to the employees or how they must get their money. I learned that the ridge had been out of fuel over the Christmas Holidays and concluded that they must have used the fuel indiscriminately for it to have finished in such a short period of time.

Shortly after my return to the ridge, I received four German lorries by the G.N.S. boat *Jaimito*. Unfortunately, one lorry had an accident eight miles from Port Kaituma when it swerved and overturned, throwing a load of 60 bags of flour onto the road and killing a passenger who should not have been on the lorry. I was asked to investigate and write a report on the incident.

Then the Regional Development Officer's driver ran his land-rover over the edge of the ridge and turned turtle. It was a miracle the vehicle had not plummeted to the bottom of the ravine of the creek. It was saved by the stump of a congo pump tree. I had to cut the road shoulder with my caterpillar D/7 tractor and build an earth ramp up which the vehicle was towed out.

The police had to investigate two murders in Pakera Village. A Guyana National Serviceman murdered his common-law wife by breaking her neck, then he drank lysol. He was caught and hospitalized in order to allow him to recover and stand trial. Then one of my mechanics went home for lunch at midday and strangled his wife.

There were more pleasant events too. I had the pleasure of meeting the American Ambassador and his wife on 10 October 1979. I had, during my spare time, been painting some portraits of the employees and some landscapes of the surrounding countryside. The Ambassador's wife said that the maids at Guyana House had informed her I was an artist and she was pleased to have seen some of my work. There was a newspaper clipping on 18 October 1979 concerning a Canadian Company drilling for oil in the Takatu Basin. This caught my attention for I had witnessed oil shale at the Essequibo River head on the Arakai Mountain foot. My father had, since the late 1800s, seen the possibilities of oil in this North West Region. A party of Engineers paid a visit to the ridge with the intention of investigating the Eclipse Falls in the Barima River for the purpose of hydropower, but due to the dryness of the lower river, they could not penetrate up to the Falls. Eddie Gonsalves, who was one of the party, had been on the Mahdia Self-Help road with me. I carried him to Papaya to show him the improvements I had made. This party travelled as far as Austin Creek, three miles beyond Papaya Training Centre, to inspect a new gold working where a tributor was getting a fair reward from his alluvial workings.

I was invited to meet a group of visiting Zambian National Service officials. Colonel Morgan invited me to lunch at Guyana House Hill 2 on the Ridge, where I met the Zambian Brigadier and his ADC. Their names have slipped me. Also present were the Director General of our own G.N.S., Colonel Roberts, Major Van Cooten and Lieutenant Parris. We travelled to the G.N.S. camp at Papaya where the Zambian Brigadier took the salute at the parade and gave our G.N.S. a talk on his National Service in Zambia. We then returned to the Officers' Club where all the senior officers of the Papaya Centre were presented to the Zambian Brigadier. The Zambian party was then escorted to Matthews Ridge Airport for their departure to the city.

I had a visit from the auditors who were very upset with the accountant, Holder, for they could find no proper records, nor were there any costings.

They borrowed my monthly, quarterly and half yearly reports, where they found itemised work and the costing for the same in my roads and utility reports. I had been doing this type of work since my sugar estate days. To report clearly and precisely takes a little more time, but it is appreciated by those that have to read the reports.

The Matarkai Authority had received two kilns in which it was proposed to make charcoal for shipment. These kilns had been lying idle behind the Papaya Saw Mills for months. Grass had grown over them and no charcoal had been made. At Major Gaskin's request, the kilns were shipped to Georgetown to be utilised by the Guyana National Service. There is a good market in the outside world for good charcoal. During the short period I was C.E.O., the Minister called a meeting in the administration office to discuss points in question with Mr. Kissoon, a labour official. Mr. Kissoon, on leaving, told me to contact him in Georgetown if I was in doubt regarding the Labour Laws.

I was kept fairly busy with complaints and applications. I made a point in tightening up some of the slackness in the administration offices and in the industrial yard. On June 18, I held a meeting in my office of all supervisors at which I asked Mr. Holder, the accountant, to explain to the staff the seriousness of the financial position of Matarkai. We had a deficit of $600,000.00 and had no money to buy parts for vehicles. Mr. Holder and Personnel Officer McEwan were also asked to explain how they proposed to pay wages. I had a meeting with the Union officials and Mr. Holder in which Mr. Holder said we should retrench some of the employees from each section. The Union argued that at least a week's notice be given before retrenchment. Mr. Holder claimed that there was not sufficient money to pay the labourers off. I said we would have to put off the Notice of Retrenchment until there was sufficient money. The Union further informed me that certain people on the administration staff had been reported to the Prime Minister as not doing a proper job. I put out a written warning that if these individuals did not improve their performance, something serious would happen to them.

I had to travel to Georgetown in search of sufficient funds for wages and salaries. I was informed by the Permanent Secretary of Regional Development that Holder 'must be mad', for nothing like retrenchment had been mentioned at the last Board Meeting. I sent a radio message to Matthews Ridge instructing Holder to withdraw all notices of retrenchment. The PS further stated that Holder had not as yet sent down the minutes of the last board meeting, neither had he sent down a proper request for wages and salaries and that no money could be released until the report on expenditure and revenue was received. I met Regional Minister Durant in town. He said that Holder and McEwan would have to go for making such a mistake.

I returned to Matthews Ridge in company with our new C.E.O.. Colonel Carl Morgan, of the Guyana Defence Force, who would take up his duties in August, Miss Carol Davis and the PS, Mr. Johnson. At the Board meeting held on Wednesday, 18 July 1979, Miss Davis questioned Mr. Holder about some missing money and advised we get a certified accountant, for Holder could not produce a proper expenditure sheet. The PS, Mr. Johnson, had taken a serious view of the shortage of money and had mentioned to me he might have to call in the police and certified accountant to check the books. Colonel Morgan has asked me to prepare a chart showing the administration structure. He also took a very serious view of the shortage of money. He came into my office after the Board meeting to have a formal chat on the general run of affairs at the Ridge. I completed the chart on 16 November, 1979 and handed it to him. I had to prepare a half-yearly report on roads and utilities for the next Board meeting.

'Doc' Hope, the dispenser of the Matarkai Hospital, asked me to give a talk to the hospital staff on the true state of affairs of Matarkai. Questions were put to me which I felt I had to answer. Mr. Sinclair, Secretary of the Guyana Agricultural Workers Union, congratulated me on the firmness of my decisions relating to the administration. He said that such had been required for a long time. Mr. Charlie King, our Guyana Broadcasting Service representative, interviewed me on my years in the interior. He said he would broadcast this on 2 October.

I received a warning from a good friend that Party members, from the Regional Minister down, did not like me as I was too strict. When the R.D.O. from Mabaruma, Mr. Morrison, came to a meeting, I addressed him as 'Sir' to which he made an objection. He wished to be addressed as 'Comrade'. I told him I had been educated at an English public school where I was taught to address my senior officers and those older than I as 'Sir' and I did not think I was yet living in a communist state where one had to use the term Comrade, and that in all of my correspondence with the Prime Minister and my Minister I addressed them as 'Sir'. I did not think he was any different.

On 1 November 1979, I was to learn of the death of Regional Minister Durant at his home in Georgetown. He and I had crossed swords on many occasions, but he and I had lived a similar way of life in the jungle working both diamonds and gold. He was ten years younger than I. There was the death of McEwan too on the 4 November 1979; he had been sick in the Pakera Hospital before being transferred to the Georgetown Hospital. I was also to learn of the death of Gregory Gaskin's father, an old friend. I travelled to Georgetown to attend his funeral.

As the year drew to an end and the first anniversary of the Peoples' Temple massacre approached, memories came back of that one week I shall never forget. On one of my visits to Georgetown, I had met Charlie Touchette, Lee Ingram, a young coloured woman and the Afro-Guyanese lorry driver who had slept a night in my house on the ridge whilst awaiting court the following day. Charlie Touchete had been one of the earliest settlers of the People's Temple who had laid out and prepared accommodation for those who were to follow. He had been out of the country (and his companions had been in Georgetown) when the massacre happened. I asked Charlie Touchette what were his plans now that the Peoples' Temple was no more. He replied that he was going to get back the ship *Albatross* which had been seized by the Government. He would then approach the Government for permission to ply the ship from Guyana to trade with the neighbouring islands. This ship, the *Albatross*, was the mother ship which met the smaller trawler the *Cudjoe* at sea, supplying her with cargo for the People's Temple at Port Kaituma. This trawler brought in food stuffs, rifles, and ammunition but was never discharged at Port Kaituma during the daylight hours. One young woman who failed to catch the train into Matthews Ridge had to sleep in a railway carriage near the docks. She reported to me that she had witnessed the unloading operations in the dead of night and had seen a burlap bag burst open which contained a number of rifles. I wondered what hold these people had over the Government that they were permitted to bring in cargo without paying any customs duties.

Heavy June rains set in, bombarding the ridge with some terrific thunder storms. The terrific claps of thunder sent vibrations through my house and the lightning could be seen and heard like the crack of a whip. These heavy downpours played havoc with my roads. I was called out to view a cutaway at Pakera Creek crossing where the six foot galvanised aqueduct must have been blocked, for all I saw was a rushing torrent of creek water flowing across the road, five feet deep and twelve feet wide. I sent for some forty foot lengths of hardwood planks with which to span the gap to allow land-rovers to cross. I then sent some axemen to fell some timbers at the 6 mile area. These were hauled to the spot to form bridge timbers. Round wood posts had to be driven down to the edge of the broken road on both sides of the gap and hardwood beams were fitted behind the posts and pinned with hardwood pickets to prevent further breakage. Men were set on to cut away bushes in the tailing where the creek made an abrupt turn to allow a free passage for the creek water. The men also cleared bushes from the upper reaches of the Creek.

CHAPTER XXXVII

A Final Retirement: Guyana Memories – 1980

In 1980, at the age of seventy-five, I decided it was finally time to retire from active service and in that year my wife and I left Guyana to be with our family in Canada. It was a decision we took with much regret, but it gave me opportunity to reflect on, and begin writing about, my experiences.

I have over the years cut and walked through many miles of raw jungle in the hinterland of Guyana in company with Amerindians on my reconnais-sance surveys: climbing mountains, swimming creeks and rivers, penetrat-ing some vast forests, vine-entangled lowlands, tick-infested swamps and the wide open grass lands of the Rupununi Savannah. I have traversed the area east of the Dutch frontier, south to the Brazilian frontier and west to the Venezuelan border. I have travelled for days and weeks up our various wa-terways, portaging boats across rapids and falls, in my search for both gold and diamonds.

A few years before my retirement I had the opportunity to take a plane flight over the land that had demanded so much physical energy to journey across by boat, land-rover and a great deal by foot. It was hard to believe such distances could now be covered in two hours by plane flight, to reach in so short a time the magnificent upland country of the Pakarima area where the land ranges from great forest-covered flats and rolling savannahs two thousand feet above sea level, to precipitous mountains towering a mile high in the clouds. It was a journey which brought back many memories of the places I had struggled to reach over what was almost sixty years of working life.

It was a dull cloudy day when at 11:00 a.m. in company with a consult-ing engineer and a surveyor, I took off from the Demerara river in one of the small high-powered planes of the B.G. Airways piloted by Harry Wendt, an American. Flying at about 800 feet, wisps of smoke-like clouds already floated below us as we skimmed over the West Coast, two sugar estates looking like miniature models below us. As we turned up the Essequibo river, the clouds thickened so we had to descend to some three to four hundred feet to keep the edge of the river in sight as our guide. Meanwhile the rain beat down on the perspex front of the cabin with such force as to make us imagine we could hear it above the roar of the motor.

Suddenly the clouds closed in all around us and the river's edge disappeared from view. Now I knew what blind flying was. When the clouds cleared sufficiently for me to recognise our position, we were passing over Kaow Island, two miles down river from Bartica and flying into the mouth of the Mazaruni River. It was now 11:47 a.m. For the next hour, having climbed to a higher altitude, the weather was sufficiently clear to be able to see the great Mazaruni a thousand feet below and follow the vast intricacy of its thousand channels. At 12:14 p.m., we crossed Kaburi Falls, just sixty-four minutes after leaving the city of Georgetown. The previous occasion on which I had seen these cataracts was after three days' hard travelling from the city.

Half an hour later we were flying over Issano landing, the terminus of the road from Bartica. Some miles below Tiboku Falls, the Mazaruni makes a sharp hairpin bend as it loops to the south; there we left the river and flew across the legs of the hairpin, reaching the stream again above the long and narrow Lau-Lau Island. Now the country ahead was hidden by a mass of white cloud. We could almost feel the plane hitting the solid wall of rain that came from it. The pilot swung the plane sharply to the south in an effort to get around the storm. We continued to fly south along the edge of it, but it showed no let up. Now I remembered that some ten miles from the river was a four thousand feet wall of mountain. We were travelling at well over a mile a minute only a thousand feet above the forest plain, which could just be discerned through the clouds. I was little anxious until, watching the compass, I saw we were gradually veering around to the west. Then the mountain wall came into sight not two minutes' flying away.

As we continued our turn, I recognised beneath us the extraordinary meanderings of the Merume river and as we crossed it, we got clear of the storm and at 1:10 p.m. were flying over Kamakusa, where my elder brother had been a gold officer some years before. We now flew almost due north for six minutes cutting off the loops of the river till we reached it again at Oranapai, easily recognisable from its island. Going on above the river, I looked carefully for places I knew. Twice I looked before recognising, on the left bank, a strip of bright green 'second growth' forest where some years ago had stood the thriving mining centre of Buck Cannister sands, with its twelve shops. Two minutes later, the Government station and extensive diamond workings of Enachu came into sight and at 1:25 p.m., two and a quarter hours after leaving Georgetown, we alighted on the river at Tumereng at the low hill opposite the mouth of the Eping river.

Going ashore, I met several acquaintances. The rail fell continually as we had a picnic lunch in Mr. Cooper's country cottage where he stayed on his monthly diamond-buying visits. (I later met Mr. Cooper, living at Mahaicony in retirement, and his son who planted rice at Plantation Drill while I was manager of the estate.) For some time there were doubts as to the advisability of our continuing the flight over the mountains that day and, whilst we waited for the weather to clear, I examined several parcels of diamonds in the shops. Eventually Harry Wendt decided we could go on. We started off once more at 3:10 p.m. and headed south towards the Merume Mountains which we hoped to cross through the Eping pass. Now the top of this pass is over 3,000 feet high and is bounded on each side with precipices that rise a further thousand feet above the forest. When still only a thousand feet above the forest, the cotton wool clouds closed in below us and we were flying in the middle of a dense white mist at ninety miles an hour towards a wall of mountain that reared at least 3,000 feet above us. As I had never before flown under such conditions, I am not ashamed to say that I was distinctly nervous. Indeed by the time the altimeter registered another thousand feet and glimpses of dark brown precipices at and above our own level became visible here and there through the clouds on either side, I really began to feel uncomfortable. On at least two occasions I had to remind myself that the pilot's life was as sweet to him as mine to me and that, despite appearances, he was taking no risks, though to a novice this seemed very much to the contrary. As we got into the pass, the great rock walls on either side were less than a mile from us.

The clouds closed in again and, by the tilt of the plane, I knew we were circling to come out. Twice again we attempted the pass and after the third turn I saw the altimeter registering over four thousand feet. So, although I could see nothing but thick clouds around, above and beneath us, I knew we were going to fly over the summit of that flat-topped range. Some minutes later, I happened to look down and there, through a hole in the cloud carpet, I got a faint glimpse of what looked like a green pasture but which was actually the savannahs of the upper Mazaruni. Swiftly we dropped, the clouds disappeared and there, beneath us, was the winding, rock-filled course of the Partang river with, just below its confluence with the Mazaruni, a neat little doll-house looking building near a long white landing strip clearly marked on the savannah. This was Imbaimadai or 'Sawari Nut Savannah', the then headquarters of Mr. Peabody, Field Officer for Amerindian Affairs.

Making a wide circle we swooped down on the long black reach of the upper Mazaruni river where we alighted at 4:20 p.m., one hour and one minute after leaving Tumereng. Although we were once more on the ground, the altimeter stayed at 1,700 feet. We taxied up to a small steep sand bank by which was moored a large, brightly-painted canoe and on which stood the lean, brown-bearded figure of Mr. Peabody surrounded by half a dozen Akawoi Amerindians. We climbed on board the big canoe and were ferried across the river to the far bank, steep and covered by bush. Climbing up through this, we came out on an undulating savannah where, a couple hundred yards away, stood the temporary headquarters, a large and comfortable thatched house with wattle walls, a kitchen of similar material and an Amerindian 'round house' constructed around one of the aerials of the station's radiotelephone.

The evening was spent in home-made easy chairs, conversing on many subjects. We were put up in canvas cots and retired for the night. Because of the altitude, the night was far from warm and we were more than glad that we brought out blankets.

Awakening at dawn, we had coffee, then walked across the savannah for a quarter of a mile for Harry Wendt to examine the landing strip that Mr. Peabody had made. It had been our intention to fly south-west from here over Mt. Ayanganna, thence to strike for the head of the Potaro river and follow the stream down to the Essequibo and then home. But as the summit of Ayanganna was still wrapped in cloud, the pilot shook his head and said he would not decide before eleven o'clock whether to take that course or not. As it turned out, the decision did not have to be made as a message came over the radiophone from a Government geologist, asking us to pick up an injured employee at Tumereng and take him down to hospital. So, with breakfast over and after bidding farewell to our hosts, we climbed aboard the little plane at one o'clock and were soon roaring away over Imbaimadai Savannah and then heading west down the Mazaruni.

The savannahs soon came to an end and were succeeded by a great forested plain surrounded by precipitous mountains. Fourteen minutes after starting, we passed the confluence of the Kukui River with the Mazaruni, seven minutes later that of the Kako and after yet another seven minutes, that of the Kamarang. All these large tributaries entered the main river on its left bank. Looking up the valley of the Kamarang, I saw a whisp of smoke where people at the Seventh-Day Adventist Mission were apparently burning a field. We had now swung towards the north and ahead of us lay a great gap in the mountains through which the Mazaruni dropped close on two thousand feet down the peneplain. Three minutes below Kamarang we saw the mouth of the little Membaru Creek, the usual route from the Kurupung to the upper river. Forty minutes after starting we entered the great gorge and flew over the Siperimer Falls. That twenty minutes I shall never forget, as I lodged it in the place in my mind where I kept my first impressions of Kaieteur Falls from my visit of almost fifty years ago.

Imagine a great river, no puny creek, dropping in fall after fall, each close on half a mile long in little more than ten miles. Stretches of smooth water, two or three miles in length, separated the individual falls making the latter all the steeper. Over Arawai Falls, apparently the biggest of the series, there floated a permanent cloud of mist through which we had to fly blind. We were flying at a distinct downward angle between the sandstone walls of the gorge and minute by minute the altimeter registered a lower level. At one point, the pilot circled round to view a miniature Kaieteur where a branch stream fell perpendicularly over a ledge several hundred feet high.

At last, one minute before two o'clock, we were over still water, once more below Peaima Falls, 1,700 feet below our starting point. Just below Peaima, the Mazaruni swings suddenly from its northern course to the south-east and this bend forms its nearest approach to the Cuyuni river, a distance of some twenty-two miles. The engineer thought that this might be a suitable place for a road joining the two rivers. I had earlier to cut a line north from Awarapari Creek mouth to Makapa Hills in the Cuyuni River when I was prospecting for gold and I had found no mountain range dividing the two rivers as was believed to be the case. We decided to have a 'look-see'. Judging from the map, one would have surmised the existence of a range of mountains to have caused this sharp deflection in the course of the Mazaruni, but as we flew north-north-west over gently undulating country, we found that the mountains stopped abruptly to our left. I had climbed this mountain from the head of the Awarapari Creek, and cut across the flat savannah to the Ekereku river where I had washed out two $\%_{6}$th diamonds in a battel. Later, there had been a diamond shout there, causing a landing strip to be built on top of the mountain. There was a clear unobstructed view straight ahead to the Cuyuni river valley and from this point we returned to the Mazaruni river, arriving at Tumereng at 2:50 p.m.

Having refuelled and taken the injured man on board, we resumed our journey downriver at 3:34 p.m. A little over an hour's flying brought us to Kaburi Falls where I was most interested in getting a bird's eye view of the numerous cataracts I had so arduously examined by boat some two years before. Now I saw I was correct in two surmises I had made at that time, that the Mazaruni at this point is at least two miles wide from bank to bank and that by far the greater volume of the river flows not over Pairimap, Warra-

Warra and Kaburi Falls themselves, but over Glass Falls, adjacent to the left bank. Compared to its maelstrom of seething, tortured water, the former three falls, fearful enough when viewed at close quarters from a boat, appeared as mere ripples.

It was just forty-five minutes after five when we dropped gently down on the Demerara river. It was one of the most interesting flying trips I had made, reminding me of how much I had encountered and seen in my many visits to the interior. Writing this now, however, I am struck by the irony that it was the district in which I was born which was least known to me but which arouses in me the deepest feelings.

I was born at Mabaruma Hill on the left bank of the Aruka River in the North West District of British Guiana on December 22, 1905. My father, a Scotsman, settled there in the late 1800s and planted citrus groves, provisions and rubber trees. My mother died in 1909. My father sold out to the British Consolidated Rubber company and moved to Georgetown where he died in 1911. He was buried near his wife under the rubber trees he had planted. Sixty-nine years later, my very last job as the Superintendent of Roads for Matthews Ridge had brought me back to the North West District, but it was an earlier visit, when I was prospecting for iron-ore deposits in Hosororo, which now comes to mind. This was when, in December 1956, I went to visit my father's grave, and the late Mr. Broomes Snr., who was our neighbour, greeted me with these words –

'Son of the soil, you have come home'